W9-ARM-242

THE COMPLETE VEGETARIAN CUISINE

Revised and Updated

ROSE ELLIOT

PANTHEON BOOKS

NEW YORK

Text copyright © 1988, 1996 by Rose Elliot
New photographs copyright © 1996 by David Armstrong
Photographs and illustrations copyright © 1988 by
William Collins Sons & Co. Ltd.

All rights reserved under International and Pan-American Copyright Conventions.
Published in the United States by Pantheon Books, a division of Random House, Inc.,
New York. Originally published in Great Britain as *Rose Elliot's Vegetarian Cookery* by
HarperCollins Publishers, London.

A Cataloging-in-Publication record has been established for this title by the
Library of Congress.
ISBN: 0-679-75896-8

Printed in Italy
First American Revised Edition
2 4 6 8 9 7 5 3 1

Foreword

Much has happened since I wrote the first edition of this book in 1988. New ingredients have become available, fresh ideas have developed. The popularity of vegetarianism has increased enormously and continues to do so. Concern over the safety of meat and the way in which animals are raised has definitely been a factor in this, as have the results of research which has shown the vegetarian diet to be a positive factor in reducing the risk of heart disease and certain types of cancer. The need for information on vegetarian cooking and good, reliable recipes has never been greater.

Revising a book is always something of a challenge. There are difficult decisions about what new recipes, ideas and ingredients to put in - but even more difficult ones about what to take out to make room. Some recipes inevitably had to go. If you are familiar with the original edition, I hope that I haven't removed too many old friends and that you will find many more new ones - and that this book will prove to be as useful and well loved in its new edition as it was in the old.

Contents

Acknowledgments

I would like to express my warmest appreciation to all the people who helped to create the first edition of this book. To my agent, Vivienne Shuster and to Joan Clibbon and Robin Wood of Collins who gave me the opportunity to write it and for their care and support throughout the project. Thanks are also due to my text editor Helen Dore and Art Director Janet James, as well as to Felicity Jackson, Barbara Dixon and Jillian Haines. I would also like to thank Nick Carman for his superb photography, his assistant Edward Allbright, and home economists Judy Bugg and Janice Murfitt, for making the food look and taste so good. I am grateful to my daughters Katy, Margaret and Claire for help with recipe testing and my husband Robert for his understanding and support throughout the project.

I am delighted with the new American edition of my book and I would like to thank very warmly all those who were involved – Jane Middleton, photographer David Armstrong, home economists Hilary Guy and Janice Murfitt, as well as Shelley Wanger, Marjorie Anderson and Gia Kim of Pantheon Books.

Introduction

This book has grown out of many years of cooking vegetarian food, and originating, testing and also demonstrating vegetarian recipes. During that time I have had the delight of seeing the great increase in interest in this style of cooking, with a dramatic and continuing swing towards vegetarianism, and many people becoming "demiveg," if not changing completely.

I like to think that vegetarian cooking has now become a cuisine in its own right. That cuisine embraces nonmeat and nonfish dishes from all over the world, as well as whole-food, macrobiotic and its own idiosyncratic recipes. It happily embraces ingredients as different as tofu and whole-wheat pasta, tempeh and rice noodles, Indian spices and sea vegetables, legumes and exotic fruits. The only qualification is that fish and other animals are not used. The result is a lively, colorful, eclectic mix which I hope I have represented here.

One of the delights of being involved with cooking is that it is a living art; novel ingredients, new recipes, a dash of herbs here, a sprinkling of spice there, an unfamiliar ingredient, spark off fresh ideas, inspire creativity. . . . Ideas are constantly changing and evolving, as are our shopping and eating habits.

In writing this book, my aim has been to provide the information, recipes and techniques needed in vegetarian cooking, both for those who are new to it, and for more experienced cooks who want to try something different. For those strict vegetarians, vegans, I have also included many recipes and these are marked with a Ⓥ, together with vegan versions of standard recipes where possible. There is every reason for vegan food to be as exciting and delicious as vegetarian food.

The initial inspiration for the book was, for me, as is so often the case for cooks, the marketplace. Week after week, as I did my shopping, I noticed the increasing range of wonderful, often weird and wonderful, ingredients, particularly fruits, vegetables, nuts, beans, herbs and spices.

These were a godsend to vegetarian cooking, rooted as it is so deeply in the raw ingredients, and dependent on herbs and spices for flavoring. What was needed was information on identifying them, storing, preparing and cooking them. . . . And so the Ingredients section of this book was born. This led on naturally to the Recipes section, with more detailed ways of using the ingredients.

Although I hope this book will be used as a reference book, I decided to put comments, tips and techniques in the margins, by the appropriate recipe, rather than in a separate chapter. This way they have relevance and immediacy, and too much formality is avoided. I do hope you will find the arrangement good to use.

The book begins with information on the nutritional side of vegetarian and vegan cooking, and on planning meals which are well-balanced, healthy and nourishing, as well as pleasant to eat. This theme of meal-planning is continued throughout the book, both in the Special Menu spreads, which appear at intervals throughout, and in the menus which, taking my publisher at his word, I've frequently included in the margins! I hope you'll enjoy them, and, indeed, the whole book.

Nutrition

In vegetarian eating, meat, fish and poultry are replaced by fresh-tasting meals based on vegetables and herbs, grains and pasta, dried beans and lentils, fresh fruits and nuts, with or without dairy products. Many people are enjoying the benefits of eating like this some of the time, while continuing to eat meat and fish occasionally: these are the demi-vegetarians. Others are switching completely to vegetarianism, and some are going still further, excluding all dairy products, and becoming vegans. Any of these ways of eating can supply all the nutrients needed for vibrant good health. In fact many people find their health improves when they become vegetarians. The key lies in planning meals around a good variety of fresh, unprocessed foods.

Eating for health

Studies of people in different parts of the world have shown that those who eat mainly unrefined foods, high in fiber, low in sugar and fat, do not succumb to illnesses like high blood pressure, heart disease, diverticulitis, cancer of the bowel and diabetes. Experts now agree that a healthy diet is one which is high in fiber and low in fat, sugar and salt. This was the kind of food which was commonly eaten in Europe before industrialization and mass food production. Contrary to popular opinion, meat was not eaten in large quantities by the majority of the population, for whom cereals and vegetables were staples. Vegetarian eating, with its emphasis on cereals, legumes and vegetables, is not therefore as far removed from what our forebears ate as is sometimes thought, and is naturally high-fiber, low-fat and low-sugar.

Protein

Part of every body cell, protein is essential for healthy growth and repair of cells, for reproduction and for protection against infection. Daily requirements are, however, small and there is no problem in getting enough protein on a vegetarian or vegan diet. Main sources of protein for vegetarians are:
- *Dairy* – cheese, milk and milk products such as yogurt; eggs
- *Nuts and seeds*, such as almonds, cashew nuts, hazelnuts, Brazil nuts, walnuts, pine nuts, pecans and peanuts; sunflower seeds, sesame seeds and pumpkin seeds
- *Legumes* – dried peas, beans and lentils, including soybeans and their products
- *Cereals and their products*, such as rice, oatmeal, whole-wheat flour and pasta

Complementary proteins

Protein consists of about twenty-two parts, called amino-acids. Eight of these are particularly important, because they cannot be manufactured by the body. These are called the essential amino-acids. Some foods, such as eggs and oatmeal, contain these in nearly the right proportions for the body to use straight away. Other foods, such as dried beans and lentils and most cereals, do not have them in such convenient proportions. But this doesn't matter, because during digestion the amino-acids from all the foods eaten at the same meal get mixed up and the body puts them together again in the right proportions. So even if a protein doesn't contain exactly the right amino-acid balance, the chances are that the shortfall will be supplied by something else eaten during the day – such as potatoes, a green vegetable, or milk in a cup of tea or coffee.

Proteins from the four groups listed above complement each other, so you can make more protein available to yourself by eating foods from two or more of the groups at the same meal, such as lentil soup with a whole-wheat roll. A reasonably varied vegetarian or vegan diet containing sufficient calories for your energy-needs will naturally supply enough protein without conscious combining.

Carbohydrates

Carbohydrates are used in the body for energy. They are found in starches and sugars, which are present in grains and flour and in products made from these, such as bread, cookies and cakes; and in sugar, honey, jams and preserves. Potatoes are also a good source, while most vegetables (especially legumes), milk and nuts contain small amounts. Many carbohydrates, in their natural, unrefined state, also contain fiber. This means that the body can draw the sugar out of the fiber gradually, as it passes through the digestive tract, resulting in a steady stream of energy.

Fat facts

Fats and oils have been an essential ingredient throughout history – the Egyptians even extracted oil from radishes. There are two sources of fat: animals and plants. The only animal fats which are used in a vegetarian diet are those found in egg yolks or in milk or its products such as cream, butter and cheese. The rest of the fats are of plant origin and include a range of oils and products made from these, namely margarine and hard vegetable fats. Fats can be saturated, unsaturated or polyunsaturated, depending on their chemical structure.

Saturated fats are the ones which are solid at room temperature. Chemically, all their "bonds" have been filled with hydrogen atoms. Most animal fats are saturated and are thought more likely to raise the level of fats in the blood. Unsaturated fats are thick, but not solid, at room temperature. These fats have room for a few more hydrogen atoms. Unsaturated fats are thought to have a neutral effect on the level of fat in the blood: they do not lower it, but neither do they raise it. Olive oil is an example of an unsaturated fat, and countries where this is the main fat used, such as Italy and Spain, have a much lower incidence of heart disease than countries where saturated fats are used.

Polyunsaturated fats are completely liquid at room temperature. These could take many more hydrogen atoms. Many vegetable oils, including safflower, sunflower, corn and soy, are polyunsaturated and thought to help lower the amount of fat in the blood. Polyunsaturated fats can be made more solid, and similar to, but not chemically the same as, saturated fats, by filling up the spare bonds with hydrogen. This process is called hydrogenation and is used in the manufacture of margarines and hard

The sugar question

Refined sugar is an energy food – but that is all it is. It does not supply fiber, to regulate the pace at which the body absorbs it, nor does it contain any vitamins or minerals. It is "empty calories." Real Barbados sugar – the sticky, molasses type – does contain some minerals, vitamins and trace elements. Honey does not contain fiber, but its sugar is mainly in a form which is slowly absorbed by the body. All forms of sweetening, honey included, are best used with discretion. Make sure that any sugar you eat is through positive choice, such as the occasional favorite dessert, rather than through unquestioned habit, such as sprinkling it unthinkingly into tea or coffee or over breakfast cereal. The majority of the recipes in this book are low in sugar, but some "sweet indulgences" are included for the occasional treat, which in my opinion does no harm at all – indeed, is to be recommended, so you don't get too rigid and fanatical – if you eat a healthy diet most of the time.

vegetable fats. However, fats which have been hardened in this way may be more harmful to the body than ones which are naturally saturated.

The unsaturated fats are generally considered to be healthiest, although this is a complicated issue, and there are many experts (and I agree with them) who consider that the naturalness of butter makes it preferable to margarine, which is a processed food. However, most authorities agree that the important thing is to reduce our total fat intake. Although a small amount of fat is needed for health, most people in developed countries eat too much fat and of the type which the body does not require. Much of this may be in the form of "hidden fat" in foods like pies, crackers, cookies, chocolate and cakes. Some foods, such as milk, can be confusing, because although the percentage of fat is low, they are eaten in relatively large quantities, and the fat intake increases. The kind of fat which the body does need is found in cold-pressed unsaturated oils, seeds, nuts, olives and avocados. Apart from these, I think the important thing is to be aware of the amount of fat you're eating and to reduce it where you'll miss it least. Cereal and whole-grain dishes, pasta, legumes, fruit and vegetables are all low in fat, and including generous quantities of these in your meals will automatically reduce the amount of fat you eat.

Fiber

Fiber is found only in fruit and vegetable products; it is the wood, cellulose and gums which make up their structure. Dairy products do not contain fiber, nor do meat and fish, although they have a chewy texture. Fiber is needed to enable the digestive system to function effectively and is therefore essential for good health. A typical vegetarian diet is naturally high in fiber. Good sources are peas and beans (both dried and fresh); most vegetables, especially cabbage, carrots, potatoes in their skins, spinach and corn; oats and other whole-grain cereals, including products made from them such as whole-wheat bread; dried fruits, especially apricots; fresh fruits, especially apples, bananas, blackberries and raspberries. Try to include at least one good source of fiber at every meal.

Minerals and trace elements

Iron

Iron is essential for making red blood cells, and a lack of iron in the diet can lead to anemia. This is one of the nutrients which needs watching, although a properly balanced vegetarian diet can provide enough. Iron is found in all legumes, lentils and soybeans being particularly rich; in whole grains and their products, such as whole-wheat bread and pasta; in nuts and seeds, especially pistachios and pumpkin and sesame seeds; in dark green leafy vegetables; and in dried fruits, apricots and prunes (also prune juice) being particularly good sources. Seaweeds are also rich sources, as are brewer's yeast, molasses, wheat germ and egg yolk.

Zinc

An important trace element, zinc is essential for healthy growth and healing, for sexual maturity and reproduction, and for the digestion of protein and carbohydrates. A shortage of zinc is often manifested in white flecks on the fingernails, and sometimes in skin problems. There also seems to be evidence of a link between a zinc deficiency and the eating disorders anorexia nervosa and bulimia. Whole grains appear to be good sources of zinc, as do legumes, but these all contain a substance called phytic acid which can bind the zinc so that we cannot absorb it all. It is not known to what extent this happens, and there is evidence that the body quickly adapts to the phytic acid when whole grains

are eaten regularly. Also, when bread is made with yeast, the proving process appears to inhibit the phytic acid. Adding some vitamin c to the dough also helps. Best sources of zinc for vegetarians and vegans are wheat germ, oatmeal, peanuts and brewer's yeast, and, for those eating dairy products, cheese and skim milk. Dried figs are a good source, as are nuts and seeds (especially sesame seeds and pumpkin seeds), corn and peas. Small but useful amounts are found in most green and yellow vegetables and fruits, such as spinach and mangoes.

Calcium

Calcium is essential for the healthy formation of bones and teeth, and for normal functioning of bones, nerves, muscles and heart. Best sources are cheese, milk and milk products. Other good sources are legumes, especially soybeans and soy flour; eggs; dried fruits, especially figs; almonds, sesame seeds and tahini, and sunflower seeds; most dark green vegetables, especially watercress and broccoli; brewer's yeast, carob and molasses. Seaweeds, especially hijiki, arame and wakame, are particularly rich, and Japanese bancha twig tea, from Japanese shops and some health food stores, is another useful source. In an area where the water is hard, some calcium is absorbed from it. White bread, cookies and cakes, and brown (but not whole-wheat) bread supply useful amounts, because the flour is fortified with calcium. Whole-wheat flour and bread contain a small amount of calcium, but it is not known how well the body can absorb it because of the phytic acid also present.

A balanced vegetarian diet, including some cheese and milk, is unlikely to be short of calcium. Vegans, or vegetarians eating very little dairy food, can get enough by eating plenty of the calcium-rich nondairy foods mentioned above.

Magnesium

Magnesium is needed for many important roles in the body, including the metabolism of carbohydrates. It is found in a wide range of foods and is not damaged by heat, though it is soluble, so may be lost if the water in which vegetables have been cooked is thrown away. A deficiency of this mineral alone is rare, except as a result of disease or where there is general malnutrition. Best sources are nuts and seeds, whole grains and products made from them, dried fruits, legumes (especially soybeans), brewer's yeast, fresh fruits and vegetables.

Iodine

A vital trace element, iodine is essential for the healthy functioning of the thyroid gland. The most reliable sources of iodine are seaweed and iodized sea salt. Sea salt contains iodine but it disappears during storage. Getting enough is not a problem.

Vitamins
Vitamin A

Vitamin A is needed for healthy skin, eyes, hair, nails and mucous membranes, and for resistance to infection. It is found in dairy products, eggs and margarine, and in all dark green and some yellow vegetables, as carotene, a substance which the body can convert into vitamin A. Carrots are a particularly rich source of carotene, as are apricots (fresh, canned and dried). Prunes, cantaloupes, red bell peppers, spinach, parsley and watercress are also good sources. A normal vegetarian diet, with its emphasis on fresh fruit and vegetables, is unlikely to be deficient in vitamin A.

B Vitamins

The B vitamins are important for the metabolism of other foods, the healthy working of the nervous system, the production of red blood cells and many other vital functions. They are found in whole-grain cereals and products made from them such as whole-wheat bread and pasta. Wheat germ, brewer's yeast and yeast extracts are other excellent sources of B vitamins, as are nuts and seeds, eggs, dried and fresh peas and beans, leafy green vegetables, potatoes, avocados and dried and fresh fruits.

Best sources of B1, thiamine, are dried and fresh peas and beans (especially soybeans and soy flour), wheat germ, oranges, dried fruits, sunflower seeds and Brazil nuts.

Milk is a major source of vitamin B2, riboflavin, so vegans and vegetarians who are not eating much dairy food need to make sure their diet includes other foods that are rich in this vitamin: leafy green vegetables, mushrooms, soybeans and soy flour, nori (p. 81), almonds, prunes and fresh dates.

Vitamin B3, niacin, is also found in the foods mentioned above. One of the richest sources of all is mushrooms, and dried peaches, plums, sesame seeds, sunflower seeds and wholegrains, peanuts, wheat and brewer's yeast are also particularly good.

The salt question

We all need some sodium, the main ingredient of table salt, but because of the amount of salt added during food processing and cooking and at the table, most of us ingest two or three times more than is considered healthy. Too much salt can encourage high blood pressure, which, in turn, can make us more vulnerable to heart attacks and strokes. Eating natural high-fiber foods, such as fresh vegetables, dried beans and cereals, while using salt sparingly, helps protect against these problems. Potassium-based salts have been greatly improved over recent years and can be very useful in reducing your sodium intake. Using fresh herbs, spices and lemon juice as seasonings also helps to reduce the need for salt. It is surprising how quickly you get used to the flavor of less salty food.

An adequate supply of B6, pyridoxine, is important for preparation for pregnancy, and studies have found it can also help alleviate premenstrual tension. So there's every excuse for eating avocados, which are a particularly good source, as are bananas, currants, raisins and sultanas, sunflower seeds, and soybeans and soy flour.

Folic acid is another vital B vitamin, especially during pregnancy. In addition to the sources mentioned above, leafy green vegetables are rich in this vitamin, especially chicory and lettuce; also avocados, oranges, almonds and walnuts. Up to 50 percent of folic acid is destroyed by heat, so there is obviously an advantage in eating these foods raw. B12 is found in dairy products and eggs, yeast extracts, fermented foods, alfalfa sprouts and seaweeds. Some soy milks are also fortified with this vitamin. A B12 supplement may be advisable for vegetarians who are not eating many dairy products and for vegans, unless they are eating good quantities of the foods mentioned above.

Vitamin C

Vitamin C protects against infection, speeds healing and the growth and repair of tissues, and is needed for the absorption of iron. It is found in a wide range of fruit and vegetables and getting sufficient vitamin C is not usually a problem for vegetarians. Particularly good sources are leafy green vegetables, tomatoes, peppers, potatoes, black currants, kiwi fruit, strawberries, papayas, cantaloupe and oranges.

continued on p. 16

MENU
Sunday Brunch

SERVES 8

Gratin Dauphinois
190

Wild Mushrooms in Cream with Pastry Leaves
272

Pipérade
215

Dried Fruit Compote
102

The preparation for this brunch can mainly be done the night before so that you can sleep late on Sunday morning if you feel like it. Don't forget to put the Gratin Dauphinois into the oven in good time. Move it to the coolest part of the oven (or take it out and keep warm) when you want quickly to bake the pastry leaves for the Wild Mushrooms in Cream with Pastry Leaves; these can be cut out the night before and kept overnight in the refrigerator. The Dried Fruit Compote can also be kept in the fridge, chilling, until the last minute.

Make the vegetable part of the Pipérade the night before, too. Then all you have to do at the last minute is bake the pastry leaves, heat the wild mushroom mixture, and finish making the Pipérade after your guests have arrived. To drink, you could serve good spicy Bloody Marys, made by flavoring tomato juice with salt, pepper, lemon juice and a good dash each of Worcester sauce (choose a vegetarian one, without anchovy extract) and Tabasco, and serving in tall wine glasses with ice and vodka. Or, better still, offer a Mimosa, made from equal parts of freshly squeezed orange juice and non-vintage champagne or dry sparkling wine, or a fruit juice-based cup using apple or orange juice.

Vitamin D

Vitamin D is necessary for the absorption of calcium, which is needed for strong and healthy bones and teeth. It is not damaged by heat, but is found only in a quite restricted group of foods. The richest sources are margarine; fortified dried, skim and evaporated milk; eggs; and fortified breakfast cereals. If you are using soy milk, it is a good idea to find one which contains vitamin D: read the label. Seaweeds are the only vegetable source of vitamin D (p. 81).

In white-skinned people, vitamin D is also formed by the action of sunlight on skin, but this does not happen in dark-skinned people, so they can become deficient in this vitamin if they are not getting enough in their diet. Vitamin D supplements are available and some experts recommend these for everyone, particularly children and old people (who do not get out into the sun very often). Vitamin D is toxic in large doses, so if you take a supplement, do not exceed the recommended dose, and check first whether any multivitamin you may be taking contains vitamin D.

Vitamin E

Vitamin E is needed for the elasticity of tissues, for general vitality and healing, and for the healthy functioning of the heart and arteries. It may also increase fertility and help to prevent high blood pressure.

Vitamin E is found in a wide range of foods and deficiency in this vitamin is rare, especially in a vegetarian diet, which generally contains plentiful amounts. Heat does not damage it significantly, but processing and prolonged storage can. Best sources are cold-pressed corn oil, wheat germ, nuts and seeds (especially almonds, hazelnuts, peanuts and peanut butter), avocados, blackberries and sweet potatoes. Also valuable are eggs, all whole grains, dried peas and beans and leafy green vegetables.

Vitamin K

Vitamin K is needed for the metabolism of proteins and for the clotting of blood. It is made by the intestinal bacteria and is also found in leafy green vegetables, cauliflower, tomatoes, egg yolk, peas and beans, potatoes, carrots, seaweeds and alfalfa. It is not thought to be damaged by cooking processes. A vegetarian diet supplies the requirements of this vitamin, especially if it includes a daily serving of leafy green vegetables.

Vitamin supplements: to take, or not to take?

Opinion is divided between those who say vitamin supplements are a necessary protection in these days of pollution and artificial fertilizers, and those who say that taking concentrated doses of nutrients is unnatural and alien to a pure way of eating. And no one knows how well vitamin supplements are actually assimilated by the body.

Personally I don't take any, although I think that they can be useful in certain cases where there is difficulty in eating healthy foods in the quantity needed to give enough vitamins and minerals – with fussy children, for instance, or older people, or after illness or during periods of rapid growth.

A vitamin D supplement is recommended for young children and older people who do not see much sun (see left). Yeast tablets are useful if you find it difficult to eat plenty of the B vitamin foods, but you really have to take them by the handful to make any impact. And B12 is a good idea for vegans and for vegetarians who are eating only small amounts of dairy products. I have a great deal of faith in the ability of a healthy body to adapt to the foods it is given (provided always that these are natural and unprocessed) and to utilize the nutrients available. I also believe that if you're eating a healthy diet, with plenty of variety, your body will let you know if it is lacking anything vital, by making you fancy certain foods that have the nutrients you need at that time.

Learning to love the soybean

Soybeans and soy flour are rich sources of nutrients, but, in my opinion, so difficult to make palatable! However, sprouted soybeans are delicious and make an excellent crunchy addition to salads, stir-fries and sandwiches. They are easy to produce at home (p. 207) so you can always ensure you have a supply of them handy.

Try a vitality salad of soy sprouts, alfalfa sprouts, shredded lettuce, chopped tomatoes, grated raw beets and carrots, layered into a bowl and topped with mayonnaise.

Creamy soy milk (p. 106) and tofu (p. 108), which can both be made at home, are other palatable ways to eat soy.

Planning vegetarian meals

When you're changing to vegetarian eating, or trying out some vegetarian meals, it's probably easiest to think of the meal you'd normally eat and then swap the meat or fish for a vegetarian main course: nut or lentil burgers instead of beef burgers; steamed vegetable pudding instead of steak and kidney pudding; savory nut or lentil loaf instead of meat loaf. Once you've planned the main course, the vegetables and a sauce if needed can be chosen to go with it.

Vegetarian eating can follow the conventional daily pattern of breakfast, one light meal and one more substantial meal; or it can be based on several light snack meals, or whatever schedule suits you. I do think that for anyone interested in healthy eating, whether a meat eater or a vegetarian, it's helpful to think of the fat content of the day's – or even the week's – eating as a whole, balancing a high-fat meal, such as a cheese tart, with a low-fat meal, such as a mixed salad dressed with lemon juice, or a platter of steamed vegetables with chopped fresh herbs. I personally find breakfast an easy meal to make fatless – fresh fruit and weak tea without milk is my favorite – and this allows scope for the rest of the day. Other low-fat breakfasts would be a whole-grain cereal with skim or low-fat milk (or soy milk) or whole-wheat toast with honey.

Vegetarianism in pregnancy

Ideally, preparation for pregnancy should begin several months before conception, and not only with the prospective mother, but with the father too, as the diet of both determines the health of the baby. During this time of preparation it's a good idea to rely on some form of contraception other than the pill, as this is known to affect the body's ability to metabolize vitamins B6, B2, B12 and folic acid, as well as zinc and iron. Make sure that your diet contains plentiful sources of these vitamins (see above) and consider supplements of vitamins D and B12 if your diet is low in dairy products. Eat plenty of the foods rich in vitamin E and include sea vegetables or seaweed-based jelling agents whenever you can (see p. 81) for iodine and other trace minerals, or take kelp tablets two or three times a week. It's also advisable to cut out or reduce the amount of alcohol you drink, and to stop smoking.

Nutritional requirements increase dramatically

A typical day of healthy vegetarian eating

Breakfast

Orange or grapefruit juice
Whole-grain muesli with milk and raisins
Whole-wheat toast with honey or marmalade
or
Fresh fruits in season
Tea, coffee or herb tea

Lunch

Salad sandwiches
or
Baked Potato (p. 190) with grated carrot and watercress
or
A vitality salad of shredded lettuce, chopped tomatoes, grated carrots and beets, sprouted soybeans and chopped nuts
or
A bowl of Leek and Potato Soup (p. 134) and whole-wheat bread
or
Hummus (p. 41) with Crudités (p. 143) or pita bread
Apple
Tea, coffee or herb tea

Evening meal

Tagliatelle Verde with Lentil Sauce (p. 252)
Green salad with avocado and fresh herbs
Apricot and Orange Fool (p. 282)
Tea, coffee or herb tea

Snacks

Whole-wheat bread
Nuts
Fresh and dried fruit

during pregnancy and lactation. Extra iron, folic acid and other B vitamins, and vitamins A, C, D, and E are needed, as well as about 50 percent more calcium than normal. You can meet this by having an extra serving of cheese or yogurt, or by taking an extra 2 cups of skim milk or calcium-fortified soy milk. Or you could step up the amount of nondairy sources of calcium in your diet, such as broccoli, kale, dried figs, almonds, sesame seeds, soybeans and soy flour, arame and hijiki. A couple of glasses a day of the creamy almond milk on p. 238 is another delicious way to take extra calcium as well as plentiful B vitamins, iron and other minerals.

If you don't mind brewer's yeast, having 1 heaping tablespoon of nutritional yeast flakes each day is a convenient way to boost your intake of the important B vitamins. Sprinkle this over your breakfast cereal or stir it into some fruit juice. This will also supply the additional thiamine, riboflavin, niacin, B6 and folic acid needed during both pregnancy and lactation, together with some useful iron, zinc and a little calcium and magnesium, while supplying only 46 calories.

A well-balanced vegetarian diet is probably naturally rich enough in vitamins A, C and E to cover the additional requirements for these during pregnancy. However, you could make doubly sure by having a piece of melon, an extra orange or half-cup of orange juice, a large banana or an extra serving of green vegetables each day, to supply vitamins A and C, and by using cold-pressed corn oil, for vitamin E, in salad dressings.

Vegetarian babies

For the first six months of life, breast milk supplies all the nutrients a baby needs and ideally solid food should not be introduced before then, although it can be given, with care, when the baby is four months old, if he no longer seems satisfied with breast milk, but certainly not before then. The reason for avoiding the early introduction of solid foods is that the baby's digestive system is immature and an allergic reaction is therefore more likely; also, the baby needs the closeness and emotional satisfaction which breast-feeding gives.

Start to introduce the baby to solid food by giving half a teaspoon of a fruit or vegetable purée, either before or after one of the main feedings of the day: lunchtime is often most convenient. Either cooked or raw fruits and vegetables can be used: mashed

---

High-vitality foods

There are certain foods which are particularly rich in a number of nutrients, and worth including in your meals as often as possible. These are:

- [ ] Legumes *especially soybeans and soy sprouts, lentils, chick peas, and red kidney beans*
- [ ] Whole grains, *especially oatmeal and millet, whole-wheat flour and bread, pasta, wheat germ*
- [ ] Nuts, *especially pistachios, almonds, Brazil nuts, hazelnuts and walnuts*
- [ ] Seeds—*sunflower, pumpkin and sesame seeds*
- [ ] Fresh fruits, *especially apples, bananas, oranges, dates, blackberries, strawberries, cantaloupe, kiwi, mango, papaya*
- [ ] Dried fruits, *especially dried peaches*
- [ ] Vegetables, *especially fresh peas, beans, corn, mushrooms, avocados, alfalfa sprouts, potatoes, tomatoes, carrots, red bell peppers and sweet potatoes*
- [ ] Dark green leafy vegetables, *especially broccoli and other brassicas, chicory*
- [ ] Seaweeds, *especially hijiki and nori*
- [ ] Brewer's yeast and yeast extract
- [ ] Milk and cheese

---

avocado, ripe banana, ripe peach or mango; very finely grated raw apple, pear or carrot; or cooked and puréed carrot or mashed potato. These first spoonfuls are really to get the baby used to the texture of solid food; breast milk will still be his main source of nourishment, and he also still needs this for the emotional satisfaction which comes from sucking.

Once the baby is happy with these small quantities of solid food, you can gradually increase the amount so that after two or three weeks he is having perhaps two tablespoons at a time. Babies of over six months can also have a little bread mashed into the food; remove the crusts and use either a 100 percent whole-wheat bread, or, if this proves to be too laxative (as it can for some babies), try an 81–85 percent whole-wheat bread, perhaps with added wheat germ.

Gradually, as the baby takes more solid food, he won't need so much milk, so that when he is about eight months he will naturally give up one feeding completely. Then you can add extra protein ingredients to the basic fruit and vegetable purées to enrich them. Try adding mashed cooked beans, mashed drained tofu, cooked and puréed lentils, tahini, smooth peanut butter, low-sodium yeast extract, finely ground nuts and seeds, wheat germ, brewer's yeast, low-fat smooth white cheeses such as farmer's cheese, "live" natural yogurt, hard cheese, and egg yolk, thoroughly cooked and mashed, to avoid any danger from salmonella.

You can gradually increase the quantities that you give to the baby for this meal of solids, and if you like you can give a savory course, of, say, puréed lentils or mashed cooked vegetables with some protein added, as suggested above, followed by a "dessert" course of finely grated fresh fruit, yogurt or egg custard. Once the baby gets used to the texture of solid food, you will probably be able to mash rather than purée his foods.

Solid foods can be introduced before or after the other main feedings of the day in the same way, so that gradually these too can be dropped. When the baby is about nine months old the bedtime feeding may be the only one left. Let the baby go on enjoying this for as long as possible; it is important for the bonding with you and the emotional satisfaction which sucking gives. The baby will give it up spontaneously when he is ready. Sometimes this happens by the time he is around a year old, but often babies need to continue for longer. My daughter Claire had just managed to give it up by her second birthday!

"Finger foods" such as fingers of bread, rusks, or raw apple or carrot can be given from about nine months, and can be helpful if the baby is teething. Never leave a baby alone with these foods, and be ready to hook them out with your little finger or to turn the baby upside down and smack him gently in the small of his back if he starts to choke.

Soon you will find that the baby can eat a little of what you as a family are eating. Make sure that this is not too highly seasoned, either with salt or spices, because of the danger of putting too much strain on the baby's kidneys. You could take a little out for the baby before adding these to the mixture. Other things to avoid are foods which contain preservatives, coloring or other additives, and foods which are high in fat, such as pastry and deep-fried foods. Watch, too, the level of fiber; as a vegetarian diet is naturally high in this, make sure the baby has, in addition, some sources of concentrated protein such as egg, cheese, smooth peanut butter or tahini, ground nuts, yogurt or brewer's yeast.

Vegetarian children

A well-planned vegetarian diet can supply all the nutrients which growing children need. Deficiencies would show up as stunted growth, listlessness, poor appetite, lack of energy, slow healing of cuts and wounds, cracks and sores around the mouth, and mouth ulcers. As long as children are healthy, full of energy and growing well, they are almost certainly getting the nourishment they need. It is, however, important that you watch their diet carefully and make sure it is rich in all the essential nutrients.

Few parents manage to get through the child-rearing process without worrying about their child's diet at some point. One of my daughters was so fussy that I sometimes wondered how she managed to keep going, but we came through this phase and she's bright, happy and healthy. I did get her to take vitamin tablets, and I think that a vitamin tablet, including vitamins B12 and D, is a good idea – for the parents' peace of mind as much as the children's nourishment! In my opinion it's best to let them have the foods that they will eat, provided these are reasonably healthy, rather than to try and make them eat what you think they ought to be eating. There are several good sources of most nutrients, so if they balk at one it's usually possible to find an alternative.

Try to include in their diet as many of the high-energy foods as you can, keeping everything as fresh and unprocessed as possible. Keep a strict eye on how much sugar and fat they eat and make sure there are plenty of wholesome snack foods available, such as fresh fruit, whole-wheat bread, rice cakes, nuts and dried fruits, crudités, cubes of cheese and

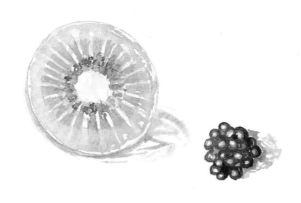

Children's favorites

Children have their own individual tastes, but these are the dishes which I've found to be generally popular with children:

Watercress Soup (p. 130)

Golden Lentil Soup (p. 134)

Leek and Potato Soup (p. 134)

Cheese and Fresh Herb Dip (p. 143)

Chili con Carne Vegetariana (p. 208)

Favorite Coleslaw (p. 161)

Baked Potatoes (p. 190)

Stuffed Baked Potatoes (p. 191)

Potato and Cheese Layer (p. 200)

Savory Lentil Loaf (p. 213)

Cheese Fondue (p. 217)

Cheese and Parsley Fritters (p. 217)

Pizza (p. 218)

Spaghetti with Green Lentil Sauce (p. 253)

Tagliatelle Verde with Lentil Sauce (p. 252)

Macaroni and Cheese (p. 257)

French Onion Tart (p. 261)

Savory Cheshire Cheese and Onion Pie (p. 265)

Spiced Potato and Chick Pea Turnovers (p. 264)

Any of the ice creams, but the Chocolate Ice Cream (p. 280) particularly (and it's healthy)

Fresh Fruit Salad (p. 286)

Old-fashioned Treacle Tart (p. 294)

Country Apple Pie (p. 294)

Steamed Pudding (p. 298)

Pancakes (p. 299)

Any sponge cakes, and particularly Quick Cupcakes (p. 310)

Parkin (p. 308)

flavored yogurts, to keep them off the sweets and potato chips. Encourage them to drink water or unsweetened fruit juice diluted with water or soda water instead of sweetened canned or bottled drinks. If you have the time, pleasing presentation of the food does help; I found that my youngest daughter, Claire, always ate her food better if I took the time to arrange it attractively on the plate or to bake a mini-savory in a ramekin dish. She loved a supper platter – small amounts of all her favorite foods arranged on a plate – cubes of cheese, thin slices of apple, some dates stuffed with almonds, a few crisp lettuce leaves, some carrot sticks. Sometimes I've arranged a salad or an open sandwich in the shape of a face, with grated carrot hair, tomato mouth and so on. If you go to this trouble, you have to take care not to over-react if your lovingly arranged offering is rejected, though in my own experience it usually isn't.

Vegetarian teenagers

As with younger children, it's most helpful to concentrate on the foods that are liked rather than to get into a situation of conflict. Some teenagers may wish to experience eating meat and junk foods if they have always had wholesome vegetarian food at home. If they're into junk foods, try and get them to take some kind of vitamin supplement, and have readily available any natural snacks, such as apples, nuts, whole-wheat bread or cake, that they will eat. The less intense the emotional atmosphere, the more quickly they will be able to discover what they as individuals really want to eat and make their own responsible decisions.

During this period of rapid growth teenagers, especially boys, may have a big appetite; plenty of whole-wheat bread, pasta, rice and potatoes will fill them up, while giving good nourishment. Include as many of the high-vitality foods as possible; soy is a particularly good food if they'll eat it, perhaps in the form of tofu, well sprinkled with a good-quality, naturally fermented soy sauce. Whole-wheat peanut butter or tahini sandwiches, perhaps with sprouted soybeans, or pita breads packed with red kidney beans, salad and any other ingredients they particularly like, are quick snacks which I've known to be popular with this age group, as are vegetarian burgers (pp. 210 and 232) served with a good supply of burger buns and perhaps some baked beans.

At the opposite end of the scale, weight reduction is another issue which frequently arises with teenagers, especially girls. This can be healthily achieved on a vegetarian diet. Include as many iron-rich foods as possible. Zinc is also important; shortage of this mineral has been linked with the eating disorders anorexia nervosa and bulimia. Include plenty of the zinc-rich foods (which are also good sources of iron), such as peanuts, corn and cheese.

Weight reduction on a vegetarian diet

The key to successful weight loss lies in finding a diet which suits your life-style and which can become a permanent way of eating for you once you're slim, to prevent the endless fluctuation of weight and constant dieting that leads nowhere. I've known people to lose weight and to keep it off when they turned vegetarian. The trick is to eat plenty of the foods which are high in fiber and nutrients and low in fat, particularly saturated fat: legumes, grains, fruit and vegetables. Avoid all refined carbohydrates such as white flour, rice and pasta, sugar and even honey. Aim to cut back your fat intake so that it accounts for no more than 10 per cent of the calories you consume, which means avoiding dairy products, nuts, olives and avocados and being careful about the amount of oil you use in recipes. Use skim milk or soy milk. For sweetening purposes use fruit juices, apple or pear juice concentrate or a little real maple syrup.

Research has shown that it is easier to lose weight if you eat the majority of your calories during the first half of the day. Enjoy a really good breakfast of fresh fruit and fruit juice, whole-grain cereal or oatmeal with skim milk or soy milk, and bread or toast with pure fruit preserves. Make lunch your main meal of the day, basing it on legumes, grains or potatoes with cooked vegetables or salad, followed by fresh fruit. Then eat lightly in the evening, avoiding fat: a light vegetable soup or some steamed or raw vegetables, or some fresh fruit, for instance. Eat as much as you want at your meals but do not eat between them, and drink plenty of water – at least 8 glasses a day.

It's best to lose weight gradually – ½–2 pounds a week, not more. When you lose weight at this rate on a high-fiber, low-fat diet, combined with some exercise, you are losing fat, not muscle. You will therefore look and feel fitter while enjoying hearty, delicious meals of healthy foods.

continued on p. 24

Main courses for dieters

Choose recipes that are high in complex carbohydrates (whole grains, legumes, potatoes) and low in fat. Reduce the amount of fat used to not more than 1 tablespoonful and substitute oil for butter or margarine.

Golden Lentil Soup (p. 134)

White Bean Soup with Scarlet Rouille (p. 135)
Pistou (p. 136)

Mixed Bean Salad with Spicy Dressing (p. 157) – reduce the oil and serve with crusty bread and green salad dressed with lemon juice

Rice Salad with Fruit and Nuts (p. 158) – go easy on the pine nuts and oil; serve with green salad dressed with lemon juice

Courgettes with Carrot, Ginger and Almond Stuffing (p. 193)

Stuffed Tomatoes (p. 195)

Sweet and Sour Vegetable Stir-fry with Almonds (p. 199)

Vegetable Curry (p. 202), with brown rice

Chili con Carne Vegetariana (p. 208)

Spicy Lentil Burgers (p. 210)

Lentil Shepherd's Pie (p. 210)

Wild Rice and Chestnuts (p. 240), with steamed Brussels sprouts and potatoes

Saffron Rice (p. 241) and Spiced Rice (p. 241)

Bulgur Wheat Pilaf with Red Peppers and Feta Cheese (p. 242) – leave out the cheese and olives; add plenty of chopped parsley

Rice Pilaf (p. 242)

Vegetarian Paella (p. 243)

Biriani (p. 244) – reduce the oil

Millet Pilaf with Nuts and Raisins (p. 245)

Mixed Rice with Glazed Root Vegetables (p. 246) – sprinkle the root vegetables with lemon or lime juice instead of oil and butter

Couscous with Spicy Chick Pea Stew (p. 247) – use whole-wheat couscous and go easy on the oil

Wholewheat Fusille Colbuco with Eggplant and Wine Sauce (p. 255)

MENU
Spring Dinner Party

SERVES 6

Mushroom and Herb Terrine with Melba Toast
146

Paella Vegetariana with Artichokes
243
Mixed-Leaf Salad with Guacamole Dressing
54 and 73

Glazed Red Fruit Tart
292

This is a relaxed, informal dinner party with fresh flavors. It is also very easy to prepare. Both the Mushroom and Herb Terrine and the Glazed Red Fruit Tart can be made in advance. The melba toast can also be made the day before and wrapped in aluminum foil to keep it crisp, although it doesn't take long to do on the day. Serve guacamole as a salad dressing and garnish it with chopped tomato, onion and chili. The main course of paella is informal but delicious, and looks attractive served from the pan in which it was cooked (if this is presentable!); otherwise, transfer it to a warmed, shallow dish just before serving.

Choose a wine to reflect the informal nature of the meal; I would be inclined to go Spanish and choose a Rioja, or choose a medium-dry white wine with enough power to cope with the flavors of the paella – a Chenin Blanc or a young Riesling, perhaps.

Using the Freezer

The freezer is as much of a boon in vegetarian cookery as it is in conventional cookery and can be used to save both time and money. It is perhaps particularly useful to vegetarians because our main dishes have to be made from scratch. So making a double quantity and freezing half, or freezing some of the components of favorite dishes, such as tomato sauce, pancakes, breadcrumbs for stuffings and toppings, ready-grated cheese and cooked peas, beans and lentils, is really worthwhile. It is also useful to have a supply of commercial frozen foods.

Foods which freeze

- ☐ *Fresh fruit and vegetables*
- ☐ *Cooked legumes*
- ☐ *Dairy products with a fat content above 40 percent*
- ☐ *Soups, savory bakes and pastries, sauces*
- ☐ *Cakes, cookies and breads*

Foods which do not freeze

- ☐ *Leafy salad vegetables such as lettuce; also raw tomatoes*
- ☐ *Hard-boiled eggs, raw eggs in their shells – store raw egg yolk and white separately to prevent the yolk toughening*
- ☐ *Dairy products with fat content below 40 percent*
- ☐ *Food strongly flavored with garlic or celery, as garlic may develop "off" flavors and celery intensifies*
- ☐ *Dishes containing cooked potato, which toughens, although mashed potato is satisfactory*

Freezer standbys

Commercial frozen foods

Frozen foods which I find useful are frozen peas, petits pois, corn kernels, spinach, puff pastry and phyllo pastry. Frozen raspberries and cream can be used to make a last-minute special dessert.

Homemade dishes

The majority of vegetarian dishes freeze well; either make up a double quantity, and freeze one, or have a cooking session to stock up the deep freeze.

Soups, casseroles and stews freeze well, but don't use garlic or celery to flavor soups and savories. Freeze in a container which allows enough room for expansion. Allow plenty of time for thawing: 6–8 hours for a quantity to serve 4–6 people. Most vegetable and bean dishes freeze successfully; Red Cabbage Casserole (p. 180) and Ratatouille (p. 187), for instance; also Chili con Carne Vegetariana (p. 208) and Lentils and Mushrooms au Gratin (p. 207).

Both savory and sweet pies and pastries freeze well; I think they are best frozen uncooked; do not make any holes in the top – add these just before cooking. Mushroom Pâté en Croûte (p. 270) is a useful dish to freeze for a special occasion.

Burgers and croquettes freeze exceptionally well. They are best open-frozen. To open-freeze, place on a tray or baking sheet, freeze until solid, then pack. Spicy Lentil Burgers (p. 210), Nut Burgers (p. 232), Cheese and Parsley Fritters (p. 217) and Felafel (p. 208) are all worth freezing.

Spinach Lasagne (p. 256) (frozen before baking) and Little Twice-Baked Soufflés (p. 223), are successful, as are Brie Parcels with Cranberry Sauce (p. 227), Gruyère Profiteroles (p. 216), and Gruyère Roulade with a vegetable filling (not avocado) (p. 224). Nut and lentil roasts are superb cooked until three-quarters done, then cooled and frozen. To use, thaw, then cook for about 30 minutes. Of the puddings, cheesecakes, ices, sorbets, pies and tarts freeze well, as do cakes and biscuits. Both scones and breads are good partially cooked before freezing, then thawed and cooked before eating.

Ingredients

It's very helpful and time-saving to have some much-used ingredients in the freezer, as well as sauces and other things which are needed for making up dishes.

Stock can be frozen in 1-cup quantities. Any leftover lemon juice can be poured into ice cube containers and frozen.

There are many uses for spare egg yolks and egg whites. Stir a pinch of sugar or salt into each egg yolk (depending on whether you want to use it for sweet or savory dishes) to stabilize it. Then freeze yolks and whites separately in ice cube containers.

Basic much-used sauces such as Fresh Tomato (p. 170), Italian Tomato (p. 171), and any others that you particularly like and use often such as Sauce Soubise (p. 173), Béchamel Sauce (p. 175), and Cheese Sauce (p. 175), are also handy to have in the freezer.

Cooked beans (p. 40) can be packed in 1½-cup portions and frozen, as can cooked crêpes. Interleave the crêpes with wax paper before freezing so that you can take them out individually as needed.

Pastry shells can be baked blind (p. 266) and then frozen. They are handy for filling with vegetables in a creamy sauce or a light egg custard mixture for quick meals.

Chopped parsley, fresh breadcrumbs and grated cheese can all be frozen in plastic bags. Grate up any additional cheese and just add it to the bag.

Secrets of successful freezing

Freeze food which is of good quality; if it is hot, cool quickly, package carefully, freeze as rapidly as possible.

Pack foods carefully to protect them and to prevent strongly flavored foods from tainting others.

Allow room for liquid contents to expand.

When sealing plastic bags, make sure that as much air as possible has been extracted.

Label each package with as much information as possible, include contents, date frozen and servings.

Freezer storage times

Bread	3 months
Butter: salted	3 months
unsalted	6 months
Cakes, plain or iced with butter icing	3 months
Cheese	6 months
Cookies	3 months
Cream	3 months
Eggs	6 months
Fruit prepared with sugar	9 months
Fruit without sugar	3 months
Ice cream	3 months
Margarine	5–6 months
Vegetables	6–9 months
Vegetarian savory dishes	3 months

Freezing vegetables

For best results, vegetables need to be blanched before freezing. Prepare the vegetables in the usual way. Bring a large saucepan of water to a boil. Put 1 pound prepared vegetables into a wire basket and plunge this into the boiling water. When the water comes back to a boil, start timing the vegetables: 2–3 minutes for leafy vegetables, peas and beans, broccoli, small cauliflower florets, small carrots, Brussels sprouts, zucchini; 7–10 minutes for corn on the cob, depending on size. Remove from the water immediately and put the vegetables under a cold running tap until they are cooled through. Drain well, then package individually and freeze immediately.

To freeze fresh herbs, see p. 118.

Freezing fruit

Perfect fruit can be frozen raw, or it can be sprinkled with sugar or covered with a syrup made by heating 1¾ cups sugar in 2½ cups water until the sugar has dissolved, then cooling. Less perfect fruit can be stewed in the normal way (p. 84), sweetened with sugar to taste, then frozen; ripe, soft fruits such as strawberries, mangoes and peaches can be puréed raw, sweetened, and frozen. A little lemon juice can be added to prevent the fruit from discoloring. Fruit for making jam or marmalade can be kept in the freezer until you are ready to use it.

Using the Microwave

Another time-saving piece of equipment, the microwave oven can be used to speed preparation of dishes and also to defrost and quickly reheat prepared dishes. The dishes suggested for freezing can be reheated successfully in the microwave oven if they are frozen in microwave-proof containers.

Microwave power

The power of microwave ovens ranges from 500 to 700 watt outputs. Many have a variety of settings, ranging from "warm" (100 watts) and "defrost" (230 watts) to "full power" (600–700 watts). Personally I do not think there is any advantage in having numerous settings; I find "defrost" and "full power" are the only ones needed. I do think, however, that there is a great advantage in having an oven which combines microwave with a conventional oven and broiler. They are more expensive but give excellent results, combining speedy microwave cooking with traditional browning and crisping.

Microwave containers

Choose shallow dishes, preferably round or oval in shape, made from pottery or heatproof glass: dishes sold as suitable for dishwashers are usually suitable for the microwave too. Do not use dishes made of metal or with metallic decorations, and avoid covering food with aluminum foil, as these can damage the magnetron.

Cooking in the microwave

Arrange the food around the edges of the dish, with the thickest part of the food towards the outside of the dish; do not pile the food up. Some foods need stirring during cooking time; this helps even distribution of heat. Many dishes need to be allowed to stand (usually for about 5 minutes) after microwaving, to give the heat time to penetrate the food fully. The more food in the microwave oven, the longer the cooking time. When cooking savory dishes or vegetables, the food cooks more quickly if it is covered; a dinner plate is good for this, and it gets warmed through at the same time, ready to serve the food on.

Vegetables do not cook any more quickly in a microwave oven than by conventional boiling or steaming, but they keep their color well and the goodness and flavor are conserved because of the small amount of water used. They cook best if cut into fairly small pieces, placed on a large plate and sprinkled with water, allowing about 3 tablespoons water for 1 pound of vegetables.

Dried peas and beans can be cooked in a microwave, and although you do not save much time by doing them in this way, they do cook well. Soak them as usual, if necessary (p. 40), then put them into a shallow container. Add boiling water to cover them by about ½ inch. Red kidney beans should be soaked and then boiled hard for 10 minutes before you put them into the microwave. Split red lentils and green or brown lentils do not need soaking; just cover them generously with water, and cook split red lentils for 10 minutes and the other types for 20 minutes, in each case followed by 10 minutes standing. It's a good idea to stir the lentils two or three times during the cooking time. Soaked black-eyed peas, cannellini beans or navy beans take 20–30 minutes, followed by 10 minutes standing; soaked chick peas take 30–40 minutes, plus 10 minutes standing. Red kidney beans, black beans and lima beans, all presoaked, and red kidney beans boiled hard for 10 minutes as described, take 45–50 minutes, with 15 minutes standing time after that.

Pasta and rice can be cooked in the microwave, although little time is saved. To cook spaghetti, macaroni or similar pasta shapes, put 8 ounces pasta into a suitable dish and add 2½ cups boiling water and 1 tablespoon oil. Cook, uncovered, for 12–17 minutes, until al dente. For 8 ounces lasagne, use 4 cups boiling water and 1 tablespoon oil, cook for 10–12 minutes and allow to stand for 2 minutes.

To cook rice, put 1¼ cups rice into a deep dish with 2½ cups boiling water and a knob of butter or vegan margarine; cover and microwave for 12–17 minutes for white long-grain rice, 20–25 minutes for brown rice, in both cases followed by 5 minutes standing.

Entertaining and Wine

Creating food which will give pleasure to others, and then enjoying it with them, is, to me, what cooking is all about, and, in this spirit, even a simple meal becomes a celebration. A perfectly planned dinner party can be a delight; but sometimes an impromptu meal, which you've cooked on the spur of the moment while chatting in the kitchen, and washed down with a bottle of vin ordinaire, can be even more pleasurable. The kind of meal and the degree of formality with which it is served depend very much on personal taste and the circumstances such as the people involved, the occasion, the place and the time available.

Throughout this book I have given menu suggestions for different occasions, and there are many more possibilities. The most important thing is to choose food which you like and make well; if you have particular favorites, don't feel shy about repeating them – your friends are probably looking forward to eating them again – at least, I know that's how I feel about my friends' specialties. Choose dishes which will not give you anxiety, then you will be able to enjoy your own dinner party too. A cold first course or dessert – or both – which can be prepared in advance to leave you free to cope with the main course eases the strain. So does serving a simple vegetable accompaniment with the main course, such as green beans or a green salad.

Entertaining has become much more fun now that so many exciting ingredients are available in the stores and markets. Using exotic fruits and vegetables provides a good conversation piece, too. Experiment with a new recipe or ingredients before trying them out on your friends and you will then be able to serve any dish with confidence.

I think everyone feels some degree of nervousness when entertaining others to a meal. Will the food be all right? Will they like it? Have you overlooked something, or made some obvious mistake in the planning? There are various points to look out for, to make sure that everything is as perfect as possible: see the checklist. Then, having prepared everything as carefully as you can, my advice is to relax and enjoy yourself!

Checklist for planning a balanced meal

In planning your meal, check that you have:
- *Contrasting colors within each course and within the meal as a whole; avoid starting with beet soup, for instance, and ending with a compote of red fruits*
- *A variety of different dishes; avoid more than one course based on fruit, pastry, nuts or any other ingredient*
- *Contrast of textures: crisp, crunchy nut roast with a smooth carrot purée, for instance; a creamy soup followed by a crisp main course, such as asparagus in phyllo pastry*
- *A good balance of flavors – avoid, for instance, starting with mint-flavored soup and ending with mint ice cream*
- *Foods of different shapes: don't have a loaf-shaped terrine followed by a loaf-shaped nut roast followed by a chocolate roulade. Plan a balance of round and square, and of dishes which are presented in individual portions and those which are served at the table*

Food presentation

Keep garnishing light, fresh and relevant to the dish. Generally I like to echo in the garnish one of the ingredients which is in the dish, rather than to introduce something new, unless it is witty or relevant in some way. Good food speaks for itself and does not need much garnishing. Instead of garnishing a main course such as lentil burgers or a nut loaf with slices of tomato or lemon, which do nothing for anybody, it can be nicer to serve it with a fresh, light salad, such as Tomato and Basil Salad (p. 73), which gives color to the meal and tastes good as well.

Chopped fresh herbs, the same type as used in the dish, can be sprinkled over as a garnish. It's nice to have a herb garden with a good variety of herbs so you always have a plentiful supply, but supermarkets now sell little packs of most fresh herbs.

Wicker baskets and trays and wooden bowls are most useful for presenting food attractively. A large round wicker tray, lined with leaves, makes an excellent base for crudités and a dip, and also for carrying a steaming hot casserole of food from the oven to the table, acting as tray and placemat in one. Small wicker or wooden bowls, perhaps lined with a colored paper napkin, make attractive containers not only for warm rolls but also for "finger salads," especially for children.

Or try using hollowed-out fruits and vegetables as containers for food. Lemons, red, green and yellow peppers, large zucchini or cucumbers, for example, can all be used imaginatively to give more color to the meal. Fruits such as pineapples, oranges, grapefruit and melons also make good containers for fruit salad mixtures, ice creams or sorbets, and will add that extra flavor to the food.

Arrange food in clumps of color, rather than mixing up colors. A pyramid shape is often a most attractive way to present individual items such as Stuffed Vine Leaves (p. 141), Profiteroles (p. 314) or fresh fruit.

Little extras make all the difference: crudités or fruit arranged on fresh (edible) leaves or on crushed ice; ice in a pitcher of water; a bunch of flowers, simply arranged, on the table, and candles, which immediately give a romantic glow and cover up flaws in the decor and surroundings (which you are probably acutely aware of, but which your friends probably won't even notice). An ice bucket will keep white wine chilled throughout the meal. If you can have matching or harmonizing colors in the table linen, napkins, candles and flowers, this, too, will contribute to the overall atmosphere.

Wine

Wine adds to the pleasure of any meal and gives it a celebratory feeling, while experiencing a meal with food and wines perfectly matched, to enhance each other, is perhaps one of life's greatest pleasures. The way to achieve this is really through experimentation – trying a dish with different wines to see what they do to each other. Try drinking up the last of your main-course wine with the dessert, and you'll know what I mean; the sweetness makes a pleasant wine taste overly sharp. Yet that wine would probably taste excellent with a mellow cheese like mild Cheddar or Fontina. (A very good reason for serving the cheese before the dessert whenever possible.) Equally, a sweet, honeyed wine would marry well with the dessert course.

When choosing more than one wine for a meal, it's common sense to start with the younger or less good wine; move from a young, light wine to a medium-bodied wine with some depth; and end with a full-bodied dessert wine. Choosing wine is now much easier and more interesting since some wine shops have introduced a numbering system, grading each wine from 1 to 10 – the dryest being number 1 and the sweetest number 10. As a general rule, serve white wine before red, the exception being sweet white dessert wines, which end the meal.

The aim when matching wine with food is to get a balance between the two: light dishes with light wines; sharp, lemon-flavored dishes, such as a first course, for instance, with a sharp, pointed wine, like a Sauvignon. Mellow, even slightly sweet foods, such as most vegetables, need a more rounded wine, like a Chardonnay or Chenin Blanc. Dishes with many flavors, or a robust, almost "meaty" taste, need a firm, strong wine which can hold its own beside them, but at the same time is not so good as to be spoiled by the flavorings of the dish: youngish, fruity red wines with medium body are ideal.

Some foods do not flatter any wine. Sharply flavored vinaigrette is an example of this, and it may be better to use a little wine with the olive oil to dress the salad. Strong flavorings of lemon juice, powerful herbs and spices (such as fennel or rosemary, for instance, and curry flavors), artichokes, Brie and Camembert cheese (which make the wine taste strange) and mayonnaise and cream sauces (which coat the palate) are other examples of foods that inhibit the appreciation of a good wine.

Wines with vegetarian food

The choice wine to serve with a special meal begins with the aperitif, which, ideally, should be one which will awaken the palate and prepare it for the meal to follow. My favorite aperitifs to serve (apart from champagne – the ultimate aperitif, incomparable for putting everyone in a celebratory mood before a special meal!) are light, dry to medium white wines, such as a Chenin Blanc, a dry Vouvray or Muscat, or a Sylvaner or Riesling. A dryish vermouth, such as Chambery, served with plenty of sparkling Perrier or Badoit water and a sliver of lemon is another favorite. Wine connoisseurs say that the best nibble to serve with drinks before a meal is plain biscuits, like water biscuits or other unsweetened cocktail biscuits, though I also like juicy, salty black olives.

Many vegetable-based vegetarian dishes are flattered by light-bodied, fruity and not too dry white wines, particularly if the dish also contains nuts, which have a slight sweetness to them. A wine made from the Chenin Blanc grape, such as a dry Vouvray, Anjou or – one of the most pleasant, with

an excellent balance of acidity and honeyed fruitiness – a Savennières, is ideal. The Savennières is particularly successful where there are a number of divergent vegetable flavors. An alternative would be an Australian Fumé Blanc.

Chardonnay-based wines also, with their softness and almost appley flavor, work well with nut and vegetable main courses: a Macon, Pouilly Vinzelles or Pouilly Fuissé, for instance, or a white Burgundy or Chablis from Australia; or perhaps an oaky California Chardonnay or Australian Wyndham Estate Oak Cask.

Alternatively, light-bodied, young, fruity red wines, perhaps served slightly chilled, can be delightful with these types of main course; wines such as a Saumur Champigny, Côtes-du-Rhône, Gamay de Touraine, Saint-Aubin or Beaujolais-Villages. A Brouilly, deliciously round and fruity in flavor, would be another possibility. From Australia, suggestions include Rosemount Beaujolais, Wyndham Estate Beaujolais, Merlot or Chardonnay.

For something fuller-bodied, to support strong herby flavorings, or to go with something like a special nut loaf, a Châteauneuf-du-Pape or a wine from the northern Rhône made from Syrah grapes, such as a Cornas, Saint-Joseph, Côte Rotie or Crozes Hermitage; or a red from the Loire, such as a Chinon Bourgeuil or Saint-Nicolas de Bourgeuil, with their raspberry-scented bouquet, or a Fleurie. California red wines are generally full-bodied and of reliable quality. Among the wines from Australia that have been recommended to me are Wynns Coonawarra Red from South Australia, a Cabernet Sauvignon, Penfolds Bin 389 or a Wolf Blas Yellow Label Shiraz.

For pasta dishes with an Italian orientation, such as Lasagne (p. 256) and Tagliatelle Verde with Lentil Sauce (p. 252) or Fusille Colbuco with Eggplant and Wine Sauce (p. 255), an Italian red wine would be appropriate: a Chianti Classico, Barolo or Barbaresco; or a Côte Rotie from France, or a Cabernet Sauvignon from France or elsewhere.

When it comes to choosing wines for the dessert course, the same principles apply. Sharp-flavored fruit salads and compotes do not go well with wine, although if they include a flavoring of a fruit liqueur such as Cointreau, that, well chilled, can be a good partner for them. Ice creams generally are not good with wine, either, because they numb the palate, though I have enjoyed a good sweet German dessert wine with homemade raspberry ice cream. The wine needs to be sweeter than the dessert so that it does not taste sour when drunk along with it.

Hot fruit soufflés, such as Hot Black Cherry Soufflé (p. 290), are complemented by a good sweet wine – as good a quality as you can afford: a German Beerenauslese, Auslese, Sauternes, Barsac or Montbazillac; or, from Australia, a Brown Bros Orange Muscat. One of these sweet wines complements, also, Pashka (p. 288), Apricot and Orange Fool (p. 282) and Compote of Dried Fruit (p. 102), in the latter case especially if it is marinated in a little of the sweet wine – a Sauternes would be especially good. A chilled sweet wine or harmonizing eau-de-vie or liqueur works with a sorbet; Poire William eau-de-vie with Pear Sorbet (p. 282) for instance, or, with Champagne Sorbet (p. 283) – champagne!

Ingredients

Good cooking begins with good ingredients, and the aim of this section is to provide a guide both to choosing and getting the best from well-loved basics, and to identifying and using some of the more unfamiliar and exotic ingredients. So there are fruits ranging from apples to rhamboutans; vegetables from potatoes to bok choy; and legumes from familiar white or navy beans to black chick peas and urd; plus a worldwide selection of nuts and grains. The sections on mushrooms and truffles, sea vegetables and cheeses offer further delicacies, and there is a glorious profusion of pasta, ranging from tiny stelline and convighi piccole to tortellini, cappelletti and ravioli . . . a feast of vegetarian delights.

⊲ **Fresh chestnut**   **Dried** ⊳ **chestnut**

Marrons glacés ▽

Chinese water chestnut ▽
The Chinese water chestnut is not act
nut but a tuber with a crisp texture

Chestnut △
The sweet chestnut has been cultivated for
thousands of years in southern Europe,
where it is widely used in sweet and savory
dishes

Nuts and Seeds

One of our earliest foods, nuts and seeds feature in traditional recipes throughout the world. Many nuts and seeds, such as walnuts, hazelnuts and sesame seeds, are a useful source of oil. They can also be made into butters, such as peanut butter, or ground into flour. Most nuts and seeds are an excellent source of nutrients, especially protein, iron, calcium and B vitamins. Nutrients vary from nut to nut, and by eating a mixture, you can be sure of getting a balanced range in your diet.

Brazil nut ▽
The seeds of a giant tree which
grows wild in the tropical
South American jungle, Brazil
nuts have a creamy texture

Macadamia nut/Queensland n
A delectable nut with a melting textur
native to Australia but now also grow
southern U.S., South Africa, the Cari
the Mediterranean
and Hawaii

△ **Cob nut**
One of the
varieties of
cultivated
hazelnut

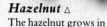

Cashew nut ▽
Native to Brazil, the cashew
nut grows in a kernel,
surrounded by toxic oil, at the
base of an apple-like fruit

Pistachio ▽
The fruit of a small tree native
to Asia and grown in southern
Italy, Sicily and the Middle
East and in California, Texas
and Arizona

Pine nut/pignolia ▽
The seed of the stone pine,
pine nuts were enjoyed by t
Romans in Britain and by t
Indians of North America

Hazelnut △
The hazelnut grows in
Europe, Asia and America
and was certainly eaten
during the Bronze Age

Pecan ▽
A relative of the walnut and a
native of North America,
where it is eaten in large
quantities as a dessert nut

⊲ **Walnut**
The walnut is native to
southeastern Europe and th
leading producer is France,
it is found in western and
central Asia, China, Austra
New Zealand, South Afric
and South America

Almond △
Native to the Mediterranean, almonds
are gastronomically the most important
nut worldwide, much used in
confectionery and baking

Sesame seeds/benne seeds ▽
The dried seeds of an annual plant, probably native to Africa, but cultivated in India and China since ancient times

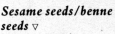

No-additive peanut butter ▷
Available either smooth or crunchy

Tahini △
Made from sesame seeds

Pumpkin seeds ▽
The seeds of a large squash native to America, pumpkin seeds are particularly rich in minerals

Alfalfa seeds ▽
A tiny legume, native to the Mediterranean

Sunflower seeds ▽
The seeds of the sunflower plant, native to Peru but now grown as a crop in many parts of the world

Poppy seeds △
These vary in color from grey-blue to cream

Shredded coconut ▽

Peanut/ground nut/monkey nut △
Native to South America, the peanut is botanically a legume, the outer shell being the pod

Coconut cream ▽

Desiccated coconut △

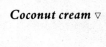

Coconut ▽
The fruit of the coconut palm which grows throughout Southeast Asia, coconut features in many tropical dishes

Tiger nut/chufa △
Native to the Mediterranean and Portugal, tiger nuts are the dried tubers of a sedge

Mixed chopped nuts △

Nuts and Seeds

Choosing and storing

Nuts are at their most delicious when eaten straight from the shell. Because of their high oil content, they go rancid quickly once shelled, so buy them in small quantities from a store with a quick turnover, and, if possible, keep them in the refrigerator or freezer; otherwise store nuts in an airtight jar or canister, and use them up quickly.

Preparing and cooking

Shelled nuts can be used whole, chopped, slivered or ground. The flavor of some, such as hazelnuts and peanuts, is improved by roasting, and this also enables the outer skin to be removed. To roast, place the nuts in a single layer on a baking sheet and bake at 350°F for about 20 minutes, until the skins rub off easily and the nuts underneath are golden-brown. Cool, then rub off the skins in a clean cloth (or leave the skins on if you prefer).

The best way to chop nuts is to place them on a sturdy board and chop with a sharp knife, holding the point down and moving the knife around in a semicircle. To sliver nuts such as almonds and Brazil nuts, hold the nut down firmly on a board and slice thinly across with a knife. Nuts can be ground in a food processor, blender, electric coffee grinder or food mill, finely (consistency of ground almonds), medium (like medium-ground coffee) or coarsely (about the texture of rolled oats). Coarsely chopped nuts can be bought as MIXED CHOPPED NUTS.

Nuts can be used in sweet and savory dishes and as a nibble. They can be made into milks, creams, butters, dips and soups; used as a thickener in sauces and casseroles; added to risottos, pilafs, stuffed vegetable mixtures and salads; sprinkled on top of puddings, gratins, cakes and breads. In vegetarian cooking they can form the principal ingredient of many delicious savories, including burgers, pâtés, pies and loaves.

ALMOND *Prunus dulcis*

Almonds are particularly rich in protein, iron, calcium and vitamin B2. There are two types, sweet and bitter. Bitter almonds are small and contain prussic acid. They are never eaten raw but are made into essence and liqueurs.

Sweet almonds can be bought in the shell, SHELLED, and with the skins removed as whole BLANCHED, SLIVERED, CHOPPED (not illustrated) and GROUND almonds. For best results, buy almonds in the skin and blanch them at home. Put the almonds into a small saucepan, cover with cold water and boil for 2 minutes. Drain and pop the almonds out of their skins by squeezing them.

Almonds are perhaps best known for their use in sweets and in baking. Almonds are blanched, roasted and salted for serving as nibbles and are delicious in main savory dishes (p. 238). Almonds can be made into a particularly good milk (p. 238).

BRAZIL NUT
Bertholletia excelsa

Brazil nuts are rich in fat, protein, the B vitamin thiamine and magnesium. They have a creamy texture and a delicate flavor which makes them excellent for eating raw in mueslis and salads or as a stuffing for dates. Although not used widely in traditional cookery, they can be made into tasty vegetarian loaves, crumbles and burgers, as well as making a good addition to a fruit cake.

CASHEW NUT
Anacardium occidentale

Cashew nuts should be white and plump with a slightly sweet, bland flavor. They can be bought whole, both raw and roasted, halved, or in pieces, which is cheapest. They are useful in vegetarian cooking for both sweet and savory dishes. They can be made into a creamy and delicate milk and topping (p. 238).

CHESTNUT *Castanea sativa*

The chestnut contains more starch and less oil and protein than other nuts, although it is rich in B vitamins. Choose chestnuts which are firm with bright, shiny skins.

Chestnuts can be made into soups, added to casseroles, such as Red Cabbage Casserole (p. 180), or pies, used to make a traditional vegetarian Christmas roast (p. 233), or to stuff cabbage leaves, or served with Brussels sprouts. Puréed and sweetened, chestnuts also make the basis of some delicious desserts.

DRIED CHESTNUTS are time-saving, although their texture is less floury than that of fresh chestnuts. Dried chestnuts should be soaked and cooked like legumes (p. 40) and can then be used to replace fresh chestnuts in recipes, allowing 1 part dried chestnuts to 3 parts fresh chestnuts. Canned whole chestnuts and chestnut purée (available either plain or sweetened) are useful pantry standbys, while chestnuts preserved whole in sugar or syrup as MARRONS GLACÉS make a sweet treat or garnish.

CHINESE WATER CHESTNUT
Eleocharis tuberosa

This is a tuber which is cultivated in China, Japan and the East Indies. It is used sliced as a vegetable and outside Asia is usually bought canned.

COCONUT *Cocos nucifera*

Coconuts can be bought whole and you should be able to hear the liquid inside when you shake them. Make sure that the "eyes" look dry, with no smell of rancidity or mold. To open a coconut, pierce two of the eyes with a skewer and drain out the liquid over a cup. Then hold the coconut horizontally in both hands and bang it down on a stone or concrete surface to break it in half. Cut the flesh away from the shell using a sharp knife, and grate or chop the flesh as required. The liquid is delicately flavored and makes a refreshing, nutritious drink or a flavoring for spiced vegetables.

Coconut flesh can be eaten fresh as a snack or in salads, fruit and vegetable mixtures. It can also be bought DRIED and POWDERED (not illustrated), DESICCATED, FLAKED, SHREDDED or as COCONUT CREAM. Keep in the refrigerator or freezer, or store in an airtight jar and use quickly. Desiccated coconut can be added to cakes, cookies and Crunchy Granola (p. 45), or reconstituted as coconut milk.

HAZELNUT
Corylus avellana, C. maxima, C. colura

Cultivated hazelnuts are derived from the cob, which grows wild in Britain, the filbert, which grows in southern Europe, and the Turkish hazel, which grows in the Middle East. The COB NUT (Kentish cob), which is grown in Kent, is not really a cob but a filbert, and in Spain hazelnuts are known as Barcelona nuts. It is difficult to tell these types apart, once harvested. They can be bought in the shell, shelled but untreated, and whole but skinned.

Hazelnuts are mainly used in baking and confectionery and are a useful nut in vegetarian cookery, being the lowest in fat, a good source of vitamin E and a tasty addition to stuffings, burgers and loaves.

MACADAMIA NUT / QUEENSLAND NUT
Macadamia ternifolia

Usually sold roasted and lightly salted, this has a delicious, delicate flavor. It is expensive and so probably best served simply, as a nibble with drinks, or in a salad, where its flavor and creamy texture can be appreciated.

PEANUT / GROUND NUT / MONKEY NUT
Arachis hypogaea

One of the best sources of protein, iron and niacin in the vegetarian diet, peanuts can be bought in the shell, shelled but raw, roasted unskinned and skinned. They can also be roasted and skinned at home, as described above. Salted and roasted and dry-roasted peanuts are also available, and of course PEANUT BUTTER, either crunchy or smooth.

Peanuts also make an excellent thick sauce for serving with salads or lightly cooked vegetables: reduce roasted peanuts to a purée in a blender or food processor with chili pepper, garlic and fresh coriander to taste, and enough milk, coconut milk or stock to make a thick sauce.

PECAN *Carya illinoensis*

Pecans can be bought shelled or unshelled and are generally used as a dessert nut and in sweet dishes such as pecan pie. They are also sometimes used as a Thanksgiving turkey stuffing, and in vegetarian cooking they provide a useful flavoring and delicious mealy texture which is good in salads and hot nut savory dishes.

PINE NUT / PIGNOLIA
Pinus pinea (Not illustrated)

The most protein-rich of the nuts, pine nuts are always bought shelled and have a fresh, creamy appearance and delicate "pine" flavor. They can be used as they are or lightly roasted in a moderate oven or under the broiler. They are added to omelettes in the pine-clad Landes area of France, but they are more extensively used in Spanish, Italian and Middle Eastern cooking, in pilafs, Spinach Omelette with Raisins and Pine Nuts (p. 214) and Pesto (p. 172), the classic Genoese sauce for pasta. Pine nuts make an excellent garnish for many fruit or vegetable dishes and they can also be made into delicately flavored nut savories (p. 237).

PISTACHIO NUT *Pistacia vera*

Pistachio nuts can be bought in the shell or shelled. They can be eaten as a nibble or as a bright garnish for both sweet and savory dishes. They are rich in iron.

TIGER NUT / CHUFA *Cyperus esculentus sativus*

This dried rhizome has a sweet, almond-like flavor. It can be eaten raw, as a nibble, or made into a creamy milk (p. 238) for a different but nutritious beverage.

WALNUT *Juglans regia*

Walnuts can be bought in the shell, or shelled, as halves or pieces. Buy fresh walnuts, as older ones can become bitter. Their strong flavor is useful in savory nut dishes, perhaps combined with other milder nuts, such as cashews. Walnuts are good in salads, with pasta, and in many sweet dishes such as walnut cake or walnut cookies.

ALFALFA SEEDS
Medicago sativa

Sprinkle alfalfa seeds over bread before baking, or sprout them as on p. 207 and add to salads. Sprouted alfalfa seeds are rich in nutrients, including protein, vitamin C and B vitamins.

POPPY SEEDS
Papaver somniferum

Sprinkled over breads, salads or pasta, or added to cakes or savory dishes, poppy seeds give a pleasant, nutty flavor. In India they are ground and used to thicken curries.

PUMPKIN SEEDS
Cucurbita pepo

Rich in nutrients, particularly protein, iron and zinc, pumpkin seeds can be bought either salted or unsalted and used whole in savory rice and vegetable dishes and mueslis, sprouted (p. 207) for salads and stir-fries, or ground and added to burgers and savory loaves.

SESAME SEEDS / BENNE SEEDS
Sesamum indicum

Rich in B3, iron, protein and zinc, sesame seeds are usually white but may be brown, red or black, depending on the variety. They are delicious when lightly roasted and can be added to sweet and savory crumble toppings, sprinkled over breads, or ground with salt (p. 237). Sesame seeds can also be used in the form of a sticky beige or brown cream, called TAHINI. This is widely used in Middle Eastern cooking, in dips such as Hummus (p. 41) which make delicious additions to vegetarian cuisine. Sesame seeds are also made into the Middle Eastern confection halvah.

SUNFLOWER SEEDS
Helianthus annuus

These can be bought whole, salted or unsalted, and added to stuffings, salads and savory bakes, or ground like nuts. Their flavor is improved by roasting lightly. Sunflower seeds can also be sprouted (p. 207). They are a natural source of many nutrients, notably B1, B6 and potassium.

Green split pea ▽

Yellow split pea ◁
Split peas – dried peas which have been skinned – can be either green or yellow, and cook quickly without soaking

Pigeon pea △
Originating in Africa, pigeon peas are grown in many warm countries and are important in Caribbean cooking

Chick pea and flour ▽

Legumes

A staple food throughout the world for thousands of years, legumes are the dried seeds of pod-bearing plants of the Leguminosae family. They are also known as pulses, a word that is linked to the Latin word *puls*, porridge, and the Greek *poltos*, poultice. Rich in protein, iron, calcium and B vitamins, they are high in fiber and contain virtually no fat, making them the nutritionists' dream food! Legumes are an economical food and when well cooked can be delicious.

Black chick pea ▽
One of the several varieties of chick pea

Dried pea △
Called soup peas in the U.S. and familiar in the U.K. as mushy peas, these are soft and sweet-tasting when cooked

Orange/split red lentil ▽
Orange or red lentils are brown lentils which have had their outer skin removed

Aduki bean ▽
The seeds of a bushy annual plant native to China, aduki beans are a popular ingredient in Chinese and Japanese cooking

Lima bean / butter bean △
Native to South America and grown extensively in Madagascar and the U.S.

Puy lentil △
Popular in France and considered by some to be the best-flavored lentil

Split urd ▷
Probably native to India, where they are called urd dal and widely used, urd beans are available both whole and split

Brown lentil ▽
A tasty lentil which remains whole when cooked but needs careful checking and washing first to remove small pieces of grit

△ **Split husked mung bean**

Green lentil △
Green lentils have a savory flavor and do not break up during cooking

Urd bean △

Black bean △
Native to Mexico and a staple food in Central and South America, black beans cook to a delicious mealy texture

Black-eyed pea/cowpea ▽
Native to Africa, black-eyed peas are popular in South America, India and the Southern U.S. There are around 50 species, some with the black "eye," others without

Fava bean/broad bean △
The original bean, cultivated since the Stone Age; can be pale or mid-brown in color. Fava beans are popular in the Middle East and Italy, where they are known as *il carne del povero*, "the meat of the poor"

Pinto bean △
Also called gunga pea and toor dal, pinto beans are native to India and popular there and in the Caribbean

Lima bean/butter bean ▷
The dried variety of the lima bean is always flat and kidney-shaped but may be quite small, as here

Black haricot bean ▽

Ful medames △
Ful medames beans are native to the Middle East, where they are widely eaten

Borlotti bean △
Also known as "rose coco" beans, borlotti are the most popular dried beans in Italy

Flageolet bean △
Delicate in flavor, color and texture, the flageolet is an immature haricot bean

White bean/haricot bean ▷
Almost certainly native to Guatemala and southern Mexico, this bean is used for baked beans in Britain, and in the U.S., where it is also known as the navy bean

Mung bean △
Mung beans are widely cultivated in China and India, where they are known as mung dal. They are the beans which are made into bean sprouts

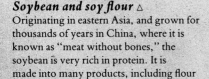

Soybean and soy flour △
Originating in eastern Asia, and grown for thousands of years in China, where it is known as "meat without bones," the soybean is very rich in protein. It is made into many products, including flour

Cannellini bean △
The large creamy white bean popular in Italian cooking

Red kidney bean △
One of the most popular beans, red kidney beans are widely used in South American and Caribbean cooking

Legumes

Choosing and storing

Legumes will keep for many years, but they become drier and harder with time. So buy small quantities of bright, shiny beans and lentils with no hint of dust, damp or mold. Keep them in an airtight container.

Preparing and cooking

Preparation of legumes is simple and involves washing, soaking (some types do not need this) and cooking in plenty of cold water until tender. If you find beans indigestible – their one disadvantage for some people – careful preparation, as described here, followed by thorough cooking, can help, as can boiling them in an uncovered pan.

1 Washing

Swish the beans around in a bowl of cold water, then drain in a colander. If you're using brown lentils, look out for little lumps of dirt and stones.

2 Soaking

Put the beans into a deep bowl and cover them with their depth again in water. Leave to soak for about 6–8 hours or overnight. Then drain and rinse again.

Alternatively, put the washed beans into a roomy saucepan, cover them with water as before and boil for 2 minutes. Then remove from the heat, cover and leave to stand for 1 hour. (This is equivalent to the long cold soak.) Drain and rinse, and cook as follows.

3 Cooking

Pour the beans into a large saucepan, cover them with their depth again in cold water and bring to a boil. Red kidney beans need to be boiled hard for 10 minutes, to destroy any enzymes which can cause stomach upsets. This isn't necessary for other beans. Then turn the heat down and simmer the beans, without a lid, until tender (see chart). Sometimes beans or lentils are added to a casserole or made into a soup after soaking but before cooking; just allow them to simmer until tender. It is best to season them after they are cooked, to

avoid any possibility of the salt toughening the outside and preventing the inside from cooking properly.

If you are short of time, canned beans, available in considerable variety, are an excellent buy.

ADUKI BEAN
Phaseolus angularis
Quick-cooking, with a pleasant, slightly sweet flavor, aduki beans can be used instead of lentils in any recipe for soups, salads, bakes or burgers. They can also be sprouted (p. 207).

BLACK BEAN *Phaseolus vulgaris*
These tasty beans are used to make American black bean soup, and, with rice, to make the Spanish dish "Moors and Christians." Good in vegetable casseroles, as a moist and tasty filling for Vegetarian Moussaka (p. 212), or in mixed-bean salads.

BLACK-EYED PEA/ COWPEA
Vigna unguiculata
These pretty little beans, often popular with children, have a slightly nutty flavor and are particularly useful because they cook in about 40 minutes, without soaking. Use in stews, soups, salads and casseroles.

BORLOTTI BEAN
Phaseolus vulgaris
Borlotti beans can be used in the same ways as any of the kidney bean family and make a pretty addition to a mixed-bean salad.

BUTTER BEAN/LIMA BEAN
Phaseolus lunatus or P. limensis
Known regionally as the lima bean and the butter bean, this legume is used in both its fresh and its dried forms. It is a tasty bean with a mealy texture which absorbs other flavors well. In the Southern U.S., it is popular in succotash.

A quick way of serving lima beans is in cream with mushrooms: fry ½ pound sliced button mushrooms in 2 tablespoons butter or vegan margarine for 3–4 minutes, then add the drained contents of one 15-ounce can of lima beans and heat gently with 1¼ cups light cream and 2 tablespoons lemon juice. Season, then serve sprinkled with paprika and chopped parsley.

CANNELLINI BEAN
Phaseolus vulgaris
Cannellini beans combine well with pasta and make a fragrant salad when mixed with a fresh herb vinaigrette. If you want to adapt chicken or fish recipes to vegetarian cooking, cannellini beans make a good replacement, as do any of the white beans.

CHICK PEA *Cicer arietinum*
Chick peas are available whole, including a BLACK variety, split, ground into FLOUR and also canned, and have a particularly savory flavor. Their cooking time is rather variable, ranging from 30 minutes to 3 hours, depending on the type. Chick peas are included in many traditional recipes, including Felafel (p. 208) and

Soaking and cooking times for legumes

Legumes can be cooked until they are just tender, al dente, or soft, as preferred

All lentils, mung beans and black-eyed peas; split peas	cook without soaking for 25–40 minutes, until tender
Flageolet beans	soak as described, cook for 30–60 minutes
Other beans, including chick peas	soak as described, cook for 1–1½ hours
Soybeans	soak as described, cook for 1½–3 hours

Couscous (p. 247). For hummus, purée 1 cup drained, cooked chick peas with 2 garlic cloves, 2 tablespoons pale tahini, 1 tablespoon olive oil, the juice of 1 lemon and enough of the chick pea cooking liquid to make a creamy consistency; add salt and pepper to taste.

FAVA BEAN/BROAD BEAN
Vicia faba
More familiar in their fresh or frozen state, dried fava beans (illustrated) have quite a strong, earthy flavor. They are widely used in the Middle East. I find their tough skin a disadvantage, but if well chopped in a food processor and blended with olive oil, garlic, lemon and parsley, they make a good dip.

FLAGEOLET BEAN
Phaseolus vulgaris
Popular in France. The fresh color and flavor make flageolet beans particularly suitable for serving as a vegetable (just boil and serve with butter and freshly ground black pepper) or as a salad.

They are also good in a creamy sauce with mushrooms, as described for lima beans (above).

FUL MEDAMES *Lathyrus sativus*
Although they are popular in the Middle East, I find ful medames one of the less useful beans because of their tough skin. But like fava beans (see above) they can be made into a good dip, using a food processor.

LENTIL *Lens esculenta*
There are several types of lentil, the most common being little BROWN LENTILS, dark greenish-grey PUY LENTILS, larger whole GREEN – sometimes called French – LENTILS and split ORANGE/RED LENTILS. Lentils can be cooked without soaking, although soaking speeds the cooking time a little. Lentils are used in the Mediterranean and Middle East to make soups, stews, bakes, sauces for pasta (p. 252) and salads (p. 158), and in India, where they are made into spicy dals (p. 209). They make a good replacement for minced meat in recipes such as Shepherd's Pie (p. 210) and Spicy Lentil Burgers (p. 210).

Whole lentils can also be sprouted (p. 207), when they become juicy with a slightly spicy flavor.

MUNG BEAN *Phaseolus aureus*
Mung beans are small, round and usually green, although there are some black and yellow varieties. They can also be bought skinned and halved to reveal their golden color. Whole mung beans make a good salad, dressed with a tangy lemon vinaigrette. When sprouted (p. 207), they are juicy and good in stir-fries and salads.

DRIED PEA *Pisum sativum*
More commonly used in their split form, whole dried peas can be used in soups and stews, taking a little longer to cook than split peas.

PIGEON PEA *Cajanus cajan*
Pigeon peas are widely used in African, Caribbean and Indian dishes, but in my opinion are not as tasty or useful as some of the other legumes.

PINTO BEAN *Phaseolus vulgaris*
These can be used like red kidney beans and are good in casseroles and to add color to mixed-bean salads such as those on p. 157.

RED KIDNEY BEAN
Phaseolus vulgaris
One of the most useful legumes, red kidney beans are available both dried and canned. They should always be boiled hard for 10 minutes before using. They are used to make the Mexican dish refried beans, in which the cooked beans are fried like a large potato cake; a delicious West Indian stew where they are cooked with carrots, onions, garlic and thyme, with a knob of coconut cream added at the end to thicken and enrich; and a tasty vegetarian chili (p. 208).

SOYBEAN *Glycine max*
Soybeans have a strong flavor and need powerful condiments, such as curry, tomato and garlic, to make them taste good. I think they're nicest when sprouted (p. 207) and added to salads and stir-fries.

Many products, such as miso, soy sauce, tempeh, soy milk and tofu, are made from soybeans and are described in other sections of this book.

SOY FLOUR is high in protein and low in starch, so it cannot be used to make a normal white sauce, although it can be stirred into savory sauces and gravies to add bulk and nutrients and is sometimes added to flour as a dough improver, in the proportion 8 parts flour to 1 part soy flour.

SPLIT PEAS, YELLOW AND GREEN
Pisum sativum
The split and skinned versions of dried peas cook quickly and can be made into a good purée for serving with vegetables, or the two colors may be combined and cooked until just tender, then mixed with a lemon or mint vinaigrette to make an attractive salad. Pease Pudding is a cheap and filling traditional British dish. To make this, see p. 207.

URD BEAN *Phaseolus mungo*
The split and skinned version of a black bean about half the size of a yellow or green pea, the urd bean is best cooked without soaking first. Urd dal is used to make dosas, the crisp pancakes of southern India, and also poppadums.

WHITE BEAN/HARICOT BEAN
Phaseolus vulgaris
White beans are useful all-purpose beans which absorb other flavors well. In France they are called haricots and are used to make the popular and filling cassoulet and Pistou (p. 136). In the U.S., where they are also known as navy beans, they are used to make another traditional dish, Boston baked beans. To make these, simmer 1 cup dried white beans as described above until almost tender, then drain and add to 1 quantity of Italian Tomato Sauce, made as described on p. 171 but not boiled after the tomatoes have been added. Stir in 1–2 tablespoons real Barbados sugar, then bake at 325°F for 2–3 hours, until the sauce is rich and thick and has been well absorbed by the beans. Stir from time to time. Serve with hot crusty bread.

▽ Brown long-grain rice
A good all-purpose, healthy
rice for savory dishes

Brown short-grain rice △
The variety of brown rice to use for puddings

◁ Brown rice flakes

Sweet brown rice ▽

Buckwheat flour △
In Russia, where buckwheat is a staple f[...]
blinis – delicious yeasty pancakes – are
traditionally made with buckwheat flou[...]

Grains

The seeds of cultivated grasses,
grains are the world's most important staple food. They are important
in the vegetarian diet, where they are
recognized as protein foods and
often mixed with other complementary proteins, such as seeds,
nuts, legumes and dairy products, to
make maximum use of their protein
(p. 10). As well as protein and carbohydrate, grains are a valuable source
of iron, zinc, calcium and B vitamins,
and, in their natural, unrefined state,
are also rich in fiber.

▽ Basmati rice, brown

Buckwheat △
Triangular-shaped seeds of a plant belor[...]
to the rhubarb and sorrel family, buckw[...]
can be bought roasted or unroasted

Basmati rice, polished ▽
A particularly aromatic long-grain rice with
slim, pointed grains

Pudding rice ▽
Sometimes called pearl rice,
this is a round-grain rice which
cooks to a creamy consistency

Millet △
The seeds of a hardy annu[...]
grass, millet is eaten as a c[...]
in Africa and Asia and use[...]
source of starch in Russia

Millet flakes ▽

Millet flour △
Millet does not contain gluten, so is useful
where there is an allergy to this

American long-grain rice ▷

Wild rice ▽
The seeds of a water grass
rather than a grain, wild rice
has long black grains which are
chewy and nutty-tasting

Ground rice ▽
Ground rice is polished rice
which has been milled

Brown rice flour ▽
Milled from the whole rice
grain, brown rice flour is useful
for gluten-free baking

Italian rice (arborio) △
The rice to use for an authentic
Italian risotto

Whole-wheat flour (100%) ▽
Milled from the whole grain. No additives (except raising agents) are allowed in 100% whole-wheat flour

▽ **Bran**
The outer husk of the grain, removed during the milling of white flour, and high in fiber

▽ **Rye grains**

Rye flakes ▽

**Whole-wheat flour
%)**
o whole-wheat flour with
e of the bran removed, or
be white flour with some
e germ and bran put back

**Coarse cornmeal or
polenta** ▷
A staple food of northern Italy, where it is used to make polenta, a thick savory porridge

Rye flour △
Widely used to make dark heavy breads (such as pumpernickel) and crispbread in Germany and Scandinavia

nbleached
te flour
consists of 72% of the
e grain

Fine cornmeal △
Milled from corn, this meal is gluten-free and is used to make tortillas, tacos and tostadas

Corn △
Indigenous to Mexico, corn is one of the world's most important cereals

Pot barley △
The whole barley grain, which can be cooked to make pilafs or salads

Pearl barley △
Barley which has had most of its outer husk removed (but still contains more fiber than brown rice!)

miny grits △
which has been steamed,
ed, dried and ground

▽ **Couscous,
whole-wheat**

Barley flour △

Barley flakes ▽

Bulgur wheat △
Popular Middle Eastern wheat which has been cracked by boiling, then redried

Oat grains (groats) △

cked wheat △
eat grains which
e been slightly
ked, good for
ng to muesli
es or sprinkling
op of loaves

Couscous, △
plain

Medium oatmeal ▷
Made by grinding the grain

△ **Whole-wheat grains**
Wheat belongs to two main groups: baking wheat and hard wheat

Semolina △
Flour made from the hard part of durum wheat. Available as whole-wheat and white

▽ **Oat flakes or jumbo
oats**

eat flakes △
e by rolling the whole
at grains to flatten them
make them easier to eat

Wheat germ △
The heart of the grain, where germination occurs, wheat germ is rich in nutrients

Rolled oats △
Oats which have been partially cooked in steam, then flattened by rollers

Grains

Choosing and storing

Grains will keep in their natural un-milled form for a year or so, but they do deteriorate and ideally should be bought fresh and used up within 6 months. Cracked and flaked grains and flours will keep for 3–6 months. Oats – with the exception of rolled oats, where heat has destroyed the enzymes – do not keep well because of their high oil content. Buy in small quantities and use within a few weeks. Oatmeal should smell and taste sweet with no rancid smell or bitterness. Wheat germ, especially if it is the best unstabilized type, which is free from additives, deteriorates rapidly; keep it in the refrigerator and use it up within 3–4 weeks. Keep other grains and flours in airtight containers in a cool, dry place.

Preparing and cooking

Whole-wheat, oat, barley and rye grains are soaked and cooked like dried peas or beans; they can then be tossed in a dressing or mixed with vegetables to make burgers, roasts or stews. Flaked grains, like jumbo oats, and also cracked wheat, make a pleasantly chewy addition to muesli mix and homemade breads; jumbo oats can be mixed half and half with rolled oats for extra-chewy oat bars.

BARLEY *Hordeum vulgare*

Barley is available in the form of whole grains, called POT (or WHOLE) BARLEY, as PEARL BARLEY, which is more refined, and as FLAKES and FLOUR. Pearl barley is often added to soups and makes a tasty casserole.

BUCKWHEAT
Fagopyrum esculentum

Buckwheat is gluten-free and a natural source of rutin, which naturopaths use to treat varicose veins and high blood pressure. It can be bought as grains, ROASTED or UN-ROASTED, and FLOUR. Unroasted buckwheat is the most useful. Wash quickly; then toast in a dry pan. To cook buckwheat, put it in a saucepan with double its volume in water and simmer for about 10 minutes, until the grains are just tender and all the water absorbed. Add butter, or vegan margarine, and seasoning.

BUCKWHEAT FLOUR is used to make pancakes. Try making pancakes as described on p. 299 using a half-and-half mixture of buckwheat and wheat flour and serving with unsalted butter, Black Olive Pâté (p. 258) and sour cream.

BULGUR WHEAT

Sometimes called burghul, cracked wheat or pourgouri, bulgur wheat is easy to prepare and delicious in pilafs or with lots of chopped fresh parsley and mint in the popular Middle Eastern salad, Tabbouleh (p. 159). To prepare bulgur wheat, put the grains into a bowl, allowing ⅜–¾ cup per person, cover with plenty of cold water and leave to soak for about 30 minutes. Then drain and put into a saucepan containing a tablespoon of olive oil, or perhaps an onion or other vegetables such as chopped red pepper and mushrooms, which have been fried in the oil for about 10 minutes, season with salt and freshly ground black pepper and stir over a gentle heat for about 5 minutes, until the wheat is hot throughout. Or put the soaked wheat into an oiled casserole, cover and bake for 15–20 minutes in a moderate oven (350°F).

CORN *Zea mays*

Corn is available as whole grains – fun for 'popping' – and as COARSE or FINE CORNMEAL, and as HOMINY GRITS. Although it is eaten as a staple food in Italy and South America, corn is not ideal for this because of its deficiency in niacin. Cornmeal is made into spoonbread in the U.S. and polenta in Italy (p. 240). It is also used to make cornmeal mush, puddings, and breads. Hominy is corn kernels that have been treated with lye, steamed and hulled; grits are coarsely ground dried hominy.

COUSCOUS

Available as PLAIN or WHOLE-WHEAT, this is made by processing semolina into tiny pellets. A quick way to prepare it is to bring 1¼ cups

---

Cooking perfect rice

There are two methods of cooking rice and each have their devotees. I find both work equally well; it's really a question of which of the methods you find works best for you.

The only rice which needs washing first is basmati, which should be put into a sieve and rinsed under the cold tap until the water runs clear.

Immersion method

Half-fill a large saucepan with water, bring to a boil and add 1 teaspoon salt. Throw in the rice, allowing ⅓ cup per person if the rice is to be served as an accompaniment, or up to ⅔ cup per person if the rice is the main dish, without much else. Simmer, uncovered, until a grain is tender when you bite it. Drain the rice into a colander and rinse it under the hot tap to remove any starch. Then put it back into the saucepan and dry the rice off over a low heat for about 5 minutes, stirring it several times with a fork to prevent sticking. Or put the rice into a shallow ovenproof dish and place, uncovered, in a cool oven (325°F) for about 10 minutes until it is dry.

Absorption method

For this you need to measure both the rice and the water, and it's handy to use the same container for this – a large mug, or a 2-cup measure. Put one measure of rice into a saucepan, add two measures of water and a little salt. Bring to a boil, then cover and turn the heat down as low as possible. Leave the rice undisturbed until it's tender and all the water has been absorbed. Then stir gently with a fork. Or, after it has come to a boil, the rice can be cooked in a cool oven (as above).

water to the boil, add 1½ cups couscous, cover and leave for 2 minutes to swell. Fork in a little butter, reheat gently for 3 minutes and season. For the traditional method, see p. 247.

MILLET *Panicum miliaceum*
Millet contains more protein and iron than any other grain. It can be bought in the form of GRAINS, FLAKES and FLOUR, and is gluten-free. The grains can be made into tasty pilafs (p. 245) and burgers, and the flakes can be cooked to make a creamy gluten-free porridge.

OATS *Avena sativa*
Oats contain more of the B vitamin biotin and more fat than wheat; they are also one of the best sources of soluble fiber (p. 12) and are gluten-free. Oats are available as whole GRAINS, called "whole oat groats", milled to fine, medium or coarse (or "pinmeal") meal, for making Porridge and Oatcakes (p. 322); as OAT FLAKES, or "JUMBO OATS", ROLLED OATS, and various pre-cooked "instant" versions. But even traditional porridge, made from oatmeal, is quick to make. To serve 2 people, bring 2½ cups water and 1 teaspoon salt to a boil, then gradually whisk in ¾ cup medium oatmeal. Simmer gently for 25–30 minutes, stirring occasionally. For Dr Bircher-Benner's original muesli soak 2 tablespoons rolled oats overnight in 3 tablespoons of water and 1 of sweetened condensed milk. Add 1 tablespoon lemon juice, grated lemon rind, ¼ pound grated apple and 1 tablespoon grated hazelnuts.

QUINOA (Not photographed)
An ancient grain dating back to the Incas, grown high in the Andes. Unusually for a grain it contains 20 per cent protein and amino-acids. It cooks to an unusual spiral shape and has a nutty flavor. Wash 1 cup quinoa thoroughly until the water runs clear, to remove a natural, slightly bitter substance which coats the grains and acts as an insect-repellent. Drain well. Bring 3¾ cups of water to a boil then add the quinoa. Cover and cook gently for 15 minutes, then remove from the heat and leave to stand for 5 minutes. It can be used like cooked rice and is good in stuffed peppers, with sautéed vegetables, or as a salad.

RICE *Oryza sativa*
Although there are many varieties of rice, these can be divided into two basic types: LONG-GRAIN, where the grain is four or five times as long as it is wide, and SHORT-/MEDIUM-GRAIN, where the grain is short and rounded. In long-grain types, which include AMERICAN LONG-GRAIN RICE and BASMATI RICE, with slim pointed grains and a particularly good flavor, the grains are more separate when cooked, so these are most suitable for pilafs and rice salads, where you want a "fluffy" texture. The round and medium grains break up more as they cook and cling together. This type includes ITALIAN RICE (ARBORIO), PUDDING (or PEARL) RICE, and SWEET BROWN RICE which is popular in macrobiotic cookery and good as an accompaniment to Japanese dishes. Many varieties of rice can be bought in a "BROWN" version, that is, with just the inedible outer husk removed, or "POLISHED" so that they are completely white (and less nutritious). BROWN RICE FLAKES, GROUND RICE and BROWN RICE FLOUR are also available.

To make traditional British Rice Pudding, put 3 tablespoons short-grain pudding rice into a shallow buttered ovenproof dish. Stir in 2½ cups milk and 2 tablespoons soft light brown sugar. Add a vanilla pod or a few drops of real vanilla extract and dot the top with a little butter. Bake for 2½–3 hours at 325°F, stirring in the skin after about 30 minutes and again about an hour later.

RYE *Secale cereale*
Rye is available in the form of whole GRAINS, FLAKES, FLOUR (white and wholemeal) and cracked grains for topping loaves. Rye lacks gluten so is usually mixed with wheat flour.

Rye flakes are delicious in a Crunchy Granola. Mix ¼ cup sesame or canola oil with 6–8 tablespoons honey or real maple syrup, 2 teaspoons vanilla extract and ½ teaspoon cinnamon, then add to 1½ cups each of rye flakes, oat flakes (rolled oats) and wheat flakes, with ⅓ cup sesame seeds and 1 cup chopped walnuts, hazelnuts, brazil nuts or almonds. Mix well. Spread out in a roasting pan. Bake at 375°F for 20–30 minutes, until crisp, stirring every 5 minutes. Cool; add ⅔ cup raisins.

SEMOLINA
Semolina is the basic ingredient for a popular vegetarian dish, Cheese and Parsley Fritters (p. 217), a variation of gnocchi. It is used to make delectable sweet puddings in Asia, and can be added to cakes and cookies.

WHOLE WHEAT
Triticum vulgare, compactum, durum
Wheat is available in a number of forms, including WHOLE GRAINS, CRACKED WHEAT, WHEAT FLAKES, and flours consisting of various percentages of grain (WHOLE-WHEAT FLOUR, 85% and 100%, and WHITE FLOUR, including UNBLEACHED, which contains fewer additives than bleached). The parts of the wheat, the GERM and BRAN, removed during the milling of white flour are also available. Wheat flour is classified as "hard" or "soft" depending on its gluten content. Gluten is the protein-rich substance which becomes springy and stretchy when water and heat are applied. Flour made from gluten-rich, hard wheat is generally considered best for making bread and for puff and flaky pastries because it produces a strong, springy dough, although soft wheat produces a better-flavored bread and is fine for making the one-rise Grant Loaf (p. 328). Soft flour produces light cakes and cookies with a melting texture.

WILD RICE *Zizania aquatica*
Particularly high in protein, and with a distinctive, slightly smoky flavor, wild rice gives a luxurious touch to a special meal. It can be cooked on its own, using the absorption method described for rice (see p. 44), or with white or brown rice, replacing some of the rice with the same quantity of wild rice.

Fresh fettuccine, plain and verde ▷

Linguine ▷

Long spaghetti ▽
Best-loved pasta, good with any sauce – lentil mixtures are particularly good – or with just olive oil, garlic and plenty of freshly ground black pepper

Spaghettini △
Slim pastas, light and refreshing mixed with colorful vegetables, cooked until just tender

Pasta

Pasta means "dough" in Italian and is the collective name for all types of spaghetti, macaroni, ravioli, vermicelli and so on. Although there is a tradition of pasta making and eating in other parts of the world such as China, Spain, Greece and Israel, the Italians are undoubtedly the world leaders and have developed hundreds of different pasta shapes. Both white and whole-wheat pasta are good sources of fiber (whole-wheat more so) and contain useful amounts of protein, iron and B vitamins.

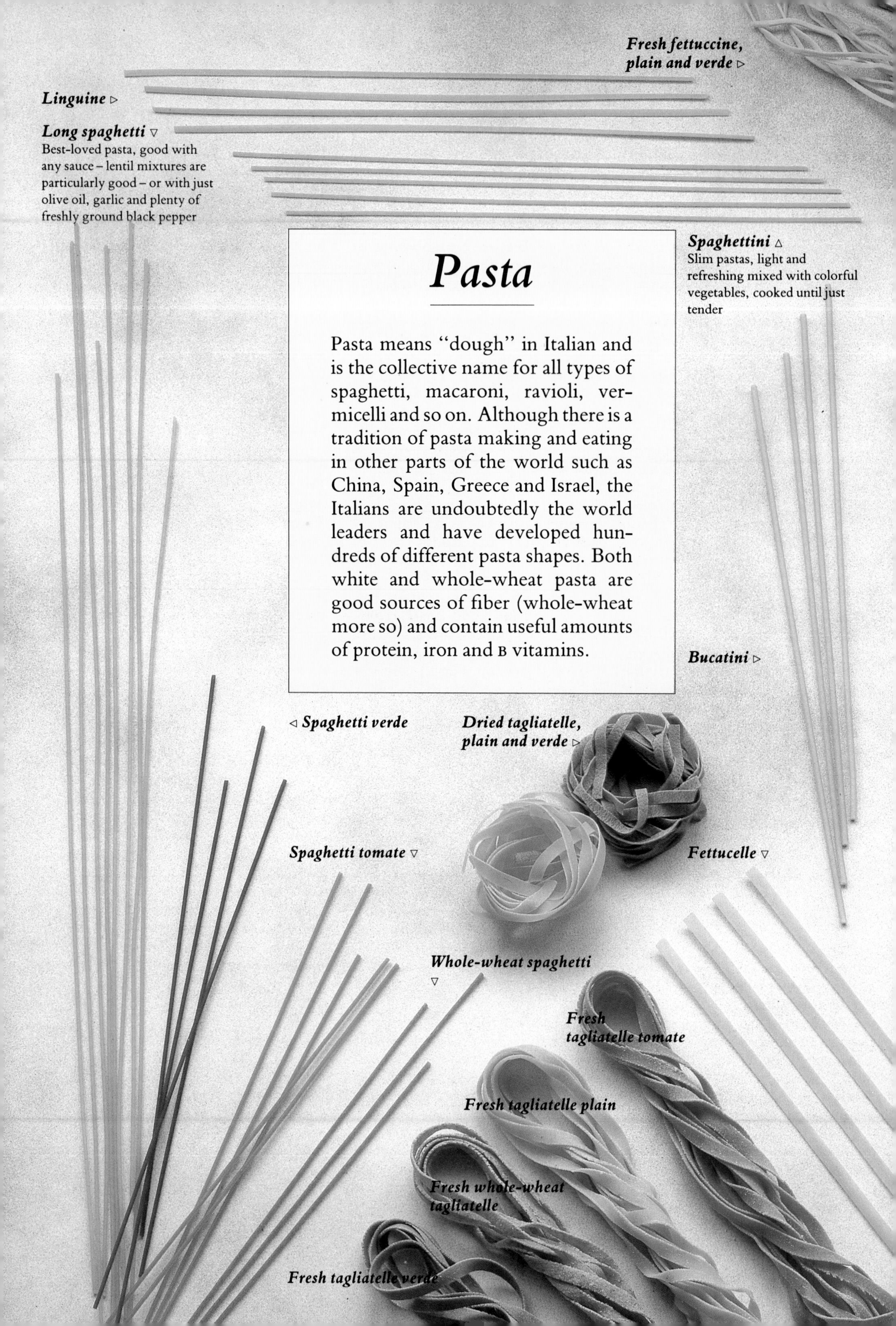

Bucatini ▷

◁ **Spaghetti verde**

Dried tagliatelle, plain and verde ▷

Spaghetti tomate ▽

Fettucelle ▽

Whole-wheat spaghetti ▽

Fresh tagliatelle tomate

Fresh tagliatelle plain

Fresh whole-wheat tagliatelle

Fresh tagliatelle verde

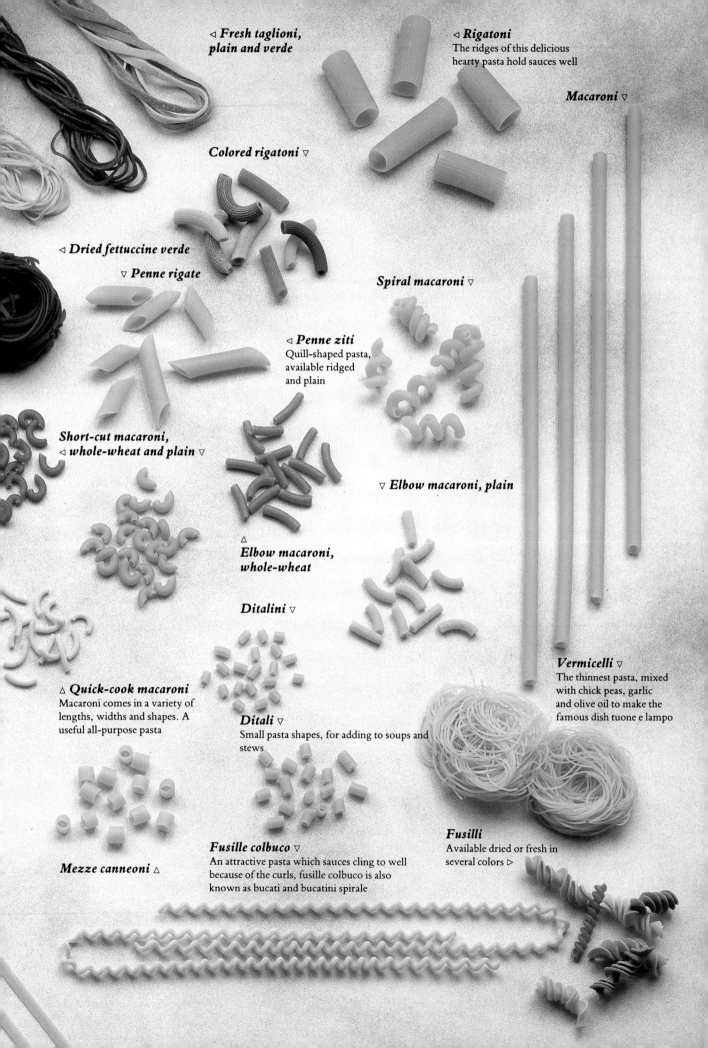

◁ **Fresh taglioni, plain and verde**

◁ **Rigatoni**
The ridges of this delicious hearty pasta hold sauces well

Macaroni ▽

Colored rigatoni ▽

◁ **Dried fettuccine verde**

▽ **Penne rigate**

Spiral macaroni ▽

◁ **Penne ziti**
Quill-shaped pasta, available ridged and plain

Short-cut macaroni, ◁ whole-wheat and plain ▽

▽ **Elbow macaroni, plain**

△
Elbow macaroni, whole-wheat

Ditalini ▽

Vermicelli ▽
The thinnest pasta, mixed with chick peas, garlic and olive oil to make the famous dish tuone e lampo

△ **Quick-cook macaroni**
Macaroni comes in a variety of lengths, widths and shapes. A useful all-purpose pasta

Ditali ▽
Small pasta shapes, for adding to soups and stews

Fusilli
Available dried or fresh in several colors ▷

Mezze canneoni △

Fusille colbuco ▽
An attractive pasta which sauces cling to well because of the curls, fusille colbuco is also known as bucati and bucatini spirale

Farfalle ▷
Pasta bows or butterflies, specially good with vegetables, either hot or as a salad
▽

Frilly lasagne verde ▽

Plain lasagne ▽

Fiochetti ▽

Lasagne verde ▽

Farfalline bows ▽
Tiny butterflies or bows, liked by children and pretty in clear soups

Pasta may be white or whole-wheat, depending on the type of flour used to make it; it can be dyed a variety of colors with vegetable purées and comes in numerous shapes and sizes. Terminology can be confusing, because often the same shape is known by several different names, and in Italy these frequently vary from province to province! Pasta can be bought dried or, increasingly, fresh. Dry pasta may contain eggs – if it does it will say *all'uovo* on the package; fresh pasta always does. Fresh stuffed pastas, such as ravioli and cappaletti, are increasingly to be found with vegetarian fillings, such as spinach and ricotta.

Cannelloni ▽
Large pasta tubes which are usually stuffed, covered with a sauce and baked

Easy-cook whole-wheat lasagne ▷
For layering with, or wrapping around, savory mixtures to make warming bakes

Lumache ▽
These "snails" make good containers for fillings such as ricotta cheese with garlic and fresh herbs, served with tomato sauce

Whole-wheat conchiglie rigate ▽

Pipe rigate △
Another hearty pasta which sauces cling to well

Wheatear whole-wheat shapes △
One of the best whole-wheat pastas, these can be added to casseroles, served simply with olive oil and seasoning or with a sauce

Conchiglie rigate (two sizes) △
Shell pasta, another good shape for serving with a sauce or in a salad with a creamy dressing

▽ **Transparent rice noodles**
This delicate pasta can be soaked for a few minutes, then added to vegetable stir-fries, or deep-fried until crisp⁻

Dried egg noodles ▷

Fresh egg noodles ▽

Fresh fine egg noodles ▷

Rice noodles ▽

Dried whole-wheat noodles ▷

Fresh oiled egg noodles △

Rice ribbon noodles ▽

Cappelletti or "little hats" ▽

Ravioli ▷
This ravioli is filled with spinach and ricotta and comes in various sizes

◁ **Tortellini**
Another example of a pasta with a vegetarian filling, available plain and verde

Conchiglie △
Attractive ridged open shells

Convighi piccole ▽
Tiny pasta, for adding to soups, come in many interesting shapes

△ **Annelli** ▷

◁ **Stelline**

Ravioli △
verde

Pasta

Quick and easy, cheap and delicious, pasta is welcoming, filling and warming. It can be made into many appetizing vegetarian dishes.

Choosing and storing
Good-quality dried pasta should feel hard and silky-smooth and when cooked should have a deliciously wheaty flavor. Store in a cool, dry place. Fresh pasta should smell fresh and look bright and slightly shiny. Store in the refrigerator and use within 24 hours if possible.

How to make pasta
Pasta is easy to make at home and worth doing if you eat a fair amount of it and enjoy cooking. You can roll the pasta out by hand, but better results are obtained by using a pasta machine. The hand-operated ones, consisting of rollers turned by a handle, are perfectly adequate for making family-sized amounts of pasta, or, for large quantities, electric machines are available.

To make 12 ounces of pasta – enough for 4 people – put 1¼ cups unbleached white flour into a bowl with ½ teaspoon salt. Gradually add 2 beaten eggs, to make a pliable dough. Set the rollers of your pasta machine to their widest position. Take a piece of pasta dough about the size of an egg, flatten it roughly with your hands, then feed it through the rollers. Fold the piece of dough in three, then feed it through again. Repeat this process six or seven times, until the dough is smooth and silky, then lay it on one side and repeat the process with the rest of the dough, keeping the pieces in the right order. Next, tighten the rollers a notch and put the pieces of dough through again, once only this time, and without folding. Repeat three times, tightening the rollers a notch each time. Cut the pieces of pasta in half if they become too long to handle, and support them as they come through the machine so they don't fall in folds and stick together.

If you want to make lasagne, cannelloni or ravioli, feed the pasta through the machine again with the rollers on the tightest setting but one. The pasta can then be cut to the required size and used straight away in savory bakes, without further drying or cooking. For ravioli, spread half the pieces of pasta out on a flat surface and put small mounds of a savory mixture (such as 1 cup ricotta cheese mixed with ¾ cup grated Cheddar cheese and ⅓ cup grated Parmesan cheese) on the pasta about 1½ inches apart. Brush around each mound with beaten egg, then cover with the rest of the pasta, pressing down around the edges and trying to exclude as much air as possible. Cut between the mounds with a pastry wheel. Put the ravioli on a lightly floured surface and leave to dry for 30 minutes. Then put the ravioli into a large pan of boiling water and cook for 4–6 minutes. Drain well, put into a hot serving dish and cover with hot tomato sauce.

To make tagliatelle, pass the pieces of pasta through one of the cutting rollers, then spread them out on a clean, lightly floured cloth, or drape over a piece of doweling, and leave to dry for about 1 hour. Then cook the pasta as described opposite, allowing 2–3 minutes only.

Preparing and cooking
Fresh or dried pasta needs no preparation before cooking.

Allow 4–6 ounces fresh or dried pasta per person for a main course, less if serving as a first course. For every 4 ounces pasta you will need 5 cups water. Bring the water to a boil in a large saucepan. Salt can be added to the water, allowing ½–1 teaspoon for every 4 ounces of pasta, but I prefer to add some crunchy flakes of sea salt to the cooked and drained pasta. When the water is boiling vigorously, add the pasta all at once.

To add long straight pasta, such as spaghetti, hold the pasta in your hand like a bunch of flowers, put the ends in the water so that it's standing up, then as the ends soften, gradually bend them, pushing more of the dry pasta into the water. When all the pasta is under water, give it a quick stir, then leave it to boil, half-covered, until tender. This will vary from type to type; smaller types cook more quickly, and fresh pasta is ready in about 5 minutes. The package will give a guide, but check it before the time is up, as cooking time can vary from batch to batch and is sometimes even affected by the weather!

To test whether the pasta is done, bite a piece; it should be tender but still slightly firm, so you can feel it on your teeth, or *al dente*, as the Italians say. When this stage is reached, remove from the heat and drain the pasta immediately. The easiest way to do this is to stand a metal colander in the sink and tip the pasta straight into it. Give the colander a good shake to make sure all the water has been dislodged from the pasta, then tip the pasta back into the still-hot saucepan.

Return to the heat with some olive oil or a knob of butter, a good grinding of black pepper, and some sea salt if you didn't add this to the water. Turn the pasta gently with a fork or spoon, so that all of it is coated with butter or oil. Serve immediately on a well-warmed serving dish or individual plates.

Dry lasagne can be cooked as described, then drained and draped over the sides of the colander and saucepan to prevent it from sticking together, ready for layering into a casserole with a tasty filling and sauce. Or it can be added to the casserole in its dry form. In this case make the filling and sauces with extra liquid for the pasta to absorb during cooking.

Fresh lasagne does not need cooking first, and, again, you should allow extra liquid because it will expand during cooking.

Cooking times for pasta	
Very thin pasta, small shapes	5–9 minutes
Larger shapes, long tubes	10–20 minutes
Fresh pasta	2–3 minutes

Serving pasta

The many varieties of pasta now available provide all sorts of serving possibilities.

The smallest, thinnest types, such as CONVIGHI PICCOLE, FARFALLINE and VERMICELLI, are good to add to soups or lightly fried vegetables as in Pasta Primavera (p. 251), while the ridged and shell-like pastas, such as RIGATONI, PENNE, PIPE and CONCHIGLIE RIGATE, all hold sauces very well. Rigatoni is also very good combined with eggplant in Eggplant and Pasta Charlotte (p. 258) or with olives in Pasta with Black Olives (p. 258).

LASAGNE and MACARONI are used with sauces in baked dishes (p. 256 and p. 257), and many of the smaller pasta shapes, MEZZE CANNEONI or WHEATEAR WHOLEWHEAT SHAPES, for example, can also be used in bakes such as whole-wheat Pasta and Mushroom Bake (p. 252).

The large pasta tubes such as CANNELLONI and RIGATONI can be stuffed with chopped mixed vegetables, or just one vegetable such as spinach, and baked in a sauce in the same way as lasagne.

The smaller shapes, such as TORTELLINI, RAVIOLI and CAPPELLETTI, can also be stuffed – cheese and nuts are good – and can be cooked in stock or water, or in a tomato sauce.

Long pastas, SPAGHETTI, SPAGHETTINI, LINGUINE, TAGLIATELLE and FETTUCELLE, are delicious served very simply, with just butter or cream, freshly ground black pepper, some chopped fresh herbs and a grating of Parmesan cheese. Or they can be dressed in numerous sauces; a lentil mixture is a good one to use (p. 252), as is an eggplant and tomato sauce (p. 254). Tagliatelle with Gorgonzola and Walnuts (p. 250) makes a delicious dish for a supper party, while linguine can be mixed with vegetables and cheese (p. 255) for a quick lunch.

Many pastas are now available colored with vegetables dyes – spinach or tomato, for example. These colored pastas can make a dish very attractive when served with an appropriately colored sauce. Children especially enjoy the COLORED RIGATONI or FUSILLI with a mushroom sauce (p. 251).

There are many varieties of EGG NOODLES available and they are best known for their use in Chinese dishes. They are often sold fresh, coiled in circles or, when dried, in square "cakes." They can be used for noodle soups, or stir-fried with vegetable mixtures after they have been boiled.

RICE NOODLES are sold as long strands and are also called rice sticks. TRANSPARENT, or cellophane, RICE NOODLES are lighter in color. They are both used in soups and stir-fries or can be deep-fried.

Quick serving ideas for pasta

Pasta with fresh herbs
Add 1–2 tablespoons chopped fresh herbs to the cooked pasta with the butter or olive oil. Tarragon and basil are delicious.

Pasta with cream
Stir a little heavy cream into the hot cooked pasta, allowing 2 tablespoons per person.

Pasta with avocado
Add a small ripe avocado, peeled and chopped, to the hot cooked pasta after draining.

Pasta with nuts
Chopped walnuts go beautifully with hot cooked pasta. They're nicest if you buy them in the shell and crack a few while the pasta cooks. Chop roughly and add to the drained and buttered pasta. A little cream mixed in as well makes this extra good.

Pasta with beans and black olives
While the pasta is cooking, heat through a can of cannellini beans in another saucepan. Drain both the beans and the pasta and mix together with a little crushed garlic, 1–2 tablespoons olive oil and a few whole black olives.

Pasta with chick peas
Add hot cooked and drained chick peas, crushed garlic and a little olive oil to hot drained pasta for a favorite Italian mixture.

Pasta with croutons
While the pasta is cooking, cut a slice of whole-wheat bread per person, remove the crusts, and cut the bread into ¼-inch squares. Fry the bread in olive oil until crisp and golden-brown all over. Drain on paper towels. Add the croutons to each serving of hot pasta.

Pasta with onions
Start this when you put the water for the pasta on to boil, to give the onions time to cook until they're really soft and slightly caramelized. Allow ½–1 large onion per person, peeled and sliced. Heat a knob of butter or vegan margarine in a saucepan or frying pan, add the onion and fry for 10 minutes, then add a sprinkling of salt, pepper and sugar, and continue to fry for a further 5–10 minutes, until the onion is golden-brown but not burned. Stir the hot cooked onion into the cooked and drained pasta.

Pasta with Fresh Tomato Sauce
Serve hot spaghetti or pasta spirals with Fresh Tomato Sauce (p. 170); snip plenty of fresh basil on top. Some diced Brie can be mixed with the pasta, to melt deliciously in the heat of the sauce.

Pasta with poppy seeds
Add a good sprinkling of poppy seeds to hot, buttery pasta; they add a nutty flavor and crunchy texture.

Sweet pasta
For a sweet pasta dish, popular in Italy, cook pasta until tender – a bit softer than the usual *al dente*, drain and add (for 12 ounces pasta, which gives 4 servings) 3 tablespoons sugar, 3 tablespoons butter and 3 ounces good quality plain chocolate, melted. Mix well and serve immediately.

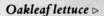

Oakleaf lettuce ▷
Also called feuille de chêne; the names refer to
the shape of the leaves

Leaf Vegetables

Crisp and refreshing, leaf vegetables
whet the appetite and cleanse the
palate. Some have been used for centuries – mustard and cress was enjoyed by the Greeks and Romans.
Today there is a wide range to
choose from, and making salads is a
particular pleasure. Several of the
leaf vegetables, such as watercress,
lettuce and spinach, make excellent
soups. Leaf vegetables contain vitamin A, calcium, iron, fiber and
chlorophyll, which, when eaten
raw, protects the body against disease.

Escarole △
A broad-leaf chicory with
the characteristic slightly
bitter flavor

Iceberg lettuce △
Iceberg lettuce has a firm heart
and a deliciously crisp texture

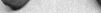

Romaine/cos lettuce ▷
Romaine lettuce has a
particularly good flavor and the
smaller leaves make good
edible scoops for dips

Lamb's lettuce △
Also known as corn salad and
mâche, the leaves of a small,
hardy plant which grows wild
in much of the Northern
Hemisphere

Chicory/curly endive ▽
With its curly leaves and
slightly bitter flavor, chicory
makes an attractive contrast
with other salad ingredients

◁ **Radicchio**
A particularly useful salad
vegetable because of its red
leaves, which lend themselves
to all kinds of stunning
garnishes and color
schemes

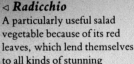

Swiss chard ▽
The thick white stem of chard
is delicious cooked with the
leaves or cooked and served
separately

Sorrel △
A hardy perennial plant often found growing
wild in Europe, sorrel has a sharp, almost
lemony flavor

Vine leaf ▷
Tender leaves from the vine
make a delicious edible
wrapping for other foods

Watercress ▷
With its hot, pungent flavor
and dark green color,
watercress makes a good
contrast to other leaf vegetables
in a green salad

Spinach ▷
One of the most useful of
the leaf vegetables, spinach
can be used raw in salads,
as well as cooked

**Boston or butterhead
lettuce**
▽

Cress △
Mild and juicy, cress appeals
particularly to children

Leaf Vegetables

Choosing and storing

These vegetables need to be bought as fresh as possible; they should be crisp and slightly damp-looking, with no sign of withering or dryness. They are best used as soon as possible, but if bought really fresh, leaf vegetables will keep in the salad compartment of the refrigerator for 2–3 days.

Preparing and cooking

Leaf vegetables, especially lettuce, are often sprayed with fungicide, so need thorough but gentle washing in plenty of cold water. Remove any coarse or damaged leaves and tough stems.

Tear, rather than cut, delicate leafy vegetables such as lettuce, and if they are going to be eaten raw, dry them carefully in a salad spinner or with a soft absorbent cloth.

Many leaf vegetables can also be very tasty when cooked and some make excellent soups.

ARUGULA / ROCKET
Eruca sativa
(Not illustrated)
Sometimes classed as an herb, arugula has a hot, almost spicy flavor and a few sprigs make an excellent addition to a green salad.

CHICORY / ESCAROLE
Cichorium endivia crispum
There are two main types of chicory, curly-leaved and broad-leaved. They all have a refreshing, slightly bitter flavor. Chicory is particularly rich in folic acid (see p. 13).

CRESS / MUSTARD AND CRESS (Not illustrated)
Lepidium sativum and *sinapis alba*
The cress widely available in the stores is not the traditional mixture of mustard and cress but often salad rape. This has a mild flavor which particularly appeals to children. All kinds of mustard and cress make a pleasant addition to a salad bowl and are useful for garnishing.

Green salad ingredients

- ☐ Lettuce (all kinds)
- ☐ Escarole
- ☐ Chicory
- ☐ Watercress
- ☐ Lamb's lettuce (corn salad/mâche)
- ☐ Tender spinach leaves
- ☐ Sorrel, arugula and tender nasturtium leaves (they're pungent, so just a few used in the salad will be sufficient)
- ☐ Scallions, raw onion rings
- ☐ Celery, cucumber, fennel, green pepper, avocado (thinly sliced)
- ☐ Fresh herbs
- ☐ Dandelion leaves (pick these carefully from a place unpolluted by dogs, cars or agricultural sprays, taking the tender leaves from near the center and washing them very thoroughly)
- ☐ Chopped walnuts or hazelnuts

GOOD KING HENRY
Chenopodium Bonus-Henricus
(Not illustrated)
Also called GOOSEFOOT, this is a perennial herb which used to be cultivated and then went out of fashion. It has small, pointed leaves growing either side of a central stem bearing small flowers like those of sorrel.

Both the leaves and the flowers can be eaten. It tastes similar to spinach and is prepared in the same way.

LAMB'S LETTUCE / CORN SALAD / MÂCHE
Valerianella locusta
Lamb's lettuce has a delicate flavor and makes a useful addition to salads, particularly in winter.

LETTUCE *Lactuca sativa*
Lettuce is an ancient cultivated crop and is probably the number one salad basic. It can be served on its own or mixed with other ingredients; shredded, it makes a good filling for sandwiches or base for other salad ingredients, and large leaves can be rolled around tasty fillings to make an interesting nibble or snack. Firm lettuce hearts can be braised in the same way as fennel (p. 182); outer leaves can be made into an excellent soup (p. 131), or used to flavor peas cooked à la Française (p. 183).

There are many different types of lettuce, some of the main ones being:

CABBAGE HEAD
These are round or flat in shape, and can be subdivided into crisp lettuces, such as ICEBERG, and the soft-leaf BOSTON or BUTTERHEAD varieties.

LEAF LETTUCE / SALAD BOWL
In this type the leaves do not form a solid heart and the leaves can be picked off individually if required while the plant is growing in the garden. This lettuce is usually particularly tender, and there are some red, bronze or variegated types available.

ROMAINE / COS
Tall, well-flavored lettuces, this group includes COS, DENSITY, and, perhaps the best-flavored lettuce of all, the hearty "LITTLE GEM."

OAKLEAF LETTUCE
Lactuca sativa
Also called FEUILLE DE CHÊNE, this attractive lettuce has a slightly bitter flavor. It makes an excellent addition to a green salad and can also be used on its own. It is particularly good with a walnut dressing and chèvre cheese (p. 150).

RADICCHIO *Cichorium intybus*
This red-leaved variety of endive has a slightly bitter flavor; it makes a useful addition to a leafy salad and is a very attractive garnish.

SORREL *Rumex acetosa*

A few sorrel leaves give interest to a green salad, and a little sorrel cooked with spinach adds sharpness. Puréed sorrel makes a good accompaniment to a nut roast, cutting the richness, and it also makes a refreshing soup. Sorrel used in a Wilted Leaf Salad makes a delicious variation on green salad. Put a mixture of green salad ingredients into a bowl, using interesting varieties such as sorrel, arugula, dandelion leaves and spinach. Fry some small cubes of wholewheat bread in butter or olive oil, to make crisp croutons; then just before you want to serve the salad, pour the croutons and their cooking fat over the salad ingredients, mix quickly and serve at once. Until the eighteenth century sorrel was popular pounded with sugar and vinegar into a green sauce, and it is still sometimes served like this in parts of Yorkshire.

Cooked sorrel should not be taken in large quantities too often because of its high level of oxalic acid.

SPINACH *Spinaca oleracea* and SWISS CHARD
Beta vulgaris, var. *Cicla*

Delicious dark green leafy plants which can be shredded raw and added to salads, cooked and served simply as a vegetable accompaniment, or made into substantial maincourse dishes. The central stem of Swiss chard is particularly good and can be shredded and cooked in a little water for a few minutes before adding the green leaves, or it can be removed, cut into lengths and cooked and served separately.

SEA KALE (not illustrated), which can be found growing wild around the coast, is a wild form of spinach beet. It can be collected and used just like spinach and has an excellent, naturally salty flavor. NEW ZEALAND SPINACH (*Tetragonia expansa*) (not illustrated) is another green leafy vegetable which is not related to spinach botanically but is similar and prepared in the same way.

Spinach is particularly rich in vitamin A, iron and calcium but, like sorrel, contains oxalic acid, which inhibits the body's ability to absorb some minerals. It's therefore best not to eat cooked spinach more than twice a week, although some natural-health experts believe that the oxalic acid in raw spinach does not have the same binding effect.

Spinach is available fresh, frozen – a useful alternative to fresh – and canned, which in my opinion is not worth eating. Fresh spinach can be very gritty, so always be sure to wash it thoroughly in several changes of cold water.

VINE LEAF *Vitis vinifera*

Vine leaves are much used as edible wrappings for foods in vine-growing countries, dolmades, or vine leaves filled with a rice stuffing, being perhaps the best-known example. They have a delicious, slightly lemony flavor.

Fresh young vine leaves, when available, need to be blanched in boiling water for a few minutes, to soften them, before being rolled around a stuffing such as cooked rice or feta cheese. Vine leaves which have been canned or packed in brine need rinsing in warm water, to wash off the salt, before use.

WATERCRESS
Nasturtium officinale

Watercress is useful in salads, soups and sauces, and can also be added to stir-fries (p. 181). Although watercress used to be gathered from the wild, it is now specially cultivated, and eating wild watercress is not recommended because of possible contamination.

Watercress should be well washed and will keep in a plastic bag in the salad compartment of the refrigerator for 2–3 days.

A tangy, bright green Watercress Sauce tastes and looks wonderful with vegetable mousses and terrines, or a white nut roast. To serve 4, fry a small onion, peeled and finely chopped, in 1 tablespoon butter or vegan margarine for 10 minutes, until soft but not browned. Add ⅓ cup dry white wine and 1 tablespoon white wine vinegar and boil until reduced and syrupy. Meanwhile chop 2 bunches of watercress, then add two-thirds of this to the reduced onion mixture, with 2½ cups Light Vegetable Stock (p. 129). Boil over a high heat until reduced to about one-third. Add the remaining watercress and purée in a blender or food processor. Stir in ¼ cup heavy or nondairy cream and reheat gently without boiling. Season to taste with salt and pepper and stir in 1 tablespoon butter or vegan margarine.

WINTER CRESSES *Barbarea vulgaris* and *Barbarea verna*
(Not illustrated)

These wild cresses grow on land—fields, roadsides or cultivated ground. Their leaves have a pungent flavor and can be cooked or used in salads.

Cooking perfect spinach

Allow 2 pounds spinach for 4 people. If the spinach is young and tender it is excellent cooked for a few seconds in olive oil until wilted (see page 180).

For spinach that is less tender, remove any tough stems; either discard these, or chop them and add to ½ inch boiling water in a large saucepan. Boil for 2 minutes, then put the spinach leaves in on top. If you are not using the stems, put the spinach straight into the pan, without any water – the water still clinging to the spinach from the washing will be enough. Push the spinach down into the pan as it cooks. A wide metal spatula is good for this if you hold it so that you can chop down with the flat part. Half cover the pan with a lid and cook for about 7 minutes, chopping the spinach with the spatula from time to time. Drain the spinach well in a strainer, using the back of a spoon to squeeze out the water. Then return it to the still-hot pan and chop it a bit more with the spatula if necessary; or turn the spinach out on a board and chop it quickly with a knife. Add a knob of butter or vegan margarine, a good seasoning of sea salt, freshly ground black pepper and perhaps a touch of grated nutmeg.

Brussels sprouts ◁
Said to have originated near
Brussels in the thirteenth
century

Kale △
Kale means "non-hearting"

Brassicas

Brassicas come in a variety of shapes
and sizes, from tiny Brussels sprouts
to big, family-sized cabbages; from
knobbly kohlrabi to beautiful purple
broccoli. They range in color from
palest greenish-white to deep burgundy red, and they span the sea-
sons. They provide useful quantities
of a range of vitamins and minerals,
including vitamins A, B and C and
useful amounts of iron and calcium.
They also contain enzymes, which
are protective and curative when the
vegetables are eaten raw.

Bok choy / mustard greens △
A variety of Chinese cabbage with a
juicy central stem and pleasantly flav
leaves, bok choy cooks quickly and i
for stir-fries

Calabrese △
One of the varieties of broccoli,
calabrese is tender, with an
excellent flavor

Kohlrabi ▷
The leaves of kohlrabi can be
eaten, but it is really grown for
its root, which is like turnip
with a delicate cabbage flavor

Flowering bok choy △

Purple cape broccoli △
A type of cauliflower, broccoli
may be in the form of a
compact head, as here, or it
may consist of individual
sprouts

Green cauliflower ▷
This beautiful vegetable is a
variety of cauliflower grown in
Europe

Cauliflower △
Probably originating in the Orient, but not
popular in Europe until the eighteenth
century, cauliflower has a delicate flavor

◁ **Savoy cabbage**
An attractive cabbage with its deeply crenellated leaves, savoy cabbage has an especially good flavor

January King Cabbage ▽

△ **Green or roundhead cabbage**

Red cabbage △
Particularly useful because it keeps well and is excellent grated as a salad or cooked slowly in a casserole

White salad cabbage△
This firmly packed head grates well and is good for making coleslaw and other raw cabbage mixtures

△ **Spring greens**
Spring greens make a good accompanying vegetable with a clean, refreshing flavor

Chinese cabbage/leaves △
A refreshing, crisp yet juicy vegetable, Chinese cabbage makes a good salad or stir-fried vegetable

Brassicas

A real kitchen basic, the brassicas provide useful all-year material for soups, salads and main courses, as well as being, if well cooked, second to none as an accompanying vegetable.

Choosing and storing

Select bright, fresh leaves, with no sign of wilting or damp, brownish patches. If there is a heart, as with cauliflower, cabbage and Brussels sprouts, look for one that is firm and tightly packed. Keep in a cool place. Brassicas are best used as soon as possible, although I find that even the more delicate varieties like broccoli, spring greens and cauliflower will keep well if stored in the refrigerator for several days.

Preparing and cooking

Wash the vegetables in cold water to which some kitchen salt has been added – this acts as a natural disinfectant. Remove hard stems and any tough outer leaves. The way brassicas are cooked makes all the difference to their palatability – and it's so easy. These are the keys to success:

- Cut the leaves up as small as possible so that they cook quickly.
- Put them into just enough fast-boiling water to prevent the greens from sticking: about ½ inch.
- Cover the pan so that the vegetables above the water will cook in the steam.
- Cook them until they're only just tender – often as little as 4 minutes, or even less for delicate varieties such as bok choy or Chinese cabbage.
- Drain them well and add any seasonings and extra ingredients you like. Personally I like to add some crunchy flakes of sea salt, a grinding of black pepper and, unless the vegetable is going to be served with a dish which is high in fat, a little unsalted butter. For other suggestions, see opposite.

BOK CHOY / MUSTARD GREENS
Brassica chinensis

This variety of Chinese cabbage is popular in Oriental cookery. Prepare and cook it as described for Chinese cabbage, above. FLOWERING BOK CHOY can be cooked in the same way, and also looks pretty in salads and as a garnish. Chinese sauerkraut is made from bok choy and is available from Chinese shops, as is DRIED BOK CHOY (not illustrated), which needs to be soaked and can then be added to soups and stews.

BROCCOLI and CALABRESE
Brassica oleracea

Sometimes described as "poor man's asparagus," this is one of the most nutritious vegetables. Voted the top by a panel of nutritionists in the U.S., it contains large amounts of vitamin A, folic acid and calcium, and is a particularly valuable vegetable for vegans.

When preparing broccoli, remove the toughest part of the stems. Then, unless it is very tender, pare the stems down a little so that they will cook in the same length of time as the more delicate heads. Or remove the stems, cut them into julienne strips (p. 184) and cook them in the water for 1–2 minutes before you put in the heads.

Broccoli is good stir-fried, too, which brings out its vivid green color. Combined with ginger and almonds, it makes a good accompanying vegetable dish. To make this, wash 1½ pounds broccoli, cut the broccoli heads in small pieces and prepare the stems as above. Peel and finely grate a small piece of fresh ginger root. Heat 2 tablespoons olive oil in a large saucepan or wok, add the broccoli, ginger, a little salt and freshly grated black pepper. Stir-fry for 3 minutes until the broccoli has heated through and softened a little. Sprinkle with ¼ cup slivered almonds and serve at once.

Broccoli tastes good served simply, with melted butter, or tossed in vinaigrette, cooled and served as a salad. It is luscious with Hollandaise Sauce (p. 176) or with cream and toasted almonds, for a special occasion; or with Fresh Tomato Sauce (p. 170). Broccoli makes a good filling for a tart (p. 262) and goes well with other vegetables in a braise (p. 181).

BRUSSELS SPROUTS
Brassica oleracea

Tiny, firm Brussels sprouts are best; they take longer to prepare, but are worth it. Most people cut a cross about ¼ inch into the stalk end of the sprouts. Personally I prefer to cut them in halves (or even quarters, if they are big) before cooking, a trick I learned from my mother. This way they cook more quickly and I think they taste better and look more attractive, with their yellow centers showing.

In any case, Brussels sprouts only need the minimum of cooking – 2–4 minutes – in a very little water; take them off the heat before you think they are done, because they will go on cooking in their own heat after draining.

Brussels sprouts are excellent lightly cooked and served simply; or with cream and grated nutmeg for a special occasion. Cooked chestnuts – fresh or drained whole canned ones – are a pleasant (and, in Europe, traditional) Christmas accompaniment to Brussels sprouts. When they are young and tender, finely shredded Brussels sprouts make a good salad when combined with raisins and chopped apple, or with grated carrots and chopped dates. When they are past their best, they can be made into a delicate, pale green purée. To make this, wash and trim 1½ pounds Brussels sprouts and cook them in boiling salted water for about 10 minutes, or until they are tender. Drain them thoroughly, then purée in a blender or food processor. Put the purée back into the saucepan, add 1 tablespoon butter, and beat in up to ¾ cup light cream until the mixture is soft. Season with salt, freshly ground black pepper and grated nutmeg, then reheat gently and serve.

CABBAGE Brassica oleracea

One variety of cabbage or another is available year-round. Early in the year, SPRING GREENS, cut up small

Creative cabbage

Try these serving ideas for hot, lightly cooked cabbage:

☐ Garlic butter

☐ Crushed juniper or coriander seeds

☐ Chopped fresh parsley, coriander or dill

☐ Sour cream, caraway seeds and a sprinkling of paprika

☐ Apple purée and a pinch of cloves

☐ Caraway seeds and melted butter

☐ Chopped fried onion

☐ Chopped scallions or chives

☐ Peeled, chopped tomato and some chopped basil (or Fresh Tomato Sauce, p. 170)

☐ Grated fresh ginger

☐ Grated nutmeg

and lightly cooked, make a good accompanying vegetable with a clean, refreshing flavor. JANUARY KING, another excellent early cabbage, can be cooked in a similar way, or, if it has a firm heart, makes a particularly good salad when finely shredded and mixed with lemon juice and olive oil, or vinaigrette. GREEN or ROUNDHEAD CABBAGE is available throughout the year, useful as an accompanying vegetable or shredded to make salads such as Coleslaw (p. 161) or Technicolor Cabbage Salad (p. 162).

WHITE SALAD CABBAGE, a firm variety, good for grating and shredding, is also excellent for salads.

RED CABBAGE is good cooked gently and slowly with onions and butter in a casserole (p. 180) and served as an accompanying vegetable, or, with some cooked chestnuts and perhaps a dash of red wine added, as a main course with baked potatoes and sour cream. Red cabbage also looks particularly attractive shredded or grated in salads.

SAVOY CABBAGE is good as an accompanying vegetable or main course, hollowed out and filled with stuffing. The individual leaves can also be wrapped around a savory filling, such as mashed cooked chestnuts and fried onion, or cooked rice with nuts and chopped herbs, packed into a shallow ovenproof dish, covered with a little well-flavored stock or a sauce (such as Italian Tomato, p. 171, or Savory Coconut, p. 177) and baked for about 30 minutes in a moderate oven.

Chopped cooked cabbage is one of the main ingredients of the Russian savory pastry koulibiac. For an easy version of this, mix together 2 pounds finely chopped cooked cabbage, 1 large fried onion, 1½ pound sliced and fried mushrooms, 2 chopped hard-boiled eggs, ¼ cup chopped parsley, the grated rind and juice of ½ lemon, and plenty of salt and freshly ground black pepper. Cover with puff pastry as described on p. 271, bake in a hot oven, 425°F, for 40 minutes and serve with a Sour Cream and Herb Dressing (p. 156).

CAULIFLOWER / GREEN CAULIFLOWER
Brassica oleracea

Cauliflower has a delicious flavor so long as it is not overcooked. I think it is best to break the cauliflower into florets and cut these as necessary so that they are all about the same size. Then cook as described above, for only 4–5 minutes, until the cauliflower is just tender but still has some firmness, then drain. Cooked like this, cauliflower hardly needs any accompaniments, though some grated nutmeg, a little grated cheese or a Fresh Tomato Sauce (p. 170) go well with it. One of the tastiest ways to cook cauliflower is in the Indian style, with spices (p. 185).

To make Cauliflower Cheese, a classic vegetarian dish, mix lightly cooked cauliflower florets with a well-seasoned Cheese Sauce (p. 175), sprinkle with breadcrumbs, dot with a little butter and bake or broil until heated through and crisp on top.

Raw cauliflower florets are particularly good for scooping up dips.

CHINESE CABBAGE/LEAVES
Brassica pekinensis

Chinese cabbage is tender and, shredded, makes a good addition to a leafy salad. Or it can be the main ingredient.

A refreshing salad in which Chinese cabbage is combined with bean sprouts in a sweet-and-sour dressing can be made as follows. Soak 6 ounces fresh bean sprouts in cold water while you prepare the other ingredients. Combine 1 tablespoon clear honey, 3 tablespoons sesame oil or olive oil, 2 tablespoons soy sauce and freshly ground black pepper in a large bowl. Add 1 inch peeled and finely grated fresh ginger root and mix well. Then add 3 cups shredded Chinese cabbage and 2 coarsely grated carrots and turn them in the dressing. Drain the bean sprouts, place in the bowl and mix well.

The best way to serve Chinese cabbage as a cooked vegetable is to shred the leaves, then stir-fry for 2–3 minutes, until heated through. Chopped onion, crushed garlic, grated fresh ginger, grated lemon rind and chopped fresh herbs are good flavorings for Chinese cabbage, or it can be stir-fried in sesame oil and served with a dash of soy sauce and a sprinkling of toasted sesame seeds.

KALE Brassica oleracea

Kale is a non-hearting type of cabbage. It should be washed well, as soil and grit tend to lodge between the stems. Kale is particularly rich in calcium and B vitamins and used to be an important winter vegetable in Britain, though many people find its flavor rather strong. It can be good to eat if it is picked or bought when young, shredded (with any tough stems removed) and cooked until tender, then well drained and served with butter and freshly ground black pepper, or with a creamy sauce, perhaps flavored with a dash of nutmeg.

KOHLRABI Brassica oleracea

The leaves of kohlrabi can be cooked like kale. The root, which resembles a cabbage-flavored turnip, can be diced or cut into strips and boiled until tender. Kohlrabi is good in a julienne of root vegetables (p. 184), where it provides an interesting contrast of color and flavor.

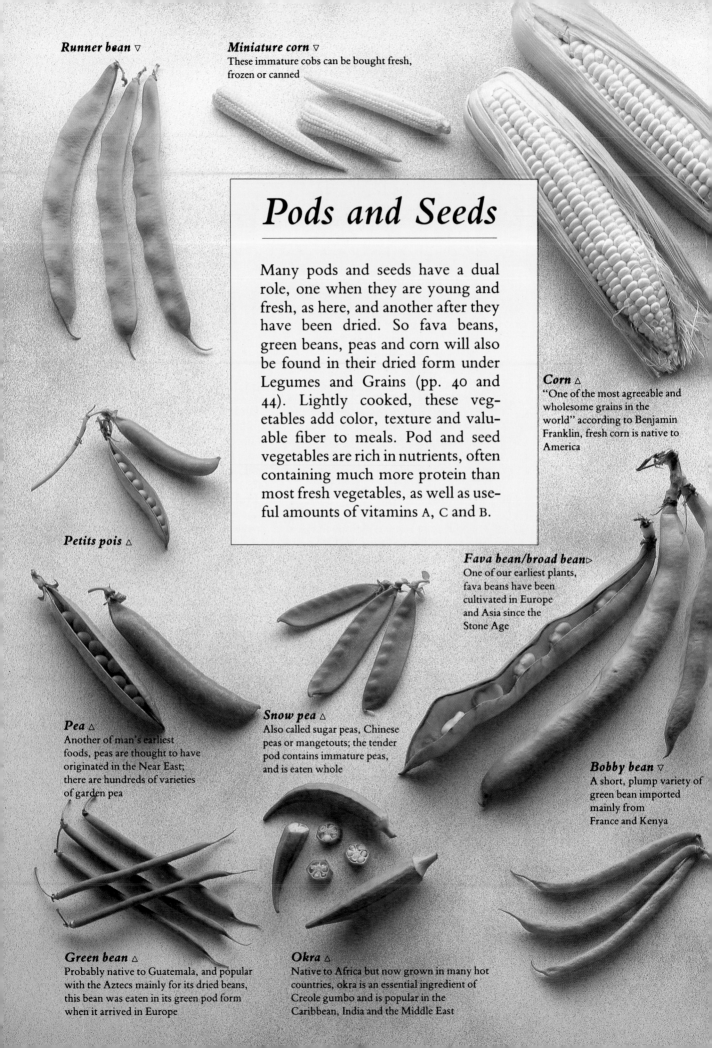

Runner bean ▽

Miniature corn ▽
These immature cobs can be bought fresh,
frozen or canned

Pods and Seeds

Many pods and seeds have a dual
role, one when they are young and
fresh, as here, and another after they
have been dried. So fava beans,
green beans, peas and corn will also
be found in their dried form under
Legumes and Grains (pp. 40 and
44). Lightly cooked, these vegetables add color, texture and valuable fiber to meals. Pod and seed
vegetables are rich in nutrients, often
containing much more protein than
most fresh vegetables, as well as useful amounts of vitamins A, C and B.

Corn △
"One of the most agreeable and
wholesome grains in the
world" according to Benjamin
Franklin, fresh corn is native to
America

Petits pois △

Fava bean/broad bean ▷
One of our earliest plants,
fava beans have been
cultivated in Europe
and Asia since the
Stone Age

Pea △
Another of man's earliest
foods, peas are thought to have
originated in the Near East;
there are hundreds of varieties
of garden pea

Snow pea △
Also called sugar peas, Chinese
peas or mangetouts; the tender
pod contains immature peas,
and is eaten whole

Bobby bean ▽
A short, plump variety of
green bean imported
mainly from
France and Kenya

Green bean △
Probably native to Guatemala, and popular
with the Aztecs mainly for its dried beans,
this bean was eaten in its green pod form
when it arrived in Europe

Okra △
Native to Africa but now grown in many hot
countries, okra is an essential ingredient of
Creole gumbo and is popular in the
Caribbean, India and the Middle East

Pods and Seeds

Choosing and storing
Look for small, crisp pods, bright and fresh-looking. Peas, beans and okra are all best when the pods are small. Corn needs to be young and tender too; pull back the leaves and look for pale yellow, shiny grains. These vegetables will keep in a cool place for a day or so, or in the refrigerator for 2–3 days, but they are all at their best when eaten as soon as possible after picking.

Preparing and cooking
See under individual varieties.

CORN *Zea mays*
Corn has a pleasantly sweet flavor, cheering golden color and chewy texture. Ideally corn needs to be picked just before cooking, because once it has been cut, the sugar in the kernels starts to turn into starch, making them tough. When buying fresh corn, pull back the leaves and look for pale yellow, shiny grains. To prepare, strip off the leaves and silky threads, then trim off the stalk end. Cook the corn in a large saucepan of unsalted water for 3–5 minutes. It is done when a kernel pulls away easily from the cob. Serve with butter and sea salt. If you need the kernels for a recipe, just cut down the cob and they will come away.

Corn on the cob makes a pleasant first course or snack for people with good teeth who don't mind getting messy as they eat. The kernels add a bright dash of color to salads and vegetable mixtures, and are also good made into fritters (p. 238). Corn kernels are available fresh, frozen and canned, though canned corn usually tastes over-sweet because of added sugar.

MINIATURE CORN, the immature cobs, can be bought fresh, frozen or canned and are pretty in salads and vegetable mixtures, especially stir-fries.

FAVA BEAN / BROAD BEAN *Vicia faba*
Fava beans can be prepared in two ways. When they are young and tender, and the pods not much bigger than green beans, they are excellent cooked in the pod; just trim, then cut into even-sized lengths and cook in a little fast-boiling water until just tender. Drain and serve with chopped parsley and butter or a creamy sauce.

Later, when the pods become too tough to eat, remove the beans from the pod and cook in boiling water until tender. If the skins of the beans are tough, and you have the time, the beans can be popped out of their skins, revealing the bright green beans inside.

Older fava beans can be made into a good soup. Whizzed in a blender or food processor with olive oil and lemon juice, they also make an excellent pale green dip, good served as a first course on top of large flat mushrooms which have been fried in olive oil and cooled, or in a salad with lettuce and grated carrot.

GREEN BEAN *Phaseolus vulgaris*
One of the most delicious vegetables, many varieties of which have been produced, including the BOBBY BEAN. Just trim and remove any strings from the side, if present (the beans are nicest if they're young enough to have no strings).

The beans can be cooked whole or cut into shorter lengths. Cook in a minimum amount of boiling water (½ inch) in a covered pan until just tender (*al dente*). Cooking time will depend on the thickness of the beans: very slender ones take only about 2 minutes, others up to 10 minutes. Drain and serve simply, as they are, or with a little butter and freshly ground black pepper. A squeeze of lemon juice and some toasted almonds are an excellent addition.

Hot green beans mixed with a vinaigrette dressing and chopped fresh herbs, then cooled, make a good first course or salad, or they can be mixed with other vegetables to make Vegetarian Salade Niçoise (p. 169).

OKRA *Hibiscus esculentus*
Also known as ladies' fingers and gumbo, okra has an intriguing mucilaginous texture and delicate flavor. Choose small, firm pods and cut off the stalk end. It is delicious prepared as on p. 186 and makes a good addition to vegetable stews, curries and spiced rice dishes.

PEA *Pisum sativum*
Unless you grow your own, it is difficult to find fresh peas that taste as good as frozen ones, which are harvested at their peak and frozen within hours of picking.

However, cooked fresh peas are a treat if they are young and tender. Simply pop the peas out of the pods and cook in a little boiling water until just tender – about 4 minutes. PETITS POIS, a small, tender, sweet variety, take less time – 1–2 minutes. Drain and serve with chopped mint and a little butter. They make a colorful addition to many vegetable and rice dishes.

RUNNER BEAN *Phaseolus coccineus*
Also called stick beans, because of the way the plants grow up sticks, runner beans originated in South America. They are the most popular green bean in Britain. If you're growing them, do pick them before they get too long; they're delicious when young and tender. Trim the beans, and if there are strings, remove these by slicing thinly down each side. Runner beans are usually cut into thin diagonal slices. Cook and serve as for green beans, or prepare in the Greek style and serve warm (p. 186).

If you have a glut of runner beans, try making some into chutney or piccalilli.

SNOW PEAS / MANGETOUTS *Pisum saccaratum*
A variety of pea, the pod of which is eaten, snow peas have a deliciously sweet flavor and, if properly cooked, a crunchy texture. To prepare them, choose young, crisp pods, trim, then cook in a little boiling water for 1–2 minutes, just to heat through and soften slightly. Drain and serve immediately. Or add them to stir-fries (p. 199). Raw snow peas make good scoopers for dips.

Globe artichoke ▷
When cooked, these giant thistles have an intriguing, subtle flavor and are excellent served either hot or cold

Asparagus △
Asparagus is the cultivated form of a type of lily and has been grown as a delicacy in Europe for over 2,000 years

Shoot Vegetables

This group includes some of the most delectable vegetables, such as asparagus, artichokes, endive, bamboo shoots and hearts of palm, which are wonderful for special-occasion cookery, or for using in small quantities to add interest to simple dishes. Alongside these are cheaper basics such as celery and fennel, which, with their clean, refreshing flavors and crisp texture, are good either cooked or raw. They all contain only small amounts of vitamins and minerals.

Bamboo shoot △
The tips of various species of bamboo, these are sold fresh in Far Eastern markets, but canned almost everywhere else

◁ **Celery**
There are basically two types of this versatile, crunchy vegetable: green-stemmed and white-stemmed

Fennel ▽
This celery-like shoot with its delicate, feathery leaves and slight aniseed flavor can be used either cooked or raw

Heart of palm ▽
The terminal shoots of certain varieties of palm, hearts of palm have a delicate flavour

Endive/Belgian endive/witloof ▷
Endive is a crisp vegetable with a slightly bitter flavor

Shoot Vegetables

Choosing and storing

Choose firm, crisp-looking specimens. With asparagus, avoid any which looks limp or has wet or dry wrinkled ends. Keep in the salad compartment of the refrigerator, or in a cool place.

Preparing and cooking

See under individual varieties.

ASPARAGUS
Asparagus officinalis

There are three basic types of asparagus, green, white and purple, and experts disagree as to which has the best flavor. Thin spears of green asparagus, called sprue, are a good buy, particularly for inclusion in dishes like Individual Asparagus Tartlets (p. 263), Pine Nut Roulade with Asparagus Hollandaise filling (p. 237), or asparagus soup.

Allow about ½ pound asparagus per person. Wash the asparagus carefully, especially around the tips, which can contain grit. Then bend each stem until it snaps – it will break at the point on the stem where it becomes tough and woody. Using a sharp knife or potato peeler, shave right down the stem, from just below the tip to the base, going deeper into the stem as you go down.

Unless you have a special asparagus pan, the best way to cook it is in a steamer, or else to tie it in a bunch and stand this in a saucepan containing 1 inch boiling water. Arrange a dome of foil over the top, to cover the asparagus tips. Either way, cook for about 10–15 minutes, until just tender. Serve hot with melted butter or Hollandaise Sauce (p. 176) or cold with Vinaigrette (p. 154), or combine with cottage cheese as a filling for crêpes (p. 197).

Frozen asparagus is useful when fresh is unobtainable, and is best steamed for about 7 minutes; and canned asparagus, while not having the same flavor or texture as fresh, can be used for garnishing or in Asparagus Rolls (p. 334).

BAMBOO SHOOT
Bambusa vulgaris

Even in China and Japan canned bamboo shoots are often used in preference to fresh ones because of their convenience. They also maintain their crispness well, drained and added to stir-fries, or cold in a salad.

CELERY *Apium graveolens*

Celery gives a specially delicious flavor to vegetable casseroles and makes an excellent soup. Break the celery head into individual sticks, trim as necessary, then scrub well under cold water.

Celery can be braised as described on p. 182, or chopped and added raw to salad mixtures. The tender stems are good for serving with dips or for topping with cream cheese or savory spreads as canapés. Crisp celery sticks are excellent with cheese, especially Stilton.

ENDIVE / BELGIAN ENDIVE / WITLOOF CHICORY
Cichorium intybus

Crisp and slightly bitter-tasting, endive makes a pleasant addition to a leafy green salad and is also good braised. Allow about 1 head per person if you're serving the endive in a salad, 2 heads for a cooked dish. Remove any damaged outer leaves. Trim the base, then insert the point of a knife into it and remove the core, which can be bitter. Wash well under cold water, but do not leave endive soaking in water as this can increase the bitterness. Cook as described for celery on p. 182, or use raw in a salad.

FENNEL *Foeniculum vulgare*

Allow 1 small fennel per person, or a larger one between 2. Trim and wash, then halve, quarter or slice.

To cook, braise as described on p. 182, or add to Spring Vegetable Braise (p. 181) or to casseroles. Steam and serve with Italian Tomato Sauce (p. 171), or cover with cream and a sprinkling of grated cheese and bake until golden-brown. Sliced or chopped fennel is refreshing with grated carrot in a salad (p. 162), in a green salad, mixed with diced cucumber, or replacing the celery in Waldorf Salad (p. 169).

GLOBE ARTICHOKE
Cynara scolymus

Very tender young artichokes can be trimmed, added to a casserole of summer vegetables and cooked gently for 20–30 minutes, until tender.

For most artichokes, however, more preparation is needed. Break off the stalk, removing with it any stringy pieces from the sides. Using a sharp knife or kitchen scissors, snip the points off the scales, then prise them apart until the soft leaves in the center and the hairy choke are revealed. Scrape the choke out firmly with a teaspoon, then rinse under cold water. Sprinkle the inside of the artichoke with lemon juice, and leave it soaking in acidulated water until you're ready to cook.

Bring a large non-aluminum saucepan of water to a boil, put in the artichokes and cook for 30–40 minutes, until a leaf can be pulled away easily. A tablespoon of lemon juice or white wine vinegar can be added to the water. Drain thoroughly and serve hot, with melted butter and lemon juice, or Hollandaise Sauce (p. 176); or cold, with Vinaigrette (p. 154). It's best not to keep cooked artichokes for more than 24 hours, as they can develop a toxin which can cause stomach upsets.

To prepare just the bottoms, or *fonds*, remove the stem and choke as described, to reveal the heart, then cut off all the leaves just above the base, and finally trim around the base. Cook in boiling water until tender. The artichoke bottoms may be topped with a creamy sauce or vegetable mixture, or served cold with a tasty dip spooned on top.

Artichoke hearts are available in cans and make a useful addition to the pantry, for inclusion in vegetable salads, casseroles and risottos.

HEART OF PALM
Sabal palmetto

Fresh hearts of palm are usually boiled until just tender and eaten hot with melted butter or cold with Mayonnaise (p. 155) or Vinaigrette (p. 154). Canned hearts of palm can be served similarly; try slicing them and mixing with diced avocado and a vinaigrette dressing.

Bulb Vegetables

Valuable in vegetarian cooking for adding flavor, bulb vegetables contain useful though not outstanding amounts of minerals and vitamins (but very little vitamin A). Their main value healthwise lies in their natural antibiotic powers and the way in which, if eaten over a period of time, onions and garlic in particular (both raw and cooked) help lower cholesterol and protect against fatty deposits in blood vessels. Both leeks and shallots have a sweet taste, less pungent than that of onion.

Spanish onion △
These large onions are the mildest in flavor

Scallion/spring onion ▽
These are tender young onions, picked before they mature

△
Pickling onion
These small onions are good used whole as well as for making into pickles

Purple or red onion ▽
Particularly useful for creating pretty color schemes and garnishes

Shallot △
A variety of onion which produces clusters of bulbs, shallots may be round or oval in shape

◁ **Leek**
Delicately flavored, with a slightly sweet taste; useful both raw and cooked

Onion △
Second to none as a vegetarian flavoring ingredient, onions are generally used in nut roasts, burgers and all kinds of savory dishes

Bulb Vegetables

Choosing and storing

Bulb vegetables should look bright and crisp; the bulbs should be firm. Avoid any onions which are sprouting, damp-looking or soft, or which smell musty. Leeks and scallions are best stored in a cool place, preferably the refrigerator, and used within a day or two. Onions will keep for at least a week if stored in a cool, dry place.

Preparing and cooking

See under individual varieties.

LEEK *Allium porrum*

Leeks need careful washing, as they may contain grit. First cut off the roots and trim the green leaves to within about 1 inch of the top of the white part. Make a slit right down one side of the leek from top to bottom and wash it under the cold tap, gently parting the layers and rinsing between them while keeping the shape of the leek intact. Then keep whole or cut into shorter lengths, or shred into fine rings for serving raw in a salad.

Alternatively, if you want a perfectly whole leek, cut a cross shape about 1 inch deep in the root end and place the leeks root end down in a deep jar of water for 30–60 minutes. After this any grit will show up as dark patches, and you can make a small incision at this point and rinse the grit away under the cold tap.

Leeks are good added to vegetable casseroles and curries, or cooked and served hot as an accompanying vegetable, either whole, sliced or puréed. I think the best way to cook leeks is to steam them or cook them in 1 inch of water in a covered pan for about 10 minutes, until tender. They can also be cooked until tender in olive oil or butter, or sautéed lightly, then braised in red wine or stock.

I very much like cooked leeks served cold as a first course, tossed in a little well-flavored vinaigrette while still hot, then served with a sprinkling of chopped parsley. For a more elaborate yet easily prepared presentation, make a leek terrine by packing the cooked and drained leeks, cut to fit, into a 1-pound loaf pan. Press down firmly, cover with several layers of paper towels and weight down. Chill for several hours, then put the terrine into the freezer for 1 hour before serving, so that it is firm enough to cut easily. Slice and pour vinaigrette over before serving.

ONION *Allium cepa*

There are many varieties of onion, ranging in color from white and yellow to shades of purple and red, and in size from minute bulbs to large ones weighing around 1 pound or more. Onions also vary a good deal in strength; some types are mild and sweet, while others are extremely pungent. Even individual varieties can change as the season goes on, changing from mild to strong, or vice versa.

To prepare onions, cut off the root and stalk end, then strip off the outer skins. Wash the onions, then chop or slice as required. If you don't need to use the onions immediately, it's best not to leave them soaking in water; either sauté them in a little oil or butter, or wrap them in plastic wrap.

Onions are included in many vegetarian dishes as a flavoring. They are also useful sliced raw in salads, for making a delectable tart (p. 261) and for soup. Large onions can be baked whole in their skins, then split open and served with butter, sea salt and freshly ground black pepper as an accompaniment, or stuffed with a nut and breadcrumb mixture and baked to make a warming winter main course.

PICKLING ONIONS can be fiddly to peel, but if you trim them, then cover with boiling water and leave for 5 minutes, you should be able to skin them easily.

The following quick method of making Pickled Onions gives an excellent result but is best done in small quantities, as the onions do not keep for more than about 4 months. Put peeled pickling onions into jars and sprinkle them with pickling spice between the layers, allowing 1 rounded tablespoon spice to a large jar. Then fill the jars with malt vinegar, making sure that the onions are completely covered. Cover with airtight, vinegar-proof lids and store in a cool, dry, dark place for at least 8 weeks before eating with cheese.

SCALLIONS (also called spring onions) make an attractive garnish and addition to salads or crudités, and are excellent added to a stir-fry or other lightly cooked mixed vegetable dishes.

SHALLOTS (*Allium ascalonicum*) can be used wherever a delicate onion flavor is needed and are also excellent for pickling. They can be peeled as described for pickling onions.

The strength of PURPLE or RED ONIONS can vary; some are quite mild, but this is not always the case.

Mild-flavored SPANISH ONIONS are ideal for slicing and adding to salads as well as for cooking, and are excellent baked with a tasty stuffing. To make stuffed onions for 4 people, rinse, but don't peel, 4 large Spanish onions. Put them into a large saucepan of water and simmer for about 20 minutes until they are tender but not cooked right through. Drain and cool, then remove the root ends and cut the onions in half horizontally. Scoop out the center of each half, making a cavity for stuffing and leaving three or four layers of onion. Arrange the onion halves in a greased shallow ovenproof dish, cut sides upward. Set the oven to 350°F.

The onions can be stuffed with a Herb Stuffing (p. 239), a nut roast mixture (pp. 235, 239), or with an unusual sweet-and-sour mixture. To make this, first chop the onion you scooped out, then crush four macaroons and add to the onion, along with 1 cup whole-wheat breadcrumbs, ¼ teaspoon each ground cinnamon, cloves and nutmeg, 2 beaten eggs, ½ cup grated Parmesan cheese and ¼ cup sultanas. Season, then heap the mixture into the onion cavities, dot with butter and bake, uncovered, for 30 minutes. A sharply-flavored cheese sauce goes well with these.

Daikon ▷
Sometimes called MOOLI, this is a type of radish popular in Japanese cooking

◁ **Rose radish**

Beet ▷

Root Vegetables

Nourishing, warming and filling, root vegetables have long been a winter mainstay because of their excellent keeping qualities and value for money. Radishes, carrots and beets add color to meals, while parsnips and turnips are delicious roasted. They contain useful quantities of iron, calcium, protein and B vitamins, and carrots are one of the richest sources of vitamin A. Root vegetables absorb flavors well and can be made into tasty soups, stews and casseroles or used in salads.

Radish
There are numerous varieties of radish; they can be the size of marbles or grapefruit, round or long, and range in color from white to red and black

△ **Burdock**
Popular in macrobiotic cooking

White radish ▷

Carrot ▷
Descended from the wild carrot

◁ **Rutabaga**
Called, confusingly, turnip Scotland and the U.S., rutabagas are larger than ac turnips and do not have rid

Turnip △
One of the oldest European food crops, turnips vary in shape and size and the skins may be white, green or tinged with purple; the flesh is usually white, juicy and pungent

Scorzonera △
Also called "vegetable oyster," because their flavor is sometimes considered similar

Parsnip △
A distinctively flavored, sweet-tasting root which was used in puddings and sweetmeats in medieval cookery

Celeriac △
A variety of celery with a bulbous root

Root Vegetables

Choosing and storing
Look for bright, firm root vegetables, with no signs of wrinkling. Store in a cool, dry place; the more delicate roots, such as radishes, keep best in the refrigerator, and I prefer to store carrots there too, if there's room.

Preparing and cooking
Radishes and tender young carrots, turnips and beets only need scrubbing; older ones need scraping. Celeriac, turnips, rutabagas, parsnips and older beets, if used raw, need peeling quite thickly. Cut into even-sized pieces, place in a saucepan, cover with cold water and bring to a boil, then simmer gently until tender. Drain, saving the cooking water for a well-flavored and nutritious stock, and add seasoning, butter or vegan margarine, chopped herbs and perhaps a squeeze of lemon juice. Salsify, scorzonera and beets are cooked in the same way (beets may require 1–2 hours, depending on size, although a pressure cooker speeds the process) until tender, when the skins will slip off quite easily.

BEET *Beta vulgaris*
Beets are usually red, although white and golden varieties are also grown. When preparing beets for cooking, if the leaves are still attached, break these off about 6 inches from the root and do not cut or pierce the skins, or the color may seep out during cooking. The leaves can also be cooked and taste like spinach. Cooked beets can be served in salads, dressed with vinaigrette, or mixed with other ingredients such as apple and celery in a dressing of horseradish, sour cream, yogurt or mayonnaise. In Russia and Poland beets are made into borscht and served with buckwheat (p. 44) – good, cheap, filling food! For a lighter version of Beet Soup, see p. 138. Young cooked beets are good served with butter, black pepper and a little orange juice and grated rind.

Beets can also be eaten raw: peel, grate and mix with an equal quantity of grated apple and some raisins, or sliced onion rings and vinaigrette for a very healthy salad which is said to help break up fat deposits in the body.

BURDOCK *Arctium lappa*
A tough root vegetable with a distinctive flavor which is an acquired taste. It should be scrubbed, sliced thinly and boiled for 30–40 minutes until tender, or it can be added to vegetable stews.

CARROT *Daucus carota*
One of the most useful and nutritious vegetables. Delicious either raw or cooked, carrots are useful in salads, soups, stews and casseroles, for serving with dips and even for making into cakes (p. 306). Baby carrots can be cooked whole, while larger ones can be cut into rounds or julienne strips (p. 184), finely or coarsely grated, shaved lengthways into ribbons with a potato peeler or "turned" as shown on p. 182. Simply cooked, as a side vegetable, carrots are good with a flavoring of chopped parsley, caraway or anise; or they can be glazed (p. 182).

CELERIAC
Apium graveolens, var. *rapaceum*
This delicious celery-flavored root is good both raw and cooked. To serve it raw, cut into fine julienne strips or grate coarsely, then mix with a well-flavored vinaigrette (p. 154). If you like, celeriac can be blanched for 1 minute in boiling water, then refreshed under cold water to soften slightly before adding the dressing. Cooked celeriac mixed with an equal quantity of potato makes a delicately flavored purée.

DAIKON *Raphanus sativus*
Daikon has a slightly hot taste, like a cross between a turnip and a radish. It can be sliced and added to root vegetable mixtures or stir-fries, diced or shredded and combined with salad ingredients, and it can also be used to make a particularly attractive garnish; see Japanese Flower Salad (p. 164).

HORSERADISH
Armoracia rusticana
(Not illustrated)
See p. 124.

PARSNIP *Pastinaca sativa*
Parsnips can be roasted like potatoes, cooked and mashed or puréed, added to a julienne of mixed root vegetables (p. 184), made into a winter soup or added to casseroles and stews.

RADISH *Raphanus sativus*
Thinly sliced radishes make a colorful and pungent addition to salads – try adding them to cooked, cooled corn, along with some chopped scallions. Radishes, with their green leaves still attached if possible, make a good addition to a crudités selection, and radish flowers are easy to make for garnishing (p. 164).

RUTABAGA
Brassica napus
Rutabagas have a sweetish flavor but they also absorb other flavors well and are good in casseroles, diced as part of a macedoine of root vegetables or mashed with carrots or potatoes. "Mashed neaps" are traditionally served with haggis at Burns Night suppers in Scotland. Raw, rutabagas make a good salad, coarsely grated and mixed with mayonnaise and chopped dates.

SCORZONERA
Scorzonera hispanica and
SALSIFY
Tragopogon porrifolius
(Not illustrated)
Cooked and served hot with cream and Parmesan, or cold mixed with vinaigrette or mayonnaise, these delicately flavored vegetables make a good first course. Or they can be dipped in batter or egg and breadcrumbs and fried until crisp, then served with lemon wedges. Frozen or canned salsify is available.

TURNIP *Brassica rapa*
Turnips can be served in any of the ways described for rutabagas. Baby turnips can be glazed with butter and sugar (p. 183). The tops, cooked like spinach, are strongly flavored and extremely nutritious.

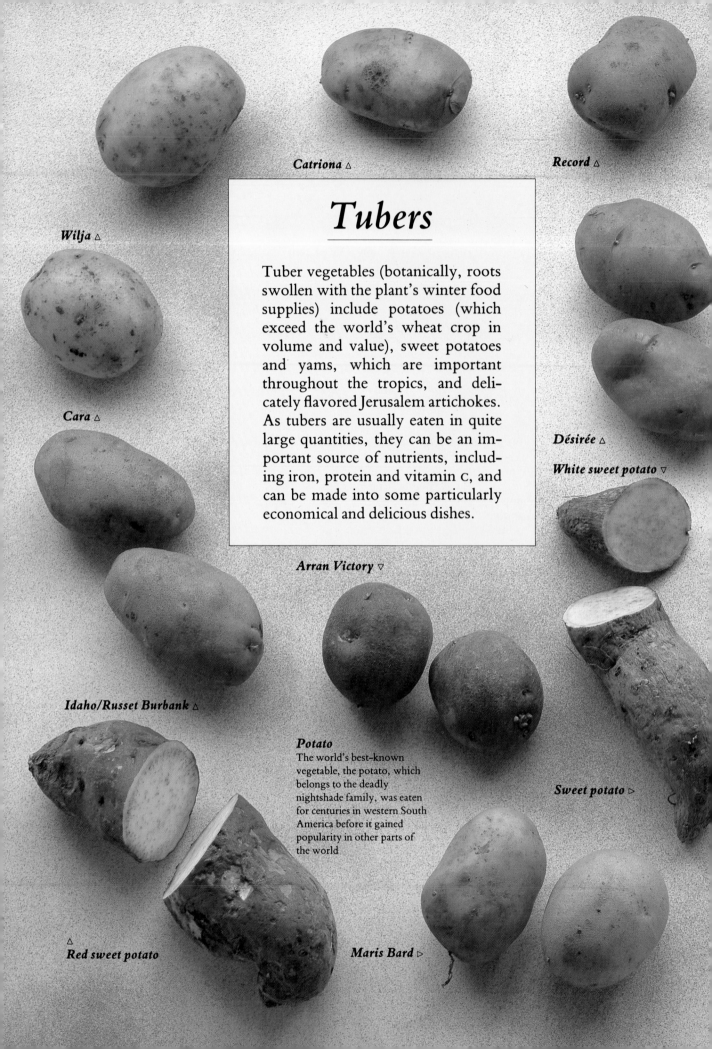

Catriona △

Record △

Wilja △

Cara △

Désirée △

White sweet potato ▽

Tubers

Tuber vegetables (botanically, roots swollen with the plant's winter food supplies) include potatoes (which exceed the world's wheat crop in volume and value), sweet potatoes and yams, which are important throughout the tropics, and delicately flavored Jerusalem artichokes. As tubers are usually eaten in quite large quantities, they can be an important source of nutrients, including iron, protein and vitamin c, and can be made into some particularly economical and delicious dishes.

Arran Victory ▽

Idaho/Russet Burbank △

Potato
The world's best-known vegetable, the potato, which belongs to the deadly nightshade family, was eaten for centuries in western South America before it gained popularity in other parts of the world

Sweet potato ▷

△
Red sweet potato

Maris Bard ▷

Vanessa ▽

◁ *Maris Peer*

Estima △

Yam ▷
Probably native to the Orient, and
popular in Chinese, African and
Caribbean cooking, the yam is a
starchy tuber often confused with
the sweet potato

Maris Piper △

Pentland Squire ▷

Jerusalem artichoke ▽
Related to the sunflower and
thought to be named after it

Romana △

Diana △

King Edward △

Cyprus new ▷

Italian new △

Ulster Sceptre ▷

Tubers

Choosing and storing

Look for firm tubers with no wrinkles or damp patches. Choose firm, even-sized, dry-skinned potatoes (prewashed potatoes do not keep as well as unwashed ones). When choosing Jerusalem artichokes, look for ones without too many knobbly bits – it makes peeling easier. Store tubers in a cool, dry, dark place.

Preparing and cooking

See under individual varieties.

JERUSALEM ARTICHOKE
Helianthus tuberosus

These can be peeled either before or after cooking. If you peel before, you will need to cut off the smaller knobbles along with the peel. Put the peeled artichokes straight into cold water, with a dash of lemon juice added to help preserve their color. Alternatively, give them a quick wash, then boil them and slip off their skins, using a small sharp knife, after cooking.

Jerusalem artichokes have a distinctive flavor reminiscent of globe artichokes (hence the 'artichoke' in the name), but not as delicate. They are good mashed to a creamy purée, served cold in a vinaigrette or hot with butter and chopped parsley. They also make a soothing winter soup and go well with Fresh Tomato Sauce. To assemble the dish, first prepare the Fresh Tomato Sauce (p. 170). While it is cooking, peel 1½ pounds Jerusalem artichokes as above and cut into even-sized pieces. Put in a saucepan with 1 tablespoon butter, 4 tablespoons water and salt. Cover and cook over a gentle heat for about 20 minutes until just tender. Drain the artichokes, pour over the tomato sauce and serve.

POTATO *Solanum tuberosum*

Nutritious staple vegetables, rich in vitamin C and potassium, and containing useful amounts of particularly good-quality protein, potatoes are made into some of the most delicious and economical dishes throughout the world.

They are sometimes loosely divided into "waxy" types, which are moist, even slightly translucent after cooking, and those which have a dry, fluffy texture, known as "floury." Generally speaking, waxy potatoes are best for salads and for frying, because they stay firm, and floury potatoes are best for mashing, boiling and baking in their jackets.

There are, however, many varieties which are good all-rounders. New potatoes, or young potatoes dug early in the season, such as the ITALIAN NEW POTATOES and CYPRUS NEW POTATOES shown, are best when they are from varieties grown specially for this purpose. They are waxy, tender and excellent for boiling and salads, but not for baking, roasting and French-frying.

The color of potato flesh varies from white through to gold. As advancements are made in preserving and shipping techniques, an extraordinary new variety of potatoes are becoming available around the world. So don't keep using the same kinds just because you're used to them.

New varieties of potato are continually being developed. Some, such as DIANA, make a brief appearance and then fade out; others survive to become well-loved favorites. These include WILJA, which is particularly good for boiling and has pale yellow flesh; MARIS PIPER, the most popular white potato in the U.K. today and a good all-rounder; KING EDWARD, which is making a comeback on account of its popularity with housewives; DÉSIRÉE, another very widely grown red potato in Europe and another excellent all-rounder; MARIS BARD, which has average cooking qualities and needs plenty of flavoring to enliven it; ESTIMA, a Dutch variety, which is growing in popularity; and RECORD, also Dutch, and with very yellow flesh, but a superb potato for making into chips and indeed for boiling and roasting.

The demand for varieties of potato also varies from area to area. The RUSSET BURBANK, also known as the IDAHO, is well-known and loved in the U.S. Many potato-lovers in America wouldn't dream of ever serving another variety on Thanksgiving or Christmas! Another type, ARRAN VICTORY, is liked in Scotland and Ireland, but not in England, on account of its blue skin. This potato was bred to celebrate the victory of the 1914–18 war and has very white floury flesh.

Potato salad is an ideal use for leftover baked potatoes. Add chopped chives, parsley, plenty of fresh-ground pepper, and a mayonnaise or vinaigrette dressing.

Varieties which are popular with show judges such as the purple-eyed CATRIONA are not always so well-favored by customers. MARIS PEER, VANESSA (bred from the popular Désirée) and ULSTER SCEPTRE, which have been favored in the past, are now being replaced by varieties such as ROMANA (also bred from Désirée and with similar qualities). CARA, which was developed in the Republic of Ireland as Oakpark Beauty, and has pink eyes like a King Edward, is growing in popularity and is being widely grown in Cyprus and Egypt.

New potatoes are good just scrubbed and boiled in their skins until just tender, then served hot with butter and chopped herbs, or mixed with vinaigrette and served cold. More mature potatoes can be scrubbed and boiled or baked in their jackets, or peeled before use.

Baked Potatoes, cooked so that their skins are crisp (p. 190), and served with butter, sour cream or a variety of toppings (p. 190), accompanied by a salad, are one of my favorite quick and easy meals. Bircher Potatoes are also popular with children: scrub medium potatoes, cut them in half lengthways and place them cut side down on an oiled baking sheet. Bake in a hot oven, 425°F, for about 45 minutes, until the tops of the potatoes are soft and the underneath golden-brown and crisp.

Another delicious way with potatoes is to cut well-scrubbed medium ones into ⅛ inch slices and arrange overlapping like roof tiles on an oiled baking sheet. Brush the potatoes with olive oil, sprinkle with chopped thyme or rosemary and a little crushed garlic, and bake in a hot oven, 425°F, until golden-brown and crisp.

Potatoes mashed until very light and creamy, with hot milk, or cream for special occasions, butter or vegan margarine and a good seasoning of salt and freshly ground black pepper, are one of my favorite ways of serving them. Mashed potatoes can be used as a topping for vegetarian shepherd's pie, and any left over can be fried to make crisp potato cakes, a good quick snack for children, especially with some grated nuts added.

I start off most soups by frying an onion and one or two potatoes together in butter, then adding the other vegetables: the potato thickens the soup and gives it body. I find that children like a plain potato soup, without other vegetables except for a flavoring of onion, whizzed to a smooth creamy purée.

Every national cuisine has its own range of potato dishes: delicious Spiced Potatoes from India (p. 185); Hashed Browns from the U.S. (p. 191); Rösti from Switzerland (p. 189) and Gratin Dauphinois from France (p. 190), to mention just a few.

Potatoes are available fresh or frozen in the form of the ubiquitous French-fries, canned, and in various dried and powdered forms.

Potato flour makes a lighter, healthier thickening for sauces than flour and butter, and it is also good for thickening clear fruit soups, using ingredients such as cooked black cherries or raspberries.

SWEET POTATO
Ipomeoa batatas
A member of the morning-glory family, the sweet potato has sweet, mealy flesh. There are two main types, one with yellow flesh and a dryish texture, and the other with particularly sweet orange flesh and a more watery texture. (The latter variety are often, incorrectly, called

---

How to make perfect roast potatoes and French-fried potatoes

Roast potatoes
Set the oven to 425°F. Peel even-sized potatoes, allowing about 1½ pounds for 4 people, and cut them into halves or quarters. Parboil the potatoes for 5 minutes.

Meanwhile, pour into a roasting pan just enough oil to cover the base. Don't make it more than ⅛ inch deep. Heat the oil in the oven.

Drain the potatoes. Make sure that the potatoes and the oil are both piping hot; a good way of doing this is to put the roasting pan over the gas flame or hotplate while you put the hot potatoes into it – but stand back, as the oil will sizzle and splutter.

Turn the potatoes in the oil, then put the pan back into the oven and bake the potatoes for 45–60 minutes, until they are golden and crisp, turning them over after about 30 minutes.

If they are ready before you are, turn the heat of the oven down to 325°F, but don't cover the potatoes or they will soften. Drain them well on paper towels before serving.

French-fried potatoes
There are two ways of making crisp French-fried potatoes. One is to fry them in oil heated to 375°F until they are soft but not browned, then to reheat the oil to 390°F and give the potatoes a final quick dip to brown and crisp them. The other way is to fry them steadily in the oil until they get past the soft stage and become crisp and brown.

Personally I use the first method if I am cooking a large number, because I can get them all partially cooked and then give them their final quick frying in batches just before they're needed; and I use the second method when I'm making just a small quantity which can be cooked in one batch.

Cut the potatoes into strips about ½ inch wide and ½ inch thick and rinse in cold water, then thoroughly dry them before frying. After cooking, drain the potatoes well on crumpled paper towels.

Désirée, Maris Piper, King Edward or Majestic are the best potato varieties for French-frying.

"yams" in the U.S.) The skins vary in color and may be white, red or purple. Sweet potatoes can be quite large, and it is usually possible to buy just a piece.

They can be boiled, roasted, fried or mashed and are enhanced by a sprinkling of sweet spice: cinnamon, nutmeg, ground cloves or allspice. Sweet potatoes are also delicious baked in their skins or "jackets" and served with butter. In the U.S., they are boiled and then candied and served as a traditional accompaniment with the Thanksgiving dinner.

Perhaps the nicest way to serve them (but not the most slimming!) is glazed with butter and brown sugar; simply parboil them, then put them into a shallow casserole, dot with butter and sprinkle with brown sugar. Bake in a fairly hot oven – 400°F – for about 40 minutes until they're golden-brown and glazed. Or follow the recipe for Glazed Carrots on p. 182. Cooked in either of

these ways, they make an excellent accompaniment to an almond nut roast for a special autumn meal.

YAM
Dioscorea rotundata, D. cayenensis
The yam is a staple food widely consumed in West Africa and the Caribbean. Yams have brown, woody skins, and their flesh is moist and sweet. They come in a variety of shapes and sizes and are usually cooked in the same way as sweet potatoes. They can be made into casseroles or boiled and served with spicy vegetable mixtures. They absorb other flavors well.

They can also be used instead of ordinary potatoes in potato salad. Peel the yams and quarter them. Boil for about 15 minutes until tender, drain and cool, then dice them. Continue as for any of the other Potato Salad recipes on p. 166.

Yams are also good peeled, sliced and fried like sauté potatoes.

Tomato ▷
An indispensable flavoring, thickening and salad ingredient. Also delicious cooked in a variety of ways

Eggplant △
Originally egg-like in both shape and color (hence their name), eggplants nowadays are more likely to be shiny, purple-skinned and a good deal larger than eggs

Fruit Vegetables

Originally from tropical or sub-tropical countries, fruit vegetables offer vibrant colors, succulent textures and intense – sometimes hot – flavors. They are nutritious – avocados outstandingly so, being rich in protein and in vitamins E and B6 (particularly good for women), while raw sweet or bell peppers are high in vitamin C, green peppers containing twice, and red peppers four times, the amount in oranges. Fruit vegetables are available year-round but are plentiful in summer.

Beefsteak tomato △
These large tomatoes are ideal for stuffing and slicing for salads

Cherry tomato △
Baby cherry tomatoes make a pretty addition to salads and casseroles, or can be hollowed out and stuffed with cottage cheese or a dip

Kenyan chili
▽

Avocado ▷
The fruit of an evergreen tree, avocados range in color from green with yellow or reddish flecks to almost black, and may be round or pear-shaped

Sweet pepper / bell pepper △
Peppers start off green, then become yellow or red as they ripen; very dark, almost black, peppers are also available, as well as cream-colored ones for pickling

Ancho chili
▽

Chili pepper ▷
There are many varieties of chili pepper, ranging in hotness from mild to very fiery, and in color from green to yellow or red

Fruit Vegetables

Choosing and storing

Eggplants, sweet or bell peppers and tomatoes should be bright and firm, with no signs of withering or discolored patches. They vary a good deal in shape and size, so look for ones which are suitable for your purpose; choose squarish peppers, for instance, and medium-sized eggplants, if you plan to stuff them. Store in a cool place – the salad compartment of the refrigerator is ideal. When choosing an avocado, either choose one which will yield all over to gentle pressure, or buy a hard one and allow up to a week for it to ripen at room temperature. Ripe avocados will keep for 1–2 days in the refrigerator.

Preparing and cooking

See under individual varieties.

AVOCADO *Persea americana*

It's best to use a stainless steel knife to cut avocados as a steel one can leave a metallic taste. Cut the avocado in half lengthways, then hold one side in each hand and twist in opposite directions to separate them, and remove the stone. With their delicate, buttery flesh, avocados are delicious halved and served simply with a good vinaigrette, or stuffed and served either hot or cold. They can be added to salads (p. 163), or made into delicious tarts (p. 263), chilled soup (p. 138) or creamy dip. To make classic guacamole, finely chop ½ a bunch of coriander, 4 medium tomatoes and 3 chili peppers. Just before serving, peel and pit 2 ripe avocados, mash them and add to the other ingredients, with seasoning.

Avocado flesh discolors after an hour or so, though coating it with lemon juice will help prevent this. One-half of an avocado will also keep its color if you leave the stone in it, cover with plastic wrap and keep in the refrigerator overnight. Undeveloped baby avocados, without stones, can be sliced into rings as a garnish or in salads.

CHILI PEPPER
Capsicum annuum

Chilis vary in hotness and a general guide is the smaller the chili, the hotter. ANCHO CHILIS are sweet and only fairly hot; KENYAN CHILIS are hot and delicious fried in oil and sprinkled with salt, as a first course.

Really HOT CHILIS need careful handling. One is ample in a dish for 4–6 people. If the recipe requires chopped chili, cut it and remove the seeds under running water. Do not touch your eyes or skin, as chili juice can cause irritation; wash your hands well afterwards. Dried red chilis are used in chutneys and pickles.

EGGPLANT
Solanum melongena,
var. *esculentum*

Eggplants are usually salted before cooking, to draw out any bitter juices: cut into cubes or slices, then sprinkle with salt and place in a colander for 30 minutes, then rinse under cold water and dry with paper towels. Recently I have been doing this less and less and have never come across a bitter eggplant, but salting does also prevent the eggplant from absorbing too much oil if it is fried.

Eggplants are usually cooked with the skin on, though this can be removed with a potato peeler if you prefer for dishes like Parmigiana (p. 202). Cut eggplants into rounds, short lengths, or cubes or dice. Eggplants for stuffing should be cut in half lengthways, and the cut sides scored diagonally in both directions, without piercing the skin. Salt can then be pressed into the cuts and the eggplants allowed to stand for 30 minutes. The flesh will then have softened and can be scooped out with a small knife and a teaspoon.

Eggplants are excellent stuffed (p. 192), in stews and casseroles, (p. 211), and in dips. To make a dip, bake 2 eggplants at 400°F for 40 minutes until tender, or broil them until soft and charred, then scrape off the charred skin. Purée the eggplant with 2 garlic cloves and 4 tablespoons each of lemon juice, chopped parsley and olive oil; season to taste. Some pale tahini is also good in this; add 1–2 tablespoons with the oil.

SWEET PEPPER / BELL PEPPER
Capsicum annuum

With their bright colors and fresh flavor, sweet peppers are useful both raw, in salads, as part of a crudités selection, and as a garnish, and cooked, in casseroles, stir-fries and vegetable mixtures. Cored and deseeded peppers make a perfect container for a stuffing. To prepare peppers, cut a thin slice off the stalk end. Remove the seeds, rinsing out any stray ones under the cold tap. Use the peppers as they are, for stuffing, or cut into rings, strips, diamond shapes or dice.

If you want to remove the outer skin, and end up with a semicooked pepper, which is good in salads, put the whole peppers under a hot broiler and turn them from time to time until the skin is charred, blistered and rubs off easily. Rinse off the skin and seeds under the cold tap.

TOMATO
Lycopersicon esculentum

There are many varieties of tomato, ranging in size from the baby CHERRY TOMATO to the large BEEFSTEAK variety. PLUM (or EGG) TOMATOES (not illustrated), which are much grown around the Mediterranean, have an intense, sweet flavor and make excellent sauces and salads. Sundried tomatoes (whole and puréed) make a useful flavoring for pasta, sauces and salads.

Tomatoes can be used with or without their skin, depending on the recipe and how tender the tomato is. To skin tomatoes, cover with boiling water and leave for 1 minute, then drain and cover with cold water. Use a small sharp knife and your fingers to peel off the skin.

Sometimes recipes suggest deseeding tomatoes, but I very rarely do this as so much of the tomato is wasted and I find that difficult to do, especially as the jelly around the seeds is a valuable form of soluble fiber. To make tomato salad to serve 4 people, slice 1½ pounds tomatoes, put into a shallow dish and sprinkle with 1–2 tablespoons of olive oil and salt, freshly ground black pepper and chopped basil to taste. A little sliced raw onion can also be added.

Ridged cucumber ▷
Has a delicious, slightly
lemony flavor,
though it can
sometimes
be bitter

Baby cucumber △
Used for making into pickles

**Golden nugget or
onion squash** ▷
One of the winter
squash, with
delicately flavored
flesh

Cucumbers and Squashes

The name *squash* originates from the
American Indian *askoot-asquash*, and
is the name given to the members
of a very varied family of fruiting
vegetables which includes pump-
kins, gourds, zucchini and cucumbers. One of the most ancient vegetable families of the world, squashes
are not particularly nutritious, although the yellow-fleshed varieties
contain useful amounts of vitamin A
and some fiber.

Butternut squash ▽
Has fairly dense, golden flesh
and makes an excellent purée

Cucumber △
Should be firm with a bright
skin; one of the most
refreshing vegetables

Pumpkin △
With its glowing, golden flesh,
this is equally good in sweet
and savory recipes

Chinese winter melon ▷
This can be used in the same
way as marrow

◁ Buttercup squash
Similar to turban squash, and can be used in the same way. Also known as yellow button squash

◁ Hokkaido pumpkin
Can be served as a vegetable or made into a soup

Ridge or acorn squash ▽
A particularly useful squash, as it can be halved and baked in the skin

◁ Doody or white pumpkin
Has pale greenish-white flesh and a delicate flavor

Turban squash ▽
This can be used in the same way as pumpkin

Zucchini ▷
Best when not more than 4–5 inches long, delicious lightly cooked

△ Marrow
The British term for the more mature version of zucchini, with a delicate flavor

Spaghetti squash ▷
A type of marrow with fibrous flesh which looks like spaghetti when cooked

Cucumbers and Squashes

Cucumbers

CUCUMBER *Cucumis sativus*
One of the first vegetables to be cultivated by man, and one of the most refreshing, cucumbers were a great favorite with the Roman emperor Tiberius, who demanded a constant supply, even in winter. Various types of cucumber are available, including RIDGED and BABY.

Choosing and storing
Cucumbers should be firm and tender with a bright shiny skin. They need to be stored in a cool place, preferably the refrigerator, and used within a few days.

Preparing and cooking
The skin should be scrubbed well before use, or if the cucumbers have been waxed, it should be removed with a peeler. The cucumber can then be grated, sliced or diced for use in salads: it is particularly good in a sweet-and-sour dressing using a little vinegar, fresh dill and white mustard seeds, or prepared in the Middle Eastern manner, with yogurt or sour cream and chopped mint (p. 167). Cucumber can also be used as a garnish, formed into cones to hold a savory filling for a cocktail nibble, or cut into sticks for serving with a savory dip.

A chilled cucumber and yogurt soup (diced cucumber mixed with plain yogurt, chopped fresh herbs and seasoning) makes a delightful start to a summer meal. Cucumber is also delectable, gently sautéed in butter with some fennel or dill seeds and a bay leaf, in a covered pan, until the flesh is almost translucent.

Cucumber can also be stuffed and baked; try cutting a good plump cucumber into 4-inch lengths, removing the skin, scooping out the seeds and filling the cavity with a mixture of finely chopped walnuts, onions, tomatoes and garlic. Bake in a well-buttered casserole, with a lid, for about 45 minutes in a moderate oven, and serve with Sour Cream and Herb Dressing (p. 156).

Dill-pickled cucumbers are widely available and make a piquant addition to salads and sandwiches. Small fresh cucumbers are sometimes available for making your own pickles (p. 342).

Squashes

Squashes come in varied colors, shapes and sizes, but they can be roughly divided into summer and winter types. Summer squash have soft skins – they are said to be too old to eat if you cannot pierce the skin with your fingernail – and watery flesh, while winter squash have hard skins and firmer, more mealy flesh. It was this hard, protective skin developed by the winter squashes which made them such useful vegetables to store for the winter in the days before refrigerators.

Choosing and storing
The more delicate summer squashes should be firm and tender, with a smooth, shiny skin. They need to be stored in a cool place, preferably the fridge, and used within a few days. The more robust winter type should be shiny and hard, with no blemishes. As a rough guide, allow 1 pound summer squash, or 2 pounds winter squash, for 4 people.

Preparing and cooking
See under individual varieties.

MARROW *Cucurbita pepo*
Marrows and larger types of summer squash are nicest when the skin is tender enough to eat; they can then be cut into small dice. If the seeds are very tender, these can be cooked along with the flesh; if not, they should be scooped out. Marrow can be cooked as described for zucchini (the butter or oil method suits marrows especially well, giving a tender, translucent, golden result). A finely chopped shallot or some grated fresh ginger or crushed garlic can be included for extra flavor. Marrow cooked in this way is good served with a crunchy topping of roasted cashew nuts. Béchamel Sauce (p. 175) with chopped herbs is a fine complement to plainly cooked marrow, steamed until just tender.

Marrows with the seeds removed make excellent containers for stuffing, either hollowed out from one end, or halved lengthways, or cut crossways into sections and stood on end. A marrow which has been allowed to mature on the vine can be made into a spicy chutney or that traditional old British favorite, marrow and ginger jam. Warwickshire cottagers used to decorate such marrows with streamers, suspend them from the rafters in the autumn and keep them until Christmas!

Small, individual-size summer squash such as the delectable little PATTYPANS (not illustrated) should be boiled in their skins until tender; the top can then be sliced off, a little butter and seasoning added, and the flesh scooped out with a spoon. The CHINESE WINTER MELON and the DOODY or WHITE PUMPKIN can be prepared like marrow, but it may be necessary to remove the skin unless this is tender. Use a paring knife or potato peeler.

PUMPKIN *Cucurbita pepo*
A pumpkin probably looks more exciting than it tastes, with its rounded shape and golden-orange skin and flesh. Pumpkin can, however, be made into an excellent smooth and creamy soup that is delicious eaten with hot garlic bread on a chilly autumn day. It is of course a traditional ingredient in Thanksgiving celebrations in the form of spicy Pumpkin Pie (p. 292) – a good way to use up your Hallowe'en decoration! Pumpkin can be served as a vegetable, and I like it best layered in a shallow gratin dish with garlic butter, topped with crumbs and baked in the oven, or cooked with some grated fresh ginger and garlic, then puréed. Spicy pumpkin bread is another popular harvest time side dish, or spread with cream cheese for a winter breakfast. TURBAN, BUTTERNUT and ACORN SQUASH, HOKKAIDO PUMPKIN, HUBBARD (not illustrated), GOLDEN NUGGET or

ONION SQUASH, and BUTTERCUP (or YELLOW BUTTON) SQUASH can all be prepared in a similar way.

SNAKE GOURD
Tricosantes cucumerina
(Not illustrated)

This unusual-looking green squash is native to Southeast Asia and Australia, and although sometimes grown in the U.S. and Europe, it is not easy to come by. It is much used in Indian vegetarian cooking and has a firm texture and an excellent flavor. It has a white down on the skin, which can be removed by rubbing the gourd all over with coarse salt. It is then cooked without peeling, and is delicious in lightly spiced vegetable dishes and curries.

The snake gourd is sometimes confused with the BOTTLE GOURD (not illustrated), a much tougher squash, which is pointed at both ends.

SPAGHETTI SQUASH
Cucurbita pepo

This has fibrous flesh which looks like spaghetti (but tastes like squash) when cooked. Halve or quarter the squash without peeling, then boil until the flesh is tender and can be scraped out. Toss the flesh in a little butter or olive oil and season well before serving.

ZUCCHINI Cucurbita pepo

These young squashes, which can be green or gold, reach their peak of perfection when they are no more than 4–5 inches long. At this point they are tender, with flesh which almost melts in your mouth, and only need trimming. They can then be cooked whole, sliced into rounds or matchsticks, or coarsely grated. Some recipes suggest salting zucchini, as described for eggplant on p. 73, and this can be helpful if you are planning to sauté them in butter because it makes them less absorbent. My favorite way of cooking them is to steam them, either in a vegetable steamer or by cooking them in a deep, covered saucepan containing only ½ inch of water, so that most of the zucchini are above the water, cooking in the steam. As soon as they

are just tender – 2–4 minutes – drain them and add coarse sea salt, freshly ground black pepper, fresh chopped herbs – parsley, mint, tarragon or basil – and a little butter. You can also serve them with a Fresh Tomato Sauce (p. 170). Zucchini can also be cooked in butter or oil, in a covered pan, over a low heat: this gives a luscious result, but I find this can be rather too rich and fatty unless the zucchini are served with something very plain.

Zucchini are excellent cooked with onions, garlic, peppers, eggplant and tomatoes, in Ratatouille (p. 187). And Provençal Zucchini and Tomato Gratin makes a delicious light supper or lunch dish. Grated zucchini (2¼ pounds for 4 people) are fried lightly in butter, then layered in a shallow ovenproof dish with Fresh Tomato Sauce (p. 170) and sprinkled with breadcrumbs mixed with grated cheese. They are

then baked in a moderate oven for 30–40 minutes.

For another excellent Provençal dish, Rice and Zucchini Gratin, cook 1¼ cups brown rice. Fry a large onion and 4 diced zucchini in 2 tablespoons of oil until tender, then add to the rice with ½ cup grated cheese, an egg and seasoning. Spoon the mixture into a gratin dish, sprinkle with grated cheese and bake at 350°F for 45 minutes.

Larger zucchini make a good base for tasty stuffings, and these squashes are always a pleasant addition to vegetable pilafs and casseroles. They are best added towards the end of cooking time so that they do not overcook.

If you are able to obtain them, SQUASH BLOSSOMS make a delicious treat dipped in a light batter and deep-fried, or filled with one of the nut roast mixtures (p. 230) and baked.

Cooking and serving ideas for winter squashes

- Winter squashes make an excellent purée; steam until tender, then whizz to a cream in a blender or food processor. Season with salt, pepper and garlic. Good with a crisp hazelnut roast or burgers.

- For a richer version, stew the diced squash gently in butter with a sliced onion, some garlic and grated ginger, until tender, then purée in a blender or food processor.

- Winter squashes, and pumpkin in particular, make an excellent soup, creamy and golden. Allow 2¼ pounds pumpkin to make a soup for 6 people. Remove the skin and seeds; dice the flesh. Fry 2 large onions in 2 tablespoons butter for 10 minutes, then add the pumpkin and 2 crushed garlic cloves and fry for a further 5 minutes. Add 6 cups water and simmer for about 20 minutes, then reduce to a purée in a blender or food processor and add a generous ½ cup light cream and seasoning to taste. Delicious sprinkled with chopped parsley or crunchy croutons.

- All the winter squashes absorb flavors well and are enhanced by the flavor of garlic and warming spices: ginger, curry powder, allspice, chili, cinnamon, cardamom.

- Pumpkin, or any winter squash, is excellent baked in a casserole. Allow 1 pound pumpkin (weighed with the skin and seeds) per person, peel and cut into ½-inch dice. Toss in seasoned flour, add a generous sprinkling of chopped parsley and crushed garlic, then pack into a well-greased casserole, dot with butter or oil and bake in a cool oven (325°F) for 2–2½ hours, until the top is crisp and brown and the pumpkin underneath is tender. Cover loosely with flour if the top browns too quickly.

- For an unusual dessert, try pumpkin in orange-flavored syrup. For 4 people, peel and slice 3½ pounds pumpkin, then cook very gently, for about 10 minutes, in a syrup made from 1¼ cups water, ½ cup sugar and the grated rind of 1 orange. Serve chilled.

Fresh shiitake ▽
These Chinese and Japanese fungi need to be gathered and eaten when young, or they become tough

Cèpe or bolete ▽
One of the most delicious mushrooms, cèpes are found in beech and oak woods in the summer and autumn

Oyster mushroom ▽
These fungi grow on tree trunks or stumps and are increasingly being cultivated

Champignon de Paris ▽
The first cultivated mushroom, grown in Paris at the turn of the eighteenth century

Dried shiitake △

Mushrooms and Truffles

Wild mushrooms have long been used to add interest and nourishment to meals. Mushrooms, whether wild or cultivated, are among the most useful flavoring ingredients in vegetarian cooking, as well as being filling and substantial if cooked in quantity. Mushrooms are interesting nutritionally, being unusually rich in vitamins B2 and B3 (which vegetarians need to be sure of including in their diet).

Pleurotte ▽
An attractive mushroom with a delicate flavor

Chanterelle or girolle △
With the color and aroma of apricots, the chanterelle is found in deciduous woods from summer until midwinter

Button mushrooms ▽
Tender and delicately flavored

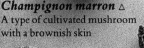

◁ Black truffle
Black truffles, from the Périgord region of France

Bottled mushrooms ▽
Mushrooms can be bought bottled, but the flavor and texture of most are not good

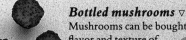

Champignon marron △
A type of cultivated mushroom with a brownish skin

White truffle △
These are canned and not as white inside as fresh ones

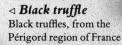

△
Oyster (bottled)

Large flat cultivated mushrooms ▽
Excellent for frying, broiling and stuffing

◁ Morel
The morel needs careful washing

△
Chanterelle (bottled)

◁ Small open-cup cultivated mushrooms
More strongly flavored than button mushrooms

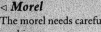

Girolle (bottled) △

△
Cèpe (bottled)

△
Funghi porcini
Available from Italian shops, these are dried cèpes

△
Dried wood ear
Used in Chinese dishes, with a gelatinous texture after soaking

Chinese straw mushroom △
A very tasty mushroom and one which survives the bott process well

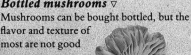

Mushrooms and Truffles

Choosing and storing

Wild mushrooms can be found in woods and fields if you know where and exactly what to look for; or they can sometimes be bought from specialist greengrocers and markets, but the supply is usually erratic: grab them when you see – or can afford – them. If buying cultivated mushrooms, avoid any that are brownish-looking. Choose mushrooms which smell fragrant and look fresh, almost with a slight bloom on them. Use quickly; they do not keep well, although they can be stored in the refrigerator for 24–36 hours.

Preparing and cooking

Wild mushrooms should be carefully washed – personally I like to wash cultivated mushrooms, too – and any tough bits should be cut out. Field mushrooms should have the top layer of skin removed.

Most mushrooms are best sliced as necessary and then cooked simply by frying lightly in butter, for about 5 minutes, until cooked through. If mushrooms exude a great deal of liquid during the frying process, you can either pour this off and save it as a flavoring for a soup or sauce, or thicken it by adding a small quantity of cornstarch mixed with water. Or – the best way, I think – continue to cook the mushrooms over a high heat until all the liquid has disappeared and you are left with very tasty, tender mushrooms: this may take 20–30 minutes. They are also delicious stuffed, in pâtés and tarts, and raw in salads.

For Mushrooms in Cream, prepare as described above, allowing 2 pounds mushrooms for 4 people. Fry in 2 tablespoons butter over a high heat for 20–30 minutes until all the liquid has disappeared, then add a generous ½ cup heavy cream and season with salt, freshly ground black pepper, a squeeze of lemon juice and a grating of nutmeg.

BLACK TRUFFLE
Tuber melansporum and
WHITE TRUFFLE
T. magnatum
A wildly expensive delicacy, small amounts of black truffles are chopped and added to dishes as a flavoring. White truffles are cut into fine slivers over the top of dishes to give them an exquisite fragrance. Canned truffles do not have the aroma and flavor of fresh ones.

CÈPE *Boletus edulis*
Cèpes have tubes under their caps instead of the more usual gills. They are delicious cooked as described above and are also excellent added to casseroles. The Italian dried mushrooms called FUNGHI PORCINI are cèpes. They are expensive, but just a few mixed with cultivated mushrooms, or added to a vegetable casserole, give a pronounced flavor. Just rinse, then use as required.

CHANTERELLE or GIROLLE
Cantharellus cibarius
The trumpet-shaped chanterelle is delicious cooked as described above or added to casseroles. It has a slightly peppery flavor and remains chewy however long it is cooked.

CHINESE STRAW MUSHROOM
Volvariella volvacea
Chinese straw mushrooms, available in bottles, make a tasty addition to vegetable stir-fries.

CULTIVATED MUSHROOMS
Agaricus bisporus
These are available at various stages of development. First come the little tight white BUTTON MUSHROOMS, which are excellent in creamy sauces (p. 174), sliced in salads (p. 163), or for using whole in Marinated Mushrooms (p. 150). The next stage is MEDIUM-SIZED MUSHROOMS and SMALL OPEN MUSHROOMS. These, too, are useful for most purposes, particularly for making into fritters or adding hearty flavors to vegetarian versions of various casseroles and stews, while LARGE FLAT OPEN MUSHROOMS are ideal for stuffing, and for broiling

or frying. CHAMPIGNON MARRON and CHAMPIGNON DE PARIS are other cultivated mushrooms.

FIELD MUSHROOM
Agaricus campestris
(Not illustrated)
These have a wonderful rich mushroomy flavor, much more intense than that of cultivated mushrooms. They are delicious fried and served as is, or made into duxelles, a concentrated mixture of finely chopped mushrooms fried with a finely chopped onion for about 30 minutes, uncovered, until they become a thick purée.

MOREL
Morchella esculenta and
M. vulgaris
This tasty mushroom tends to harbor grit and sometimes insects in its honeycomb cap, so it is best to cut it up first, then wash it in salted water. Fry morels and use in any of the ways suggested above. Dried morels are well worth buying (when you're feeling rich). Soak them in hot water for 30 minutes, then strain, reserving the soaking water for use in cooking. Wash them well, then chop and add to casseroles, soups, sauces for a deliciously intense mushroom flavor.

OYSTER MUSHROOM
Pleurotus ostreatus
With their firm texture these make a useful addition to casseroles. Use like cultivated mushrooms.

PLEUROTTE *Pleurotus ostreatus*
This delicately flavored mushroom can be prepared in a similar way to chanterelles.

SHIITAKE *Lentinus edodes*
Fresh shiitake can be sliced, fried and added to rice dishes, stews and stir-fries; soak the dried ones in boiling water for 30 minutes, then drain and chop. Add the soaking water to the dish or keep as stock.

WOOD EAR or CLOUD EAR
Auricularia polytricha
These are rather tough mushrooms used in Chinese recipes. Soak in boiling water for 30 minutes before use.

Arame ▽
A delicately flavored seaweed which grows in the seas around Japan and has a slightly sweet taste

◁ Dulse
Reddish-purple in color, dulse has quite a chewy texture

Kombu ▽
From the northern seas of Japan, kombu comes in thick black strips and is useful for flavoring stocks and soups

Sea Vegetables

Seaweeds, or sea vegetables, as they are more appetizingly called, have been an important food for people all over the world since ancient times. In some poor coastal areas they were eaten as a survival food, but in Japan they are an important part of the national cuisine, many types being cultivated and used. Seaweeds are high in nutrients, including protein, iron, calcium, potassium, sodium and iodine, and are also one of the rare nonanimal sources of vitamin B12.

Wakame ▽
A mild-flavored, useful all-purpose seaweed

Laver ▽
Ranging in color from pinkish-purple to greenish-brown, laver grows on rocky north European coasts. It can be bought dried, or cooked, as here

Nori ▽
The most popular sea vegetable, and my own favorite, nori is made into sheets in Japan by pressing the seaweed out by hand after drying

▽ Carrageen
This pale-colored, branching seaweed is found on the rocky coasts of northern Europe, and on the American coast from Maine to North Carolina

Hijiki ▷
Means "bearer of wealth and beauty" in Japan, where it has been used for hundreds of years

Sea Vegetables

Choosing and storing

Seaweeds can be bought dried from health food stores, as well as shops stocking Japanese ingredients. As Japanese cooking gains popularity across America, you can also find seaweed in some supermarkets. Store your seaweed in an airtight container in a cool, dry place.

Preparing and using

Most seaweeds (with the exception of nori, see below) need soaking before use. Put the seaweed into a bowl, starting with a small amount, say ¼ cup, if this is the first time you've used it, cover with boiling water and leave for 20 minutes, then drain. The soaking water, which contains useful nutrients, can be used in the recipe or discarded if it is too salty and strongly flavored. Then put the seaweed into a saucepan, cover with fresh cold water (which can be flavored with grated fresh ginger or tamari) and simmer gently until tender – generally 20–30 minutes. Alternatively, the seaweed can be added to a vegetable stew or casserole at this point. The cooked seaweed can be added to other cooked vegetables, or cooled and mixed with fresh vegetables and a dressing to make a salad.

Seaweed is naturally gelatinous, and some types, notably carrageen and AGAR-AGAR (not illustrated), can be used to make vegetarian jellies and molds (see Carrageen below).

ARAME *Eisenia bicyclis*

Arame is cut into long thin strips after harvesting. It is a good seaweed to start with if you're unfamiliar with sea vegetables. Arame is pleasant in salads, such as Radish, Cucumber and Arame Salad (p. 164), and in vegetable side dishes. It needs only 5 minutes soaking followed by 20 minutes cooking before use.

CARRAGEEN *Chondrus crispus*

Carrageen can be cooked and served in vegetable dishes or salads. I think it is more useful as a jelling agent, producing a light, delicately flavored jelly, or blancmange – my mother often made this when I was a child and I loved its curious, delicate flavor. To make Carrageen Pudding, soak ⅓ cup carrageen in warm water for 10 minutes, then drain and put into a saucepan with 1 quart (scant) milk and a vanilla pod and simmer for 20 minutes. Strain through a fine sieve, pressing the carrageen to extract all the jelly. Add ¼ cup clear honey or sugar and an egg yolk; finally fold in the whisked egg white. Pour into molds to set. This can be made with soy milk and without the egg for a vegan version.

DULSE *Rhodymenia palmata*

Dulse never gets very soft even if you cook it for 40–50 minutes, so is not to everyone's taste, though it's a seaweed I particularly like, finely shredded and added to a soup, salad or rice dish.

HIJIKI *Hiziki fusiforme*

Sold coarsely shredded, hijiki has a sweet, delicate flavor rather like that of arame (see above). Hijiki is an outstanding source of iron and calcium, just ¼ cup supplying nearly half the recommended daily requirement for an adult. I think it is most delicious added to salads or rice and vegetable mixtures or stir-fried vegetable side dishes.

KOMBU *Laminaria japonica*

Most often used to flavor stocks, and an essential ingredient of the Japanese stock dashi, kombu is a strongly flavored sea vegetable: you will only need one strip to flavor 2½ cups water.

LAVER *Porphyra umbilicalis*

Prepare laver as described above, cooking for 50–60 minutes. Laver can also be bought ready-cooked and canned; it looks like a thick green purée. A purée of laver is mixed with oatmeal to make the Welsh delicacy laver bread. In my opinion, you have to be either Welsh or a real seaweed devotee to enjoy either laver or laver bread.

NORI *Porphyra tenera*

Another good one to try if you're not familiar with seaweeds, nori is prepared differently from the others. Take a sheet of nori and hold it close to a hotplate or gas flame for a minute or so, moving it slightly until it is toasted and crisp all over. It can then be used to wrap up tasty savory ingredients to make sushi (p. 142), or you can scrunch it up in your fingers and sprinkle it over the top of salads, soups, stir-fries or vegetable soups.

WAKAME *Undaria pinnatifida*

After soaking the wakame (see above), open up the leaves, cut out the central spine and cook the wakame as described above. Wakame is used to make the classic Miso Soup (p. 133), and is also useful for flavoring soups and stews and adding to salads and vegetable side dishes. For a tangy rice salad, add soaked and shredded wakame to cooked brown rice. Season with salt, pepper, sugar and vinegar, then add shredded fresh vegetables. Garnish with sesame seeds.

Ideas for using sea vegetables

☐ Toast nori and crumble over any salad, stir-fry or creamy dip, for a tangy, salty flavor.

☐ Soak and shred kombu, flavor with chili powder, crushed garlic, chopped scallion, vinegar, sugar, salt and pepper. Serve as a side dish with Japanese-style sweet-vinegared rice (p. 241) and stir-fried vegetables.

☐ Soak and shred wakame, mix with diced cucumber, sliced radishes, sugar, vinegar, salt and pepper. Leave for 1–2 hours (or longer) to marinate; serve sprinkled with sesame seeds, as a side dish with Japanese-style rice.

☐ For an interesting nibble or side dish, add soaked and diced wakame to beaten egg; fry on both sides to make a kind of pancake. Cut into pieces. Sprinkle with a few sesame seeds if you wish; dip into soy sauce to eat.

◁ **Hothouse grape**

◁ **Muscat grape**

Napoleon red grape △

Apples, Pears and Grapes

Apples, pears and grapes have been cultivated and enjoyed for centuries. Delicious and refreshing, they are available all year round. They contain a range of useful vitamins and minerals, and apples and pears are rich in particularly valuable fiber. There are many varieties of these fruits, although with apples and pears, in recent years, there has been a tendency to concentrate on a few outstanding ones.

Seedless grape △

Grape
Grapes are generally classified as being either table grapes, like the ones shown here, or wine-making grapes

Bartlett or Williams pear ▽

Tientsin ya pear ▽

Logipont pear ▽

Chinese pear ▽

Laxton Fortune apple ▽

Pear
There are around 5,000 named varieties of pear, but only about 20–30 are widely cultivated

Crab apple ▽

Ellison's Orange ▷ **apple**

Conference pear ▷

◁ **Comice pear**

Edward VII ▽

Crispin ◁ ▽

Spartan ▽

Red Delicious ▽

Granny Smith ▽

Bramley's Seedling △

Jonagold ▽

Yellow/Golden Delicious ▽

◁ *Greensleeves*

Starking △
Cox's Orange Pippin ▽

Egremont Russet ▽

James Grieve ▽

Apple
Descended from the crab apple, which grows wild throughout Europe, apples are traditionally divided into cooking apples and eating apples

Apples, Pears & Grapes

APPLE *Malus pumila*

Choosing and storing

One of the basics of the pantry, one variety or another of apple is available all the year round. Choose bright, firm, sweet-smelling apples with no wrinkles or bruises. They are best stored in a cool, airy place. Only late-season apples will store over the winter, and if these are wrapped individually in newspaper and put in boxes or on shelves in a cool place, they will keep for several months.

Preparing and using

Good eating apples are delightful just as they are, or with cheese, such as a piece of aged Cheddar. They can be sliced and added to fruit salads and compotes, or mixed with vegetables in a savory salad such as the famous Waldorf (p. 169). If you need to keep raw cut apple for any length of time, either dip the pieces in a light salt and water mixture, or toss them in lemon or orange juice, to preserve the color. Grated apple forms the basis of the original Bircher Muesli (p. 240). Eating apples can also be used for cooking; in fact I prefer them to the sharper-flavored cooking apples for some dishes because their natural sweetness means that less sugar is needed. Sliced and peeled COX'S ORANGE PIPPIN apples are delightful stewed with raisins, baked in a pie (p. 294) or made into an open tart: follow the recipe on p. 292 but use lightly poached apple slices instead of red fruit, and glaze with sieved and warmed apricot jam.

Another widely cultivated apple is the YELLOW/GOLDEN DELICIOUS, firm, crisp, and some would say tasteless when young, becoming golden and sweeter when more mature. Like Cox's, Golden Delicious apples can be used for making pies and tarts, and are frequently used for this purpose in France. The

GRANNY SMITH apple is another variety which you either like or you don't, green in color, very crisp, with a clean, refreshing flavor. The STARKING apple has a red skin. It is a delicious eating apple, very crisp, with sweet, white flesh. Another popular red-skinned apple is the RED DELICIOUS, a firm, sweet variety developed in the U.S. This apple can be eaten raw or baked. The MCINTOSH (not illustrated) is another popular all-purpose American variety. This has a slightly sharp flavor, good for eating raw or baking. SPARTAN apples, developed in Denmark, can be used for both cooking and eating and have a custard-like flavor. Other good eating apples are LAXTON FORTUNE, EDWARD VII and ELLISON'S ORANGE, with a flavor not unlike a Cox apple; the brown-skinned EGREMONT RUSSET with its deliciously mellow flavor; CRISPINS, JAMES GRIEVE and GREEN-SLEEVES; and JONAGOLD, which has a long season, lasting from autumn until the spring.

Cooking apples are best used if a sharp flavor is required; some cooking apples, such as BRAMLEY'S SEEDLINGS, also collapse when cooked, so these are best if you want a soft purée. Large cooking apples are excellent cored, scored around the middle to prevent bursting, stuffed with dried fruit or mincemeat, or honey and chopped nuts, and baked whole for 40–50 minutes in a moderate oven. Or they may be peeled, cored, wrapped in shortcrust pastry and baked to make apple dumplings.

Cooked apple is used as a basis of many excellent desserts: apple crumble and apple meringue, apple fool and apple amber, to mention just a few. I like to make apple purée into ice cream (p. 281), to serve with a Blackberry Coulis (p. 300) or Sorbet (p. 282). Cooking apples are also used to make apple sauce, which makes an excellent accompaniment to Savory Lentil Loaf (p. 213). To make Apple Sauce, cook 1 pound peeled, cored and sliced cooking apples in 2 tablespoons butter or vegan margarine in a covered pan for about 10 minutes until pulpy. Cooking apples can be used, too, to make herb-flavored apple jelly, one of the best preserves, and also a sweet and spicy chutney (p. 342).

CRAB APPLES, the original apple, are small, more the size of large cherries than of apples as we know them, and very sharp. They range in color from yellow to red and are mainly useful because they are full of pectin, so they can be made into an excellent ruby-colored jelly which is delicious for serving with nut roasts (instead of red currant or cranberry jelly). They can also be mixed with mint to make, for very little expense, a delicious sweet-and-sour jelly. To make this you need 5 pounds of crab apples, or crab apples and ordinary apples mixed. Cook the apples in a little water until tender. Add 5 cups distilled vinegar and cook for 5 minutes longer. Strain, preferably through a jelly bag, for at least twelve hours. Measure the liquid and return to the pan with 2 cups sugar for each 2½ cups liquid, heat gently until the sugar is dissolved, then boil until setting point is reached as described on p. 339. Then add 8 tablespoons chopped mint.

Stewing fruit

Juicy fruits such as apples (also black and red currants, blueberries, blackberries and rhubarb) are best cooked in a minimum of water, or none at all. Put the fruit into a heavy-bottomed saucepan with 2 tablespoons water to each 1–1½ pounds fruit. Cover the saucepan and then heat gently until the juices run and the fruit is tender – this will probably take around 10 minutes.

Instead of water, butter can be used for stewing apples, and red currant jelly for rhubarb. When the fruit is soft, add sugar or honey to taste. Do not put this in sooner or the outside of the fruits may toughen before the inside is properly cooked.

PEAR *Pyrus communis*

Choosing and storing
Pears need choosing carefully, because once perfectly ripe they deteriorate very quickly. It is best to buy them slightly underripe and keep them at room temperature for a day or two until they are just right, when they should give slightly when pressed at the stalk end. Once this stage is reached, they will keep for a day or two in the refrigerator, but bring them to room temperature before serving, to draw out all the flavor.

A good dessert pear can be really superlative, with a delicate flavor, natural sweetness and melting flesh.

Preparing and using
Pears like this really need no accompaniment, although they do complement a good ripe cheese, such as a Brie, and make a delicious first course with a Roquefort Dressing (p. 149), or with a cream and yogurt dressing flavored with tarragon vinegar to give a hint of sharpness (p. 148).

Perfectly ripe pears can be peeled and served in some of the combinations for which cooked pears are traditionally used, such as Poire Belle Hélène, where they are filled with vanilla ice cream and topped with Hot Chocolate Sauce (p. 300).

Perhaps the most delicious dessert pear is the COMICE, delicately flavored, juicy and very sweet when at its best. The yellow-skinned BARTLETT or WILLIAMS pear is another popular dessert variety. The CONFERENCE pear has a rather tough brownish-green skin, and this, too, has a delicious flavor, especially when fully ripe, but it also cooks well (see below) as does the PACKHAM (not illustrated) and indeed many dessert pears, including the LOGIPONT. Poached as described, then drained and chilled, these pears are delicious served with some whipped cream or in the traditional ways described above. They are also excellent, deeply stained and delicately flavored, when poached in a syrup made with cheap red wine instead of water. Cooking pears can also be pickled or made into chutney.

Poaching fruit
This method is best for pears and other firm fruits such as apricots, peaches and plums. First make a sugar syrup. For 1–1½ pounds fruit you need 1¼ cups water, or other liquid such as wine, cider or fruit juice, and ½ cup granulated sugar. Honey can be used instead of sugar but will add its own strong flavor. Put the sugar and water into a heavy-bottomed saucepan and heat gently until dissolved. Then turn up the heat and boil rapidly for 2 minutes. Put in the prepared fruit, bring back to a boil, then simmer gently, half-covered, until the fruit feels tender when pierced. It's important to give large fruits like whole or halved peaches or pears time to cook right through to the center or they may discolor. Allow at least 20–30 minutes for whole pears and 15–20 minutes for the others. Let the fruit cool in the syrup, or remove the fruit with a draining spoon and thicken the syrup by boiling rapidly until it is reduced in quantity.

It is also possible to buy Asian pears, such as the TIENTSIN YA PEAR and the CHINESE PEAR. These are eaten when they are still firm, and can be used raw, adding a crisp texture to fruit and vegetable salad mixtures, or cooked as described above.

GRAPE *Vitis vinifera*

Choosing and storing
Many varieties of table grape are grown, ranging in color from white through red, as in the NAPOLEON RED, to deepest purple, of which the HOTHOUSE GRAPES are an example. Grapes also vary in sweetness, and the only way to be sure of what you are buying is to try one. The green MUSCAT GRAPES are particularly sweet, with the characteristic "muscat" flavor, and SEEDLESS GRAPES, too, are particularly sweet.

Once bought, grapes need to be used quickly, although they will keep for 2–3 days in the refrigerator. Bring them out and allow them enough time to get back to room temperature before serving.

Preparing and using
A bunch of grapes makes a decorative addition to a fruit bowl or cheese board, and, like apples and pears, grapes are excellent all put together in a salad, with watercress and walnuts too. They make an attractive addition to a fresh fruit salad – choose the color to complement the other fruits – and can also be made into a delicate jelly with grape juice set with agar-agar (p. 286). Black and white grapes, arranged in alternating circles, make an attractive filling for a tart or topping for a cheesecake. A white nut roast made from pine nuts or almonds is good served with a garnish of fresh green grapes, while little bunches of seedless grapes are a mother's best friend as lunch-box fillers and replacements for sugary sweets.

Ideas for using a glut of pears or apples
- Spiced pears are easy to make and go well with a nut or lentil loaf.
- Both pears and apples can be made into excellent ice cream, following the recipe on p. 280. These are good served with a sauce or sorbet that complements their flavor: pear ice cream with pear sorbet; apple ice cream with blackberry sorbet; pear ice cream with chocolate or raspberry sauce; apple ice cream with blackberry or orange sauce.
- If you make wine, both pears and apples can be made into good medium-dry white wine.
- Make pear or apple jelly or jam, perhaps flavored with fresh herbs.
- Pear or apple sauce goes well with a savory lentil loaf.

◁ Peach
Peaches may be white- or
yellow-fleshed and freestone,
clingstone or semi-clingstone,
depending on how firmly
attached the pit is to the flesh

Date ▽
Fresh dates are much more succulent than
their dried counterparts (p. 101)

U.S.A. Golden date ▷
A juicy sweet variety

Stone Fruits

This group includes some of the
most delectable fruits, many of
which delighted the people of China,
Greece and Rome thousands of years
ago. At the peak of perfection, these
fruits all make a fine dessert, served
fresh and without any adornment.
They are health-giving, containing
useful amounts of a range of vitamins and minerals. Peaches and apricots are particularly good sources of
vitamin A, while dates are rich in B
vitamins (especially B2 and B3) and
iron.

Nectarine △
This smooth-skinned variety of
peach has juicy flesh and a
fresh, sweet flavor similar to
peaches

Lichee ▽

Golden Cape plum△

Apricot ▽
This fragrant, delicately flavored fruit
originated in China, where it has been grown
for 4,000 years

Cherry ▽
One of the delights of early
summer, ripe, sweet cherries
are a delight to eat just as
they are

Red Ace plum △

Plum
Plums, like peaches, are divided into
freestone and clingstone types

Greengage △
A variety of plum and one of
the sweetest and best to eat raw

Santa Rosa plum △

△ Prune plum

△ Burbank plum

Damson △
Small plums with an intense,
slightly bitter flavor

Switzen plum △

Stone Fruits

Choosing and storing

Superb when perfectly ripe, these fruits are soon past their best, so need buying and storing carefully. As they are soft, stone fruits are particularly susceptible to damage during transport, so look for sound fruits without bruises. When buying fresh dates make sure that they really are fresh, with no sign of "sweating" or flaking. If they have a slightly winey flavor, they are "off," and while they won't hurt you, they are certainly not at their best. If you need to store these fruits, keep them in a cool place (or the refrigerator).

Preparing and using

Perfect fruits can be served as they are, or the pits can be removed and the fruit sliced and added to a fruit salad. Peaches can be peeled in the same way as tomatoes (p. 169). Underripe peaches, apricots and nectarines can be poached in a sugar syrup (p. 85); plums can be stewed (p. 84), baked into pies and made into crumbles.

APRICOT *Prunus armeniaca*

Perfectly ripe apricots make one of the best dessert fruits; they are also pleasant with cream cheese in a salad or as part of a fruit compote. Less perfect fruits are good poached in vanilla-flavored syrup and served with thick yogurt or cream, or in a pie or little tartlets. Apricots are used in savory recipes in the Middle East and go well with chick peas and white beans; an apricot sauce is good served with a savory nut roast instead of apple sauce, and I also like apricot sauce with Deep-fried Camembert (p. 221) instead of the more usual gooseberry sauce.

Cooked, drained apricots can be topped with an all-in-one cake mixture (p. 304) and a scattering of slivered almonds and baked to make an apricot sponge pudding, and they are included in Danish pastries. They can be pickled or made into jam or chutney. Apricot jam, melted and sieved, makes a useful glaze for fruit dishes and is often used to make almond paste adhere to a fruit cake (p. 312). Apricot brandy makes a delicious addition to sweet apricot dishes such as compotes and fools. Apricots are available fresh, dried (p. 102), canned either in syrup or their own juice or made into preserves or chutney (p. 342).

CHERRY *Prunus avium*

Sweet juicy cherries make an easy and refreshing dessert. Ones which are less than perfect, or the sour MORELLO CHERRIES (not illustrated), can be poached to make a compote or jelly, or covered with batter to make a clafoutis, a popular French cake. In central Europe cherries are made into chilled soups, and they are also excellent made into a tart, or served hot and flambéed with ice cream. The famous Black Forest cake, consisting of layers of the lightest chocolate sponge, black cherries and cream, with a liberal sprinkling of cherry liqueur, may have been devalued by the popularity of synthetic-tasting versions, but is still a wonderful cake when properly made.

Cherry brandy, and kirsch, an eau-de-vie made from the pits of cherries, are delicious flavorings for any cherry dish, and kirsch is also traditionally added to Cheese Fondue (p. 217). Cherries are available fresh, frozen, canned and made into preserves; black cherry preserve is one of the most delectable.

DATE / U.S.A. GOLDEN DATE *Phoenix dactylifera*

Fresh dates are one of the best sweet-substitutes, either as they are or with their pits removed and replaced by a freshly cracked Brazil nut or a mixture of whipped cream, cream cheese, ground almonds and honey or orange flower water. They make a good addition to a fresh fruit salad, or they can be served with thick Greek yogurt with a topping of a clear honey and, for a really superlative dessert, a little heavy cream.

LICHEE *Litchi chinensis*
See p. 92.

NECTARINE
Prunus persica, var. *Nectarina*
Particularly juicy and well flavored, nectarines can be used in similar ways to peaches. They are available both fresh and dried.

PEACH *Prunus persica*
A sweet, ripe, juicy peach is a delight and needs no accompaniment. Not-so-perfect peaches can be peeled (as described for tomatoes, p. 169), sliced and added to fruit salads and compotes, or sliced, covered with sweet white wine and chilled.

Peach Brûlée is also good: put sliced peaches into a shallow heat-proof dish, cover with whipped cream and an even layer of brown sugar, and chill. Just before serving, put under the broiler until the sugar caramelizes.

Ripe peaches make excellent ice cream (p. 281). This is good served with raspberry sorbet (made as for Blackberry Sorbet, p. 282) or Raspberry Coulis (p. 300). Spiced peaches (made as for Orange Slices, p. 343) and peach chutney (made as for Sweet Spiced Apricot Chutney, p. 342) are other good ways of using less than perfect specimens. Peaches are available fresh, dried (p. 103) and canned in syrup and in fruit juice.

PLUM/GREENGAGE
Prunus domestica, P. institia
Like the other fruits in this group, sweet and tender plums and greengages are excellent eaten *au naturel*. VICTORIAS are an example of excellent dessert plums, and when at their peak need no accompaniment. Other good dessert varieties are the SANTA ROSA, RED ACE and GOLDEN CAPE plums. Many varieties, such as the SWITZEN, BURBANK and PRUNE PLUM, can be eaten fresh when ripe or used for cooking, though sour varieties like the tiny DAMSON (*Prunus institia*) need to be stewed in a sweetened syrup, perhaps with a touch of cinnamon added (p. 84), or made into crumbles (p. 295) or pies (p. 294). Plums are available fresh, dried (in the form of prunes, p. 103) and canned, and also in the form of preserves, crystallized fruits and liqueurs.

▽ **Cranberry**
Hard, bright red shiny berries with
an acidic, slightly spicy flavor

Blackberry ▽
Picking blackberries – and
eating them, still warm from
the sun – is one of the pleasures
of late summer

Raspberry ▷
Exquisitely flavored, and the
most delicate of all the berries

Berries and Soft Fruits

These luscious fruits are also some of
the most nutritious. Black currants
contain a useful amount of calcium
and are one of the best of all sources
of vitamin C, and strawberries, too,
are unusually rich in this vitamin.
Raspberries, blackberries and all the
currants contain high levels of fiber.
Rhubarb contains calcium but also
oxalic acid, preventing its absorption, so it is inadvisable to eat rhubarb more than twice a week.

Blueberry ▽
Related to the bilberry,
blaeberry or whortleberry,
which grow wild in Europe
and northern Asia, the
blueberry is very popular in the
U.S.

Rhubarb △
Technically an edible
stem, but treated as
a soft fruit in the
kitchen

Black currant
Named after dried currants because black
currants were thought to resemble them,
currants grow wild throughout Europe

Gooseberry ▽
A sharply flavored fruit of early summer in
countries with a fairly cool climate,
gooseberries can be yellow, green or
red/purple, smooth or hairy

Strawberry △
Sweet and juicy berries of summer

Red currant △
Red currants have a sharp flavor and a
juicy texture

Wild strawberry △
Tiny fruits with perhaps the best flavor of all
the strawberries

Berries and Soft Fruits

Choosing and storing

With the exception of cranberries and rhubarb, these fruits are delicate and need gentle handling. Look for bright fruit that is firm but not hard, with no sign of bruising, wetness or mildew. Check the baskets to see if they are stained with juices, and avoid any that are. Rhubarb should be crisp and bright and the sticks not too large (or they could be tough). Use the fruit as soon as possible; if necessary, keep it in a cool place, preferably the refrigerator. Most of these fruits are available frozen, bottled and canned, as well as fresh.

Preparing and cooking

Many people advise against washing soft fruit, but I prefer to do so, to remove dust and any residues of sprays. Pat them dry on paper towels. For further preparation, see under the individual fruits. To cook these fruits, put them into a pan over gentle heat without water for a few minutes until the juices run. A little sugar or honey can then be added to taste, and rhubarb is good cooked with a few tablespoons of red currant jelly. This group of fruit is particularly good for preserving.

BLACKBERRY
Rubus macropetalus
Plump juicy berries make a delicious pie, perhaps combined with apples (p. 294). Blackberries can be made into one of the best sorbets (p. 282), or an excellent coulis (p. 300).

BLACK CURRANT and RED CURRANT
Ribes nigrum, R. sativum
Unless they are going to be sieved, currants need to have the stems and flower ends removed. This is easily done with bunches of currants by drawing the prongs of a fork down through the clusters. A few raw currants can be added to a fruit salad or compote, but generally currants are best cooked and can be made into pies, tarts, ice cream and sorbets and the famous Danish red fruit pudding rödgröt, where a mixture of red fruits is stewed, then puréed, thickened with cornstarch, arrowroot or potato flour and allowed to become cool, when it will have a soft, slightly jellied texture. Summer Pudding is another traditional use for currants: Stew them with other red fruits, then dip thin, crustless slices of bread into the juices and use to line completely the sides and base of a pudding mold. Fill the mold with the drained fruit, then put more juice-soaked bread on top. Put a plate and a weight on top, then leave for several hours. Turn out of the mold and serve with thick yogurt or cream.

BLUEBERRY
Vaccinium corymbosum
Fat, juicy blueberries are delicious served with cream or thick yogurt and a little sugar or honey, or they can be made into pies, crumbles, tarts, cheesecake toppings and muffins, or stewed to make a filling for crêpes.

CRANBERRY
Vaccinium macrocarpum
This is perhaps best-known in the form of Cranberry Sauce (p. 174). It is, by the way, as delicious with a white, delicately flavored Christmas nut roast as it is with turkey. Cranberries can also be made into pies and tarts, but they need a lot of sugar to make them palatable.

GOOSEBERRY *Ribes uvacrispa*
Dessert gooseberries just need to be trimmed before eating. Cooking varieties can be stewed gently with a few tablespoons of water to prevent them from sticking to the pan. A few sprigs of elderflowers added to the pan give a delicate muscat flavor. Puréed stewed gooseberries make a good sauce for a Brazil nut roast and also for deep-fried Camembert or Brie. Or add to the puréed gooseberries cold custard, yogurt, cream, or a mixture of these, to make a fool (p. 282). Gooseberries can also be made into excellent pies (p. 294) and crumbles.

LOGANBERRY
Rubus ursinus var. *loganobaccus*
(Not illustrated)
A natural hybrid between the raspberry and blackberry, these were first discovered in the garden of Judge J. H. Logan at Santa Cruz in California and named after him. Loganberries have a sharp flavor and can be eaten cooked or uncooked, in ways similar to blackberries and raspberries. Loganberry ice cream and sorbet are especially good.

RASPBERRY *Rubus idaeus*
Raspberries are wonderful eaten as is, with sugar and cream, or made into ice cream (p. 281), sorbet or a coulis (p. 300). They do not need initial cooking for these, just rubbing through a sieve (nylon, not metal) to purée and remove the seeds.

RHUBARB *Rheum rhabarbarum*
Rhubarb has a tart flavor and has to be cooked with sugar before it can be eaten. To prepare rhubarb, cut off the leaves (which are poisonous) and trim the base. Peel off any tough skin, then cut the rhubarb into manageable lengths and cook as described above. Rhubarb is complemented by the flavor of cinnamon, ginger or orange and can be made into a pie, a creamy fool or an excellent quick crumble (p. 295), or covered with all-in-one sponge mixture (p. 304) and baked to make rhubarb upside-down cake.

STRAWBERRY
Fragaria x ananassa
Strawberries are good simply hulled and served with cream and sugar. They also make an attractive addition to a summer fruit salad or a luscious topping for a cheesecake or little tartlets. The French way of serving them with light, heart-shaped molds of cream cheese is as delectable as it is pretty. Less perfect strawberries can be made into jam, ice cream or fools and mousses. Little WILD STRAWBERRIES (*Fragaria vesca*) or ALPINE STRAWBERRIES make a pretty decoration for something delicately colored like a Champagne Sorbet (p. 283), or for a compote of summer fruits.

Green banana ▽
Filling and nutritious, the banana is a staple food for poor people in some places where it is grown

Prickly pear ▷
Prickly pears grow around the edges of the large succulent leaves of the prickly pear cactus

Tropical and Exotic Fruits

Often vividly colored and with intriguing flavors, fragrances and textures, tropical and exotic fruits bring a welcome touch of variety and luxury to the vegetarian table. Some are rather expensive, but many are also rich in valuable nutrients: bananas are an excellent source of magnesium and B6; passion fruit, of protein, fiber and B1; kiwi fruit and guavas, of vitamin C; and mangoes, of vitamin A and zinc.

Golden passion fruit △

Mango ▽
My favorite fruit, the mango has deliciously juicy, deep golden, soft-textured, fragrant flesh

Banana ▷
Botanically an herb rather than a tree, the banana is said to be one of the first fruits to be cultivated

Kiwi ▷
One of the marketing success stories of the 1980s, the kiwi fruit comes mainly from New Zealand

Custard apple ▷
A fruit belonging to the same family as the papaya

Japonica △
Fruits of the orange-flowered garden japonica, with an exquisite, heady fragrance which will scent a whole room

Fig ▷
One of the most delicious of fruits, and one of the most ancient

Quince ▷
A small, hard fruit, golden when ripe, with an intense, heady fragrance, like the japonica

◁ Plantain
One of the 400 varieties of banana, the starchy plantain is used for cooking in India, South America and the Caribbean

▽ Pomegranate
Technically a large, thick–skinned berry, the pomegranate grows on a small tree and is common throughout the Middle East

▽ Passion fruit
Inside its leathery skin is a fragrantly flavored greenish pulp containing many seeds

Papaya ▽
Usually a pretty pink inside, though it can be yellow, with sweet, fragrant, slightly melting flesh and shiny black seeds

Persimmon ▽
Native to China, this fruit ripens and becomes deep orange on the tree after the leaves have fallen, a striking sight

◁ Tamarillo
The tamarillo can be red or yellow and is related to the kiwi fruit and the tomato

Pineapple △
A pineapple is really a cluster of fruits which weld together as they grow

◁ Guava
A tart fruit with a strangely exotic flavor and juicy flesh which can be pink, white or yellow

Rhamboutan △
Very similar to the lichee but with a hairy skin

◁ Lichee
The fruit of a tree which originated in Thailand and southern China, the lichee has translucent flesh inside a hard, heavily indented skin (illustrated also on p. 86)

Carambola ▷
Also called star fruit, with a delicate fragrance and juicy texture

Tropical and Exotic Fruits

Choosing, storing, preparing and using

See under individual fruits

BANANA *Musa sapientum*

Bananas for exportation are cut when they have reached their full size but are still green, and sometimes they are still slightly green and underripe when they reach the stores. Bananas will ripen if left at room temperature for a day or two. As they become riper they become softer and develop brownish spots on the skin; peeled and well mashed, very ripe bananas are a good early food for babies and can also be made into moist cakes and tea breads (p. 330).

Buy bananas in bunches attached to the stalk, as the skins of loose bananas are easily torn and the flesh will discolor.

In Europe, America and Australia, bananas are mainly used in sweet dishes, although they may be served as a side dish with a curry. They contrast well with other fruits, so are a popular addition to a fruit salad mixture. More luxuriously, bananas can be split lengthways and served with Vanilla Ice Cream (p. 280) and Chocolate Sauce (p. 300), or flambéed with rum, or made into fritters and served with slices of lime – all rich and fattening ideas, these, although bananas can be a dieter's friend too, because one or two of them make a complete, filling, easy, transportable and nutritious meal of around 200 calories.

In India, South America and the Caribbean, GREEN BANANAS are used in savory dishes. The leaves of the banana plant are also used in Mexico and India for wrapping food before cooking, as we might use aluminum foil, with the added advantage that the banana leaf adds a delicate flavor to the dish. The leaves are used to make disposable plates, too. Bananas are available fresh and dried (see p. 102).

CARAMBOLA or STAR FRUIT *Averrhoa carambola*

The carambola looks better than it tastes. Look for plump yellow fruits without blemishes. To use, wash, then cut into slices with a sharp stainless steel knife. The slices will be star-like in shape and make a pretty decoration for a cake, cheesecake, sorbet, jelly, or fruit salad.

CUSTARD APPLE *Anonacea squamosa*

Widely used in the tropics, custard apples are ripe when they feel soft to the touch. They have a creamy, custard-like flavor and texture and can be used in compotes or made into fools and ice creams.

FIG *Ficus carica*

The best figs I ever ate were left on our verandah early one morning by the gardener when we were staying in Corfu. We did wonder where he had found them, but they made a fabulous breakfast. There are several types of fig and they vary in color from golden to red and purple. They need to be completely ripe, when they are fairly soft, but they are highly perishable, so are best used immediately, although they will keep in the refrigerator for 24–48 hours.

Figs are good to eat at any time of the day, either on their own or served simply: quartered, for instance, with some cream cheese or thick Greek yogurt and a little clear honey. They are delicious cut almost in half from the pointed end, then almost in half again, gently opened, topped with a little Greek yogurt or whipped cream and served on a raspberry coulis (p. 300). In North Africa and other Mediterranean countries, figs are commonly made into a preserve. Figs are available fresh, canned and dried (p. 102).

GUAVA *Psidium guajava*

In my experience fresh guavas can be rather disappointing, because it's not easy to buy one that is sweet and ripe. If you do, use it immediately or keep it in the refrigerator briefly. The whole fruit is edible, although guavas are usually peeled, and can be eaten fresh or stewed. They are frequently made into jellies and preserves. Guavas are available fresh and canned: I think canned guavas are a safer buy than fresh ones, and their pink color looks especially nice in a fruit salad.

JAPONICA *Chaenomeles*

These fruits are hard and only suitable for cooking. They are difficult to cut and peel, but only need halving or quartering if you are going to make them into a jelly preserve, the most common way of using them; follow the recipe for Crab Apple Jelly on p. 340. This sweet, scented preserve is good for serving with nut roasts, or for eating on bread.

KIWI *Actinidia sinensis*

These little furry fruits are ripe when they yield to slight pressure. They keep well, either at room temperature or in the refrigerator, and should be peeled thinly with a sharp knife before using. The greatest asset of the kiwi fruit is its stunning bright green flesh and attractive central arrangement of seeds, which give it a flower-like appearance when sliced. So slices of kiwi fruit make an attractive garnish and decoration for dishes ranging from a tropical fruit salad to a cheesecake, and, of course, the traditional use for kiwi fruits, Pavlova or fruit meringue (p. 285). Kiwis are extremely high in vitamin C and can be a good way of getting children to take this; try slicing the top off a ripe kiwi fruit and letting them scoop the flesh out with a teaspoon, like eating a boiled egg. Kiwi fruits are available fresh and canned.

LICHEE *Litchi chinensis* and RHAMBOUTAN *Nephelium lappaceum*

Ripe lichees are about the size of a small plum with a red knobbly skin which becomes brown and hard; rhamboutans have spines, reminiscent of a small hedgehog. The skin comes away quite easily if you pull it back with your fingers, like peeling an orange. Inside the flesh is white, juicy and translucent-looking with a distinctive, scented (and very pleasant) flavor, and there is a large shiny brown pit in the middle.

Lichees make a delicious addition to an exotic fruit salad: try a mixture of lichees, ripe segments of orange, with all the skin removed, and slices of kiwi fruit. Available fresh (see illustration on p. 86) and canned (p. 91). Canned lichees lack the crisp texture of fresh ones but make a good sorbet or jelly.

MANGO *Mangifera indica*

Choose a mango which feels just soft all over, or buy one when it is hard and let it ripen at room temperature for a few days. I think the rounded, greeny-red variety of mangoes are better than the flatter, more oval yellowy ones. The mango has a large pit in the middle, so it is best to slice it down each side of the pit (see opposite). You can eat the skin, but it is generally peeled off, as it is very chewy. Mango is excellent on its own, and I like making it into a compote; for this, put slices of mango into a bowl, then blend half a cup of chopped mango with enough water to make a thin purée and pour this over the mango slices. Serve chilled, for a special breakfast or brunch. Or allow half a mango for each person and "turn" the halves as shown above right. Mango makes an excellent fool, sorbet or ice cream (p. 281); the flesh does not need cooking before use. Mango also goes well with other sweet fruits in a salad or compote.

PAPAYA *Carica papaya*

Look for a papaya which is slightly soft all over – like a good dessert pear or perfectly ripe avocado. Papaya can be served for breakfast or as a first course; cut in half, scoop out the seeds from the center, and serve with a slice of lime: halved papaya is eaten with a spoon, like an avocado. Peeled and sliced, papaya, with its pink flesh, makes an attractive addition to fruit salads.

PERSIMMON *Diospyrus kaki*

Persimmons must be very ripe and soft before eating, because until then their tannic content makes them unpleasantly acidic. When ripe they are good puréed and made into ice cream, or added to a fruit compote.

PINEAPPLE *Ananas comosus*

Most of the pineapples which are available outside the tropics are poor examples of the fruit, because the sugar which is stored in the stem only enters the fruit when it is ripe, and pineapples for export are picked before this stage. When choosing a pineapple, look for one which has a strong "pineapple" smell and try pulling out one of the leaves: if it comes out, the pineapple is ripe. To use, cut off the leafy top and peel the pineapple thickly to remove the skin and "eyes" too. Then slice, removing any hard central core. Pineapple makes a juicy and refreshing addition to sweet and savory salads and can be made into ices and sorbets. Baby pineapples are pretty halved right through the leaves with the flesh scooped out, diced, mixed with strawberries and liqueur and then spooned back into the skins again. A large pineapple, hollowed out, makes an attractive container for a party fruit salad, or for ice cream or sorbet (made from the scooped-out flesh), with the leafy top replaced for serving. Pineapple is available fresh, dried (p. 103), as juice, canned in syrup or its own juice, crushed or in slices, cubes or pieces.

PLANTAIN *Musa paradisiaca*

Plantain is widely used in savory dishes in India, South America and the Caribbean. It is often thinly sliced and fried like potato chips.

POMEGRANATE
Punica granatum

The pomegranate is full of seeds surrounded by shiny, jewel-bright pulp which is sweet and very juicy and arranged in irregular compartments divided by tough skin. The seeds can be scraped from the skin with a teaspoon or sharp knife and make an attractive topping for desserts or salads. They are widely used in Persian cooking.

PRICKLY PEAR
Opuntia magacanlaa and
O. fiscus-indica

These fruits have prickly skins and you need to wear gloves to handle them. Cut off all the skin, then slice

PREPARING AND TURNING
A MANGO

the flesh. Sometimes the flesh is a vivid pink and makes a striking addition to a fruit salad, but it can also be paler and less interesting. The flavor is fairly boring.

PURPLE PASSION FRUIT
Passiflora edulis and
GOLDEN PASSION FRUIT
P. laurifolia

Buy passion fruits when the skin is wrinkled, as this denotes ripeness. Cut the fruits in half and scoop out the pulp and seeds. This passion fruit pulp makes a delectable addition to a fruit salad, which it permeates with its flavor, or sauce for a sorbet or arranged fruit salad, but is at its most delicious, I think, in a sorbet – one of my very favorites (p. 282).

QUINCE *Cydonia oblonga*

Like japonicas, quinces need cooking before use. Peel, quarter and slice them as you would apples, then simmer them in a little water and add sugar to taste. They can be made into compotes, fools and pies and are widely used in Middle Eastern cooking. In the sixteenth and seventeenth centuries they were popular in Britain for making into preserves. Quince jelly has a pleasant and distinctive flavor.

TAMARILLO
Cyphomandra betacea

When ripe, the tamarillo feels soft to the touch and can be peeled and sliced and added to fruit salads. The seeds are edible and the fruit has a sweet-sharp flavor.

◁ Honeydew melon
One of the winter melons; the skin can be green, yellow or white, and the flesh is greenish-tinged

Gallia ▽
Gallia melons have a rough, bark-like skin which looks as though it has a white net over it, hence the name of "netted" (or "musk") melons

Melons

Melons, with their high water content, are one of the most refreshing fruits. They belong to the same family as cucumbers, and there are many different types of varying size, flavor and coloring. They can, however, be divided into three basic groups: winter melons, cantaloupe melons, and musk or netted melons. Watermelons belong to a different branch of the family and contain useful minerals. Melons with golden flesh (especially cantaloupes) are exceptionally rich in vitamin A.

Watermelon △
Characterized by their smooth, shiny skin and watery, melting flesh, watermelons are often dark-green-skinned with crimson flesh and dark brown seeds, though there are many varieties with other colorings, some with pale seeds or even seedless

Ogen ▷
Named after the kibbutz in Israel where they were developed, these small round melons with greenish-yellow striped and mottled skin and pale green flesh belong to the cantaloupe group

Cantaloupe ▽
This small, orange-fleshed melon, deeply ridged as if to show where it might be cut into segments, has given its name to the cantaloupe group of melons. In the U.S. the melon called a cantaloupe is actually a netted melon

Charentais △
The charentais, with its fragrant, sweet orange flesh, is the most famous of the cantaloupe melons

Melons

Choosing and storing

Cantaloupe melons, including the CANTALOUPE (or ROCK MELON) itself and the CHARENTAIS and OGEN melons, smell deliciously fragrant when they're ripe, and yield to a little pressure at the stalk end. Netted melons, too, of which the GALLIA is one of the best, are ripe when they give a little if pressed at the stalk end. CASABA MELONS (not illustrated) and HONEYDEW MELONS are ripe when they will yield to a little pressure at the end opposite to the stalk.

It is difficult to tell when a WATERMELON is just right for eating. One way is to look for a matte-skinned (rather than a shiny) melon, and to rap it with your knuckles: it should sound hollow, like a drum; alternatively, you can usually buy cut melon slices, in which case go for bright red flesh without any white streaks or a pale-looking middle. The seeds should look shiny and hard. Never buy cut melon slices from foreign markets because they may be contaminated.

Fully ripe melons should be used as soon as possible; others can be kept for a few days if stored at room temperature.

Preparing and using

Unless you want to marinate melon flesh in a syrup or flavoring liquid, which is useful for melons which are underripe or dull-flavored, it's best to prepare the melon just before you are ready to eat it.

Large melons can be cut down from the stalk end into sections; smaller melons can be cut in half at right angles to the stem. With very small ones, such as small Ogens, allow a whole one per person, slice the top off, like a boiled egg, and carefully scoop out all the seeds. The melon flesh can also be served without the skin, scooped out into balls using a melon baller; or you may simply remove the skin and cut the melon flesh into small dice.

Melons are very low in calories and are therefore an ideal choice if you are trying to lose weight. There are many different ways of serving melon for a low-calorie first course or dessert: see some ideas below.

Watermelon contains less vitamin C than other melons, but is wonderfully refreshing on a hot summer's day. If you are feeding a lot of people, at a summer barbeque, for example, you could buy a small whole watermelon. Scoop out the flesh and remove the seeds. Mix the chopped flesh with other fruit and serve it in the hollowed-out shell. You can also use the halved and hollowed skins of any of the smaller melons for individual servings filled as suggested below.

Melon is best served chilled, but do not let it get too cold, or the flavor will be dulled. Prepare the melon, then chill it in the refrigerator for no more than 30 minutes before serving. Or if the melon has been stored in the refrigerator, take it out about 30 minutes before you are ready to serve it.

If you have to store cut melon in the refrigerator, cover it carefully with plastic wrap, as it easily absorbs the smell and flavor of other foods. Use the melon as quickly as possible, as it will soon deteriorate.

Melon seeds are not usually eaten with the melon, although they are in fact a good food and in some parts of the world are dried and used in cooking or as a nibble.

Serving ideas for melon

- Marinate diced melon and diced peeled cucumber in a mint and honey vinaigrette for a refreshing appetizer.

- Scoop out the flesh of halved Ogen melons and mix with small strawberries; spoon back into the melon shells for a pretty dessert.

- Fill halved charentais melons with ginger ice cream, top with chopped preserved stem ginger and a little of the syrup.

- Marinate the diced flesh of winter melons, sliced kiwi fruit, green grapes and slices of green apple in a ginger-sugar syrup (1 tablespoon grated fresh ginger added to 1¼ cups sugar syrup) for several hours (or overnight) to make green ginger fruit compote.

- Cheer up a poorly flavored melon by topping each portion with some port, ginger wine or chopped stem ginger with a little of the syrup.

- A whole melon makes a delightful picnic food, cooling and refreshing on a hot day. Take plenty of paper towels and a container to put the seeds in.

- Mix balls of bright orange melon flesh (such as charentais) and pale green melon (such as honeydew or Ogen) for a pretty, simple and low-calorie first course.

- For a pretty and refreshing soup, purée two melons, one with green flesh and the other with orange flesh. Put the mixtures into separate pitchers, thin with enough water to make a pouring consistency, and sweeten slightly, if necessary. To serve, hold the pitchers at either side of a chilled bowl and pour from them at the same time, to create a two-colored effect. Garnish with fresh mint.

- Watermelon mixed with plenty of chopped mint makes a refreshing first course.

- Try a red fruit salad made from cubes or balls of watermelon, halved and seeded black grapes, sliced figs and strawberries.

- To make Melon Jelly, put cubes of melon into a large bowl or individual bowls. Bring 2½ cups fruit juice—grape, apple or orange—to a boil and sprinkle in 2 teaspoons agar-agar, whisking well until dissolved. Boil for 1 minute. Cool slightly, pour over melon and leave to set.

Navel orange ▷
Navel oranges, so-called
because of the navel-like
swelling at the flower end, are
sweet and juicy

Citus Fruit

Valued not only for their juicy flesh
but for the oils they contain which
are used for making flavorings and
perfumes, and for citric acid, citrus
fruits bring tangy flavors to the
kitchen and a sharpness which helps
to draw out the taste of other ingredients. They are one of the best
sources of vitamin C, and oranges are
also rich in B1, vitamin A and folic
acid, while the bioflavinoids in the
white skin and pith of citrus fruit are
thought to be particularly helpful to
women with menstrual problems.

Valencia sweet orange △
Sweet and very juicy oranges

Jaffa orange △
The shamouti variety, or Jaffa
orange, which originally came
from Israel, juicy and slightly
sharp-tasting

Clementine △
The clementine is a cross
between the tangerine and the
orange. It has no seeds

Tangerine △
The skin of the tangerine is a
deeper color than mandarins

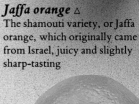

Satsuma △
Identified by their easily
peelable, loose skins and sweet,
juicy flesh. Some types are
seedless

Lemon △
Together with oranges, the
most important citrus fruit and
indispensable as a flavoring

Kumquat ▽
Sharp-tasting miniature oranges, useful for
garnishing or making into preserves

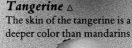

Lime △
Very sour small green citrus
fruits with their own almost
perfumed taste

Jaffa sweetie ▷
A cross between a grapefruit
and a lime

◁ **Pink grapefruit**
Pink and red grapefruit are
available; the flesh of these
ranges from pale pink to ruby
red and is sweet and juicy

Mineola ▽
A hybrid type of sweet orange
with a deep color and
smooth skin

Seville orange △
These sour oranges, for making into
preserves, actually reached Europe before
sweet oranges

Pomelo or shaddock ▽
The fruit from which the
grapefruit is descended

△ **Ugli fruit**
Like a big, rather lumpy
grapefruit, this is a cross
between a grapefruit and a
tangerine and tastes like a
particularly juicy, sweet
grapefruit

White grapefruit △
The most widely grown citrus
fruit, sharp and refreshing

Citrus Fruit

Choosing and storing

Citrus fruit should look bright and plump, with no brown patches or shriveled skin. The fruits, especially grapefruit, should feel heavy, so pick them up before you buy them – it's surprising how they vary.

Preparing and using

Citrus fruits should be scrubbed well if you are going to use the skins, as these are often treated with sprays. Adding a tablespoon of cider vinegar to the washing water is said to help counteract the harmful effect of any chemical residues on the skins.

Leftover citrus juices can be frozen for future use; just put them into ice cube containers, freeze, then transfer to a plastic bag. Slices of lemon, orange and rind also freeze well and can be added straight to drinks without defrosting. Freeze them until solid on a plate or tray, then put them into a plastic bag or container.

GRAPEFRUIT and PINK GRAPEFRUIT
Citrus x paradisi

This is probably most often served halved as a first course. For variety, the rind can be vandyked (see below) and the flesh scooped out and mixed with chopped orange segments and mint. Or the grapefruit can be halved and the segments loosened (see below) and the top sprinkled with brown sugar, then placed under the broiler until the sugar is melted and the fruit warmed through. One of my favorite grapefruit dishes is a salad of grapefruit and orange segments, avocado and watercress. Pink grapefruit are particularly sweet and juicy as well as being an attractive color.

Canned grapefruit is available; also grapefruit juice, natural and sweetened.

JAFFA SWEETIE *Citrus* spp
One of the citrus hybrids which have recently been developed, this has a sharp, refreshing flavor.

KUMQUAT *Fortunella margarita*
These are delicious stewed whole in a sugar syrup, or made into a preserve (p. 343), then spooned over home-made Vanilla Ice Cream (p. 280).

LEMON *Citrus limon*
Both the juice and the rind of lemons are indispensable in the kitchen for flavoring; lemon juice brings out the flavor of other foods, and the rind gives a subtle tang. A strip of lemon rind added to a bouquet garni is good in soups and vegetable casseroles. Lemon juice can be used to make salad dressings, and I often use it with fruity olive oil instead of wine vinegar. Lemon juice also helps to preserve the color of other fruits and vegetables which discolor easily; brush the cut surfaces, or dip them in a cupful of water which has had the juice of ½ lemon added. Lemon is used to flavor cakes and puddings; one of the most delicious is traditional Sussex pond pudding, in which a whole lemon is surrounded by a suet crust, then steamed, resulting in a delicious lemony syrup filling. Cut into circles, wedges or tiny pieces, lemon makes one of the most refreshing and attractive garnishes.

The candied peel is best bought in whole pieces: it's expensive, but there's no comparison between this and the chopped variety. Bottled lemon juice is a useful pantry item, although not as good as fresh.

To make Lemon Barley Water, old-fashioned but soothing, refreshing and easy to make, put 4 tablespoons pearl barley into a saucepan with 1½ cups water and the pared rind of half a lemon and bring to a boil. Simmer gently, uncovered, for 20 minutes, then strain and cool. Add the juice of ½ lemon and sugar or honey to taste – about 1 tablespoon. Serve chilled, with ice if you wish.

LIME *Citrus aurantifolia*
Lime is a wonderful flavoring ingredient; try it squeezed over exotic fruit or hot sugary pancakes, or in avocado dips. It has many uses in sweet dishes, including Key Lime Pie and as a flavoring for ice cream, parfaits and cheesecake.

ORANGE *Citrus sinensis*
There are a number of types of dessert oranges, including NAVEL ORANGES, which are deliciously sweet and have the characteristic navel at the flower end; the juicy

VANDYKING A GRAPEFRUIT

PREPARING HALVED GRAPEFRUIT FOR SERVING

JAFFA (or SHAMOUTI); and the VALENCIA. Oranges are good to eat just as they are, cut into segments, with all the rind and pith removed. Sprinkled with orange flower water and a little orange blossom honey, and chilled, they make one of the most refreshing desserts, good served with an almond or cashew nut cream (p. 238) rather than dairy cream. Alternatively the sliced oranges can be sprinkled with crushed caramel for a sweet crunchy topping. Oranges also make an excellent addition to a fresh fruit salad, and their juice helps pale fruits, such as apples and pears, to keep their color. Whole oranges can be simmered in sugar syrup, then cooled and served with shreds of the peel, blanched and drained.

Orange peel is included in chopped mixed peel, but the best way to buy it is in whole pieces. Most packaged orange juices are made from frozen concentrate. Try to find fresh squeezed juice if possible.

BLOOD ORANGES (not illustrated) are small oranges shot with red; the juice and a little shredded peel are added to Hollandaise Sauce (p. 176) to make Maltese sauce, traditionally served with asparagus.

POMELO or SHADDOCK
Citrus grandis
Probably the fruit from which the grapefruit evolved, it has a sour, slightly bitter flavor. It can be used like an ugli fruit.

SEVILLE ORANGE
Citrus aurantium
These oranges are unsuitable for eating raw, but they are used in marmalade and to make liqueurs and orange flower water. The grated rind and juice can also be used as a flavoring.

TANGERINE, MANDARIN, MINEOLA, CLEMENTINE, SATSUMA *Citrus reticulata*
These members of the citrus family are all very easily peeled, and their flesh separates readily into segments. Clementines are the smallest, have a good flavor and, like satsumas, have no seeds. They all have a more delicate flavor than oranges. Mandarin segments can be bought canned, either whole or in pieces. Delicious for eating just as they are and a popular way of making sure children get their daily requirement of vitamin C, these are also good in fruit salads. You can also add a few sections to a green salad.

UGLI *Citrus* spp
A cross between a tangerine and a grapefruit, the ugli is native to the East Indies. It tastes like a superb grapefruit and can be prepared in the same ways. In fact, an ugli can be a better choice than grapefruit if you want sweet, juicy segments for a breakfast compote or salad.

Its lumpy, mottled skin peels easily and the flesh can be segmented very quickly. It is very juicy and has few seeds. Don't be put off by its unfortunate name!

How to make candied peel

Homemade candied peel, for use in cakes and puddings, can be made at home using grapefruit, orange or lemon skins. You will need the skins of 6 oranges or lemons, or 4–5 grapefruit, or an equivalent amount of more than one type.

Scrub the fruit thoroughly, halve and remove the pulp, leaving only the zest and white peel. Or use the (well-scrubbed) skins of fruits after you have squeezed the juice from them.

Put the skin halves into a saucepan, cover with cold water, bring to a boil and simmer until tender. This takes 1–2 hours, and it's a good idea to change the water 3 times to remove any trace of bitterness, especially with grapefruits.

Drain the skins thoroughly, reserving the liquid. Increase the liquid to 1¼ cups with water if necessary, then pour into a saucepan and add 1 cup sugar. Heat gently until the sugar has dissolved, then bring up to a boil. Add the peel, remove from the heat and leave for 2 days.

Remove the peel from the syrup with a perforated spoon; add another ½ cup sugar to the syrup, heat gently until dissolved, then add the peel and simmer gently until translucent.

Leave the peel to soak in this syrup for 2 weeks, then remove the peel with a perforated spoon and place it on a wire rack to drain and dry. Once the peel is dry, it can be stored in an airtight jar.

PEELING AN ORANGE

SEGMENTING AN ORANGE

Banana chips ▷

Dried bananas ▽
Dried bananas are sweet with a true banana flavor. The "chips" are made from slices of unripe banana which have been deep-fried in a mixture of oil and sugar

Apple rings △
Creamy white rings or slices of apple have a slightly rubbery texture when dry. They are nearly always treated with sulphur dioxide (hence the pale color)

Dried Fruit

Fruit has been preserved by drying in the sun for the last 5,000 years, and when the early settlers traveled to America, they took with them supplies of dried apples, nectarines, peaches, apricots, quinces and grapes. Today, dried fruit is still an important ingredient and a concentrated source of nutrients. Dried fruit is high in fiber, rich in B vitamins and minerals, apricots and peaches being notable for their iron content and also for vitamin A, and apricots for calcium as well.

Dried papaya △
Like banana chips, these chunks of papaya and pineapple have been sugar-dipped

Dried figs ▽
Usually whole and generally sun-dried and unsulphured, figs sometimes have a white powdery look – this is natural sugar which has seeped through the skin

△ **Dried pineapple**

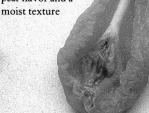

Dried pears ▷
These may be whole or halved and have usually been treated with sulphur dioxide. They have a delicious, true pear flavor and a moist texture

Prunes ▽
A variety of black-skinned plums which used to be grown mainly in France. Now produced in other places, notably California

Dried peaches △
Usually sold in halves, dried peaches do not taste particularly like fresh peaches but have their own charm

Muscatel raisins ◁

These are the original raisin –
muscatel grapes,
purplish-black in color, dried
in the sun and with a delicious
muscat flavor

Lexia raisins ▽

Another delicious raisin, the
lexia type comes from
Australia; it is sold seeded and
is particularly juicy and sweet

Sun-dried raisins ▷

The smaller, more common
"seedless raisin" does not have
the flavor or the moist texture
of the other two types, but is
widely available and a useful
all-purpose raisin

Hunza apricots ▽

Apricots are available whole or
in halves or pieces; small dried
Hunza apricots are sold whole
still containing their kernels. If
the apricots are orange or
yellow in color, they have most
likely been treated with sulphur
dioxide

▽ Sun-dried apricots

◁ Dried apricots

Dates ▽

Very sweet and nutritious,
dates can be bought whole,
pitted and unpitted, or
pressed into a block for use in
cooking

Currants ▽

Originally grown around Corinth, these are
small sweet grapes which are dried and
packaged without the addition of sulphur
dioxide

Sultanas △

These are dried seedless white grapes, similar
to small seedless raisins. They originated in
Izmir (later called Smyrna) in Turkey and are
now widely grown in other places, notably
Australia

Dried Fruit

Choosing, storing, preparing and using

Fruit is dried either in the sun or in dehydration chambers, where the moisture is evaporated by hot air. Dried fruit may be treated with sulphur dioxide gas during the drying process to prevent its becoming too dark in color. Sulphur dioxide interferes with the body's ability to absorb vitamin B1 and has been linked with digestive upsets and possibly genetic mutations, so look for unsulphured fruits if possible. The effect of the sulphur dioxide can be reduced if you first wash the fruit well in warm water, then cover it with cold water and bring to a boil. Allow the fruit to simmer without a lid for 5 minutes, then drain off the water and rinse the fruit again. It can then be used, or soaked in cold water, or covered with fresh water and simmered gently until tender.

Many fruits are also coated with mineral oil in order to prevent them from sticking together. This, too, is an additive which is not recommended, as it can interfere with the body's ability to absorb some nutrients. The oil can be removed by washing the fruit in several changes of warm water, or can be avoided altogether by looking for fruit which has been packaged without oil, or with vegetable oil rather than mineral oil (although I prefer to wash this off, too, before using the fruit). Drain the rinsed fruit in a colander, then spread it out on a tray lined with paper towels and leave it in a warm place overnight to dry.

When buying dried fruit, check the date stamp on the package, buy in fairly small quantities and keep the fruit in an airtight jar.

APPLE RINGS

These can be eaten as they are or chopped and added to cakes and puddings. They are often included as part of a dried-fruit salad mix and make a pleasant addition to fruit compotes.

APRICOTS

Dried apricots can be eaten as they are or soaked (and cooked until tender, if preferred) and served simply with yogurt or cream, or made into purées, fools (p. 282) and other desserts. Sun-dried HUNZA APRICOTS have a particularly good flavor and make a wonderful compote, just soaked and simmered gently until tender if necessary.

Dried apricots can be made into an excellent jam all the year round. To make about 2½ quarts, put 1 pound dried apricots into a bowl, cover with 8 cups of water and leave to soak overnight. Next day, put the apricots and their water into a preserving pan, add the juice of 1 lemon and simmer until the apricots are really tender – about 50–60 minutes. Then remove from the heat and add 6 cups of granulated sugar and ½ cup roughly chopped almonds. Heat gently until the sugar has dissolved, then boil for 20–25 minutes, stirring often. Test for a set (p. 339) and when this is reached, remove from the heat and add a knob of butter. Let the mixture cool slightly, then spoon into warm, sterilized jars.

BANANAS

Ordinary DRIED BANANAS, which look like slim (or flattened) dark brown versions of fresh bananas, make a pleasant nibble or addition to homemade dried fruit bars and bonbons. They can be reconstituted by soaking in water, but the texture is rather soggy and not particularly pleasant. Soaked and puréed dried banana could be used to make a tea bread (p. 330) instead of mashed fresh banana.

BANANA CHIPS, slices of banana prepared with a crisp sugar coating, are also available and make a relatively healthy sweet treat which many children like.

CURRANTS

A very useful ingredient, currants are used extensively in baking, for instance in currant buns, Eccles cakes, fruit cakes (p. 310) and Christmas pudding (p. 296); they are also often added to savory pilafs and stuffings in Middle Eastern cooking.

Mixed with almonds and spice, they make sweet crisp cookies. Sift a generous ¾ cup plain whole-wheat flour, ½ teaspoon baking powder and ½ teaspoon allspice into a large bowl. Tip the bran from the sieve into the bowl and add 4 tablespoons butter, 2 tablespoons ground almonds, and ⅓ cup currants. Mix well, then stir in 1 tablespoon water to make a dough. On a lightly floured board, roll the dough out to about ¼ inch thick, then stamp into rounds of 2 inches. Prick each round, place on floured baking sheets and bake for 10 minutes at 400°F.

DATES

Dates make a pleasant sweet treat or nibble, either as they are or with the pit replaced with an almond or Brazil nut, some almond paste or cream cheese.

Dates can be added to cakes and puddings and made into very good cookies (p. 321). If you're buying cooking dates, check that they're not "sugar-rolled," an unnecessary treatment in view of the intense sweetness of dates. Pitted dates need looking over before use, because the odd pit or hard stalk end does creep in.

FIGS

Often sold squashed in blocks, figs are high in fiber. They can be eaten as they are, soaked as part of a fruit compote, or made into wholesome candies and cookies. Steamed fig pudding with rum sauce is a warming winter dessert.

DRIED-FRUIT SALAD

(Not illustrated)

This is a mixture of a number of the fruits shown overleaf; usually prunes, apple rings, apricots and perhaps peaches and pears. You can buy it ready-made or make it up yourself from your favorite varieties.

Dried-fruit salad mix can be made into an excellent compote. To do this, cover the mixture with boiling water and leave to soak overnight. Allow one pound of fruit to serve 4 people. Next day, simmer gently, half-covered, until the fruit is tender and all the liquid reduced to a glossy syrup. Serve hot or chilled. If you are serving it cold, some fresh fruits can be added for contrasting flavor and texture. It's a pleasant dish for serving at breakfast as well as for dessert. A friend of mine makes an alcoholic version with brandy added, which is excellent, though perhaps not for breakfast.

PAPAYA

This is perhaps not as healthy as naturally dried fruit, because of the added sugar, but is still a pleasant and relatively healthy sweet treat.

PEACHES

You can eat dried peaches as they are, but I prefer them lightly soaked, or soaked and simmered until tender. They make a pleasant addition to savory dishes such as pilafs as well as being delicious in cakes, puddings and compotes.

PEARS

Pears can be eaten as they are, or soaked and cooked; chopped, they make an unusual and delicious addition to a fruit cake and are one of the ingredients in the famous Swiss Christmas fruit pastry Birnbrot.

To make Birnbrot, make up a half-quantity of dough as described for Quick Rolls on p. 328. While the dough is rising for the first time, make the filling. Chop 1⅓ cups dried pears and ⅔ cup dried pitted prunes and put them into a saucepan with ⅓ cup seedless raisins and 1¼ cups cold water. Bring to a boil, then simmer uncovered gently until the mixture is thick and dry. Sieve or purée in a blender or food processor, then add the grated rind and juice of half a lemon, ¼ cup soft brown sugar and a little ground cinnamon and grated nutmeg.

Knead the risen dough, then roll it out to a square about 15 by 15 inches and not more than ¼ inch thick. Spread the pear mixture to within about 1 inch of the edges. Fold the edges over to enclose the filling, then roll it up firmly, like a jelly roll, and put it onto a baking sheet. Prick the roll all over, then cover it with a clean cloth and put it into a warm place for 30 minutes, to rise.

Heat the oven to 350°F. Brush the bread all over with beaten egg and bake it in the center of the oven, for about 35 minutes, until golden-brown and crisp. Serve it while it's still warm. It's an excellent pastry for serving with coffee, or as a dessert after something rich like fondue.

PINEAPPLE

Crunchy cubes of pineapple preserved in sugar syrup make a delicious addition to rich fruit cake mixtures, tutti-frutti ice cream or a platter of bonbons to serve with after-dinner coffee.

PRUNES

Prunes are not usually treated with sulphur dioxide but may have undergone other processes to tenderize them or soften the skins, and they are often coated with mineral oil, so wash them carefully.

Prunes are one of those things you either like or you don't; if you still have unfortunate childhood memories of them, do try them as part of a boozy compote of dried fruits, extra-light Christmas pudding or ice cream – you may have a pleasant surprise! Prune mousse is surprisingly good, as is the classic French prune tart.

Prune juice is available and is extremely rich in iron, one of the best sources of this mineral if you're feeling run down.

RAISINS

Any of the types of raisins shown overleaf are excellent for eating with nuts as a snack or for adding to mueslis or fruit or vegetable salads. Raisins are also indispensable in baking, for fruit cakes, puddings and cookies.

SULTANAS

Some sultanas are treated with sulphur dioxide, others are not: check the label. They are useful in baking for cakes, Christmas pudding (p. 296) and mince pies (p. 297), as well as in salads, puddings and mueslis.

Drying fruits and vegetables

Drying fruits and vegetables involves drying out the natural moisture present in all fruits and vegetables so that the enzymes which cause decay are inhibited. This can be done in the sun or in an oven. Oven-drying can be done over several days, perhaps in the residual heat of the oven after it has been used for something else. The drying temperature needs to be between 120 and 150° F; leave the oven door ajar to allow moisture to escape.

Fruits and vegetables to be dried in the sun need to be spread out on clean mesh or trellis trays, slats of wood or wire trays. Raise them off the ground and turn the produce over twice a day so that it dries evenly. Cover the produce with clean cheesecloth to keep off flies and dust. Bring the fruit in at night because the increased moisture in the air then will affect the drying process. Alternatively, fruits and vegetables can be threaded onto string and hung up to dry.

Preserve the color of fruits such as apples and pears by plunging them into a bowl containing 2 teaspoons citric acid to every 4 cups of water; drain and pat dry, then dry in the oven or in the sun as described.

Vegetables such as mushrooms, onions, garlic and peppers can be dried as they are; others, such as runner or green beans, need blanching for 2 minutes in boiling water before being patted dry with a cloth and then dried as described above.

Store dried fruits and vegetables in an airtight jar or canister. They will keep for a year. Use dried fruit as it is; soak dried vegetables for a few hours first, then cook in the soaking water, or add them to stews and casseroles without pre-soaking. Soak dried tomatoes in boiling water for 30 minutes, drain, put into jars and cover with oil.

Aromatic dried tofu △
A well-flavored dried tofu; a plain version is also available

Smoked tofu △
Smoking adds flavor to tofu

Firm tofu △
Firm tofu comes in a block (like a block of cheese) and can be cut into cubes or slices and fried

Soft tofu △
Tofu is a white curd product made by cooking a curdling soy milk

Dried deep-fried tofu △
One of a number of varieties of dried tofu

Dairy and Nondairy Ingredients

These foods enrich and fortify vegetarian cooking. Some are concentrated and high in fat, so they are generally used in small quantities. They include dairy and nondairy products as well as a range of high protein foods, some of which have been used in countries in the East for thousands of years but are relatively new to the West.

Seitan △
This original "textured vegetable protein" can be bought as pâtés and pastes (below)

△
Textured vegetable protein
Chunks and "chopped," made from soy

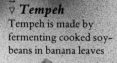

△
▽ Tempeh
Tempeh is made by fermenting cooked soybeans in banana leaves

◁ **Cow's milk**
Another basic food which has been used for centuries, milk is a useful source of protein, calcium and the B vitamin riboflavin in the lacto-vegetarian diet

Soy milk △
This liquid is made from soybeans

Nonfat dry milk ▽
A useful pantry standby

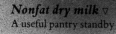

Goat's milk △
Considered by some health experts to be more digestible and healthy than cow's milk

Buttermilk ▷
Traditionally the milk which is left over after butter-making, low in fat and with a sour flavor

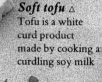

Light cream ▽
Light cream will not whip

Heavy cream ▽
Heavy cream has a
high fat content
and whips up to a
thick consistency

△
Clotted cream
Thick cream, being the fat
skimmed from rich Devon
milk after it has been
heated and cooled rapidly

◁ **Whipping cream**
This cream whips to a light
consistency

Nondairy cream ▽
Made from water and
vegetable oil; the flavor varies
from brand
to brand

Sour cream ▽
Has a similar fat content to
light cream, a thick texture
(although it will not whip)
and a sour flavor

◁ **Soy cream**
May be sold as
soy cream, or you
can use a
concentrated type
of soy milk
without diluting it

Greek yogurt ▽
Available strained (left)
and unstrained, this is made
from ewe's milk

Quail's egg ▽
An attractive ingredient, which
makes a delightful garnish

Smetana ▷
In Russia, a mixture of sour cream and heavy
cream; outside Russia, it is usually made from
light cream and skim milk

◁ **Hen's egg**
A nutritious ingredient in the
lacto-vegetarian larder.
Free-range eggs do not involve
cruelty

Parev ▷
A cream replacement made from water,
vegetable oil, sugar and flavorings,
available from Jewish food stores

Duck's egg △
As nutritious as hen's eggs, and, some say,
with a finer flavor

Live yogurt △
A soured milk product made by
culturing milk with a bacterium
called *Lactobacillus bulgaricus*

Dairy and Nondairy Ingredients

MILK

MILK is a basic ingredient, containing a balanced range of nutrients including protein, calcium, riboflavin and vitamins A, D and B12, and is available in various forms. Most milk is pasteurized, which means it has been heated to 160°F for 15 seconds, to destroy bacteria. Milk is available with all the cream remaining, with some removed, low-fat or fully skimmed. NONFAT DRY MILK is also available and is useful for adding to drinks and other dishes to increase their nutritional value; I prefer the powder (from health food stores and not to be confused with milk powder with added fat) to the granules. Skim milk may have been fortified with the fat-soluble vitamins, A, D and E, which are lost when the fat is removed. GOAT'S MILK, thought by some experts to be healthier and more digestible than cow's, is also available in both liquid and powdered form.

HOMOGENIZED MILK has been mechanically treated so that the cream does not separate from the milk and rise to the surface, while UHT MILK has been heated to 270°F for 1–2 seconds, then rapidly cooled and packed under sterile conditions.

EVAPORATED MILK, a useful pantry item, has been homogenized and had half its water removed by evaporation. It is then sterilized and canned. CONDENSED MILK is whole or skim milk which has been boiled down to about a third of its original volume and then, usually, sweetened with sugar and canned. It's useful for making fudge (p. 345) and a wonderful ice cream (p. 280), as well as being the binding ingredient in the traditional Bircher Muesli (p. 45). If you boil an unopened can of condensed milk for 4 hours, then cool the can, beat the contents lightly and pour into a crumb crust or pastry shell and chill, you have Gypsy Tart. It's also useful for making Toffee Shortcake: boil the contents of a small can of condensed milk with ¼ pound each of sugar and butter and 2 tablespoons light corn syrup for 5 minutes, then pour on top of Easy Shortbread (p. 320). When it's cool, spread 6–8 ounces of melted chocolate on top! Wicked, but delicious.

BUTTERMILK is mainly useful in making certain breads and cakes, as in Soda Bread (p. 330), where it helps the bread to rise. The SMETANA sold outside Russia is like a low-fat sour cream and can replace sour cream in recipes. Various brands of SOY MILK are available. The nutritional content of most is not the same as that of cow's milk, although the taste is similar; if the milk is for babies, children or old people, I recommend buying a soy milk which has been fortified with vitamins so that it has the same nutritional value as cow's milk. Check the labels; you may need to go to a health food store.

YOGURT

Look for "live" YOGURT cultured from *Lactobacillus bulgaricus*. Avoid those which contain thickeners or have been pasteurized after culturing. Although the bacterium does not survive in the gut, yogurt is more digestible than milk. Good yogurt should be sweet and thick, not thin and sour. GREEK EWE'S MILK YOGURT, both the normal version and the thicker, strained type, are excellent. If you think you don't like yogurt, try these before finally writing it off! NONDAIRY SOY YOGURT, suitable for vegans, is available from health food stores, and can also be made at home from soy milk (p. 280).

Yogurt is easy to make at home, in a wide-necked thermos which will hold 2½ cups. Bring 2½ cups milk to a boil, then remove from the heat and leave to stand until you can comfortably dip your little finger into it. Whisk in the skin on the top of the milk together with ¼ cup nonfat dry milk powder or granules and 1 teaspoon real live yogurt. Pour into the scalded thermos, screw on the lid and leave overnight or for 10–12 hours, until thick and creamy. Store in the refrigerator, where it will thicken further, and save a teaspoonful for starting off your next batch.

You can make yogurt from any kind of milk; whole milk gives the creamiest result, but use skim milk if you want to reduce the calories. When you leave the mixture to stand, make sure you put the thermos in a place where it won't get touched, and don't open it for 10 hours or so, because for some reason knocks and rough movements can upset the fermentation process. You may find you need to buy a new container of real live starter yogurt from time to time if the finished mixture does not get as thick as usual.

For fruit yogurt, make the yogurt as described. When it is ready, simply add chopped fresh fruit, cooked fruit purée or good-quality jam and sugar or honey to taste. Reduced-sugar jams are excellent stirred into yogurt.

For gloriously thick, Greek-style yogurt, line a large sieve or colander with cheesecloth. Scald the cheesecloth by pouring a kettleful of boiling water through it. Set the sieve or colander over a bowl, pour the yogurt into the sieve or colander and leave to drip overnight.

CREAM

CREAM, a concentration of the fatty part of the milk, comes in various concentrations. HALF-AND-HALF (not illustrated) is the lowest in fat, containing around 12 percent; LIGHT CREAM and SOUR CREAM contain 18–20 percent; HEAVY or WHIPPING CREAM contains 36–40 percent. CLOTTED CREAM contains 55 percent fat. Obviously, in view of its relatively high fat content cream needs to be used with discretion, but it is useful for adding richness to soups and sauces, making a quick sauce for pasta, and in special desserts such as ice cream and parfait. CRÈME FRAÎCHE is a sharp-tasting cream, the flavor somewhere between heavy cream and sour cream. It goes particularly well with sweet fruits, such as strawberries, and it makes a good alternative to sour cream (though higher in calories) when a dish is going to be cooked, as it doesn't separate. You can make crème fraîche by whipping together equal quantities of heavy and sour cream, then leaving at room temperature for 24 hours. Refrigerate after this, which will make the cream thicker. Crème fraîche will keep in a covered container in the refrigerator for 2 weeks. SOY CREAM, with the consistency of light cream, and various nondairy whipping creams, including the kosher PAREV, are available and can replace dairy cream in recipes. All fresh dairy products need to be kept in a cool place, preferably in the fridge, as do canned and packaged milks once opened. Use within 1–3 days.

EGGS

When buying hen's eggs, look for genuine free-range eggs, which are becoming easier to find – many supermarkets now supply them. All the recipes in this book assume the use of free-range eggs. Store in the refrigerator or in a cool place for 7–14 days. Always bring eggs to room temperature before use. DUCK'S EGGS should be well cooked before eating because shells are porous and ducks are not always choosy about where they lay their eggs! Tiny QUAIL'S EGGS can be hard-boiled (for 4 minutes), then shelled (which needs patience!) and used either whole or sliced as a pretty luxury garnish for appetizers, salads and savories. They look charming set into a clear jelly made from 1¼ cups boiling Dark Vegetable Stock (p. 132), with 1 teaspoon agar-agar (p. 286) whisked into it and boiled for 1 minute. Add a few sprigs of leafy tarragon and any small lightly cooked vegetables you fancy.

In the U.S., hen's eggs are graded according to weight. Small eggs, for examples, weigh 1½ ounces; medium eggs, 1¾ ounces; large eggs, 2 ounces; extra-large, 2¼ ounces; and jumbo, 2½ ounces. Most recipes call for large to extra-large eggs.

VEGETARIAN PROTEIN FOODS

SEITAN is a chewy, high-protein food made from protein-rich wheat gluten. It is available frozen and in cans, jars and vacuum packs; various types of SEITAN PÂTÉ and spreads are also available. It is also easy (but rather messy) to make seitan at home by making dough out of a high-gluten flour and water, soaking it under water for 1 hour, then rinsing it under cold water until all the white starch has come out and you're left with an elastic, thread-like mass. This is then simmered in seasoned stock to which some tamari (p. 184) has been added. The resulting seitan is a brownish color because of the tamari. It can be cut into cubes or slices, marinated in more tamari and other tasty ingredients such as garlic and fresh grated ginger, then fried or used to make kebabs. You can also grate seitan and use it as a substitute for ground or minced meat in burgers, shepherd's pies, spaghetti sauce, chili, or casseroles of all sorts.

TEMPEH is another nutritious, high-protein food and has antibiotic properties. It is much liked by some wholefood cooks, but not by me: I find the flavor of soybeans too strong and the texture too stodgy. It needs to be soaked in, or served with, a good strong marinade of crushed

---

Four simple ways to cook an egg

Boiling an egg
For foolproof boiling, it helps to prick the rounded end of the egg to allow the air to escape and prevent bursting. You can buy a special egg-pricker for this purpose, or pierce the rounded end of the egg with a needle. Then, three-quarters-fill a small saucepan with water and bring to a boil. Put the egg into the water and start timing, keeping the water at a steady simmer. Remove the egg with a slotted spoon.

Timings for boiled eggs
These timings are for large-sized eggs at room temperature:
For a runny yolk 4 minutes
For a slightly runny yolk 6 minutes
For a lightly hard-boiled egg 8 minutes
For a dry yolk and set white 10 minutes
When hard-boiling an egg, plunge the egg straight into cold water once the time is up; this will prevent overcooking and the formation of a grey mark between the egg yolk and the white.

Frying an egg
Pour enough oil into a nonstick frying pan to lightly cover the base, then heat it until it sizzles. Break an egg and slip it into the oil. As the egg cooks, spoon over some of the hot oil, to cook the top. As soon as the white in the center of the egg, around the yolk, is set, slip a metal spatula under the egg, lift the egg out and hold it over the frying pan for a moment or two to drain off excess oil. Put the egg straight onto a warmed plate.

Poaching an egg
Fill a wide, shallow pan, such as a deep frying pan, with water. Add 1 tablespoon vinegar and bring to a boil. Break an egg into a cup, then slip it into the water. Immediately turn up the heat so that the water boils vigorously and the bubbles help draw the white around the yolk, then lower the heat and poach gently until set – 2–3 more minutes. Remove the egg with a slotted spoon, and trim the edges to neaten if you wish.

Scrambling eggs for 2
Beat 4 eggs, and, for perfection, pass them through a strainer to remove threads. Season with salt and pepper. Melt 1½ tablespoons butter in a medium heavy-bottomed saucepan. When it sizzles, add the eggs. Cook over low heat, stirring. For creamy scrambled eggs, remove from the heat just before the eggs set. They will cook a little more in the heat of the pan. If you want firmer scrambled eggs, cook for a moment or two longer, until no longer runny. But don't overcook: remember they'll go on cooking in their own heat. Serve immediately on warmed plates.

garlic, grated ginger and soy sauce, maybe some Dijon mustard, too. It is usually cut into cubes or slices and shallow-fried in oil.

FIRM TOFU can be treated in any of the ways described for seitan and tempeh; it should be kept covered with water in a bowl in the fridge before use. SOFT TOFU, in a vacuum pack, can be kept outside the fridge until opened. It can be beaten to a smooth consistency for dips, dressings, pie and tart fillings and fools. Various other types of tofu such as SMOKED TOFU, AROMATIC DRIED TOFU and DRIED DEEP-FRIED TOFU can sometimes be obtained, and these make an interesting addition to stir-fries.

Tofu absorbs flavors well and benefits from being soaked in a marinade before use. Wine, herbs, spices, garlic, oil, citrus rinds and juice, mustard, soy sauce and strongly flavored stock can all be used.

A stock made by simmering a sea vegetable such as wakame in water, until the water has reduced well, then straining it, makes a very pleasant marinade when you feel like giving tofu a taste of the sea.

TEXTURED VEGETABLE PROTEIN is available in various meat flavors as well as natural, and comes in assorted shapes and sizes. It is easily rehydrated in hot water according to the instructions on the package, but has more flavor if left to soak in stock overnight. QUORN (not illustrated) does not need rehydrating. Many vegetarians find these useful products when making the changeover from meat-eating. Nonvegetarians can stretch chopped meat and make it healthier by adding or replacing one-third to one-half with reconstituted textured vegetable protein. Reconstituted textured vegetable protein can be added to nut and lentil dishes, such as roasts, savory loaves, burgers and shepherd's pies, to add bulk, nourishment and flavor. It is useful because it adds moisture and also a chewy texture, which not only can be pleasant but is particularly valuable in vegetarian cooking, where a lot of the ingredients lack those qualities.

How to make tofu

This is best when made from the super soy milk (p. 280). You also need nigari, a white powder which, when added to the soy milk, makes it separate into curds and whey.

You can buy nigari at some health food stores. If you cannot get it, Epsom salts can be used, but the result is not as good.

Put 2½ cups super soy milk (p. 280) into a saucepan and bring to a boil. Dissolve ½ teaspoon nigari (or Epsom salts) in about 4 tablespoons hot water and add to the milk. Leave for 5 minutes for the mixture to curdle. Line a sieve with a piece of cheesecloth, then pour the curdled mixture through, separating the curds from the liquid. The liquid will not be needed. Fold the cheesecloth over to cover the curds and place a weight on top. Leave for at least 1 hour, then remove the curds – which are now tofu – from the cheesecloth and store in cold water in the fridge.

Ideas for using tofu and vegetarian protein foods

☐ Make Vegetarian Toad-in-the-Hole: set the oven to 425°F. Put 2 tablespoons of oil into a 8 by 8 inch roasting pan and heat in the oven until smoking hot. Put ¾ cup plain 85% whole-wheat flour into a bowl with ½ teaspoon salt and 2 eggs. Gradually mix in 1¼ cups milk, to make a batter. Have ready ½ pound seitan or tempeh, cut into cubes, or reconstituted textured vegetable protein cubes. Quickly pour the batter into the pan containing the hot oil, add the cubes of seitan, tempeh or vegetable protein and return to the oven. Bake for about 35 minutes, until puffed up and golden-brown. Serve with a vegetarian gravy and cooked vegetables.

☐ Thread cubes of firm tofu, seitan, tempeh or textured vegetable protein onto skewers with mushrooms, tomatoes and onions.

Marinate in a mixture of 1 tablespoon each of soy sauce, brown sugar, mustard and wine vinegar, then brush with oil and grill or broil to make tasty kebabs.

☐ Whizz tofu with strawberries and honey to make a smooth, dairy-free fruit fool.

☐ Dip slices of firm tofu, tempeh or seitan in flour which has been seasoned and flavored with a crushed garlic clove, shallow-fry in olive oil until crisp on both sides and serve with wedges of lemon.

☐ Any of these protein foods can be mashed, then mixed with fried onion, garlic, herbs and spices, formed into burgers, coated in flour, or egg and breadcrumbs, and fried in oil, or baked on an oiled baking sheet.

☐ Simmer textured vegetable protein in red wine with a bay leaf, then drain, reserving the liquid. Fry a chopped onion, a crushed garlic clove and some button mushrooms in butter or vegan margarine for 10 minutes, then add the protein chunks and stir over the heat until they are heated through. Add a very little flour, to take up any excess fat, then add the reserved cooking liquid and simmer for 10 minutes. Add a small carton of sour cream and cook over gentle heat until the cream is hot (but don't let it boil). Season and serve.

☐ For a vegetarian-style mixed grill, fry chunks of seitan, textured vegetable protein or tempeh in oil and serve with broiled tomatoes, fried potatoes, onions and mushrooms.

☐ For a tasty dressing, whizz together some tofu with fresh herbs such as basil or coriander, lemon juice and seasoning.

◁ Farmhouse Cheddar
Cheddar cheese made in the traditional way and allowed to mature naturally, with a strong, distinctive flavor

Parmesan ▷
One of Italy's most famous cheeses, a hard cheese with a granular texture, used for grating and cooking

Gjetost ▷
A Norwegian cheese with a fudge-like consistency and slightly sweet flavor

Cheese

Cheese was first made by herdsmen as a convenient way to carry milk, and contains all the nutrients present in milk in a more concentrated form. Cheese was made by the Sumerians 6,000 years ago, then by the ancient Greeks and by the Romans, who brought their cheese-making skills as far as Britain. Delicious to eat as it is or to use in cooking, cheese is a very nutritious food, being one of the best vegetarian sources of protein, calcium, vitamins A, B (including B12), D and E, and zinc.

△ Vegetarian Cheddar
Cheddar cheese made with vegetarian rennet

Pecorino △
Can be used as a grating or table cheese

Tilsit ▷
A strongly flavored, semihard cheese made in Germany

▽ White Stilton
This is a traditional Stilton before the mold has been allowed to develop

Raclette △
A semihard cow's milk cheese from Switzerland with a sweet, mild flavor

Provolone △
A smoked Italian cheese

Gruyère △
Cow's milk semihard cheese from Switzerland with a nut-like flavor

◁ Monterey Jack
A variety of American jack cheese with a high moisture content and creamy flavor

Emmenthal △
Fairly sweet, nutty-flavored semihard cheese from Switzerland

Fontina △
Has a slightly smoky flavor

Cantal △
Semihard cheese, good for cooking, the French equivalent of our cooking Cheddar

Edam ▷
Famous semihard Dutch cheese made in a ball shape with distinctive red wax covering

Gouda ▷
Semihard Dutch cheese which can be eaten fresh or matured

Petit Suisse ▷
This unripened cream cheese is good with fresh or poached fruit

Mozzarella ▷
Originally made from buffalo's milk, mozzarella is an unripened Italian cheese with a soft, moist consistency and a mild, creamy flavor; buy genuine Italian mozzarella

Boursin △
An unripened cream cheese which comes with various flavorings added; this one is flavored with herbs and garlic

Fresh, unripened cheeses are for eating shortly after they are made. Soft cheeses, which have been matured for a short period of time and contain less moisture than fresh cheeses, are firmer but still spreadable. Blue cheeses are ripened by the growth of mold from within them, giving them their characteristic sharp, tangy flavor and dappled blue-green appearance. The fat content of these cheeses, which is usually given on the wrapping in the form of a percentage of the whole cheese, varies from very low to high, depending on the type of milk or cream they are made from.

Chèvre △
A goat cheese from France which comes in a range of shapes and sizes

Fromage frais △
This smooth low-fat cheese from France has a light texture, almost the consistency of whipped cream

Farmer's cheese ▷
Smooth unripened cheese. Different types are available with varying fat contents

Chèvre Lezay ▷
Mild, larger log shape with edible rind

Chèvre ▷
Small soft goat cheese coated in various herbs and spices

Ricotta cheese △
Unripened Italian cheese, made in the classic pudding-mold shape

Cream cheese △
A soft, unripened cheese with a high fat content

Low-fat cottage cheese △
A low-fat white cheese with a lumpy texture and creamy flavor

▷ **Soft skim-milk cheese**
A smooth, rathe bland cheese with a minimum of fat

◁ **Cottage cheese**
Often applied to soft unripened cheeses in general, this name is used specifically for a low-to-medium-fat soft cheese with a pleasantly tangy flavor

Stilton ◁
A relative newcomer to the blue-cheese scene, Stilton first became known in the eighteenth century and is said to have originated in Leicestershire, in England

Feta ▽
A fresh soft Greek cheese, made from ewe's milk, with a crumbly texture and a sharp, tangy flavor

Dolcelatte ▷
Made in Italy from cow's milk, similar to Gorgonzola, and good with pasta

Danish blue △
Made in rounds from homogenized cow's milk, with a good sharp, tangy flavor

Camembert ▽
Similar to Brie, although often stronger-flavored, Camembert, also from France, is made in small, deep rounds and sold in halves and portions as well as whole

Roquefort △
Called the "king of cheeses" by some, Roquefort is made from ewe's milk in the Causses area of France

Brie ▷
A French fresh soft cheese, made in a large flat round, with a soft, almost "runny" texture, an edible rind and a mild, creamy flavor

Gorgonzola △
Probably the world's most famous cheese and certainly one of the best, Gorgonzola has been made in Italy since the ninth century. It is made in large cylinder shapes

Cheese

Choosing and storing

All cheese is best bought at its peak and used as soon as possible, within twelve hours, if practicable. This applies especially to unripened and fresh soft cheeses, though semihard and hard cheeses will keep for longer.

A cold cupboard is said to be the best place to store cheese, lightly covered. I keep mine, in small quantities, in a plastic container in the refrigerator for up to a week. If stored in the refrigerator, the cheese should be removed and allowed to come to room temperature for an hour or so before serving.

Hard, semihard and fresh soft cheeses which contain over 45 percent fat, such as full fat and cream cheeses, can be wrapped in plastic wrap and kept for up to 3 months in the deep freeze. Grated Cheddar or Parmesan keeps well in a container in the freezer and can be used from frozen. I grate up leftover pieces of cheese and add them to the container, to save waste and ensure a supply of grated cheese when I need it. Unripened cheese with a high fat content will freeze, but the low-fat ones like fromage blanc and farmer's cheese will not.

In order to separate milk into curds and whey, cheese-making rennet is added to milk in the proportions 1 part rennet to 5,000 parts milk. The rennet most commonly used is a digestive juice taken from the stomachs of calves. This means that many cheeses are not totally vegetarian. However, now that vegetarian rennet is available (and gives cheese makers more reliable results than traditional rennet) it is possible to buy vegetarian versions of a number of cheeses, and the range is increasing. However, cheese made with vegetarian rennet is not always labeled as such, so it's well worth your while to make inquiries.

Cooking and using

See under individual sections.

UNRIPENED CHEESES

Delicious to eat just as they are, with vegetable or fruit salads or as fillings for cherry tomatoes, pitted apricot halves or juicy fresh dates; beaten with fresh herbs and garlic, coarsely crushed black peppercorns or paprika as a dip or topping for crisp crackers; or shaped into small balls or rolls and coated with crushed roasted nuts as a cocktail nibble.

Low-fat cheeses such as FARMER'S CHEESE, FROMAGE FRAIS and SOFT SKIM-MILK CHEESE are particularly useful as cream substitutes to reduce the fat in traditional dishes such as fools, tart fillings and uncooked cheesecakes. They can be diluted to a creamy consistency with skim milk, flavored with a dash of honey and vanilla, and served with desserts instead of cream. For cooked cheesecake, COTTAGE CHEESE or RICOTTA give just the right moist texture, and ricotta is also excellent with pasta, as a filling for ravioli or layered into a lasagne bake (p. 256).

COTTAGE CHEESE, CREAM CHEESE and BOURSIN are good in salads; cream cheese with pineapple is a classic salad mixture, served on a base of crisp lettuce, with tomato and cress. Boursin makes a particularly pleasant addition to a cheese board and is available with different flavorings. MOZZARELLA, too, is particularly good in salads; with avocado and tomato in the famous Italian tricolor salad, for instance, and it is the best cheese to use as a topping for Pizza (p. 218) or Eggplant Parmigiana (p. 202), because it melts to a delectably soft, creamy consistency. PETIT SUISSE, served as it is, or with fresh fruit, makes a pleasant and easy dessert course.

SOFT CHEESES

These cheeses make an excellent addition to a cheese board, and, like the unripened cheeses, are good in salads; the mixture of cubes of FETA cheese with tomato, cucumber, onions and black olives in a Greek salad is a classic. Hot BRIE or Deep-fried CAMEMBERT is a favorite first course or light main course (p. 221).

A whole Brie baked in phyllo pastry makes a spectacular (and easy) dish for a supper party. Either Camembert or Brie can be mashed with walnuts and cream to make a dip or a filling for open mushrooms, which are then baked. CHÈVRE, or goat cheese, comes in a range of shapes and sizes, and may be mild or strong, creamy or firm. CHÈVRE LEZAY is a mild variety of the larger log-shaped chèvre; CHÈVRE BOUCHERON (not illustrated) is more strongly flavored. Small logs of chèvre sliced into little circles just ask to be made into pretty salads. Slices of large chèvre logs are excellent just melted under the broiler; try broiling them on top of tomato slices and serving on a base of crisp lettuce and watercress for supper.

BLUE CHEESES

Blue cheeses, such as STILTON, ROQUEFORT, DANISH BLUE, GORGONZOLA, and DOLCELATTE (available from specialty cheese shops), are ripened by the growth of green molds which develop inside them, giving the characteristic flavor and color. These cheeses are excellent eaten with crispbread or fruit – they have a special affinity with pears. They are also useful in dips, dressings, salads, soups and sauces for pasta. In this way blue cheeses are invaluable in vegetarian cooking because they are one of few very strongly flavored ingredients.

Making cottage cheese

You can make your own cottage cheese from milk which has turned sour; or sour it yourself by adding lemon juice and boiling for 10–15 minutes, using 2 tablespoons lemon juice to about 4 cups of milk.

Pour the sour milk through a metal sieve or colander lined with a double layer of cheesecloth. Leave the sieve over a bowl until it stops dripping – this should take an hour or so. The residue in the sieve is your cottage cheese; add salt and flavorings, such as chopped fresh herbs or crushed garlic, to taste.

SEMIHARD AND HARD CHEESES

Semihard and hard cheeses contain less moisture than soft cheeses; they cut easily but do not spread. They have been ripened from within by the action of enzymes and bacteria over a period of months. Most can be used either for grating and cooking or as a dessert cheese. CHEDDAR, Britain's best-known cheese, is an example of this adaptability. A fine Cheddar is one of the best cheeses to serve for dessert, but is also one of the best cooking cheeses, because it melts well and has a good flavor. Cheddar is available in various strengths, mild as well as strong and well aged. A piece of mature FARM-HOUSE CHEDDAR, some crusty bread and pickled onions (p. 65), washed down with a glass of beer, makes a traditional plowman's lunch. EDAM and GOUDA, the famous Dutch cheeses, and MONTEREY JACK, originally from California, are other cheeses which are particularly good eaten with crusty bread, crisp crackers or salad.

For another quick snack meal, try putting a round slice of PRO-VOLONE on top of a lightly fried large, open mushroom or a thick slice of large beefsteak tomato; broil until the cheese has melted, then serve with salad and French bread.

EDAM, with its red skin, is another popular cheese, particularly with dieters, because it is lower in fat than many cheeses. I find Edam a good cheese for making fondue, although EMMENTHAL is the classic for this. GRUYÈRE, another Swiss cheese which is also made in France, has a nutty flavor and a smooth, uniform texture containing some holes, much smaller than those in Emmenthal. Gruyère, too, is used for fondue and is a useful cheese for cooking, because of its fine flavor and good melting qualities.

Other cheeses which melt well are CANTAL, the French cheese quite similar to Cheddar, and FONTINA, which is used to make, among other things, an Italian version of cheese fondue with eggs and truffles. A less well known but interesting cheese is RACLETTE. It is melted to make a Swiss dish which is eaten with potatoes and accompanied by pickled gherkins.

PARMESAN cheese is an important cheese for cooking because of its strong, sharp flavor. It can be bought ready-grated, but for the best flavor, buy a piece of aged Parmesan, if possible, and grate it yourself as needed. PECORINO is another excellent hard, pungent cheese from Italy, suitable both for cooking and eating as it is.

One of the more unusual cheeses is GJETOST, from Norway. This looks like fudge and has a slightly sweet, floury taste. It can be eaten with bread or made into appetizers and desserts.

Selecting a cheese board

When choosing cheeses for a cheese board, I prefer to concentrate on one or two perfect pieces of cheese rather than offer a great variety. An excellent, generous sized piece of matured Cheddar, for instance, really needs no accompaniment except some crisp crackers or crusty bread and perhaps some fresh celery. A "white" cheese board made up of just three or four chèvre cheeses is another favorite of mine, especially if it is served before the dessert and there is some dry white wine to be finished up with the cheese.

Alternatively, try making up a cheese board of a complementary pair of cheeses, one soft and creamy, such as Brie or a creamy chèvre, and one hard or semihard – perhaps a red one, like DOUBLE GLOUCESTER or LEICESTER, or a superb piece of STILTON or, another of my favorites, WENSLEYDALE.

If you happen to have a large gathering of cheese lovers at Christmastime, it can be fun to offer them a whole wheel of Stilton, but make sure everyone slices it across and no one wrecks the cheese by pouring port into the middle!

Quick serving ideas for cheese

Cheese is one of the most useful convenience foods; here are some ideas for using it:

☐ Form cream or softened Cheddar cheese into a log shape; roll the log in a mixture of sesame seeds and chopped parsley.

☐ Alternatively, roll Cheddar cheese into balls the size of walnuts and then roll in chopped herbs, sesame seeds or ground nuts.

☐ Make raw kebabs: spear cubes of firm cheese onto skewers with wedges of tomato, cubes of cucumber or pineapple, scallions, radishes, baby button mushrooms, gherkins, pitted olives, or any other fruit or vegetable you fancy. The skewers can be coated with a vinaigrette marinade before serving, if you like.

☐ Slice the top off green peppers and scoop out seeds and core, then pack peppers with a mixture of cottage cheese and raisins or scallions, press down firmly and chill until required, then cut into slices and serve as part of a salad.

☐ Make cheese spread for sandwiches by mixing very finely grated Cheddar or Cheshire cheese with milk to make a soft paste. Flavor with chopped chives or scallions, curry powder or a pinch of chili powder.

☐ For a sweet-and-sour salad with a crunchy texture, mix 3 cups shredded cabbage with 1 cup diced cheese, ¾ cup chopped dates and ½ cup roasted peanuts. Dress with natural yogurt.

☐ For Cheese Curry, melt 2 tablespoons butter in a saucepan and sauté a chopped onion for 10 minutes. Then stir in 4 tablespoons flour and 2–3 teaspoons curry powder. Add 1¼ cups water, stirring over the heat until the sauce thickens. Simmer gently for 10 minutes, then add 1 cup cubed cheese and ¼ cup sultanas. Serve immediately, with hot cooked rice.

Herbs

Herbs have been used for centuries, both for flavoring and for healing. Some, like parsley, which is rich in iron, potassium, calcium and vitamin C, are unusually high in nutrients; others have medicinal and curative properties. Thyme and rosemary (which is an excellent hair tonic) are natural disinfectants, dill is sleep-inducing, fennel is helpful for nursing mothers, mint aids digestion, and sage not only makes a good hair rinse but is said to promote a healthy old age.

◁ Summer savory
More delicate in flavor than winter savory, summer savory goes well with fresh beans

Lemon balm △
Delicately flavored with lemon, and soothing to the digestion, lemon balm is good in tea and added to fruit cups

Winter savory △
Winter savory is known as "the bean herb" in Germany, because its spicy, peppery flavor complements them so well

Borage ▽
An unusual herb in that the flowers are used, giving a cucumber flavor and attractive color to salads and summer punches

Camomile △
A popular herb for making in tea, camomile is soothing and sleep-inducing

Feverfew △
Hot and peppery, a few leaves of feverfew, eaten each day in a sandwich, has been found to be helpful to migraine sufferers

◁ Sweet cecily
A sprig of sweet cecily added to stewed fruit reduces the need for sugar

Salad burnet ▷
With a cucumber fragrance when crushed, salad burnet is a popular salad herb in Southern European countries

Hyssop ▷
A warm, aromatic herb which grows wild in Southern Europe and is used in liqueurs such as Chartreuse

Lovage △
A delicious herb, which tastes like spicy, lemony celery and deserves to be more widely used

▽ **Comfrey**
Comfrey leaves have healing properties and were formerly used to treat wounds

Angelica △
Best-known in its crystallized form, angelica has a musky scent and can be used fresh in salads and vegetable dishes

Curry plant ▽
The leaves of this herb smell and taste of curry and are widely used in Indian, Malaysian and Indonesian cooking

Coriander △
A most popular herb worldwide, with a strange but addictive flavor, widely used in South America, China and Japan, Southeast Asia and India, and the Middle East

Fenugreek △
A spicy, rather bitter-tasting herb, popular in Indian cooking

Chervil △
Chervil has a fresh, delicate flavor and is one of the herbs (along with parsley and chives) which make up the classic *fines herbes* mixture

Flat-leaved (or Italian) parsley △
Flat-leaved parsley is considered to have a superior flavor to the curly type

Curly parsley △
The most widely used herb. There are various varieties of parsley

Chives ▽
Chives have a delicate onion flavor and are at their best in raw or very lightly cooked dishes

Tarragon ▷
One of the most important herbs, tarragon comes in two varieties; choose French tarragon rather than Russian, as it has a finer flavor

Basil ▽
The favorite of many cooks, chopped fresh basil brings a taste of summer sunshine and is the classic flavoring for tomatoes and for pesto sauce

◁ **Apple mint**
A delicately flavored mint, for seasoning apple dishes, adding to fruit cups, making into teas

Sage ▽
A popular herb in traditional British cookery, sage has a strong, camphor-like flavor and makes a good tea

◁ **Spearmint**
The best all-purpose mint, along with round-leaved Bowles mint (*M. rotundifolia* var. Bowles, not illustrated)

◁ **Ginger mint**
One of the many interesting varieties of mint

⊲ Fennel
Golden-flowered,
anise-flavored fennel is a classic
flavoring for fish but is useful
for vegetarians too, especially
combined with lemon and
olive oil

Dill △
Although native to southern
Europe, by adoption dill is
Scandinavian, in which cuisine
it is widely used

Oregano ▽
Widely used in Italy, oregano
has an intense, savory flavor

Rosemary △
Widely used in the Mediterranean, rosemary
has a delicious pine-like flavor that can
enhance both sweet and savory dishes

Bay △
One of the bouquet garni
herbs; the intense flavor of bay
gives depth to casseroles,
stocks and soups

⊲ Thyme
A fragrant herb, one of the ingredients of a
classic bouquet garni

Sweet marjoram ▷
Related to oregano, marjoram
has a sweet, slightly spicy
flavor, making it a useful
all-purpose herb

Lemon thyme ▷

Herbs

Choosing and storing

The best way to experience herbs is freshly picked. Once picked, they should be kept in a jar of water or loosely wrapped in a plastic bag in the refrigerator for a day or so. Dried herbs lack the aroma of fresh herbs, but are useful when fresh ones are unavailable, and bay leaves actually taste better when dried. Keep dried herbs in small airtight bottles, in a dark place if possible.

Preparing and using

Fresh herbs should be lightly washed, then patted dry before use. Handle them gently to preserve their fragrant oils. Then use them whole, or chop them, according to the recipe. To chop herbs, remove any coarse stems, then put the herbs on a board and chop with a sharp knife, holding the point of the blade down with one hand and pivoting the knife from the point in a quarter-circle. Herbs can also be chopped in a food processor; this is excellent for chopping large quantities.

As dried herbs are more strongly flavored than fresh ones, a smaller quantity is needed: only a quarter to a third of the amount of fresh herbs. Dried herbs can be added to a dish at the beginning of cooking, as can a bouquet garni and the robust fresh herbs such as bay, rosemary and thyme, but the fresh delicate green herbs are better added towards the end of the cooking, to make the most of their flavor and color.

To make a bouquet garni, tie a sprig of parsley, one of thyme and a bay leaf together. Sometimes I like to include a strip or two of lemon peel also, for a fresh, citrus flavor. Alternatively, one of the best ways to make a bouquet garni is to slit a trimmed, washed leek down one side, pop the herbs inside the leek and tie it to hold the herbs in place.

Chopped fresh herbs make an excellent flavoring for butter or vegan margarine; just mix finely chopped herbs into soft butter or margarine, together with a few drops of lemon juice, if you like. Keep in the fridge for a day or two; or freeze for several weeks. Add to hot cooked vegetables, use to make herb bread, or swirl into hot cooked pasta.

Drying and preserving

Pick herbs for preserving at the height of their season, before they flower, on a sunny day after the dew has dried. Cut them with long stems and hang up in bunches in a cool, dark place to dry naturally. Keep different herbs apart so that the flavors do not merge. When the herbs are completely dry and brittle, store them in dark, airtight containers.

Alternatively, herbs can be deep-frozen. Cut them as described, then blanch them by dipping them briefly into a deep pan of boiling water. Refresh immediately in cold water, pat dry, then freeze on open trays. When frozen, pack in plastic bags. Or chop the herbs, put into ice cube containers, top up with water and freeze. When frozen, transfer to a plastic bag, keeping individual types together.

One of the best ways of preserving the flavor of basil is to chop the leaves, then put them into a jar in layers, sprinkling each layer with salt. Cover with olive oil and keep the jar in the fridge. Although the leaves darken, the flavor remains.

Or make basil-flavored oil, to bring a summer taste to winter salads. Put several sprigs into a bottle and fill up with olive oil; the oil will be impregnated with the flavor after several weeks. Herb-flavored vinegars can be made in a similar way.

ANGELICA
Angelica archangelica
Best-known in its crystallized form, angelica has a musky scent and can be used fresh in salads and vegetable dishes.

BASIL *Ocimum basilicum*
Best-known as a flavoring for tomatoes and for the classic Italian sauce Pesto (p. 172), basil is good in any salad mixture or chopped over lightly cooked vegetables.

BAY *Laurus nobilis*
Bay can be used either dried or fresh. It is usually included in a bouquet garni and is good in vegetable casseroles, soups and stews, and to flavor the milk used to make sauces such as Bread Sauce (p. 175). A bay leaf is an old-fashioned flavoring for rice pudding. Fresh bay leaves, if you can find them, make an attractive garnish for fresh cheeses or sorbet in fresh orange skins.

BORAGE *Borago officinalis*
An unusual herb in that the flowers are used, giving a cucumber flavor and attractive color to salads and summer punches. Try adding the flowers to ice cubes.

CAMOMILE *Anthemis nobilis*
A popular herb for making into tea, camomile is soothing and sleep-inducing.

CHERVIL *Anthriscus cerefolium*
Chervil has a fresh, delicate flavor and can be used lavishly in salads and over lightly cooked vegetables. As part of the traditional *fines herbes* mixture, it is a delicious flavoring for an omelette.

CHIVES *Allium schoenoprasum*
Very useful wherever you need a subtle onion flavor, chives are also one of the most useful garnishing herbs; just snip them over the top of pale-colored soups, dips and salads. Chives are a particularly good flavoring for egg and cheese dishes and are added to some cheeses.

COMFREY *Symphytum officinale*
Cucumber-flavored, like borage, comfrey can be chopped into salads or dipped in batter and fried as a nibble. The flowers can be used in fruit cups.

CORIANDER
Coriandrum sativum
Similar in appearance to flat-leaved parsley, this is the world's most popular herb, widely used in South America, Asia and the Middle East. In the U.S., fresh coriander is sometimes called cilantro or Chinese parsley.

CURRY PLANT
Murraya koenigii
The leaves of this herb smell and taste of curry and are widely used in Asian cooking.

DILL *Anethum graveolens*
A pretty, feathery herb, attractive as a garnish as well as a flavoring, dill is good in any cucumber dish or chopped into sour cream as a topping for baked potatoes.

FENNEL *Foeniculum vulgare*
This herb, with its aniseed flavor, helps to cut the oiliness of foods; sprinkle it over fried potatoes or eggplant, add a little to nut burgers. Fennel is good in a green salad dressed with lemon and olive oil.

FENUGREEK
Trigonella foenum-graecum
This is a spicy, rather bitter-tasting herb, popular in Indian cooking.

FEVERFEW
Chrysanthemum parthenium
Feverfew is a useful cure for migraine. Eat a few leaves each day in a sandwich.

HYSSOP
Hyssopus officinalis
This warm, aromatic herb grows wild in Southern Europe and is used in liqueurs such as Chartreuse.

LEMON BALM
Melissa officinalis
Delicately lemon-flavored and soothing to the digestion, lemon balm is good in tea and added to fruit cups, or used to flavor a cake by sprinkling it on the lining paper before putting in the cake mixture.

LEMON GRASS
Citronella sereh (Not illustrated)
Lemon grass looks a bit like a scallion and gives an exquisite citrus flavor, much used in Asian cooking. Use the bulbous 4–5 inches of the stem. Discard the toughest layer; shred or crush.

LOVAGE *Levisticum officinale*
This unusual but delicious herb is good in a lettuce or cabbage salad, or added to celery soup to intensify the flavor. Use lovage sparingly.

SWEET MARJORAM
Origanum marjorana
A useful herb, marjoram is best added towards the end of cooking time, to preserve its sweet flavor. It is also excellent in nut and lentil roasts (pp. 239, 213) and savory bakes, in stuffings and burgers.

MINT *Mentha*
One of the most important and widely used flavorings. There are many varieties of mint, including APPLE MINT, SPEARMINT and GINGER MINT. It is a traditional flavoring for peas and new potatoes and is chopped to make fresh Indian chutneys and mint sauce, which is good as an accompaniment to a lentil roast. To make Mint Sauce, mix 4 tablespoons chopped mint with 1 tablespoon superfine sugar, 1 tablespoon boiling water and 2 tablespoons wine vinegar.

OREGANO *Origanum vulgare*
This is one herb which retains its flavor well when dried. It is useful in any dish where you want quite an intense taste, and is widely used in Italian cooking, in sauces to serve with pasta and lasagne bakes, and sprinkled on top of pizza (p. 218). Oregano is also pleasant in a nut or lentil roast or burgers.

PARSLEY *Petroselinum crispum*
The most commonly used herb in European and American cooking, parsley comes in CURLY and FLAT LEAF (or ITALIAN) varieties. Parsley has a fresh, mild flavor, and can be used lavishly, added to sauces and stuffings, sprinkled over cooked vegetables and pasta, and included in salads. It is used almost like a vegetable in the Middle Eastern salad Tabbouleh (p. 159). Parsley stalks make an excellent flavoring; tie them together and add to any soup or casserole.

ROSEMARY
Rosmarinus officinalis
This fragrant herb, with pine and camphor notes, is good in pilafs and nut dishes; as a natural "skewer" for kebabs and as a flavoring for bread, egg custards and ice creams.

SAGE *Salvia officinalis*
A strongly flavored herb, traditionally used with onions to make a stuffing (which can be baked between layers of a cashew nut roast or used to fill a squash). Sage complements split peas and split orange/red lentils, and is a good flavoring for savory apple jelly; it is found in cheeses and is a good addition to homemade cheese dips.

SALAD BURNET
Poterium sanguisorba
With a cucumber fragrance when crushed, salad burnet is a popular salad herb in many Southern European countries.

SUMMER and WINTER SAVORY
Satureja hortensis and *S. Montana*
These peppery herbs go well in any savory dish, particularly any which include split peas or lentils. Try adding winter savory to lentil soups; chop summer savory over tender young fava beans or add to a white bean salad.

SWEET CECILY *Myrrhis odorata*
A sprig of sweet cecily added to stewed fruit reduces the need for sugar.

TARRAGON
Artemisia dracunculus
Tarragon is good in omelettes or any delicate egg dish. Try adding it to a savory jelly, delicately flavored flan filling, omelette or mildly flavored cheese soufflé. Or add some chopped tarragon to the filling for stuffed eggs, then serve them on a base of fresh tarragon leaves. It's also good chopped into salads, including rice salad, and added to butter for serving with fresh summer vegetables or pasta.

THYME and LEMON THYME
Thymus vulgaris and *T. serpyllum*
Excellent for adding to any long-cooking casserole or stew, and one of the components of bouquet garni, thyme is an herb which survives the drying process well. It makes an excellent addition to almost any savory mixture.

Caraway seeds ▽
Caraway has a sweet, slightly aniseed flavor

Aniseed △
The fragrant seeds of an umbelliferous plant

Allspice △
The dried berries of an evergreen tree native to the West Indies

Cardamom △
The pods of a perennial plant of the ginger family, and the second most expensive spice in the world, cardamom has a eucalyptus-like scent and flavor

Spices

Spices are the dried buds, flowers, fruits, leaves and barks of aromatic plants, mainly from tropical countries. They have been used for centuries, highly revered for their rarity and use in the preservation of food and the making of medicines and perfumes. For hundreds of years spices were a precious trading commodity. Today they are an essential ingredient in good cooking, and especially in vegetarian cooking because of the strong flavors they provide for so many dishes.

Cayenne pepper △
A powder made from dried small hot red chili peppers from Central America

Celery seeds △
The dried seeds of the celery plant, native to Italy

Chinese five-spice △
This is made from equal parts of finely ground fennel, cloves, cinnamon (or cassia), star anise and anise, and is subtly aniseed-flavored

Chili △
The dried fruit of a hot and spicy pepper from South America

Cloves ▷
Cloves have antiseptic and preservative properties and can be bought whole or ground

Coriander seeds △
These dried seeds are the world's most-used spice

Cumin seeds △
These dried seeds of plant related to the parsley family have slightly bitter flavor

Cinnamon △
The dried bark of an aromatic evergreen of the laurel family

Dill seeds △
These have a slightly sweet flavor

Fennel seeds △
The aniseed-flavored seeds of the fennel plant

Fenugreek △
Rectangular yellowish-brown seeds

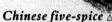
Garam masala △
A blend of roasted ar ground spices

△
Curry powder
A blend of several spices, in varying strengths

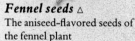

Garlic ▷
The bulb of a perennial plant native to Asia

Ginger △
When fresh, this has citrus-like smell and

◁ **Horseradish**
The root of a plant native to southeastern Europe, horseradish has a hot, pungent flavor

Mace ▽
Mace can be bought whole, as "blade" mace, or ground

Mixed spice ▽
Usually consists of four parts each ground nutmeg and cinnamon, two parts ginger and one part ground cloves

Juniper berries ▷
The berries of a small prickly shrub which grows wild in many parts of the Northern Hemisphere, including Britain

Nutmeg ▽
The dried kernel of an apricot-like fruit; see mace. Nutmeg is available whole and ground and has a slightly sweet, aromatic flavor

◁ **Black mustard seeds**
The hottest of the mustard seeds

Paprika ▽
A sweet mild powder made from a variety of peppers

◁ *Whole-grain mustard*
Contains whole brown mustard seeds

△
White mustard seeds

◁ *Dijon mustard*
A hot prepared mustard from France

◁ **Brown mustard seeds**

Dried green peppercorns ▽

Pink peppercorns ▽

Pickled green peppercorns ▽

Fresh green peppercorns ▽

▽ **Black peppercorns**
The sun-ripened berries of the pepper vine

△

Green peppercorns
The unripened berries of the pepper, available dried, pickled and sometimes fresh, with a sharp, hot flavor

◁ *White peppercorns*
Peppercorns which have been ripened, then skinned

Pickling spice ▽
A mixture of spices for chutneys and pickles

Star anise △
The dried fruit of an evergreen tree

Tamarind ▽
Tamarind has a sharp flavor, rather like lemon juice

Poppy seeds △
The seeds of the opium poppy, native to the Middle East

Saffron △
Saffron is the dried golden stamens of a crocus-type flower

Turmeric △
A rhizome belonging to the ginger family, but with a different flavor

Vanilla △
The black, snake-like pods of a climbing orchid native to Central America, vanilla has a sweet, delectable flavor

Spices

Choosing and storing

Buy spices in small quantities – just enough to use up within six months – from a store with a rapid turnover. Keep the spices in airtight jars. Strictly speaking, they should be kept away from the light, or stored in dark jars, but I like the decorative look of them on an open shelf and find I experiment with them more if I have them in front of me. Prices vary, and although it's worthwhile spending extra for high-quality spices, make sure that you're not really paying for fancy packaging. Indian and Middle Eastern food stores often sell excellent spices, simply packaged and reasonably priced.

There's no doubt that many spices are best bought whole so that you can grind them as you need them. This is easy and practical with some of the spices, such as black and white peppercorns, which can be kept in separate grinders, and whole coriander, which you can also grind in a pepper mill. Nutmeg is easy to grate as you need it, either on a special nutmeg grater (which may have a handy compartment for keeping the pieces of half-grated nutmeg) or on the finest blade of a box grater. Most other spices can be pounded in a mortar with a pestle, or – easier – whizzed to a powder in an electric coffee grinder.

Using

Spices are used to flavor both sweet and savory dishes, and some can also be added in large quantities to thicken sauces. The basic spices are black peppercorns and fresh nutmeg; others can be added as you need them for individual recipes. One way of getting to know spices is to cook a new spicy recipe every week or so and buy the spices needed for it, then see how they taste added to other dishes.

Spices can also be used as flavorings for ice creams or for hot and cold milk, and as toppings and garnishes.

ALLSPICE
Pimenta diocia

Allspice can be bought whole or ground and tastes like a mixture of cinnamon, nutmeg and cloves. It is useful in baking instead of mixed spice (of which it is often an ingredient). A few whole berries make an interesting addition to stews and casseroles.

ANISEED *Pimpinella anisum*

Aniseed is available whole or ground, but is most useful whole, when it can be added to cooked vegetables (it goes particularly well with carrots). Aniseed can also be used in baking, to flavor cakes, pastries and cookies. It also lends the distinctive, licorice-like flavor to ouzo, Pernod and Ricard (pastis).

CARAWAY SEEDS *Carum carvi*

The curved seeds of a plant native to Europe and Asia, caraway is popular in German and Austrian cooking. It is famous in England for its use in seed cake, which was popular in Victorian times. Caraway can be sprinkled on top of bread or savory pastries, included in coleslaw and sprinkled over cooked cabbage. It is used in goulash and in liptauer cheese, a flavored cheese dip from Hungary. Some cheeses contain caraway seed, and caraway is used to make certain liqueurs, such as kümmel, made in Germany, Denmark and Holland.

CARDAMOM
Elettaria cardamomum

Cardamom pods range in color from white or pale green to almost black (which are an inferior type). Cardamom is available whole or ground and is a fragrant spice, one of my favorites. It can be used to flavor spiced vegetable dishes and pilafs, or the small black seeds can be taken out of the pods and crushed. Cardamom also makes a pungent and unusual flavoring for sweet dishes such as the Indian ice cream kulfi and the Middle Eastern sweetmeat halvah.

Ground cardamom is available, but it is better to buy it in the pod and crush the seeds to a powder yourself in a mortar with a pestle.

CAYENNE PEPPER
Capsicum annuum

Cayenne is useful for giving a kick to bland dishes such as an avocado dip or cream cheese dip; it is good in cheese dishes.

CELERY SEEDS
Apium graveolens

Used whole or in the form of celery salt, these can be added to any dishes requiring a celery flavor – soups, appetizers, casseroles, even a salad dressing – or sprinkled on top of loaves. But use with discretion, as too many can taste bitter.

CHILI *Capsicum annuum*

Chili can be bought whole, flaked or ground. The pungency of ground chili varies from mild to very hot, depending on the blend. Use in vegetarian chili and other Mexican and Southwestern dishes; like cayenne pepper, chili can be used to give a kick to mild dishes.

CHINESE FIVE-SPICE

This slightly aniseed-tasting flavoring is used in Chinese dishes; try adding a pinch to vegetable stir-fries.

CINNAMON
Cinnamomum zeylanicum

Cinnamon can be bought as pieces of bark, "quills" made from the inner bark, and powder. This warm, fragrant flavoring is good in both sweet and savory dishes. The bark and quills can be used to flavor pilafs and spiced vegetable dishes; the quills are also useful for flavoring poached fruits and fruit compotes. Cinnamon is difficult to grind at home, so it's useful to buy it ready-ground too, for adding to cakes and cookies. A cinnamon stick can be kept in a jar of superfine sugar to flavor it; this sugar, or sugar mixed with cinnamon, is good for cheering up a bland melon, and sprinkled on top of hot buttered toast makes cinnamon toast.

CLOVES *Syzygium aromaticum*
and *Eugenia aromatica*

Cloves are the dried flower buds of a tall aromatic evergreen of the myrtle family native to Southeast Asia. It is useful to have both whole and ground cloves, since cloves are difficult to grind at home, and ground cloves are useful in fruit cakes and in some bean dishes. Whole cloves make a delicious flavoring for apple pie, whole baked onions, bread sauce and cheese fritters.

Cloves also have natural antiseptic and preservative properties, as I discovered for myself recently when my young daughter had half made a pomander: the half of the orange studded with cloves was still dry and perfectly preserved, while the other side was rotten.

CORIANDER SEEDS
Coriandrum sativum
Coriander seeds have a slight burnt-orange flavor and are available whole and ground. I find it useful to keep both on hand. Coriander complements many vegetable, grain and bean dishes. The whole seeds can be roasted in a dry saucepan, then lightly crushed or finely ground before use; or you can keep a pepper mill full of coriander, or it can be bought ready-ground.

Ground coriander is used to flavor spicy Pakoras from India. These can be served as a first course or as a side dish. To make Pakoras, put ¾ cup chick pea flour into a bowl with 1 teaspoon each salt and grated fresh ginger, ½ teaspoon each chili powder and ground coriander, ¼ teaspoon turmeric, and enough water to mix to a thin batter – ¾ to 1 cup. Leave the batter to stand for about 30 minutes. Meanwhile, peel and slice into rings 2 large onions. Dip the onion rings into the batter, then fry in deep or shallow fat until crisp; deep fat gives the crisper result. Drain the onion rings on paper towels and serve immediately.

As it is mild, coriander is often used in quite large quantities to thicken as well as flavor Indian or Middle Eastern vegetable dishes. Mushrooms or vegetables can be flavored with coriander to make a delicious first course (Marinated Vegetables, p. 150). Coriander is also an essential ingredient of curry powder and garam masala (see below).

CUMIN SEEDS
Cuminum cyminum
The whole seeds are best if roasted in a saucepan before use to mellow the flavor. Along with coriander, cumin is frequently used in curries and spiced vegetable dishes. I find it useful to have both the whole seeds and ground cumin on my kitchen shelf.

CURRY POWDER
A popular flavoring in the West, but not much used in India, curry powder consists of a blend of spices, usually including coriander, turmeric, fenugreek, cumin and chili. It can be bought in varying strengths from mild to hot. I find it quite useful for perking up some bland mixtures such as the filling for deviled eggs, or to flavor mayonnaise, but not for making curries; for these a mixture of coriander, cumin, fresh ginger, chili, garlic and other spices gives a much better flavor.

DILL SEEDS Anethum graveolens
Probably best-known as the flavoring in dill pickles, dill seeds have a refreshing flavor. They are a popular flavoring in Scandinavian cooking. Like fresh dill, dill seeds are excellent in any cucumber dish, such as cucumber soups and salads, as well as with cabbage, carrots and any of the root vegetables.

FENNEL SEEDS
Foeniculum vulgare
Fennel seeds are much used in Indian cooking and when added to bean dishes are said to counteract any indigestibility, though I have never had any proof of such effectiveness. They are best if lightly roasted in a dry pan before use.

FENUGREEK
Trigonella foenum-graecum
Fenugreek is an ingredient in curries and Indian dishes, but you do not need much, as it has quite a harsh flavor. I think the whole seeds are best to use, and they should be lightly roasted in a saucepan first. The seeds can also be sprouted (p. 207), but watch your teeth when you eat them.

GARAM MASALA
Garam masala can be bought ready-blended, although in India cooks make up their own mixture, often to old family recipes. The mixtures usually include coriander, cumin, cloves, cinnamon and black pepper. Add to curries at the end of the cooking, to flavor and thicken.

GARLIC Allium sativum
Garlic is indispensable for subtly enhancing the taste of other ingredients or giving its own wonderful flavor to savory dishes. It can be used in a whole range of dishes, from soups and salads – rub a salad bowl with a cut clove of garlic for a delicate flavor – to casseroles, bakes, accompaniments such as hot buttery garlic bread, and dips and sauces such as the famous aïoli of Provence.

Garlic Potatoes are delicious. Peel and cut potatoes into even-sized chunks and boil for about 15 minutes until just tender. Drain and spread the potatoes in a shallow ovenproof dish. Crush one or two garlic cloves with some butter and dot over the surface of the potatoes. Season and cook in a fairly hot oven for about 40 minutes, turning the potatoes from time to time to coat them in the garlic butter.

Garlic can be bought fresh, as a paste in a tube, as flakes, as powder or as a salt. Fresh garlic is by far the best, and worth the small effort involved in peeling and crushing the individual cloves from the bulb.

A bulb of garlic will keep well for several weeks in a dry kitchen. When I can, I like to buy a string of garlic – it looks attractive hanging up in the kitchen and means there's always plenty available. Choose firm bulbs with no sign of powderiness and look for nice big fat ones made up of fat individual cloves – they're so much easier to peel and crush. To crush garlic, either use a good-quality, sturdy garlic press with nice large holes, or crush with the side of a knife on a small board, adding a little salt to help grind it into a paste.

Garlic is a natural antiseptic, excellent for cleansing heavy metals from the body and keeping colds (and, alas, probably one's friends) at bay.

GINGER *Zingiber officinale*

Ginger is the rhizome of a flowering plant which is native to Southeast Asia but has been grown in China for thousands of years. It can be bought fresh, dried and ground. FRESH GINGER has a deliciously fresh, citrus-like smell and flavor, along with the characteristic hotness, and is used in Chinese, Caribbean and Indian dishes. It transforms a dish of simple root vegetables into a gourmet feast and can give a wonderful lift to a winter compote of dried fruit. DRIED GINGER ROOT is useful when making preserves and chutneys, and POWDERED GINGER is a popular flavoring for cakes (such as gingerbread, Parkin (p. 308) and fruit cakes, biscuits and cookies. Gingerbread Men are a perennial children's favorite. To make about 12, set the oven to 350°F. Melt 2 tablespoons butter or vegan margarine, ¼ cup Barbados sugar, 1 tablespoon molasses and 2 tablespoons golden syrup or light corn syrup gently in a saucepan, then cool until you can put your hand against the saucepan. Sift in a generous ¾ cup fine 100% whole-wheat flour and ½ teaspoon each bicarbonate of soda and ground ginger. Mix to a pliable dough. If the dough is too soft to roll, chill in the refrigerator for about 20 minutes; otherwise roll it out about ¼ inch thick and cut into gingerbread men shapes. Put the gingerbread men on the baking tray and bake for about 10 minutes, until firm and beginning to darken around the edges. Cool on a wire rack.

Ginger is available preserved in syrup and crystallized, both excellent for adding to ice cream, cakes, fruit salads or a compote of dried fruits.

HORSERADISH *Armoracia rusticana*

Finely grated horseradish can be added to mayonnaise or cream to make horseradish sauce. Or it can be made into a dressing for sliced tomato salad. To make this, combine in a bowl ½ cup cottage cheese, 2 tablespoons natural yogurt, 2 teaspoons olive oil, ½ teaspoon wine vinegar and 1 teaspoon grated horseradish. Mix until creamy, then pour over sliced tomatoes and garnish with chopped fresh herbs. Horseradish is pungent and can make your eyes water as you grate it. I think a jar of preserved grated or creamed horseradish is a better bet.

JUNIPER BERRIES *Juniperus communis*

Juniper berries take three years to ripen, so the bushes carry berries at different stages of development. Juniper berries can be used fresh or dried, and a few berries added to casseroles and vegetable dishes give an intriguing flavor. Juniper is used to make gin, and in Germany juniper is added to sauerkraut and preserves.

MACE *Myristica fragrans*

Mace is the lacy covering surrounding the kernel inside the apricot-like fruit of an evergreen tree of the myrtle family. A BLADE of mace is useful for flavoring Béchamel Sauce (p. 175) and delicate soups; while a pinch of GROUND MACE enhances many savory mixtures and is especially good in delicate nut roasts made from white nuts (p. 239).

MIXED SPICE

The flavor of different brands of mixed spice varies, so it's worthwhile experimenting to find your favorite. A useful flavoring for cakes, cookies and fruit mixtures such as mincemeat.

MUSTARD SEEDS *Brassica hirta* and *B. nigra*

WHITE, BLACK and BROWN mustard seeds are used in curries and Indian dishes, and the white ones make a delicious addition to cucumber and dill salad, cucumber pickle and chutneys. MUSTARD POWDER (not illustrated) is a mixture of varieties together with wheat flour and turmeric. A pinch or so brings out the flavor of cheese dishes: it should be blended with cold water for the best flavor. Many types of prepared mustard are available, often with intriguing additions like fresh herbs and green peppercorns. These are fun ways to jazz up a sandwich or spread, but the essential basics to have in the pantry, in my opinion, are DIJON MUSTARD, which is delicious in salad dressings, and a whole-grain mustard, especially MOUTARDE DE MEAUX, which, as well as being a useful ingredient, is a good accompaniment to many cold savory dishes.

NUTMEG *Myristica fragrans*

Traditionally, nutmeg was used for sweet dishes such as milk puddings, egg custards and custard tarts, while mace was used in savory dishes. However, nutmeg is equally at home with vegetables such as mushrooms, spinach and cabbage, and in dishes such as onions in cream sauce. The flavor of freshly grated nutmeg is much better than that of ready-ground nutmeg.

PAPRIKA *Capsicum tetragonum*

Paprika makes a cheering garnish to any pale dishes such as Hummus, Guacamole, Cheese and Fresh Herb Dip (p. 143) or mashed potatoes. Paprika is useful for its subtle, peppery taste as well as its color, and is an essential ingredient in many Hungarian recipes, where it is used to thicken, as well as flavor. The best paprika is Hungarian noble sweet, followed by semisweet, rose, strong and commercial, in descending order of quality.

PEPPERCORNS *Piper nigrum*

GREEN PEPPERCORNS are included in some special dishes, for their color as much as their flavor. BLACK PEPPERCORNS have a mellow flavor and, when freshly ground, give an appetizing piquancy to food. WHITE PEPPERCORNS have a sharper, more astringent flavor, which is useful at times, and some cooks prefer to use white pepper for seasoning pale mixtures which would be discolored by flecks of black pepper. MIGNONETTE (not illustrated) is a mixture of white and black peppercorns and is widely used in France. You can make up your own mignonette mixture by putting both white and black peppercorns into a pepper mill. This gives a pleasant flavoring, worth trying. The other flavoring which is based on either black or white pepper and is popular in France (where it can be bought at any supermarket) is quatre épices, a mixture of ground peppercorns, cloves, nutmeg and cinnamon – a pleasant mixture to experiment with.

PINK PEPPERCORNS (*Schinus molle*), also known as Baie rose and false pepper of America, are the fruits of a small ornamental tree of the cashew family. They can be used to make an attractive garnish because of their pretty color.

PICKLING SPICE

An essential ingredient in chutneys and pickles, a little pickling spice can also be added to a casserole, or ground in a mortar with a pestle and used to add piquancy to a nut roast.

POPPY SEEDS
Papaver somniferum

Widely used in Indian and Jewish cooking, poppy seeds have a nutty flavor and a crunchy texture and make a pleasant addition to curries, hot vegetable dishes and salads, and sprinkled over hot buttery pasta. They are also used as a topping for breads (p. 329) and as an ingredient in the famous Jewish poppy seed cake.

SAFFRON *Crocus sativus*

The world's most expensive spice, saffron has an aromatic flavor and will color pale ingredients (such as rice) soft yellow. Classically it is used in Paella (p. 243) and in Cornish saffron cake. Buy the dried stamens (rather than "powdered saffron" which is almost always a dye) and soak a few in a couple of tablespoons of boiling water for 15 minutes before use, then add to the dish, together with the soaking water.

STAR ANISE *Illicium verum*

This star-shaped fruit is a pod which contains shiny golden-brown seeds. It is added whole to casseroles and stir-fries and has a delicate aniseed flavor. It is used particularly in China, where it is believed to have a beneficial effect on the digestive system.

TAMARIND *Tamarindus indica*

The dried fruit of the tamarind tree, native to East Africa and known as "Indian dates" because of its sticky, fibrous appearance, tamarind can be added to curries and Indian dishes to give sharpness.

To use, soak a small piece in water until pulpy, then press through a sieve and use the liquid and pulp which come through.

TURMERIC *Curcuma longa*

Turmeric is a rhizome. It is sometimes available fresh, when it looks rather like fresh ginger, but it is normally bought dried, either whole or ground, when it is bright gold. Ground turmeric is useful for adding flavor and a vivid golden color to rice and vegetable dishes and is much used in Indian cooking. It is also used in some chutneys and pickles.

A traditional British use for turmeric is in piccalilli, a piquant pickle for serving with cold savory nut or lentil dishes. To make piccalilli, prepare 1 pound each of pickling onions, cucumber, cauliflower florets and runner beans, cutting them into bite-sized pieces. Put the vegetables into a large dish or onto a plastic tray, sprinkle with ¾ cup salt and leave for 24 hours. Meanwhile, put 5 cups white vinegar into a saucepan with 4 dried chilis, 4 cloves, 2 tablespoons dried ginger, bruised with a rolling pin, and ¾ cup granulated sugar. Heat gently until the sugar has dissolved, then bring to a boil. Remove from the heat, cool and strain. Rinse and drain the vegetables. Put ⅔ cup flour into a bowl with 2 tablespoons mustard powder, 1 tablespoon turmeric and 2 crushed garlic cloves. Add enough cooled vinegar to make a smooth paste. Bring the rest of the vinegar to a boil, add some of this to the flour mixture and stir, then add the flour mixture to the vinegar in the pan and stir well until thickened. Add the vegetables to the pan. Cook for 5 minutes. Spoon the mixture into warm, sterilized jars. Cover with vinegar-proof tops. Keep for 3 months before using. Makes 5–6 pounds.

VANILLA *Vanilla planifolia*

Vanilla pods are expensive, but they can be used over and over again. Break a vanilla pod in half and bury the pieces in a jar of superfine sugar to make a delicate vanilla-flavored sugar for using in ice cream, delicate fruit dishes and egg custards. Or simmer a whole pod in a sugar syrup or milk which you're going to use to make egg custard. The vanilla pod can later be extracted, rinsed in warm water, patted dry with a paper towel and left to dry on an airy shelf in the kitchen before storing in an airtight jar. A more extravagant use is to grind up the whole vanilla pod with cashew nuts, carob powder and honey to make rather superior healthy sweet treats (p. 344). Vanilla extract, made by extracting the vanilla flavoring from the pods with alcohol, is available but expensive. Cheaper vanilla essence contains a synthetic vanillin made from eugenol, which is found in clove oil.

Recipes

In choosing recipes for this section, I've aimed for a balance between traditional vegetarian basics, such as Nut Roast, Lentil Soup, Cheese Flan and Soufflé, and more contemporary dishes such as Warm Thai Noodle Salad, Roasted Cashew Nut Roulade with Wild Mushroom Filling, and Roasted Mediterranean Vegetables with Mozzarella and Basil. I have also borne in mind the dictates both of healthy eating and of the palate, which are not by any means always contradictory. However, some indulgences have crept in, like Profiteroles and Summer Fruit Meringue, as have some particularly health-conscious recipes, including Sugarless Dundee Cake and Reduced-Sugar Jam. None of the recipes are unduly difficult or time-consuming to make; I hope you will enjoy both making and eating them.

Soups

Thick, warming and filling, thin and elegant, or ice-cold and refreshing, soup is one of the most versatile dishes. It is also economical and quick and easy to make. Vegetarian soups are flavored with vegetable stocks, herbs, spices, and, for more intensity, miso (p. 133) or yeast extract (p. 232). Using homemade stock produces an excellent soup, but if you haven't any, don't let this deter you; use ordinary water and season carefully, for a delicate soup which lets the flavor of the vegetables sing out.

Making Stock for Soup

Many recipes for soup call for stock, and for vegetarians this of course means a vegetable stock. While some good vegetable stock powders and cubes are available, if you use these regularly, all your soups tend to have a similar flavor. On the other hand, homemade vegetable stock has a delicate flavor which varies from batch to batch and is easy to make.

Ⅴ ROASTED BUTTERNUT SQUASH SOUP Ⅴ WITH CARAMELIZED ONION RINGS

Butternut squash, with their firm, sweet, golden flesh, make a satisfying soup for chilly days. It is also delicious made with pumpkin. The vegetables can be roasted in advance, when the oven is on for something else, if this is more convenient.

SERVES 4

2 butternut squash
2–3 celery stalks
2 onions, peeled
2 tablespoons olive oil
3¾ cups Light Vegetable Stock (p. 129)
salt and freshly ground black pepper

1 Preheat the oven to 400°F.
2 Halve the squash and scoop out the seeds, then peel the squash and cut into 1-inch chunks. Cut the celery and one of the onions into rough chunks.
3 Put the prepared vegetables in a roasting pan, sprinkle with 1 tablespoon of the oil, then mix them with your hands to distribute the oil evenly. Roast the vegetables in the oven for about 45 minutes, until they are tender and lightly browned.
4 Purée the vegetables in a blender or food processor with some of the stock; if you want a very smooth soup, pass the purée through a strainer into a clean pan. Add the rest of the stock, season to taste and heat gently.
5 To make the garnish, cut the remaining onion into thin rings and fry in the remaining oil for 10–15 minutes, until brown and crisp.
6 Reheat the soup and check the seasoning. Serve in warmed bowls, topped with the onion rings

ⓥ CARROT AND GINGER SOUP ⓥ

A delicately flavored soup with a beautiful color.

SERVES 4

1 onion, peeled and chopped
2 tablespoons butter
1 pound carrots, scraped and sliced
½ pound potatoes, peeled and cut into
*   ½-inch dice*
1 teaspoon grated fresh ginger
salt and freshly ground black pepper
3¾ cups water
TO GARNISH (OPTIONAL)
4 tablespoons light cream

1 Fry the onion gently in the butter in a large saucepan for 5 minutes, then add the carrots, potatoes, grated ginger and a sprinkling of salt. Cover and cook for about 10 minutes, stirring from time to time.

2 Add the water and bring steadily to the boil, then simmer gently for about 15 minutes, until the vegetables are tender. Purée in a blender or food processor, then return the soup to the rinsed-out saucepan and thin with a little more water if necessary.

3 Reheat gently and season with salt and pepper. Serve in warmed individual bowls, each topped with a spoonful of cream, if liked.

Variations
CARROT, APPLE AND GINGER SOUP
Make as described, adding 1 pound peeled, cored and chopped dessert apples with the carrots, increasing the amount of water to 4⅓ cups and adding 3 tablespoons sherry with the water. Serves 4–6.

Variation
CARROT, LIME AND CORIANDER SOUP
Make as described but omit the ginger. Using a zester, remove the rind of 1 lime in long strips (or grate it finely). Flavor the puréed soup with the juice of the lime, adding it gradually until it is to your taste. Garnish the top with coriander leaves, coarsely crushed coriander seeds and the lime rind.

SPICED PARSNIP SOUP
Use parsnips instead of carrots and add 1 tablespoon curry powder to the onions when you sauté them. A swirl of light or nondairy cream is good on top of this version, and add some crisp croutons for extra flavor.

Light Vegetable Stock

Put an onion, a couple of garlic cloves, a celery stick, a carrot and a bouquet garni into a saucepan. Cover generously with water and bring to a boil. Simmer, half-covered, for about 1 hour, then strain.

Other vegetables and flavorings, such as leeks, thinly pared lemon rind and allspice berries, can be added. Peelings from well-scrubbed potatoes also give a particularly pleasant flavor to vegetable stock.

White Bean Soup with Scarlet Rouille (p. 135); Carrot, Lime and Coriander Soup; Roasted Butternut Squash Soup with Caramelized Onion Rings (p. 128)

TOMATO SOUP WITH BASIL

Made with fresh tomatoes and basil, this is one of the most
delicious soups, wonderful for supper in
the cool of a summer evening.

SERVES 4

Garnishes for Soup

□ Fresh parsley or chives, snipped,
on top of a bowl of soup, looks
attractive, tastes good and goes well
with most soups.

□ Snip fresh basil over tomato soup,
mint over pea soup, dill or fennel
over cucumber soup.

□ A swirl of cream or sour cream
looks good on a dark soup such as
ruby-red beet soup, or on carrot and
ginger soup, or chilled avocado
soup.

□ A few roughly chopped walnuts
or toasted slivered almonds or pine
nuts go well with creamy soups such
as cauliflower or Jerusalem
artichoke.

□ Whole-wheat croutons add a
pleasant crunch to vegetable soup.
Make these by frying ¼-inch dice of
whole-wheat bread in a little oil until
golden-brown and crisp all over;
drain on paper towels.

□ Top mushroom soup with a few
slices of fried mushroom, and
asparagus soup with one or two
asparagus tips, cooked at the
beginning of the soup-making
process and reserved.

1 onion, peeled and chopped
1 tablespoon butter or vegan margarine
2 medium potatoes, peeled and diced
1 pound tomatoes, peeled and sliced, or one
   14-ounce can tomatoes
1 quart Light Vegetable Stock (p. 129) or
   water
salt and freshly ground black pepper
TO GARNISH
basil sprigs

1 Sauté the onion in the butter or vegan
margarine in a large saucepan, covered,
for 5 minutes, without browning.
2 Add the potatoes, cover again and
cook gently for a further 5–10 minutes,
then add the tomatoes and cook for 4–5
minutes more. Stir from time to time
and do not allow the vegetables to
brown.
3 Add the stock or water, cover the pan
and leave the soup to simmer for 15–20
minutes, until the potatoes are tender.
4 Purée the soup in a blender or food
processor and if you want it really
smooth, sieve it to remove the tomato
seeds – this isn't essential. Reheat the
soup gently without boiling.
5 Serve in warmed bowls, garnished
with basil sprigs.

WATERCRESS SOUP

The all-time most popular soup in my family, and very quick and
easy to make. I like to add the watercress at the end of cooking, as
this gives the soup a better flavor and color. If you are using a
bunch of watercress with stems, separate the stems from the leafy
tops and cook the stems with the potatoes. Watercress soup, with
all its variations, is excellent served chilled, as well as hot.

SERVES 4

1 onion, peeled and chopped
1 tablespoon butter or vegan margarine
1½ pounds potatoes, peeled and diced
1 quart Light Vegetable Stock (p. 129) or
   water
1 bunch of watercress
salt and freshly ground black pepper
3–4 tablespoons heavy or nondairy cream,
   optional

1 Sauté the onion in the butter or vegan
margarine in a large saucepan, covered,
for 5 minutes, without browning.
2 Add the potatoes, cover again and
cook gently for 5–10 minutes more. Stir
from time to time and do not allow the
vegetables to brown.
3 Stir in the stock or water, cover the
pan and leave the soup to simmer for
about 20 minutes, until the potatoes are
tender.
4 Reserve 4 small watercress sprigs for
garnishing, then purée the soup in a blender or food processor with the rest of the
watercress. Season to taste with salt and
pepper, reheat without boiling and serve
in warmed bowls, each topped with a
swirl of cream and a watercress sprig.

Variations

LETTUCE SOUP

For this delicious summer variation, omit the watercress, and cook 1 pound chopped outside lettuce leaves along with the potatoes. Some fresh chopped mint or parsley stirred in at the end of cooking is pleasant, and a little light or nondairy cream swirled on top is even better.

SPINACH SOUP

Omit the watercress and cook 1 pound chopped spinach leaves with the potatoes. Flavor the soup with a little freshly grated nutmeg.

SORREL SOUP

A sharp, refreshing variation, made by substituting for the watercress 3 ounces chopped sorrel leaves, which are added with the potatoes. Season with plenty of salt, freshly ground black pepper and freshly grated nutmeg. A swirl of light, nondairy or sour cream on top of each bowl makes this soup extra good.

FRESH HERB SOUP

For this fragrant variation, purée the soup with a small bunch of herbs instead of the watercress. Parsley, tarragon and chives are particularly good.

Ⅴ GREEN PEA AND MINT SOUP Ⅴ

This soup is refreshing and quick to make. It's equally good served hot or chilled. Use frozen petits pois, if possible, for their delicious sweet flavor.

SERVES 4

1 onion, peeled and chopped
1 tablespoon olive oil
1/2 pound potatoes, peeled and cut into
   1/2- inch dice
1 pound frozen petits pois or peas
4–5 good sprigs of mint
3 3/4 cups water or Light Vegetable Stock
   (p. 129)
salt and freshly ground black pepper
1–2 tablespoons freshly squeezed lemon juice
TO GARNISH
chopped fresh mint
fresh or soured cream (optional)

1 Cook the onion in the oil in a large saucepan for 5 minutes, being careful not to brown it.

2 Add the potato, stir well, then cover and continue to cook gently for a further 5–10 minutes, again being careful not to brown the vegetables.

3 Add the peas, mint and water or light vegetable stock. Bring to the boil, then cover and simmer for 15–20 minutes, or until the vegetables are very tender.

4 Purée the soup in a blender or food processor, then transfer it to a clean saucepan. If you want a very smooth texture, pour it through a fine strainer.

5 Adjust the consistency with extra water if necessary. Season with salt, pepper and the lemon juice to taste. Reheat and serve with sprinkled chopped fresh mint and cream, if desired.

CELERY AND STILTON SOUP

SERVES 4–6

MENU

A Japanese Meal

Miso Soup with Bean Curd

Vegetable Tempura with Dipping Sauce
198
Sweet Vinegared Rice
241
Stir-fried Carrots with Watercress and Sesame Seeds
181

Tangerine and Lichee Fruit Salad
286

1 head celery
1 onion, peeled and chopped
1 tablespoon butter
1 quart Light Vegetable Stock (p. 129) or water
1 cup grated Stilton cheese
salt and freshly ground black pepper

1 Trim, wash and chop the celery, reserving a few of the leaves as a garnish.
2 Sauté the onion in the butter in a large saucepan, covered, for 5 minutes, without browning. Add the celery, cover again and cook gently for a further 5–10 minutes. Stir from time to time and do not allow the vegetables to brown.
3 Add the stock or water. Cover the pan and leave the soup to simmer for 30 minutes, until the celery is very tender.
4 Purée the soup, together with the cheese, in a blender or food processor, until smooth. Season to taste, return to the rinsed-out pan and reheat gently.
5 Serve the soup in warmed bowls and snip the reserved celery leaves on top.

Variations
CELERY AND CHESTNUT SOUP
For this vegan version, add ½ pound fresh peeled chestnuts (p. 233) or the drained contents of one 14-ounce can of chestnuts to the onion with the celery. Use 5 cups of stock or water for this variation.

CELERY AND PEAR SOUP WITH TARRAGON
Another vegan version which sounds strange but tastes good. Add 1 pound pears, peeled, cored and diced, with the celery. Use 5 cups stock or water. Snip some fresh tarragon on top of the soup before serving.

CAULIFLOWER SOUP WITH CHEDDAR CHEESE
Use a medium-large cauliflower instead of the celery, and grated Cheddar cheese instead of the Stilton. A few chopped walnuts make a pleasant garnish.

Ⓥ   FRENCH ONION SOUP   Ⓥ

This soup is very filling, and makes a good main course, followed by fruit or a light dessert.

SERVES 4–6

Dark Vegetable Stock

Wipe and chop ½ pound mushrooms, then put them into a saucepan with a sliced onion, a bouquet garni and 5 cups water. Bring to a boil, then cover and simmer gently for 1 hour. Cool, then leave overnight before straining. This makes just under 1 quart.

The water that vegetables have been cooked in makes good stock and contains useful nutrients. Strain it into a container, cool and keep in the fridge for 2–3 days.

2 pounds onions, peeled and thinly sliced
2 tablespoons oil
4 teaspoons sugar
salt and freshly ground black pepper
2 quarts Dark Vegetable Stock (left)
2 garlic cloves, crushed
a few drops of lemon juice
TO GARNISH
chopped parsley or chives

1 Sauté the onions in the oil in a large saucepan for 10 minutes until soft. Add the sugar and salt and pepper to taste and cook for a further 15–20 minutes, until the onions are a deep golden-brown, but don't let them burn.
2 Add the stock, garlic, and lemon juice. Bring the soup to a boil and let it simmer for about 10 minutes. Check the seasoning.
3 Serve the soup in warmed bowls, sprinkled with parsley or chives.

Variations
GOLDEN ONION SOUP
Make as described, adding 3 tablespoons sherry and 2–3 tablespoons Dijon mustard along with the stock.

FRENCH ONION SOUP GRATINÉE

Ladle the soup into a warmed heatproof tureen (or large casserole dish) or individual bowls for this non-vegan version.

Top with a slice of French bread sprinkled with about ¼ cup grated Gruyère or similar cheese per person. Place under a hot broiler until the cheese is melted and golden-brown.

MISO SOUP WITH BEAN CURD

This Japanese soup is light but sustaining and has a savory flavor. It is particularly good as part of a Japanese menu, perhaps followed by Vegetable Tempura with Dipping Sauce (p. 198) and Sweet Vinegared Rice (p. 241).

SERVES 4

½ pound firm bean curd (tofu, p. 108)
2 scallions, trimmed and finely chopped
1 quart Light Vegetable Stock (p. 129)
4 tablespoons miso (right)
1 teaspoon soy sauce

1 Cut the bean curd into 16 equal cubes and divide between warmed soup bowls. Divide the chopped scallions between the bowls too.

2 Heat the stock in a saucepan, then take out a little and blend with the miso, to soften it and give a creamy consistency. Tip this back into the saucepan with the rest of the stock.

3 Bring the soup almost to a boil, but do not let it boil, or valuable enzymes in the miso will be destroyed. Add the soy sauce, then pour the soup into the bowls on top of the bean curd and scallions. Serve immediately.

Variation
MISO SOUP WITH BEAN CURD AND WAKAME

This is made exactly as above, except that wakame seaweed (p. 81) is added to the bowls.

Soak 4 pieces of wakame in cold water for 10 minutes, then cut out the spine and any hard pieces and snip the wakame into rough pieces with kitchen scissors. Put into the bowls along with the bean curd and scallions. Serve the soup immediately.

Miso

Miso is a thick brown paste made by fermenting soybeans, barley or rice under pressure for up to 2 years, then adding a little salt. Miso is rich in nutrients, including protein and B vitamins. There are various types: light-colored miso has a more delicate flavor than darker ones, but they all have a deliciously savory taste and are useful in soups, casseroles, sauces and gravies. Miso should be added at the end of the cooking time to conserve the vitamins.

Miso Soup with Bean Curd; Vegetable Tempura with Dipping Sauce (p. 198); Sweet Vinegared Rice (p. 241)

LEEK AND POTATO SOUP

This makes a thick soup, a real meal in itself on a cold day. For a lighter result, add enough extra stock or water to give the consistency you want. For real luxury, add an extra spoonful or two of cream and top with some snipped chives.

SERVES 4–6

Main Course Soup

Some soups make warming and satisfying main courses, especially welcome for a winter lunch or Sunday supper around the fire. The thick bean and lentil soups, and those which contain cheese, such as Celery and Stilton (p. 132) and Cauliflower and Cheddar (p. 132), make a filling meal with just some warm crusty bread or rolls, or (especially with lentil soup) Garlic Bread (p. 137). I like French onion soup with a small side salad or some crudités; grated cheese is good on top of tomato soup or thick leek and potato soup, and for a really hearty meal, add tasty whole-wheat dumplings to vegetable soup.

Lentil Soup Ideas

Lentil soup lends itself to experimentation. Here are some ideas:

Fry 1–2 teaspoons curry powder with the onions when making the soup; purée the soup with 1 tablespoon coconut cream.

Fry an onion and some garlic, and perhaps a teaspoon of ground cumin, in a little butter or vegan margarine and add to the soup after puréeing.

Garnish with plenty of chopped parsley or some croutons made as described on p. 130 and tossed in a little curry powder or crushed garlic.

3 leeks, washed and sliced
1½ pounds potatoes, peeled and diced
2 tablespoons butter or vegan margarine
1 quart Light Vegetable Stock (p. 129) or water
3–4 tablespoons heavy cream or nondairy cream (optional)
salt and freshly ground black pepper
TO GARNISH (OPTIONAL)
chopped parsley

1 Sauté the leeks and potatoes very gently in the butter or vegan margarine in a large saucepan, covered, for 10 minutes, stirring often.
2 Cook gently, without browning, still covered, for a further 10 minutes, stirring from time to time to prevent the vegetables from sticking to the pan.

3 Add the stock or water, stir, then simmer for 5–10 minutes, until the vegetables are tender.
4 Purée in a blender or food processor, adding the cream if using. Season to taste with salt and pepper, stir, and serve in warmed bowls, sprinkled with a little chopped parsley if you like.

Variations
VICHYSSOISE

For this creamy, chilled version of Leek and Potato Soup, purée the mixture, adding 1¼ cups milk or soy milk and 1¼ cups light or nondairy cream. Sieve, then chill the soup. Season carefully with salt, pepper and grated nutmeg. Serve in chilled bowls, sprinkled with snipped chives. Serves 8.

GOLDEN LENTIL SOUP

A satisfying, comforting soup which makes an excellent cheap, filling main course with crusty whole-wheat rolls or garlic bread. If you have a pressure cooker, you can make it in about 10 minutes.

SERVES 4

1 large onion, peeled and chopped
1 tablespoon butter or vegan margarine
½ pound dried split red lentils
1 quart (generous) Light Vegetable Stock (p. 129) or water
1–2 teaspoons lemon juice
salt and freshly ground black pepper
TO DECORATE
lemon butterflies

1 Sauté the onion in the butter or vegan margarine in a saucepan or pressure cooker for 10 minutes, until it is soft but

has not browned.
2 Add the lentils and stir for 1–2 minutes, then add the stock or water. Bring to a boil, then half cover the pan and leave the soup to simmer gently for 20 minutes, until the lentils are very tender and pale-colored; or cook in a pressure cooker for 5 minutes.
3 Beat the soup with a spoon to break up the lentils and make it smoother, or purée in a blender or food processor. Add the lemon juice and salt and pepper to taste. Decorate with lemon butterflies to serve.

ROASTED HAZELNUT SOUP

SERVES 4

1 onion, peeled and chopped
2 tablespoons butter or vegan margarine
1 pound potatoes, peeled and diced
1 garlic clove, crushed
salt and freshly ground black pepper
1 quart Light Vegetable Stock (p. 129) or
    water
3/4 cup roasted, skinned hazelnuts
    (p. 36), finely ground
1 tablespoon lemon juice
TO GARNISH
a few chopped, roasted hazelnuts
chopped chives

1 Sauté the onion in the butter or vegan margarine for 5 minutes, until lightly browned, then add the potatoes, garlic and a little salt and pepper. Cook gently, covered, for a further 5–10 minutes.
2 Add the stock or water, bring to a boil, then leave to simmer gently for 15–20 minutes, until the potatoes and onion are tender. Purée the soup in a blender or food processor and stir in the ground hazelnuts, lemon juice and salt and pepper to taste.
3 Serve the soup in warmed bowls, each topped with a sprinkling of chopped hazelnuts and chives.

Variation
ALMOND SOUP
Use ground almonds instead of hazelnuts.

Dumplings for Soup

Put 1 1/3 cups plain whole-wheat flour into a mixing bowl with 1 1/2 teaspoons baking powder, 1/2 teaspoon salt and 5 tablespoons grated cold butter. Mix well. Dissolve 1 teaspoon yeast extract in 2 tablespoons water and add to the flour mixture, then add more water, just enough to make a soft dough. Form the mixture into 8 dumplings, then drop them into half a panful of gently simmering water and simmer for 20 minutes, until puffed up. Remove with a slotted spoon and serve them in a vegetable soup.

WHITE BEAN SOUP WITH SCARLET ROUILLE

Lima beans, cannellini beans and haricot beans are all suitable for
this soup, and you can use either canned or dried ones.

SERVES 4

1 onion, peeled and chopped
1 tablespoon olive oil
2 garlic cloves, crushed
2 × 15-ounce cans lima beans or cannellini
    beans, drained and liquid reserved, or 1
    cup dried beans, soaked in water for 8
    hours, then drained
salt and freshly ground black pepper
lemon juice, to taste
FOR THE ROUILLE
1 large red pepper, quartered
1/4 cup white breadcrumbs
1 tablespoon olive oil
1 dried red chili, crumbled

1 Fry the onion gently in the oil in a large saucepan for 10 minutes, then add the garlic and cook for a minute longer.
2 Add the drained canned or soaked beans and 1 quart water (if using canned beans, make the reserved liquid up to this quantity with water). Bring to a boil and simmer until the beans are very tender – about 20 minutes for canned beans or 1–1 1/2 hours for dried beans – adding more water if necessary.
3 Meanwhile, make the rouille. Place the pepper under a hot broiler until the skin has blistered and blackened in places, turning as necessary. Cool, then remove the skin and seeds. Purée in a blender or food processor with the breadcrumbs, oil, chili and seasoning to taste. The mixture should be the consistency of mayonnaise. Transfer to a small serving bowl.
4 Purée a cupful or two of the soup, then return it to the pan so you have a mixture of puréed soup and beans. Season and add lemon juice. Reheat gently, pour into warm bowls and serve with the rouille.

Left to right: Golden Lentil Soup (p. 134); Pistou; Roasted Hazelnut Soup (p. 135)

PISTOU

A wonderful filling vegetable soup from southern France. Serve it with crusty bread for a complete main course. If you're using dried beans, you need to soak and cook them first. You could also add a small handful of barley – put it in along with the haricot beans. This soup reheats well and tastes even better the next day.

SERVES 4

1 onion, peeled and chopped
2 tablespoons olive oil
2/3 cup dried navy or other white beans, soaked and cooked, or one 15-ounce can cannellini beans, drained
2 carrots, scraped and diced
2 potatoes, peeled and diced
3 leeks or small zucchini, washed and sliced
one 15-ounce can tomatoes
2 garlic cloves, crushed
1–2 tablespoons chopped fresh basil or 1 teaspoon dried basil
salt and freshly ground black pepper
1 quart Light Vegetable Stock (p. 129) or water
2 ounces thin pasta or pasta shapes

1 Sauté the onion in the oil in a large saucepan for 5 minutes, then add the drained beans, all the vegetables, the garlic, the dried basil, if used, and salt and pepper to taste, and cook for a further 5 minutes.

2 Add the stock or water, cover and simmer for 20–30 minutes, then add the pasta and cook for a further 10 minutes. If you're using fresh basil, add this now and check the seasoning. Serve the soup in warmed bowls.

Variations
VEGETABLE AND LENTIL SOUP
Use lentils instead of dried beans. Omit the pasta, or not, depending on how hearty you want the soup to be.

SIMPLE VEGETABLE SOUP
For this lighter version (which makes a good basis for dumplings, p. 135) make as described, but omit the navy or cannellini beans and pasta.

MIXED MUSHROOM SOUP

While this is a great way to make the most of a smallish quantity of freshly gathered wild mushrooms, if you are lucky enough to have some, it's also good made with ordinary open-cap cultivated mushrooms.

SERVES 4–6

3 tablespoons butter or vegan margarine
1 onion, peeled and chopped
1 pound potatoes, peeled and cut into ½-inch dice
3¾ cups water or Light Vegetable Stock (p. 129)
1 pound mixed mushrooms, washed and sliced
salt and freshly ground black pepper

1 Melt half the butter or margarine in a large saucepan, put in the onions and cook them gently, with a lid on the pan, for 5 minutes.
2 Add the potatoes, stir, cover and cook for 5 minutes more; then add the water or light vegetable stock. Bring to a boil. Cover and cook over a gentle heat for about 15–20 minutes, or until the potatoes are tender.
3 Meanwhile heat the rest of the butter in another pan, put in the mushrooms and cook, uncovered, for about 5 minutes, until tender. Don't worry if the mushrooms make some liquid.
4 Purée the potato mixture in a blender or food processor, then return it to the saucepan. Add the mushrooms and any liquid they have produced. Season to taste, reheat gently and serve.

Garlic Bread

Crisp, hot garlic bread goes well with many soups and also with salads, and it's easy to make. Slice a loaf of French or Italian bread at 1-inch intervals, cutting almost through so that the slices are still joined at the base. Beat 2–3 crushed garlic cloves into ¼ pound softened butter or vegan margarine and spread this on both sides of the slices of bread. Push the slices together to re-form the loaf, then wrap it in foil. Place on a baking tray and bake for about 20 minutes at 400°F, until the bread has heated through and the butter has melted. Serve immediately.

CREAMY WHITE POTATO SOUP WITH ONION

Like most of my soups, this soup is thickened entirely with puréed potato; the result is very soothing and creamy.

SERVES 4–6

4 onions, peeled and sliced
1 pound potatoes, peeled and cut into even-sized pieces
3¾ cups water
3 tablespoons butter or vegan margarine
1 tablespoon olive oil
salt and freshly ground black pepper
grated nutmeg

1 Put a quarter of the onions into a large saucepan with the potatoes and water. Bring to the boil, then cover and cook until the potatoes are completely tender – about 15–20 minutes.
2 Meanwhile melt the butter and oil in another pan, put in the remaining sliced onions and cook them gently, with a lid on the pan, until the onions are very tender: about 15 minutes. Do not let them brown.
3 Purée the potato mixture in a blender or food processor, then return it to the saucepan. Add the onions and salt, pepper and grated nutmeg to taste. Reheat gently and serve.

Variation
CREAMY ASPARAGUS SOUP
Proceed as above to the end of step 1. Replace the three remaining onions with a bunch of asparagus: trim and steam until tender; chop. Purée the soup with the butter and oil, add the asparagus and season.

V   ICED BEET SOUP   V

WITH DILL

*Although it's wonderful cold, this soup is also very good served
hot. Use cooked beets without vinegar (see p. 67 for cooking
beets). Serve with hot Herb and Onion Bread (p. 328).*

SERVES 4–6

1 onion, peeled and chopped
1 tablespoon oil
½ pound potatoes, peeled and diced
3–4 medium beets, cooked, peeled and diced
*5 cups Light Vegetable Stock (p. 129) or
    water*
grated rind of ½ lemon
1 tablespoon lemon juice
salt and freshly ground black pepper
TO GARNISH
3 tablespoons light or nondairy cream
dill sprigs

1 Sauté the onion in the oil in a large
saucepan, covered, for 5 minutes, without browning. Add the potatoes, cover
again and cook gently for a further 5–10
minutes.
2 Add the beets and stock or water.
Bring to a boil, then cover the pan and
leave the soup to simmer for about 20
minutes, until the potatoes are tender.
3 Purée the soup in a blender or food
processor, then add the lemon rind and
juice, and salt and pepper to taste. Allow
to cool, then pour into a bowl, cover and
chill until ice-cold.
4 Serve the soup in chilled bowls, each
topped with a swirl of cream and a small
sprig of dill.

Serving Chilled Soup

For a dramatic presentation, ideal for
a special summer dinner, stand each
bowl of chilled soup in an outer
bowl of crushed ice.

V   CHILLED AVOCADO SOUP WITH   V

TOMATO AND CORIANDER SALSA

SERVES 6

2 large ripe avocado pears
1 small onion, peeled and roughly chopped
1 garlic clove, crushed
2 tablespoons lemon juice
*3¾ cups Light Vegetable Stock (p. 129) or
    water*
1 tablespoon red wine vinegar
salt and freshly ground black pepper
FOR THE SALSA
½ purple onion, finely chopped
2 tomatoes, deseeded and chopped
1 green chili, deseeded and finely sliced
1 tablespoon chopped fresh coriander
1 tablespoon wine vinegar
salt and freshly ground black pepper

1 Halve the avocado pears, remove the
pits and skin. Cut the flesh into chunks
and purée in a blender or food processor
with the onion, garlic, lemon juice and a
third of the stock or water.
2 Add the rest of the stock or water and
blend again until very smooth.
3 Add the vinegar and season to taste,
then pour into a bowl and cover. Allow
to cool, then chill.
 4 Check the seasoning, then serve in
chilled bowls, garnished with the salsa,
made by combining together all the salsa
ingredients.

Variation
WITH TOMATO AND CHILI SALSA
For an attractive garnish, top the soup
with a salsa made by combining ½ finely
chopped red onion, 2 de-seeded and
finely chopped tomatoes, 1 de-seeded
and finely sliced green chili, 1 tablespoon
of wine vinegar and salt and pepper to
taste.

Iced Yellow Pepper Soup with Basil; Chilled Avocado Soup with Tomato and Coriander Salsa (p. 138)

Ⅴ ICED YELLOW PEPPER SOUP WITH BASIL

Yellow peppers make a smooth, sweet soup which is excellent served icy cold.

SERVES 4

1 onion, peeled and chopped
1 tablespoon olive oil
4 yellow peppers, de-seeded and cut into ½-inch squares
2 garlic cloves, crushed
½ pound potatoes, peeled and cut into ½-inch dice
3¾ cups water or Light Vegetable Stock (p. 129)
juice of ½ lemon
salt and freshly ground black pepper
TO GARNISH
finely chopped basil
strips of broiled yellow pepper (p. 145)

1 Cook the onion in the oil in a large pan for 5 minutes, being careful not to let it brown. Add the peppers, garlic and potatoes, then cover and cook gently without browning for 5–10 minutes.

2 Add the water or stock and bring to the boil. Cover the pan and simmer for about 15–20 minutes, until the vegetables are very tender.

3 Purée the soup in a blender or food processor, adjusting the consistency with extra water or stock if necessary.

4 Add the lemon juice, a tablespoonful at a time, and salt and pepper to taste. Chill until needed, then serve garnished with the chopped basil and broiled pepper strips.

Variation

ICED RED PEPPER SOUP WITH THYME

For an equally good variation, use red peppers instead of yellow ones and garnish with coarsely crushed black pepper and fresh thyme.

First-Course Dishes

First courses are rewarding to make because they can be perfect little works of art, with plenty of scope for imaginative use of color, flavorings and garnishes. This chapter contains a range of possibilities for both first courses and snacks. You'll also find recipes in other sections (particularly Salads (pp. 154–169), Accompanying Vegetables (pp. 180–191), Main Vegetable Dishes (pp. 192–203), and Pasta (pp. 250–259) which, served in small portions, make equally tempting first courses. Similarly, many of the first courses in this section make good light main courses, if served with suitable accompaniments such as warm bread or rolls.

LINING A LOAF PAN

Line the pan with a long strip of greased aluminum foil to cover the base and extend up the narrow sides

THREE-LAYERED OMELETTE

This is easy to make and looks very effective, either sliced into bite-sized pieces as an appetizer, or into larger pieces and served with a sauce as a first course. It can be made in advance.

SERVES 6–8 AS A FIRST COURSE, 12 AS AN APPETIZER

1 tomato, peeled and chopped
1 small red pepper, deseeded and chopped
4 tablespoons butter
2 cups wiped and finely chopped mushrooms
½ pound frozen chopped spinach, thawed
6 eggs
salt and freshly ground black pepper

1 Sauté the tomato and pepper gently in 1 tablespoon of the butter in a small saucepan for about 5 minutes, until tender, then purée in a blender or food processor.
2 Sauté the mushrooms in another 1 tablespoon of the butter for 2–3 minutes.
3 Squeeze excess water out of the spinach.
4 Have three bowls ready and break 2 eggs into each. Beat, then add the spinach to one, the mushrooms to another, and the red pepper mixture to the third. Season to taste with salt and pepper.
5 Melt one-third of the remaining butter in a small frying pan (p. 25). When hot, pour in the spinach-flavored mixture.
6 Cook until it's set on the bottom, then reduce the heat, cover and cook until the top is set – about 5 minutes.
7 Lift the omelette out with a spatula and put it onto a plate, moist side up.
8 Make an omelette with the red pepper mixture in the same way. Turn out on top of the spinach omelette, moist side down.
9 Repeat with the mushroom mixture, then press down lightly all over and leave to cool completely – about 1 hour.
10 Cut the omelette into bite-sized or larger slices and place them sideways on a plate to show off the colored stripes.

Ⅴ VEGETABLE TERRINE Ⅴ

This pretty terrine is easier to make than it looks

SERVES 6

butter for greasing
6 ounces even-sized young carrots, trimmed
6 ounces fine green beans, topped and tailed
6 ounces broccoli florets, stems trimmed
2 large red peppers, halved
¼ pound cream cheese

¼ cup milk
4 eggs
¼ cup finely grated Parmesan cheese
salt and freshly ground black pepper
FOR THE SAUCE
1 tablespoon olive oil
1 small onion, peeled and chopped
¼ pound potato, peeled and diced
½ pound carrots, scraped and sliced
1¼ cups water
freshly grated nutmeg
TO GARNISH
sprigs of chervil or dill

1 Preheat the oven to 300°F.

2 Line a deep 1-pound loaf pan with a long strip of parchment paper to cover the base and short sides, then grease the long sides with butter.

3 Half-fill a large saucepan with water and bring to the boil. Add the young carrots and boil for 10–15 minutes or until tender. Remove with a slotted spoon and cool quickly in a colander under cold running water. Leave to drain. Repeat this process with the beans and the broccoli, using the same water but cooking them for 3–4 minutes only. Keep the cooked vegetables separate.

4 Place the peppers under a hot broiler for about 10 minutes, until the skin has blistered and charred in places. Cool, then remove the skin, seeds and stems.

5 Beat together the cream cheese and milk, then add the eggs and beat well. Stir in the Parmesan cheese and season with salt and pepper.

6 Spread 3–4 tablespoons of the cheese mixture over the base of the loaf pan, just to cover it. Put in the broccoli florets, arranging them with heads down. Spoon over some cheese mixture, then cover with a layer of red pepper, trimming the pieces to fit.

7 Top with more of the cheese mixture, then follow with layers of carrot, more red pepper, and green beans, adding some of the cheese mixture between each layer of vegetables. Finish with a layer of cheese mixture.

8 Put the loaf pan into a roasting pan and pour boiling water around it, then bake, uncovered, for 1 hour or until it feels firm to the touch and a skewer inserted in the center comes out clean.

9 While the terrine is baking, make the sauce. Heat the oil in a medium saucepan and add the onion, potato and carrots. Cover and cook gently, without browning, for 10 minutes. Add the water and simmer for 10–15 minutes, until the vegetables are completely tender.

10 Blend the sauce to a smooth purée in a blender or food processor and thin with more water if necessary. Season with salt, pepper and grated nutmeg.

11 The terrine can be served hot or cold. Spoon a pool of sauce on to individual serving plates. Turn out the terrine and slice it carefully, to keep the layers intact, then place on top of the sauce. Garnish each portion with chervil or dill.

Vegetable Terrine; Spring Rolls with Dipping Sauce (p. 143)

SUSHI

Creamy-colored rice with a deep purple wrapping of nori makes piquant, intriguing-looking morsels to have with drinks, or they can be served as part of a Japanese meal. Serve them arranged around the dipping sauce, on a small tray or flat plate.

MAKES ABOUT 20

Umeboshi Plums

A popular ingredient in Japanese and macrobiotic cooking, umeboshi plums are plums that have been pickled for at least two years. During this time they develop lactic acid, which makes them a particularly healthy ingredient, cleansing the gut and aiding digestion. They have a sharp, pungent, salty flavor and can be added to dishes – particularly grain dishes – or served alongside.

MAKING SUSHI

1 Lay the nori on a raffia mat, place the filling on top

2 Roll up, using the mat to help make a good shape

3 Cut into ½-inch slices and place on a serving plate

Sushi; Three- Layered Omelette (p. 140)

2 sheets of nori (p. 81)
½ quantity Sweet Vinegared Rice (p. 241)
½ cup cooked spinach, fresh or frozen, drained and chopped
1 umeboshi plum (left), pit removed, flesh chopped
FOR THE DIP
2 teaspoons Dijon mustard
6 tablespoons shoyu (p. 184)
TO GARNISH
radish flowers (p. 164)

1 Toast the nori sheets on both sides by holding them above a gas flame or electric hot plate until they become crisp.
2 Put one of the nori sheets on a Japanese mat or double layer of paper towels and spread with half the rice, taking it to within ½ inch of the top of the nori. Place the spinach on top of the rice in a horizontal strip about ½ inch from the bottom of the nori.

3 Starting from the bottom, carefully roll up the nori so that the spinach is enclosed and the rice and nori rolled around like a jelly roll.
4 Press the roll firmly together and bang each end on the work surface to firm them up. Leave the roll for 20 minutes (or longer) to settle.
5 Using a sharp knife, carefully cut the roll crossways into ½-inch slices.
6 Repeat the process with the second piece of nori and the rest of the rice, using the chopped umeboshi plum instead of the spinach.
7 To make the dip, put the mustard into a bowl and gradually blend in the shoyu, to give a smooth consistency. Put the mixture into a small bowl, place in the center of a small tray or large plate and arrange the sushi around, alternating the 2 types of filling. Garnish with a radish flower.

CHEESE AND FRESH HERB DIP

This is a simple dip which is popular with children. We sometimes eat it with crudités (right) for a weekend lunch, with perhaps a vegetable soup as a first course.

SERVES 4

3 tablespoons butter, softened
1¼ cups vegetarian Cheddar cheese, grated
6 tablespoons milk
3–4 drops Tabasco sauce
salt and freshly ground black pepper
1 tablespoon chopped fresh herbs, such as chives, chervil or parsley
TO GARNISH
1 chervil sprig

1 Cream the butter, then gradually add the cheese and milk, beating until smooth and soft; or blend in a blender or food processor.
2 Add the Tabasco sauce and salt and pepper to taste. Stir in the chopped fresh herbs and mix well. Transfer the dip to a small bowl, smooth the surface slightly with a fork or the back of a spoon and serve, garnished with chervil.

Cheese and Fresh Herb Dip

Ⅴ SPRING ROLLS WITH DIPPING SAUCE Ⅴ

MAKES 12

1 onion, peeled and chopped
6 ounces carrots, coarsely grated
1 green pepper, de-seeded and sliced
1 tablespoon olive oil
2 garlic cloves, crushed
1 green chili, de-seeded and finely sliced
6 ounces beansprouts
1 tablespoon soy sauce
salt and freshly ground black pepper
12 sheets phyllo pastry
oil for deep-frying
FOR THE DIPPING SAUCE
½ small onion, finely chopped
2 tablespoons soy sauce
2 teaspoons rice vinegar or 2 teaspoons wine vinegar and 2 teaspoons water
2 teaspoons superfine sugar
2 teaspoons sesame oil

1 Fry the onion, carrots and green pepper in the oil for about 7 minutes, until almost soft, then add the garlic, chili and beansprouts and fry for a further 2–3 minutes, until the vegetables are cooked.
2 Add the soy sauce and season with salt and pepper. Leave to cool.
3 Make the dipping sauce by mixing all ingredients together. Put into a small bowl.
4 Fold a sheet of phyllo pastry in half lengthwise. Place a good heap of the mixture just inside one corner, fold in the sides and roll up to make a neat parcel.
5 Half-fill a saucepan or deep-fat fryer with oil. Heat until the oil is hot enough to form bubbles around the tip of a wooden chopstick or the handle of a wooden spoon.
6 Deep-fry the spring rolls a few at a time until they are golden brown and crisp all over – about 3–4 minutes. Drain on paper towels and keep warm while you fry the remaining spring rolls.
7 Alternatively, preheat the oven to 400°F. Place the spring rolls on a baking sheet brushed with olive oil. Brush the rolls lightly with olive oil and bake for about 30 minutes, turning them over after about 20 minutes so that both sides become crisp.
8 Serve with the dipping sauce.

Crudités

Crudités are popular with most people. Served with a piquant dip, they make a refreshing and easy-going starter, and are useful for serving with drinks. Choose really crisp, fresh vegetables in contrasting colors and flavors. Have at least three different types, arranged in little heaps on a leaf-lined plate or tray, or heap them up in a small basket with the dips arranged around the outside. The basic preparation of the vegetables can be done several hours in advance and the vegetables kept in a plastic bag in the salad compartment of the refrigerator until needed, but it is best to cut vegetables into matchsticks just before you want to serve them. Some possibilities are:
☐ Ruby-red radishes, with the root trimmed but the leaves left on
☐ Scallions, trimmed
☐ Matchsticks of scraped carrot
☐ Matchsticks of crisp celery
☐ Matchsticks of red, green or yellow pepper, or cucumber
☐ Sprigs of cauliflower – especially good for scooping up dips
☐ Crisp endive leaves
☐ Large juicy black olives
☐ Cherry tomatoes
☐ Baby button mushrooms

BRANDADE OF LIMA BEANS WITH BLACK OLIVE PURÉE

V   V

A brandade, or posh purée, makes a tasty first course and can be varied with different accompaniments. It's also a very quick and easy dish to make.

SERVES 4

1 tablespoon olive oil
1 onion, peeled and chopped
1 garlic clove, crushed
15-ounce can lima beans, drained
2 tablespoons light cream or soy cream
1 tablespoon lemon juice
salt and freshly ground black pepper
TO SERVE
1 bibb lettuce
olive oil
4 teaspoons black olive paté
4 slices of lemon
crostini (p. 332), rubbed with a cut clove of garlic

1 Heat the oil in a medium saucepan, add the onion and garlic, cover and cook for 10 minutes, until soft but not browned.
2 Remove from the heat and put into a blender with the drained beans, light or soy cream and lemon juice. Blend to a purée. Return the mixture to the pan, season with salt and pepper.
3 Divide the crisp lettuce leaves between four serving plates. Just before serving, reheat the lima bean brandade. Divide between the four plates. Top the brandade with a spoonful of black olive paté, a drizzle of olive oil and a slice of lemon. Serve at once, with the garlic crostini.

ASPARAGUS WITH ORANGE VINAIGRETTE

V   V

SERVES 4

1½ pounds asparagus
1 orange
2 tablespoons lemon juice
4 tablespoons olive oil
salt
TO GARNISH
dill sprigs

1 First prepare the asparagus. Remove any tough ends by bending the stalks near the base; they will snap off at the point where they become too tough to eat. Wash the asparagus well: sometimes the heads can be slightly gritty.
2 Finely grate half the orange rind and pare the rest into long strips with a zester or by peeling it off thinly with a knife, then cutting it into fine shreds. Cut the remaining skin and pith from the orange and slice the flesh.

3 Put the grated orange rind into a jar or bowl with the lemon juice, oil and some salt and pepper to taste and shake or whisk to combine.
4 Next, cook the asparagus. Bring ½ inch water to the boil in a saucepan and add the asparagus. If you use a fairly tall, narrow pan and can stand the asparagus in it with the stalks in the water and the heads above, so much the better, because the stalks, which take a little longer to cook, can boil while the heads cook in the steam – but this isn't essential if you cook the asparagus quickly. It should be only just *al dente*.
5 Drain the asparagus and put it on to a serving plate or plates. Give the dressing another shake or whisk and pour it over the asparagus. Garnish with sprigs of dill, the pared orange zest and orange slices.

Broiled Peppers; Asparagus with Orange Vinaigrette (p. 144)

BROILED PEPPERS

Broiled pepper halves make a very good first course and the filling provides plenty of opportunities for experiment. Possibilities include fried mushrooms, cubes of ripe avocado, artichoke hearts, and feta cheese with purple onion rings.

SERVES 4

2 medium red peppers
2 medium yellow peppers
1 pound zucchini, quite thinly sliced
2 tablespoons olive oil
1 pound cherry tomatoes, halved
2 garlic cloves, crushed
salt and freshly ground black pepper
TO GARNISH
sprigs of basil

1 Halve the peppers, cutting right through the stem so that half of it remains intact on each pepper half. Trim away the core and seeds carefully.

2 Place the pepper halves shiny-side up under a hot broiler and cook for 10–15 minutes, until tender and charred in places. Remove and leave to one side.

3 Sprinkle the zucchini with the olive oil and turn them with your fingers so that they are evenly coated. Broil for 5–10 minutes, until browned and tender.

4 Transfer the zucchini to a bowl and put the tomatoes under the broiler for about 5 minutes, until tender and charred in places. Add to the zucchini. You can remove the skins or leave them on.

5 Add the garlic and salt and pepper to the zucchini and tomatoes. Mix gently, then spoon the mixture into the pepper halves. Serve warm or at room temperature, one yellow and one red pepper half on each plate, garnished with the sprigs of basil.

Eggplant Dip Ideas

Eggplant dip has a delicate flavor which can be intensified in various ways.

Try adding a tablespoon of tahini to the dip before puréeing; garnish with toasted sesame seeds.

For a smoky, "mock caviar" version, grill the eggplant for 20–30 minutes until charred all over. Scrape off the charred skin, rinse the eggplant, then continue as described in the recipe.

Ⅴ   FAVA BEAN DIP WITH MINT   Ⅴ

SERVES 4–6

Serving Dips

Serve small quantities of 3 or more contrasting dips, say vivid green Fava Bean Dip with Mint (right), Mushroom Pâté with Porcini (right), Tapenade (below) and Cheese and Fresh Herb Dip (p. 143), on individual plates, or in bowls on a wicker tray, surrounded by an equally colorful selection of crudités and some big juicy black olives and lemon wedges.

Any of these dips make excellent fillings or toppings for peeled and hollowed-out tomatoes, lightly fried mushroom caps (with the stalks removed) or artichoke hearts. A selection of quickly made (or bought) dips, together with a couple of different cheeses, a basket of warm assorted rolls and a simple fresh crisp salad – say lettuce, tomato wedges, cucumber and onion rings – with fresh fruit to follow, and good coffee, makes a delicious spur-of-the-moment lunch or picnic.

1 pound shelled fava beans
leaves from 6–8 sprigs of mint
2 tablespoons lemon juice
3–4 tablespoons olive oil
salt and freshly ground black pepper
TO GARNISH
sprigs of mint

1 Cook the fava beans in boiling water for about 5 minutes, until just tender, then drain, saving the liquid.
2 Put the beans into a blender or food processor with the mint, lemon juice and oil and blend to a purée, adding enough reserved cooking liquid to make a soft consistency. Season with salt and pepper.
3 Spoon the mixture into a small bowl or heap it up in the center of a serving plate and surround with crudités. Garnish with mint sprigs.

Ⅴ   MUSHROOM PÂTÉ WITH PORCINI   Ⅴ

SERVES 4–6

½-ounce package of dried porcini mushrooms
4 tablespoons butter or vegan margarine
1 small onion, finely chopped
1 garlic clove, crushed
1½ pounds mushrooms, washed and sliced
2 tablespoons Madeira, brandy or sherry
salt and freshly ground black pepper

1 Put the porcini into a cup and cover with 2–3 tablespoons boiling water. Leave for 10–15 minutes, then drain and chop, reserving the liquid.
2 Heat the butter or margarine in a large saucepan, add the onion and garlic and cook gently, covered, for 5 minutes.
3 Add the mushrooms to the pan along with the chopped porcini and their liquid and cook, uncovered, for 10–15 minutes.
4 Add the Madeira; cook for a minute.
5 Coarsely chop the mixture in a food processor – don't let it get too fine. Season, then transfer to a serving bowl and leave to cool. Serve cold but not straight from the refrigerator. Alternatively, pack the pâté into a 1-pound loaf pan or individual ramekins; turn out to serve.

Tapenade

This vegetarian version of the classic Provencale dip (which usually includes anchovies) is excellent with crudités, on crackers or as a topping for baked potatoes or hard-boiled eggs.

Put 4 ounces pitted black olives, 1 ounce drained capers, 1 peeled clove of garlic and 1 crumbled dried red chili into a food processor and blend to a coarse purée. Add 4 tablespoons olive oil and blend again until the oil has mixed in with the other ingredients. Season with salt and pepper and spoon into a small bowl. Serve at room temperature.

Ⅴ   MUSHROOM AND HERB TERRINE   Ⅴ

SERVES 6

1½ pounds button mushrooms, washed
4 tablespoons butter or vegan margarine
1 tablespoon chopped fresh herbs, such as
    chives, parsley or chervil
salt and freshly ground black pepper
TO GARNISH
rosemary sprigs
tiny lemon wedges

1 Remove one or two perfect mushrooms and slice; set aside for garnishing. Grate the rest of the mushrooms in a food processor, or finely chop them by hand.
2 Heat the butter or margarine in a large saucepan and quickly sauté the sliced mushrooms for about 2 minutes; set aside.
3 Sauté the rest of the mushrooms over moderate heat for about 15 minutes, until all the liquid has evaporated. Add the herbs and salt and pepper to taste.
4 Press into an oiled and base-lined 1-pound loaf pan, cover with wax paper, top with a weight and leave until completely cold. Turn out and cut carefully into slices. Garnish with the reserved mushroom slices, rosemary and lemon wedges.

EGGPLANT, TOMATO AND MOZZARELLA TERRINE

This terrine is made by layering ingredients in a loaf pan, then weighing them down so they hold together. It looks impressive but is quite easy to do and makes an excellent appetizer or light main course.

SERVES 8

2 tablespoons olive oil
1 medium eggplant about ¾ pound, cut lengthwise into slices not more than ¼ inch thick
1½ pound beefsteak tomatoes
½ pound fresh mozzarella cheese
salt and freshly ground black pepper
1 basil plant
FOR THE DRESSING
2 tablespoons balsamic or red wine vinegar
6 tablespoons olive oil

1 Line a 1-pound loaf pan with a strip of parchment paper to cover the base and extend up the short sides. Brush with a little of the olive oil.

2 Brush the eggplant slices on both sides with the remaining olive oil, then broil until golden brown and tender, turning over half-way through. Cool.

3 To peel the tomatoes, cover them with boiling water and leave for 10 seconds, then test to see if the skins will split and come off easily. If not, leave them a little longer; otherwise, drain them and slip off the skins. Quarter, de-seed and slice.

4 Drain the mozzarella cheese, pat dry with paper towels and cut it as thinly as you can to make enough slices for 2 layers.

5 Cover the base of the loaf pan with a single layer of eggplant slices and sprinkle with salt and pepper. Next add a layer of mozzarella slices, then a layer of tomato slices and finally one of basil leaves. Repeat the layers, ending with a final layer of eggplant (to make 3 layers of eggplant and 2 of everything else).

6 Cover the pan with a thick pile of paper towels, put a weight on top and leave it in the refrigerator until ready to serve – the longer you can leave it, the easier it will be to slice. Meanwhile, make the dressing by putting the vinegar and oil in a

small screw-top jar with some seasoning and shaking until combined.

7 Remove the kitchen paper and turn the terrine out on to a board. Cut it into slices, using a sharp knife and a sawing movement. Put a slice of terrine on each plate and spoon a little of the dressing at the side.

Eggplant, Tomato and Mozzarella Terrine; Fava Bean Dip with Mint (p. 146); Mushroom Pâté with Porcini (p. 146)

Vegan Variation
VEGETABLE TERRINE
This version does not need baking in the oven. Return the vegetable purées to separate saucepans with ¼ cup of the cooking liquid, bring to a boil and sprinkle ½ teaspoon agar-agar powder over each, mixing well. Boil for 1 minute. Spoon the mixtures into the pan in layers as described, then leave to cool and set.

Ⓥ AVOCADO ON A RASPBERRY COULIS Ⓥ

This pretty, summery first course is simple to make but needs assembling at the last minute so that the avocados do not discolor.

SERVES 4

HALVING AN AVOCADO

1 Using a stainless steel knife, cut the avocado lengthways, cutting as far in as the large central pit

2 Holding the avocado in both hands, twist the two cut halves in opposite directions to part them

3 Ease out the pit, using your fingers or a knife point

4 Take off the skin with the help of a sharp knife. Sometimes this strips off easily, at other times you may have to peel it off thinly with the knife

1 quantity Raspberry Coulis (p. 300)
2 tablespoons raspberry or wine vinegar
¼ cup olive oil
salt and freshly ground black pepper
2 ripe avocados
TO GARNISH
thyme sprigs
a few pink peppercorns (optional)

1 Make a vinaigrette by mixing together the Raspberry Coulis, vinegar and oil. Season to taste with salt and pepper.
2 Pour a pool of this coulis onto 4 individual serving plates.
3 Halve the avocados and carefully remove the skin and pits. Place half an avocado cut side down on a palette knife, then cut it across into fairly thin slices.
4 Slide the sliced avocado off the palette knife into the center of the plate on top of the Raspberry Coulis, so that the avocado half keeps its shape.
5 Repeat this process with all the avocado halves. Garnish with thyme sprigs and a scattering of pink peppercorns. Serve immediately.

Variation
AVOCADO ON TWO PEPPER SAUCES
Make two sauces as described on p. 172, using a large green and a large yellow pepper. Add 1 tablespoon olive oil to each, with wine vinegar to taste. Cool, then put the sauces into two containers. Holding one container in each hand, pour from them both at once onto the serving plates, to create a 2-color effect. Arrange each avocado half on the plate where the 2 sauces meet.

Ⓥ PEARS WITH PIQUANT CREAM DRESSING Ⓥ

The pears for this recipe need to be perfectly ripe, so that they slice like butter. If they are a bit on the hard side when you buy them, they will ripen up if left in a fruit bowl for a day or two.

SERVES 4

½ cup (generous) whipping or nondairy cream
¼ cup plain or vegan yogurt
1–2 teaspoons tarragon or wine vinegar
a little sugar
salt and freshly ground black pepper
2 Comice pears
lemon juice
TO GARNISH
pink peppercorns
6 tarragon sprigs
TO SERVE
tender lettuce leaves

1 Beat the whipping or nondairy cream until thick, then add the yogurt and 1 teaspoon of the vinegar and beat again.
2 Add a little sugar, salt and pepper to taste, and the remaining teaspoon of vinegar if you wish.
3 Give the mixture a final beating, so that it holds its shape.
4 Halve the pears, then carefully remove the cores and peel. Brush the pears all over with lemon juice.
5 Put a lettuce leaf on each serving plate, then place a pear half on top, cut side down. Spoon the piquant cream mixture on top and garnish each with a few pink peppercorns and a tarragon sprig. Serve immediately.

Variations

CUCUMBER WITH PIQUANT
CREAM

For this delicious version, replace the pear with 1 cucumber, peeled and thinly sliced. Place the cucumber slices in a colander, sprinkle with salt and leave for 30 minutes, then rinse and drain well. Sprinkle with sugar, wine vinegar and salt (if necessary). Divide the cucumber between the serving plates just before serving. Top with the cream and garnish.

PEARS WITH ROQUEFORT
CREAM

Use the Blue Cheese Dressing (p. 154), instead of the piquant cream for an excellent (but non-vegan) version.

SLICING AN AVOCADO

1 Put the skinned avocado half on a palette knife and slice

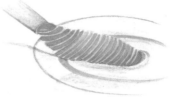

2 Lift the slices on the knife and slide onto a plate

[V] *Linguine with Tomatoes, Basil and Cream*

[V] [V]

LINGUINE WITH
TOMATOES, BASIL AND CREAM

A delicious and easy first course, excellent before a main course of summer vegetables.

SERVES 4

½ pound green linguine
1 bunch scallions, trimmed and chopped
2 tablespoons butter or vegan margarine
1 pound firm tomatoes, peeled, deseeded and chopped
generous ½ cup light or nondairy cream
salt and freshly ground black pepper
TO GARNISH
1–2 tablespoons chopped fresh basil

1 Cook the linguine in a large pot as described on p. 50, until *al dente*. Drain the pasta in a colander immediately.

2 Meanwhile sauté the scallions gently in the butter or vegan margarine in a large saucepan for 2–3 minutes, then add the tomatoes and cook for a further 1–2 minutes. Stir in the cream, remove from the heat and keep warm.

3 Add the pasta to the tomato and cream mixture. Season to taste with salt and pepper, then serve in heated deep plates, each portion sprinkled with a little chopped fresh basil.

SALAD OF OAK LEAF LETTUCE WITH CHÈVRE CHEESE CROÛTONS

Choose a baguette that is about the same circumference as the goat's cheese. You can use other types of lettuce if oak leaf is not available: frisé is very good.

SERVES 4 AS A FIRST COURSE, 2 AS A LIGHT MEAL

MENU

Quick Autumn Supper

Salad of Oakleaf Lettuce with Chèvre Cheese Croûtons

Taglioni Verde with Tomato Sauce and Eggplants
254
Crusty Bread

Fresh Fruit Bowl

Coffee

1 oak leaf lettuce
8 fairly thin slices from a small baguette
2 × ¼-pound chèvre cheese logs with rind, each sliced into 4 rounds
1 quantity Vinaigrette (p. 154)

1 Wash the lettuce and shake, pat or spin dry. Divide between 4 serving plates, tearing the leaves in half if necessary to fit and putting a few curly pieces in the center.
2 Toast the slices of baguette under the broiler, then place a piece of goat's cheese on top of each one and broil again until the cheese melts and is lightly flecked with brown.

3 Drizzle a little vinaigrette carefully over each plate of salad, then put the cheese toasts on top of the leaves and serve at once.

Variation
ARUGULA SALAD WITH CROÛTONS AND PARMESAN

Use a good bunch of arugula (three-quarters of a pound) instead of the lettuce, and fresh Parmesan cheese instead of the chèvre. Mix together the arugula, shaved Parmesan and vinaigrette. Fry the bread until crisp and add at the last minute.

[V]

VEGETABLES À LA GRECQUE

[V]

One of my favorite first courses – and a dish which I like as a light meal, too – this is good served with some good bread, to soak up the juices.

SERVES 4

1 onion, peeled and sliced
2 tablespoons olive oil
2 garlic cloves, crushed
1 tablespoon coriander seeds, crushed
½ pound cauliflower florets
½ pound trimmed leeks, cleaned and sliced
½ pound green beans, trimmed and cut in half
½ pound tomatoes, skinned, de-seeded and chopped
1–2 tablespoons lemon juice
salt and freshly ground black pepper
TO GARNISH
2 tablespoons finely chopped parsley or coriander

1 Cook the onion in the oil in a large saucepan for 5 minutes with the lid on the pan, then put in the garlic and coriander seeds and cook for 1–2 minutes more.
2 Add the cauliflower florets, trimmed leeks, green beans and tomatoes to the pan; mix so that everything is coated in the oil. Cook gently, uncovered, for 10–15 minutes, until the vegetables are tender when pierced with the point of a knife.
3 Add the lemon juice a tablespoonful at a time; season with salt and pepper. Serve hot, warm or at room temperature, with the chopped herbs on top. If you are serving the vegetables cold, check the seasoning again first.

ROASTED MEDITERRANEAN VEGETABLES WITH MOZZARELLA AND BASIL

Very quick and easy to make and delicious as either a first or a main course, this needs only some crusty bread to accompany it.

SERVES 4 AS A FIRST COURSE, 2 AS A MAIN COURSE

*1 large eggplant, about ¾ pound, or about 8
   baby eggplants*
¾ pound zucchini
2 tablespoons olive oil
salt and freshly ground black pepper
*¾ pound tomatoes, preferably cherry
   tomatoes*
½ pound mozzarella cheese
sprigs of basil

1 Preheat the oven to 400°F.
2 Cut the eggplant into pieces about ¼ inch thick, 2 inches long and 1 inch wide, or cut the baby eggplants in half. Cut the zucchini into rounds ¼ inch thick.
3 Put the eggplant and zucchini in a shallow roasting pan and sprinkle with the olive oil and some salt and pepper. Mix well with your hands so that all the vegetables are coated with the oil.
4 Put the pan towards the top of the oven and roast for about 20 minutes or until the vegetables are almost tender, turning them as necessary. Then add the tomatoes – cherry tomatoes whole, others quartered – and roast for a further 5 minutes.
5 Meanwhile cut or break the mozzarella cheese into smallish chunks, then add these to the vegetables. Roast for about 5 minutes longer, until the cheese has melted and browned lightly, then tear the basil over the top and serve at once.

Salad of Oak Leaf Lettuce with Chèvre Cheese Croûtons; Roasted Mediterranean Vegetables with Mozzarella and Basil

MENU
Summer Celebration

SERVES 6

Iced Beet Soup with Dill
138

Warm Herb and Onion Bread
328

Pine Nut Roulade with Asparagus Hollandaise Filling
237

Zucchini with Herbs
New Potatoes
Bitter Leaf Salad
54

Champagne Sorbet with Wild Strawberries
283

This is a delectable meal, but not too difficult to cope with, because the Iced Beet Soup with Dill and the Champagne Sorbet can both be made in advance. The Pine Nut Roulade does need some last-minute attention; get it all ready (except for garnishing) before you sit down to the meal so that it can be heating through in the oven while you eat your soup.

The wine served with the roulade needs to be strong enough to support the flavor of the asparagus; perhaps a mature Graves or a medium-dry wine with a honeyed flavor such as a Savennières or Chenin Blanc. Finish this off with a cheese board if you are serving one, then end the meal with a flourish by serving chilled champagne with the sorbet.

Salads

Another versatile category, salads can be as light and refreshing or as substantial and filling as you choose; they can be first courses, accompaniments or, if they are substantial enough, and perhaps served with bread, potatoes or rice, the main course itself. They are particularly healthy and slimming, too, if you use a light dressing or a richer one in moderation. This section contains a variety of salads for different occasions, as well as a selection of useful and easy dressings. When making salads, you will get excellent results if you use the freshest ingredients you can find and aim for a good contrast in colors, textures and flavors.

Walnut Oil

A delectable oil for use in salad dressings, walnut oil is high in polyunsaturates and has a rich, nutty flavor. Hazelnut oil is equally delectable – and expensive! – but both are wonderful for making the occasional extravagant salad dressing, or for tossing freshly cooked pasta in. These oils make lovely presents for avid cooks.

[V]

VINAIGRETTE

[V]

Exact proportions for this basic French dressing are very flexible. If you use good ingredients and are generous with the oil and fairly mean with the vinegar you can't go wrong!

MAKES ABOUT 60 ml/2–3 fl oz

1 teaspoon salt
2 teaspoons red wine vinegar
freshly ground black pepper
3 tablespoons olive oil

Whisk all the ingredients together until thoroughly blended.

Variations

WALNUT VINAIGRETTE
Make as described, using 3–4 tablespoons walnut oil.

GARLIC VINAIGRETTE
Add a crushed garlic clove to the mixture, blending well.

MUSTARD VINAIGRETTE
Start by mixing 2–3 teaspoons Dijon mustard with the salt and vinegar, then gradually mix in the oil, for this thick and tangy version.

LEMON VINAIGRETTE
Replace the vinegar with fresh lemon juice.

BALSAMIC VINAIGRETTE
Use balsamic vinegar instead of wine vinegar.

BLUE CHEESE DRESSING

MAKES 1 cup

2 ounces blue cheese
⅔ cup plain yogurt

Either mix the ingredients together in a food processor or a blender until they are thoroughly combined or mash the cheese into a soft consistency with a fork, then gradually beat the yogurt into it.

MAYONNAISE

Homemade mayonnaise is a delicious treat, is not difficult to make and will keep for at least a week in a covered container in the refrigerator (but it won't freeze).

MAKES ABOUT 1 cup

2 large egg yolks
¼ teaspoon salt
¼ teaspoon mustard powder
2–3 grindings black pepper
2 teaspoons white wine vinegar
2 teaspoons lemon juice
1 cup (scant) cold-pressed sunflower oil

1 Put the egg yolks, salt, mustard, pepper, vinegar and lemon juice into a bowl and whisk lightly until combined.
2 Add the oil, a drop at a time, whisking well after each addition.
3 When you have added about half the oil, the mixture will emulsify and start to look like mayonnaise. At this point you can add the oil a little more quickly.
4 Continue until the mixture is really thick, then taste the mixture and adjust the seasoning if necessary.
5 If the mayonnaise seems a bit on the thick side, you can thin it by beating in a teaspoon or two of boiling water.

Variations

BLENDER METHOD
Mayonnaise can be speedily made in a blender or food processor. Put in the egg yolks, seasonings, vinegar and lemon juice and blend for 1 minute. Then gradually add the oil, drop by drop, through the top of the globlet. When you have added about half the oil and the mixture has thickened, you can add the rest more quickly, in a thin stream.

AÏOLI
For this very delectable garlic-flavored mayonnaise, blend 6–8 peeled garlic cloves in the blender or food processor, then proceed exactly as for mayonnaise. Makes a wonderful dip for crudités.

MANGO CHUTNEY MAYONNAISE
A good variation for serving with cold lentil loaf or nut burgers. Stir in 2–4 tablespoons chopped mango chutney.

AVOCADO DRESSING

A delicious vegan dressing for salads. It can be diluted with a little water to make a thinner dressing.

MAKES ABOUT 200 ml/7 fl oz

1 ripe avocado, halved, peeled and pit removed
1 tablespoon lemon juice
1 tablespoon white wine vinegar
1 teaspoon Dijon mustard
salt and freshly ground black pepper
dash of Tabasco sauce

1 Put the avocado into a blender or food processor with the lemon juice, wine vinegar and Dijon mustard and blend to a smooth cream.
2 Season to taste with salt, pepper and a drop or two of Tabasco. Taste and add more Tabasco if wished.

Tahini Dressing

Put 4 tablespoons tahini into a small bowl with 2 crushed cloves of garlic and 2 tablespoons of water. Gradually blend the water into the tahini. When it becomes stiff and crumbly, add another 2 tablespoons of water and blend again. Continue adding water until the tahini is creamy, like mayonnaise; you will probably need to add about ½ cup in all. Add a tablespoonful of lemon juice and salt and pepper. Taste, and add more lemon juice and seasoning as required.

Dressing Tips

□ A quick and easy way to make a vinaigrette-type dressing is to put all the ingredients into a screwtop jar and shake until emulsified. If you only need a little of the dressing, the jar makes a convenient storage container for the refrigerator. Let the dressing "come to" at room temperature for 30 minutes or so before use, then give it a shake to re-emulsify the ingredients.

□ Although you can make dressing in bulk and store it in the refrigerator, it only takes a moment to make, and I think it's better made fresh when you need it. If you are making the salad in a bowl, it saves time and washing up to make the dressing right into the bowl. If it's a delicate, leafy salad, and you are not planning to serve it immediately, put a pair of crossed salad servers in the bowl, then put the salad in on top. The salad servers will keep the salad above the dressing until you are ready to toss and serve the salad, preventing it from getting soggy.

V # WARM THAI NOODLE SALAD V

SERVES 4 AS A FIRST COURSE

3 ounces egg thread noodles
¼ pound snow peas or sugar snap peas, trimmed
¼ pound baby corn, sliced on the diagonal
½ bunch of scallions, trimmed and sliced
1 bunch of radishes, trimmed and sliced
FOR THE DRESSING
grated rind and juice of 1 lime
1 tablespoon rice vinegar or red wine vinegar
2 tablespoons light soy sauce
1 tablespoon sesame oil
2–3 tablespoons torn coriander leaves
TO SERVE (OPTIONAL)
Gomasio (p. 237)
soy sauce

1 To make the dressing, put all the ingredients in a large bowl (large enough to hold the salad) and mix them carefully together.
2 Bring a large saucepan half full of water to a boil and add the noodles, snow peas and corn. Bring back to a boil and simmer for 2–3 minutes or until the noodles are just tender. Drain thoroughly in a colander and then put the noodles and vegetables into the bowl on top of the dressing.
3 Add the scallions and radishes and gently toss everything together. Serve immediately, while still warm, accompanied by some gomasio and extra soy sauce, if you wish.

Legume Salads

Legumes – peas, beans and lentils – make excellent salads, filling and full of flavor. Particularly good are all members of the kidney bean family, including of course the red and black varieties: lima beans; French, brown and puy lentils; and the always delicious chick peas. A mixture of different colors, shapes and sizes gives a particularly attractive result, great for a buffet party.

Put the dressing on these salads – a vinaigrette is delicious – when the beans are freshly cooked, drained, but still hot. Add flavoring ingredients such as raw onion rings, chopped scallions, fresh chopped herbs, grated fresh ginger, garlic, black olives – the possibilities are wide. Allow to cool to room temperature, stirring the salad gently from time to time. The beans will absorb the full flavor of the dressing and any of its ingredients, resulting in a moist, shiny salad.

SOUR CREAM DRESSING

MAKES ABOUT ½ cup

about ½ cup sour cream
salt and freshly ground black pepper

1 Just stir the sour cream and season to taste with salt and pepper, for a simple yet delicious dressing.

Variation
SOUR CREAM OR YOGURT AND HERB DRESSING
Add 2 tablespoons chopped fresh green herbs – mint, parsley, tarragon or basil, or a mixture of them – to the sour cream or yogurt.

V # RICE SALAD WITH OYSTER MUSHROOMS AND AVOCADO V

SERVES 4

1¼ cups brown rice
2 tablespoons olive oil
½ pound oyster mushrooms
2 garlic cloves, crushed
salt and freshly ground black pepper
1 ripe avocado, peeled, pitted and sliced
juice of 1 lemon
½ cup pine nuts, toasted
2–3 tablespoons chopped scallions or chives
a few sprigs of flat-leaf parsley, torn

1 Half fill a large saucepan with water and bring to a boil. Add rice and boil for 45 minutes, until tender, then drain.
2 Meanwhile heat the olive oil in a saucepan and fry the oyster mushrooms and garlic for about 4 minutes. Season.
3 Toss the avocado in the lemon juice.
4 Combine the rice, oyster mushrooms, avocado, pine nuts, scallions or chives and parsley and serve warm or cold.

MIXED BEAN SALAD WITH SPICY DRESSING

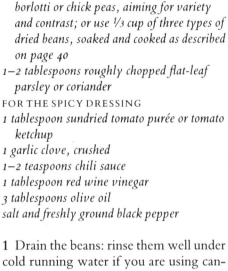

You can use dried beans which you soak and cook yourself, or canned beans. If you're cooking them, it's best to cook the different types separately to preserve the colors. This is delicious as a filling for pita pockets or soft bread rolls or with a leafy salad.

SERVES 4–6

3 × 15-ounce cans beans – choose from cannellini, red kidney, flageolet, pinto, borlotti or chick peas, aiming for variety and contrast; or use ⅓ cup of three types of dried beans, soaked and cooked as described on page 40
1–2 tablespoons roughly chopped flat-leaf parsley or coriander

FOR THE SPICY DRESSING
1 tablespoon sundried tomato purée or tomato ketchup
1 garlic clove, crushed
1–2 teaspoons chili sauce
1 tablespoon red wine vinegar
3 tablespoons olive oil
salt and freshly ground black pepper

1 Drain the beans: rinse them well under cold running water if you are using canned ones. Put them into a bowl with the parsley or coriander.
2 Make the spicy dressing: put the tomato purée or ketchup into a small bowl and gradually blend in the garlic and a little chili sauce, vinegar and finally the oil and some seasoning to taste. Check the hotness and add more chili sauce to taste.
3 You can add the dressing to the beans at this stage, or drizzle it over them, which looks pretty.

Variations
RED KIDNEY BEAN AND WALNUT SALAD
Make the salad as described, using either the basic vinaigrette (p. 154) or the walnut version instead of the spicy dressing, and adding 1 large coarsely grated carrot, 2 sliced celery sticks and ⅔ cup roughly chopped walnuts to the beans.

MIXED BEAN AND BLACK OLIVE SALAD
Use ½ cup each dried red kidney beans and navy beans, soaked, cooked and drained, or one 15-ounce can of each. Add ½ cup black olives to the mixture.

Tabasco
This is a hot flavoring liquid made from the Tabasco variety of chili pepper. It is very useful for perking up all kinds of mixtures from avocado dip to cheese sauce. It is very hot, so you need only a drop or two. Do get the original type: the imitations are not as good.

Warm Thai Noodle Salad (p. 156);
Mixed Bean Salad with Spicy Dressing

UNMOLDING A RICE SALAD

1 Slip a knife between the rice salad and the sides of the mold to loosen

2 Invert a serving dish on top of the rice mold

3 Turn the mold and the serving dish over together, giving the mold a shake to help the rice to slide out

4 Lift off the ring mold

Making a Round Rice Salad Mold

If you haven't a ring mold, make a round rice salad mold instead, using a cake pan or soufflé dish lined with well-oiled foil. This mold looks pretty if you fry 6–7 small flat open mushrooms in oil and arrange these attractively in the base of the mold before putting in the rice. Add the rice gently, to keep the pattern intact.

Any rice salad mixture can be molded in this way. Make sure your serving plate is large enough, because the salad tends to crumble once it is cut.

FRENCH LENTIL AND WALNUT SALAD

This makes an excellent winter salad, filling and satisfying.

SERVES 4

1 cup (generous) dried French lentils, cooked and drained (p. 40)
½ cup walnuts, chopped
1 garlic clove, crushed
1 bunch scallions, trimmed and chopped
1 quantity Walnut Vinaigrette (p. 154)
salt and freshly ground black pepper
TO GARNISH
1–2 tablespoons chopped parsley

1 Put the lentils into a bowl with the walnuts, garlic, scallions and vinaigrette. Mix well, season with salt and pepper, then leave to marinate for several hours.
2 Put the salad into a serving bowl, then chill until needed. Sprinkle the parsley on top just before you serve the salad.

Variations
FRENCH LENTIL, MUSHROOM AND WALNUT SALAD
Add 2 cups very fresh button mushrooms, washed, thinly sliced and sprinkled with 1–2 tablespoons lemon juice, to the mixture.

FRENCH LENTIL, CARROT AND WALNUT SALAD
Add 1–2 coarsely grated carrots to the mixture for a good contrast of color.

FRENCH LENTIL, WALNUT AND ONION SALAD
Add a mild raw onion, peeled and sliced.

FRENCH LENTIL, WALNUT AND EGG SALAD
For this excellent (but non-vegan) version, make the salad as described, put it into a shallow bowl and surround with 2–4 hard-boiled eggs cut into wedges.

RICE SALAD WITH FRUIT AND NUTS

This is good served with a lettuce, chive and avocado salad and perhaps some sliced ripe tomatoes, too. Or you could serve it with chutney, a cucumber raita and some chapattis or poppadums for an easy Indian-style supper.

SERVES 4–6

1¼ cups basmati rice
¼ teaspoon turmeric
2 tablespoons olive oil
1 onion, peeled and chopped
2 garlic cloves, crushed
1 cup blanched almonds
½ cup pine nuts
juice of 1 lemon
⅔ cup dried apricots, sliced

⅓ cup sultanas
3 tablespoons chopped coriander
salt and freshly ground black pepper

1 Half fill a large saucepan with water and bring to a boil. Rinse the rice in a sieve until the water runs clear, then add the rice and turmeric to the pan and boil, uncovered, for 10–12 minutes, until the rice is tender. Drain in a strainer, then put into a bowl.

2 Meanwhile heat the oil in a saucepan, add the onion and garlic and cook gently for 5 minutes. Turn up the heat, add the almonds and pine nuts and cook for 5 minutes longer, stirring often, until the onion and nuts are golden brown.

3 Add the onion mixture to the rice, along with 1 tablespoon of the lemon juice (which will immediately turn the rice bright primrose yellow), the apricots, sultanas, coriander and salt and pepper. Taste and add more lemon juice if necessary.

Variation
RICE SALAD WITH BEAN SPROUTS AND WILD RICE

For this particularly good version, cook ⅓ cup wild rice with the basmati rice. Omit the turmeric, fruit and nuts and lemon juice. Sauté the onion with the garlic, then add to the rice, together with a cup of bean sprouts.

Rice Salad with Fruit and Nuts (p. 158); Tabbouleh

[V] TABBOULEH [V]

This Middle Eastern salad, based on bulgur wheat, is quite substantial yet the herbs and lemon juice give it a light, refreshing flavor, making it a good hot-weather salad.

SERVES 4–6

1½ cups bulgur wheat
2½ cups boiling water
1–2 garlic cloves, crushed (optional)
4 tablespoons lemon juice
2 tablespoons olive oil
½ cup chopped parsley
½ cup chopped scallions
4-inch piece of cucumber, finely diced
¼ cup chopped mint
4 tomatoes, peeled and finely chopped
salt and freshly ground black pepper
TO GARNISH
black olives or lemon or tomato slices

1 Put the bulgur wheat in a bowl and cover with the boiling water. Leave it to stand for about 10–15 minutes, until the wheat has absorbed all the water and has puffed up.

2 Add all the remaining ingredients and mix well, seasoning to taste. Spoon the mixture into a shallow serving dish and garnish with the olives or slices of lemon or tomato.

Variation
TABBOULEH RING

To make a molded ring, put the warm tabbouleh mixture into a 2- to 2½-quart ring mold, press down firmly and leave until cold. Then turn out onto a large plate or serving platter and fill the center with some watercress, black olives or sliced tomatoes.

Rice Salad Ideas

Rice salad is easy to make: just add the ingredients to the rice. The more contrast you can get in the ingredients you add, the better.

Choose from chopped raw onion or scallions, small cubes of cucumber, chopped red or green pepper, corn kernels, cooked peas, small cubes of cooked carrot or coarsely grated raw carrot, finely chopped celery, raisins or sultanas, finely chopped dried apricots, chopped nuts, chopped peeled tomato, cooked beans, black olives, chopped fresh herbs.

Moisten the mixture with a little vinaigrette dressing or mayonnaise thinned with some milk.

LIGHT CAESAR SALAD

I like to use a good-quality, store-bought reduced-calorie mayonnaise to make this vegetarian version of Caesar salad, although you could use regular mayonnaise. It's delicious as a light lunch or first course.

SERVES 4–6

Dressing a Salad

Some salads, such as legume and grain salads and those made from cooked vegetables and firm vegetables, like cabbage, are ideal if dressed in advance and left for the flavors to blend. Others, especially delicate leafy mixtures, are best dressed at the last minute, even at the table, just before serving.

For a really good salad, leafy ingredients need to be dried of excess water. This can be done by putting them in a salad shaker or spinner, or by patting them gently in a clean, absorbent cloth or paper towels. I find a salad drier, consisting of a perforated basket which spins the salad inside a container, thus removing the water, most useful. If there is time, wash and dry the leaves, then put them into a plastic bag and chill them in the fridge for 30–60 minutes to crisp.

1 romaine lettuce, washed
¼ pound cherry tomatoes, washed
several sprigs of basil, torn into pieces
6 × ½-inch slices of French bread
1–2 tablespoons olive oil
FOR THE DRESSING
2 tablespoons reduced-calorie mayonnaise
2 tablespoons plain yogurt
½ teaspoon Tabasco sauce
⅓ cup Parmesan cheese, grated
salt and freshly ground black pepper
TO GARNISH
⅓ cup Parmesan cheese, flaked

1 Check that the lettuce has no excess water clinging to it. If there's time, wash and dry it and put it in a polythene bag in the refrigerator to chill and crisp.

2 Tear the lettuce into rough pieces and put them in a bowl. Add the cherry tomatoes, halved if liked, and the basil.
3 Make the dressing: put the mayonnaise into a small bowl with the yogurt, Tabasco, Parmesan and a little salt and pepper and mix together well.
4 Make croûtons by brushing the French bread on both sides with the oil, then broiling on both sides until golden and crisp. Cut the pieces in half.
5 Just before you are ready to eat the salad, add the dressing to the lettuce mixture in the bowl and toss until the leaves are coated. Add the croûtons and mix together gently. Sprinkle the flakes of Parmesan cheese over the salad and serve at once.

FAVORITE COLESLAW

This traditional favorite is a useful salad because it can be made ahead of time. It goes particularly well with crisp nut burgers.

SERVES 4

2 cups finely shredded green cabbage
1 cup scraped and coarsely grated carrots
1 tablespoon chopped chives
1 small green pepper, deseeded and chopped
2 tablespoons plain yogurt or water
2 tablespoons Mayonnaise (p. 155)
salt and freshly ground black pepper
TO GARNISH
chives

Put the cabbage, carrot, chives and green pepper into a large bowl. Add the yogurt or water, mayonnaise and salt and pepper to taste. Garnish with chives.

Variation
CARAWAY COLESLAW
Make as described, adding 1 teaspoon caraway seeds, for a Middle European flavor to the salad.

[V] # ENDIVE, WATERCRESS AND WALNUT SALAD [V]

This variation of green salad is good with cheese dishes.

SERVES 4

2 heads endive, washed
1 bunch watercress, washed
1 quantity Vinaigrette or Walnut Vinaigrette
  (p. 154)
½ cup chopped walnuts

1 See that the endive and watercress leaves do not have any excess water clinging to them. If there's time, wash and dry them in advance and put them into a plastic bag in the refrigerator, to chill and crisp.
2 Put the dressing into a salad bowl, cross the salad servers on top, then put in the endive, watercress and walnuts. Turn the leaves in the dressing at the last minute, just before serving.

Variation
ENDIVE, WATERCRESS, WALNUT AND ORANGE SALAD
Make as described, adding 2 oranges, peeled and cut into segments. Hold the oranges over a bowl as you cut them, to catch the juice. Use some of this (carefully removing any seeds) to make the vinaigrette dressing for the salad, instead of the vinegar.

This is a particularly good accompaniment to hot legume and nut dishes; or, topped with a blue cheese dressing and served with warm whole-wheat rolls, it makes a good light lunch or supper dish on its own.

Low-Calorie Salad Dressings

- Sprinkle vegetables with lemon juice or rice vinegar, seasoning and chopped fresh herbs or finely chopped onion.
- Use fresh orange juice to dress root vegetable salads: grated carrot and grated raw beets are particularly good with orange.
- Lemon or lime juice makes a good dressing for grated cabbage salad, perked up with herbs, seasoning and perhaps a dash of Dijon mustard.
- Plain yogurt, or the Yogurt and Herb Dressing on p. 156.
- For a low(er)-calorie mayonnaise, mix mayonnaise (homemade or bought) with an equal (or even double) quantity of plain yogurt.

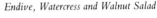

Endive, Watercress and Walnut Salad

ⓥ SWEET CARROT AND FENNEL SALAD ⓥ

SERVES 4

Fennel Tip

If you find the flavor of fennel rather strong, plunge the bulbs into boiling water for 2 minutes before slicing.

2 bulbs fennel
1 pound carrots, scraped and coarsely grated
½ quantity Vinaigrette (p. 154)
salt and freshly ground black pepper
a little sugar
TO GARNISH
fennel leaves

1 Remove any tough outer leaves from the fennel. Cut off and reserve any feathery green leaves. Slice the fennel and put it into a bowl with the grated carrot.
2 Add the vinaigrette and mix well.

Season to taste with salt and pepper, then add a little sugar to taste. I think this touch of sweetness enhances the flavor of the carrot and fennel pleasantly. Garnish with fennel.

Variations
SWEET CARROT, FENNEL AND RED PEPPER SALAD
Make as described, adding a small red pepper, deseeded and chopped, to the ingredients. This is a good salad for serving with a creamy pasta dish.

ⓥ TECHNICOLOR CABBAGE SALAD ⓥ

SERVES 4–6

Cold-pressed Oils

Oils are extracted from nuts, seeds, legumes and (in the case of olive oil) from fruits by pressing them. This is usually done several times, at first by using pressure alone and later, to extract the maximum oil, by using heat too. Cold-pressed oil is oil obtained by the early pressings and is the richest in flavor and nutrients (some of which are damaged when heat is used). Other chemicals may also be used in the later pressings and antioxidants may be added to increase the keeping qualities. Cold-pressed oil is the best for both flavor and health. It is more expensive, and should be bought in small quantities (that can be used up within about a month) and kept in the refrigerator. If the oil goes a bit cloudy or solid, don't worry; it will return to normal if you take it out of the fridge and leave it at room temperature.

3 cups finely shredded green cabbage
2 large carrots, scraped and coarsely grated
1 medium red pepper, deseeded and chopped
1 onion, peeled and finely chopped
2 tablespoons chopped parsley
½ cup raisins or black olives
1 quantity Vinaigrette (p. 154)
½ cup roasted peanuts or sunflower seeds

1 Put the shredded cabbage into a bowl with the grated carrots and the chopped pepper, onion and parsley. Stir in the raisins or black olives.
2 Add the vinaigrette and stir well to coat all the ingredients.
3 Add the nuts or sunflower seeds just before serving.

ⓥ SCANDINAVIAN-STYLE CUCUMBER SALAD ⓥ

Serve with rich dishes, or as a contrast to creamy salads in a buffet selection.

SERVES 4–6

1 large cucumber, peeled and sliced
salt
1 onion, peeled and thinly sliced
2 tablespoons white wine vinegar
1 teaspoon sugar
1 tablespoon white mustard seeds
2 tablespoons chopped fresh dill
freshly ground black pepper
TO GARNISH
1–2 dill sprigs

1 Put the cucumber slices into a sieve or colander and sprinkle with salt. Set a weight on top and leave for 30 minutes, to draw out the excess liquid. Then squeeze and pat dry with paper towels.
2 Put the cucumber into a bowl and add the onion, vinegar, sugar, mustard seeds, dill and pepper. Stir well.
3 Leave to marinate for at least 2 hours. Garnish with dill before serving.

Sweet Carrot and Fennel Salad (p. 162); Scandinavian-Style Cucumber Salad (p. 162)

WARM SALAD OF OYSTER MUSHROOMS

SERVES 2

a few green salad leaves, such as lettuce, curly endive, arugula or mâche
¼ pound oyster mushrooms
1 tablespoon olive oil
1 garlic clove, crushed
1–2 tablespoons fresh lemon juice
salt and freshly ground black pepper

1 Wash the salad leaves, shake them dry and arrange them on 2 serving plates.
2 Wash or wipe the mushrooms. Heat the oil in a pan and put in the mushrooms and garlic; fry quickly for 2–3 minutes.
3 Add the lemon juice, salt and pepper, then spoon the mushrooms and their juices over the salad leaves and serve at once.

Variations

WARM SALAD OF SHIITAKE MUSHROOMS AND PARMESAN

Use fresh shiitake mushrooms instead of the oyster mushrooms. Slice and fry in oil and garlic as described. Add 2 tablespoons fresh Parmesan cheese cut into fine shavings and spoon onto the green salad leaves.

WARM SALAD OF MUSHROOMS AND GARLIC

For this simpler variation, use ordinary white mushrooms; wipe and slice thickly. Fry in the oil with an extra crushed garlic clove and serve.

MAKING RADISH FLOWERS

1 Cut a thin petal of skin from the tip of the radish to the stem. Repeat, making 5 petals

2 To make a rose, cut a slice off the root end, then make 3 small cuts round that before making the petals

3 Drop radishes into ice water for the petals to open

MENU

Quick Late-night Supper for Two

Tsatsiki and Warmed
Pita Bread
167

Cheese Fondue with
French Bread
217

Japanese Flower Salad

Passion Fruit Sorbet
Illustrated on p. 283
282

Clockwise from top: Pink Potato Salad (p. 166); Radish, Cucumber and Arame Salad (p. 164); Japanese Flower Salad (p. 164)

[V]
RADISH, CUCUMBER AND ARAME SALAD
[V]

Don't be put off by the seaweed – arame – in this recipe. With a sweet-and-sour dressing, it makes a very good salad, full of nutrients, and looks pretty with the cucumber and radishes. Excellent for serving with Japanese-style rice dishes.

SERVES 4

¼ cup dried arame
½ cucumber, peeled and diced
1 bunch radishes, trimmed and sliced
1 teaspoon sea salt
1 teaspoon sugar
2 tablespoons rice vinegar

1 Rinse the arame in cold running water, then soak in cold water for 5 minutes. Drain the arame, place in a saucepan, cover with water, bring to a boil, and simmer gently for 10 minutes. Drain and leave the arame to cool.

2 Add the cucumber, radishes, sea salt, sugar and rice vinegar to the cooled arame and mix well to combine all the ingredients.

Variation
RADISH, CUCUMBER AND HIJIKI SEAWEED SALAD

Make this in the same way, using hijiki, another kind of seaweed, instead of the arame. Prepare the hijiki as described on p. 81.

[V]
JAPANESE FLOWER SALAD
[V]

This pretty salad makes an excellent accompaniment to a rich main course such as Cheese Soufflé (p. 222), Cheese Fondue (p. 217) or a creamy quiche. Serve Vinaigrette (p. 154) separately. If you have the time to cut the vegetables as suggested (p. 166), it adds to the charm of this salad.

SERVES 4

1 medium head chicory, leaves separated, washed and broken into even-sized pieces
1 medium head radicchio, leaves separated, washed and broken into even-sized pieces
12 radishes, cut into roses (above left)
12 cherry tomatoes, peeled
2 large carrots, scraped and cut into 8 chrysanthemums (p. 166)
one 4-inch piece of daikon (mooli), scraped and cut into 8 chrysanthemums (p. 166), or 8 cauliflower florets
8 scallions, trimmed and curled
a few parsley sprigs

1 On 4 individual plates, or in 4 small shallow baskets lined with colored napkins, make a base of mixed chicory and radicchio.
2 Arrange the radishes, tomatoes, carrot and daikon flowers, or cauliflower florets, attractively among the mixed leaves on the plates.
3 Garnish with the scallions and parsley sprigs.

Variation
Other vegetables of your choice can be used in this salad, as well as edible flowers, such as nasturtiums and borage. Garnish with parsley sprigs or flowers.

MAKING CARROT AND DAIKON FLOWERS

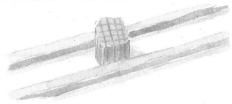

1 Cut carrot or daikon into 1-inch rectangles. Round off the corners slightly

2 Hold the rectangle between two chopsticks and cut across first one way then the other, cutting down as far as the chopsticks

3 Sprinkle salt into the cuts and leave for 30 minutes, then rinse

4 Gently open up the cuts with your fingers

Root Salads

Root vegetables – carrots, rutabagas, celeriac and raw beets – make good, substantial salads. They can be made several hours in advance if convenient, as they will not spoil. The effect can be varied according to how coarsely you grate the roots, and the dressing used. Little heaps of different-colored root vegetables on a base of lettuce, with perhaps a creamy dip or dressing in the center, and some parsley sprigs or black olives to decorate, make a colorful and vitamin-rich lunch. Or the roots can be served separately, as part of a mixed salad selection. Here are some good combinations:

- Grated raw beets and apple, dressed with orange juice or Herb Vinaigrette (p. 154)
- Grated raw beets and sliced raw onion rings, with Vinaigrette (p. 154)
- Grated rutabaga with chopped dates, dressed with a mixture of yogurt and Mayonnaise (p. 155)
- Celeriac, cut into julienne strips, dressed with Mustard Vinaigrette (p. 154) or Sour Cream Dressing (p. 156)
- Young turnips, coarsely grated, mixed with Vinaigrette (p. 154) and raisins or chopped parsley
- Coarsely grated raw carrot with apple and celery, dressed with orange juice

POTATO SALAD

New potatoes, cooked in their skins, are especially good for this salad, though I make it all the year round and find it works well with old potatoes too: the secret is to undercook them slightly, so that they still have a bit of bite to them and hold together well. And if you can get hold of an interesting, well-flavored variety, they will make this salad extra good.

SERVES 4

1 pound small, even-sized potatoes, scrubbed
3 tablespoons Mayonnaise (p. 155)
3 tablespoons plain yogurt or sour cream
salt and freshly ground black pepper
2 tablespoons snipped chives, chopped
   scallion or parsley

1 Cook the potatoes in boiling water to cover, until they are just tender when pierced with a knife – about 15 minutes, depending on the size of the potatoes.
2 Drain the potatoes as soon as they are done and, if you wish, slip off the skins with a sharp knife. (Usually I prefer to leave the skins on.)
3 Dice the potatoes if necessary and put them into a bowl with the mayonnaise and yogurt or sour cream. It's fine – indeed, best – to do this while they are still hot.
4 Allow to cool to room temperature, then check the seasoning and serve, sprinkled with the chives, scallion or parsley.

Variations
PINK POTATO SALAD
Make as described, adding 1–2 tablespoons cooked and diced beet to the mixture. This will turn the whole salad a pretty pink, making this a good salad for serving with a pale dish, such as French Onion Pie (p. 261).

POTATO SALAD WITH VINAIGRETTE DRESSING
A good vegan version. Use ½–1 quantity of Vinaigrette (p. 154) instead of the mayonnaise. A bunch of radishes, trimmed and sliced, or a little chopped red pepper, are good added to this, for extra color.

Ⅴ GREEN BEAN SALAD WITH RADICCHIO Ⅴ

This is a light salad, made from fresh rather than dried beans, and the different shades of green look pretty against the red of the radicchio leaves. This salad goes excellently with Cheese Soufflé (p. 222) for a nourishing lunch or supper.

SERVES 4–6

½ pound frozen fava beans
½ pound fresh or frozen green beans, trimmed and cut into 1-inch lengths
½ quantity Vinaigrette (p. 154)
salt and freshly ground black pepper
2 tablespoons chopped summer savory or other fresh herbs (such as chives or mint)
1 medium head radicchio, leaves washed and separated

1 Cook the fava and green beans together in a little boiling water for 5–10 minutes, until just tender and still crisp. Drain well.
2 Put the hot beans into a bowl with the vinaigrette, salt, pepper and herbs. Mix well, then cool to room temperature.
3 Just before serving, add the radicchio to the beans and stir gently to mix all the ingredients.

Ⅴ TSATSIKI Ⅴ

This Middle Eastern salad is a good accompaniment to cooked grain dishes. It also makes a refreshing starter served on small plates and eaten with strips of warmed pita bread.

SERVES 4–6 AS A SIDE SALAD, 6–8 AS A FIRST COURSE

Tsatsiki

1 large cucumber, peeled and cut into small dice
salt
1 cup thick plain yogurt, preferably Greek, or vegan yogurt
¼ cup chopped fresh mint
2 garlic cloves, crushed
freshly ground black pepper
TO GARNISH
mild paprika
mint leaves

1 Put the cucumber into a sieve or colander and sprinkle with salt. Set a weight on top and leave for 30 minutes, to draw out excess liquid which would dilute the dressing too much. Then squeeze and pat dry with paper towels.
2 Put the cucumber into a bowl and add the yogurt, mint, garlic and a grinding of pepper. Stir well, taste and add more salt and pepper if necessary. Put into a shallow serving dish, sprinkle with paprika and garnish with mint leaves.

Waldorf Salad (p. 169); Greek Salad

GREEK SALAD

Instant nostalgia for anyone with happy memories of Greece, this
makes a substantial salad for 4 people or a side salad for 8. A
generous portion of Greek salad, accompanied by warm
whole-wheat pita bread or rolls, makes a delicious
light lunch or supper.

SERVES 4 AS A MAIN COURSE, 8 AS A SIDE SALAD

1 large mild onion, peeled and thinly sliced
1 quantity Vinaigrette (p. 154)
*1 pound tomatoes, peeled if necessary, and
  sliced*
1 cucumber, diced
½ cup black olives (optional)
*1½ cups crumbled feta cheese or other dry
  white cheese such as Wensleydale or
  Cheshire*
TO GARNISH (OPTIONAL)
chopped parsley

1 Put the onion into a bowl with the
vinaigrette; mix well, then leave to
stand for 30–60 minutes, to allow the
onion to soften in the dressing. Stir
occasionally.
2 Add the tomatoes, cucumber, olives,
if used, and cheese, stirring gently to
distribute all the ingredients. Divide the
salad among the individual serving plates
and sprinkle each portion with chopped
parsley, if you wish.

WALDORF SALAD

This classic salad goes well with cheese dishes, also slices of
cold nut or lentil loaf.

SERVES 4

3 red-skinned apples, cored and diced
2 tablespoons lemon juice
3 celery sticks, chopped
4 tablespoons Mayonnaise (p. 155)
4 tablespoons plain yogurt
50 g/2 oz chopped walnuts
salt and freshly ground black pepper

1 Put the apple into a bowl, sprinkle
with the lemon juice and mix well. Add
the celery, mayonnaise, yogurt, walnuts
and seasoning to taste.

2 Serve immediately; or, if the salad has
to wait for any length of time, leave out
the walnuts until just before serving.

Variation
GRAPE, CELERY, PEAR AND ALMOND SALAD

Replace the apples with 225 g/8 oz mixed
black or red and white grapes, halved and
seeded, and 2 ripe pears, peeled, cored
and diced. Use 50 g/2 oz toasted flaked
almonds instead of the walnuts.

VEGETARIAN SALADE NIÇOISE

Served with crusty French bread, this makes an excellent light
lunch, or, in smaller portions, a refreshing first course.

SERVES 4 AS A MAIN COURSE, 6–8 AS A STARTER

1 large lettuce, washed, torn into pieces and
shaken dry
1 medium onion, peeled and sliced into rings
450 g/1 lb firm tomatoes, washed and sliced
5 hardboiled eggs, quartered
450 g/1 lb cooked French beans, cut into 2.5-
cm/1-inch lengths
12 black olives
2 tablespoons chopped parsley
1 quantity Vinaigrette (p. 154)

1 Line a large serving plate with the lettuce, then arrange all the ingredients, except the vinaigrette, on top, not too neatly.
2 Spoon a little of the vinaigrette over
the salad just before serving. Serve the
rest of the vinaigrette separately in a small
jug.

Variation
VEGAN SALADE NIÇOISE

Use the drained contents of 1 × 425-g/
15-oz can butter beans, or 100 g/4 oz
butter beans, soaked, cooked and
drained, instead of the hardboiled eggs
cut into quarters.

Onion Tip

If you want to include raw onion in a
salad, but find it too strong, blanch
the onion first by covering with
boiling water, leaving for 2 minutes,
then draining.

SKINNING A TOMATO

1 Put the tomato into a bowl and cover with boiling water. Leave for 1 minute

2 Drain. Slip off the skin with a sharp, pointed
knife

Sauces

Sauces can add the final, delicious touch to a dish, often contributing color as well as moisture; they also form an integral part of some vegetarian dishes such as Eggplant and Pasta Charlotte (p. 258) and Pine Nut Roulade with Asparagus Hollandaise Filling (p. 237). A good sauce, such as Fresh Tomato (below), Pesto (p. 172) or Cheese Sauce (p. 175) can turn plain freshly cooked pasta or vegetables into a quick and tasty meal. When making your favorite sauces, it's worth cooking extra portions which can be frozen. The sauces in this chapter are the ones which I consider the most useful both as components of recipes and for serving with other dishes.

Ⅴ   FRESH TOMATO SAUCE   Ⅴ

I find this fresh, lightly cooked tomato sauce one of the most useful. Its flavor and bright color go well with many savory dishes, and it's excellent with pasta and many cooked vegetables, especially pale ones like cauliflower. Another advantage is that, unlike many sauces, it is very low in calories. This sauce is definitely best when made with fresh tomatoes: canned tomatoes just don't give the same result. If you have to use these, make Italian Tomato Sauce (p. 171) instead.

SERVES 6

Keeping Sauces Warm

It is often convenient to make sauces in advance, to avoid feeling pressured at the last minute. Both the Tomato Sauces (pp. 170 and 171), Vegetarian Gravy (p. 172) and Cranberry Sauce (p. 174) can be reheated gently in a saucepan. Béchamel Sauce (p. 175), and its variations, can also be reheated, but keep the heat low and stir, or use a double saucepan. A double saucepan is also best for Bread Sauce (p. 175) and Sauce Soubise (p. 173) and these can be kept warm in a water bath (or a saucepan standing in a roasting tin half filled with boiling water, with foil over all). Quick Hollandaise Sauce (p. 176) can be kept warm in a water bath, too, but I think the best way is to put it in a thermos flask for up to 2 hours. Take care that this sauce does not get too hot, or it may start to curdle. (If this happens, quickly add an ice cube – or start again, adding the curdled sauce gradually to a fresh egg yolk.)

1 onion, peeled and finely chopped
1 tablespoon olive oil
2 pounds tomatoes, peeled and roughly chopped
salt and freshly ground black pepper

1 Sauté the onion in the oil in a large saucepan for 10 minutes, until softened but not browned.
2 Add the tomatoes and cook for a further 10 minutes, until the tomatoes are soft but still bright in color and fresh in flavor.
3 Purée the tomato mixture in a blender or food processor. Season to taste with salt and pepper.

Variations

FRESH TOMATO AND BASIL SAUCE
For this summery version, make as described, adding 1 tablespoon chopped fresh basil just before serving.

FRESH TOMATO AND GARLIC SAUCE
Add 1–2 crushed garlic cloves to the onion with the tomatoes.

FRESH TOMATO AND MUSHROOM SAUCE
While the tomatoes are cooking, sauté 1⅓ cups finely chopped button mushrooms in 1 tablespoon olive oil in a pan until tender. Stir into puréed sauce.

FRESH TOMATO AND CHILI SAUCE
Add 1 green chili, deseeded and finely chopped, to the onion with the tomatoes.

[V]   # ITALIAN TOMATO SAUCE   [V]

A well-flavored sauce that goes well with many vegetarian savory dishes.

SERVES 4

1 onion, peeled and chopped
1 celery stalk, finely chopped
1 carrot, scraped and finely chopped
2 tablespoons olive oil
2 garlic cloves, crushed
two 14-ounce cans tomatoes
½ teaspoon each basil and oregano
1 bay leaf
½ cup (generous) red wine, Dark Vegetable
   Stock (p. 132) or water
salt and freshly ground black pepper

1 Sauté the onion, celery and carrot in the oil in a medium saucepan for 10 minutes, until soft but not browned. Add the garlic, tomatoes, basil, oregano, bay leaf, and the red wine, Dark Vegetable Stock or water.

2 Cook gently for 20 minutes, stirring from time to time, until the tomatoes have almost reduced to a purée.

3 Remove the bay leaf, then purée the sauce in a blender or food processor. Season to taste with salt and pepper. A little extra liquid can be added at this point for a thinner sauce, if wished. Add either more red wine, Dark Vegetable Stock or water.

Italian Tomato Sauce; Pesto (p. 172)

VEGETARIAN GRAVY

This is a tasty gravy, quite like a conventional meat gravy.
The soy sauce both flavors and colors it.

MAKES JUST UNDER 2 cups

Gravy Tip

Gravy freezes well, and it is very useful to have a supply in the freezer. Make a double batch and freeze in ice cube trays; when solid remove gravy cubes and store in a plastic bag to use as required. This is particularly useful if you only need small quantities of gravy at a time.

1 onion, peeled and chopped
2 tablespoons oil
2 tablespoons unbleached white flour
1 garlic clove, crushed
*2 cups (scant) Dark Vegetable Stock
   (p. 132) or water*
1 teaspoon yeast extract
1–2 tablespoons soy sauce
salt and freshly ground black pepper

1 Sauté the onion in the oil in a medium saucepan for 5 minutes, then add the flour and cook for a further 5–10 minutes, until the flour and the onion are nut-brown and the onion is soft and slightly pulpy.
2 Add the garlic, sauté for 1–2 minutes, then gradually stir in the Dark Vegetable Stock. Bring to a boil, then simmer for 10 minutes.
3 Strain the gravy into a clean saucepan and add the yeast extract, soy sauce and salt and pepper to taste. Stir well to mix, then serve.

MENU

Speedy Supper

Asparagus with Orange
Vinaigrette
144
Spaghetti with Pesto

Sweet Carrot and
Fennel Salad
162

Store-bought Ice Cream
with Butterscotch Sauce
301

PESTO

This popular Italian sauce for pasta can also be added to vegetable soups.

SERVES 4–6

2 garlic cloves, crushed
1/3 cup finely chopped fresh basil
1/4 cup chopped parsley
1/2 cup pine nuts or cashew nuts
1/2 cup grated Parmesan cheese
1/2 cup (generous) olive oil
freshly ground black pepper

Put all the ingredients into a blender or food processor and blend until smooth.

Variation
PARSLEY PESTO
Instead of fresh basil, use an extra 1/4 to 1/3 cup chopped parsley and a teaspoon of dried basil.

SWEET PEPPER SAUCE

Like tomato sauce, this bright red sauce is low in calories and excellent with many savories. For non-vegans, it may be enriched by adding 1–2 tablespoons butter just before serving.

SERVES 4

2 large red peppers
4 garlic cloves, peeled
salt and freshly ground black pepper

1 Put the peppers into a saucepan with enough water to almost cover. Bring to a boil, then simmer until tender.
2 Remove the peppers from the water, reserve the water, and discard the stems and seeds. Chop and place in a blender or food processor.
3 Add the garlic to the peppers, together with 1 1/4 cups of the cooking water, and blend to a purée.
4 Transfer to a clean saucepan. Season with salt and pepper and reheat gently.

V ## SAUCE SOUBISE V

*Sauce Soubise; Sweet Pepper Sauce
(p. 172); Hollandaise Sauce (p. 176)*

One of my personal favorites, this delicately flavored, thick onion
sauce is excellent with crisp nut loaves, such as the one on p. 239,
and nut burgers. If there's any left it's excellent poured over hard-
boiled eggs, heated through in the oven and served with fingers of
hot wholewheat toast. You do need to use white rice for this recipe
because of its starchiness, which thickens the sauce.

SERVES 4

2½ tablespoons white long-grain rice
½ pound onions, peeled and coarsely chopped
1 tablespoon butter or vegan margarine
½ cup (scant) water
a few parsley sprigs
1 thyme sprig
1 small bay leaf
2 tablespoons heavy or nondairy cream
salt and freshly ground black pepper
freshly grated nutmeg
a pinch of sugar

1 Parboil the rice in plenty of boiling
water for about 5 minutes, then drain.
2 Meanwhile, sauté the chopped onions
in the butter or vegan margarine in a
medium saucepan for 10 minutes. Add
the drained rice, water and parsley,
thyme and bay leaf.
3 Cover the pan and cook over a gentle
heat for 20–25 minutes, or until the
onions are very soft.
4 Remove from the heat and discard
the parsley, thyme and bay leaf. Purée
the onion mixture in a blender or food
processor.
5 Reheat the sauce gently in a double
boiler or heatproof bowl set over a saucepan of simmering water.
6 Just before serving, add the cream, and
season carefully with salt, pepper, nutmeg and sugar.

Gravy Alternatives

Don't get stuck in a gravy rut! There
are many other delicious sauces that
go excellently with savory
vegetarian dishes. Both the tomato
sauces on pp. 170 and 171 make
excellent alternatives to gravy and
are delicious with many vegetarian
dishes. Other good sauces to use in
place of gravy are:

Mushroom Sauce (p. 174)
Wine Sauce (p. 174)
Sweet Pepper Sauce (p. 172)
Sauce Soubise (left)

MUSHROOM SAUCE

[V] [V]

SERVES 4

Making Quick Meals from Sauces

It's useful to have some sauce in the fridge or freezer, because it can make the basis of good quick meals. Try:

Fresh Tomato Sauce (p. 170) – over hot cooked pasta or with lightly steamed root vegetables or winter squash served with cooked brown rice and roasted sunflower seeds; or parboil halved and deseeded green peppers, fill with a mixture of cooked brown rice, sautéed onion, mushrooms and nuts, place in a casserole, pour tomato sauce around the peppers and bake

Italian Tomato Sauce (p. 171) – layered with lasagne, grated mozzarella cheese and sautéed mushrooms or eggplants, or puréed spinach

Vegetarian Gravy (p. 172) – with sautéed onion and cubed leftover nut loaf

Sauce Soubise (p. 173), Béchamel (p. 175) or Cheese Sauce (p. 175) – over cooked leeks, cauliflower or diced mixed root vegetables, or over hard-boiled eggs

Egg Sauce (p. 175) – over any steamed vegetables; particularly good with fennel or zucchini

Curry Sauce (p. 177) or Savory Coconut Sauce (p. 177) – over hard-boiled eggs, drained canned chick peas or lima beans, or lightly steamed cauliflower

¼ pound button mushrooms, washed and chopped
1 tablespoon butter or vegan margarine
1 teaspoon cornstarch
½ cup (generous) milk, soy milk or light cream
salt and freshly ground black pepper
a few drops of lemon juice
freshly grated nutmeg

1 Sauté the mushrooms in the butter or vegan margarine in a small saucepan for 4–5 minutes, until just tender, then stir in the cornstarch.
2 Cook for 1–2 minutes, then add the milk, soy milk or cream, stirring all the time. Boil for 1 minute, then remove from the heat.
3 Season the Mushroom Sauce to taste with salt and pepper, a little lemon juice and freshly grated nutmeg.

Variation

WILD MUSHROOM SAUCE

A good way of using just a few precious wild mushrooms, delicious with a special nut roast or as a filling for vol-au-vents. Replace some – or all – of the button mushrooms with wild mushrooms, well washed and chopped.

WINE SAUCE

[V] [V]

Serve this rich sauce on individual plates, with nut burgers or roasts.

SERVES 4

1 onion, peeled and finely chopped
⅔ cup finely chopped mushrooms
2 tablespoons olive oil
1¼ cups red or white wine
2 tablespoons butter or vegan margarine
salt and freshly ground black pepper
a little sugar

1 Sauté the onion and mushrooms in the oil in a small saucepan for 10 minutes, until lightly browned.
2 Add the wine and let the mixture bubble away over the heat for a few minutes, uncovered, until the liquid has reduced by about half.
3 Cut the butter or vegan margarine into pieces, then add them to the sauce. Stir gently. Season to taste with salt, pepper and a little sugar. Serve the Wine Sauce immediately.

CRANBERRY SAUCE

[V] [V]

For me, cranberry sauce, made from fresh cranberries, is an essential part of Christmas dinner.

SERVES 8

2 cups cranberries, washed
¼ cup water
½ cup sugar
1 tablespoon port or fresh orange juice

1 Put the cranberries into a saucepan with the water. Bring to a boil, then simmer for about 10 minutes, until the berries are tender.
2 Add the sugar and cook gently until it has dissolved. Remove the pan from the heat and add the port or fresh orange juice. Stir well, then serve the Cranberry Sauce at once.

V   # BÉCHAMEL SAUCE   V

This sauce will keep, well covered, in the refrigerator, for a few days.

MAKES ALMOST 2 cups

2 tablespoons butter or vegan margarine
3 tablespoons unbleached white flour
2½ cups milk or soy milk
a piece each of onion, celery and scraped
   carrot
1 bay leaf
6 black peppercorns
1 thyme sprig
1–2 mace blades
salt and freshly ground black pepper
freshly grated nutmeg

1 Melt the butter or vegan margarine over low heat in a medium saucepan. Add the flour, stir over low heat for 1–2 minutes, then add the milk, a quarter-cup at a time, mixing well after each addition.
2 Add the onion, celery, carrot, bay leaf, peppercorns, thyme and mace, then leave the sauce to simmer gently for 10–15 minutes.
3 Strain the sauce through a sieve into a clean saucepan. Season to taste with salt, pepper and nutmeg.

Variations
PARSLEY SAUCE
Add 2–4 tablespoons chopped parsley and a few drops of lemon juice to the sauce after straining.

MORNAY OR CHEESE
SAUCE
A non-vegan variation. Make as described. Add 1 teaspoon Dijon mustard and ½–1 cup grated Cheddar or Gruyère cheese to the sauce after straining. Reheat gently but do not allow to boil after adding the cheese or it may become stringy.

EGG SAUCE
Stir 2 finely chopped hard-boiled eggs into the sauce after straining for another non-vegan variation.

V   # BREAD SAUCE   V

Serve with a nut roast such as White Nut Roast (p. 239) as part of a traditional vegetarian Christmas dinner.

SERVES 4–6

3 cloves
1 onion, peeled
1¼ cups milk or soy milk
1 bay leaf
2 slices white bread, crusts removed
1 tablespoon butter or vegan margarine
2 tablespoons light or nondairy cream
salt and freshly ground black pepper
freshly grated nutmeg

1 Stick the cloves into the onion, then put the onion into a saucepan with the milk and bay leaf.

2 Bring to a boil, then remove from the heat, add the bread, cover and set aside for 15–30 minutes to allow the flavors to infuse.
3 Remove the onion and the bay leaf. Beat the mixture to break up the bread, and stir in the butter or vegan margarine, the cream, and salt, pepper and nutmeg to taste. Sprinkle nutmeg on top.

QUICK HOLLANDAISE

SERVES 6

½ cup butter, cut into rough chunks
1 tablespoon lemon juice
2 egg yolks
salt and freshly ground black pepper

1 Put the butter into a small saucepan and heat until it has melted and is boiling.
2 While this is happening, put the lemon juice and egg yolks into a food processor or blender with a good pinch of salt and whizz for 1 minute to make a pale, thick mixture.
3 With the machine running, pour the melted butter in a steady stream into the food processor or blender through the top of the feeder tube, and whizz for a further 1 minute. Then let the mixture stand for a minute or two, before using it.

Blender Béarnaise Sauce

A blender or food processor can be used for a no-fuss, labor-saving version. Have the butter melted and cooled. Put the egg yolks into a blender or food processor with the strained reduced vinegar. Whizz until combined and thickened a little. Then add the melted butter through the top of the blender or food processor, a little at a time. The mixture will thicken. Add the lemon juice and seasoning to taste.

Ⅴ # AVOCADO AND RED PEPPER SALSA Ⅴ

SERVES 4–6

1 ripe avocado, peeled, pitted and diced
½ small red pepper, de-seeded and chopped
4 scallions, sliced
juice of ½ lemon
1–2 tablespoons chopped fresh coriander
salt and freshly ground black pepper

Put the avocado, red pepper and scallions into a bowl. Stir in the lemon juice, chopped coriander and seasoning to taste.

BÉARNAISE SAUCE

Another rich sauce, though a little goes a long way. It's wonderful with crisp nut or lentil burgers. For a quick and easy blender version, see above left.

SERVES 6

½ small onion, peeled and chopped
1 bay leaf
6 black peppercorns
¼ cup white wine vinegar
1 tarragon sprig, or a pinch of dried tarragon
2 egg yolks
1 stick (¼ pound) unsalted butter
salt and freshly ground black pepper

1 Simmer the onion, bay leaf, peppercorns, vinegar and tarragon in a small saucepan until the liquid has reduced to 1 tablespoon.
2 Put the egg yolks into the top of a double boiler, or into a heatproof bowl set over a saucepan of gently simmering water (with the base of the bowl above the level of the water).
3 Strain the reduced vinegar liquid over the egg yolks, pressing against the sieve to extract as much as possible.
4 Whisk the mixture until the egg yolks begin to thicken slightly.
5 Add the butter, about a teaspoon at a time, whisking well after each addition. The sauce will thicken and become creamy. Season to taste with salt and pepper. Serve warm.

TOMATO SALSA

A salsa is a kind of raw relish made from fresh vegetables and/or fruit, which are finely chopped and mixed with vinegar, fruit juice or oil. Other ingredients such as herbs, spices and capers are added for extra piquancy. You can go on adding ingredients until you have a mixture which tastes right to you, aiming for a balance between the different flavors and textures. A salsa can add a fresh and colorful note to almost any dish. Here is a basic recipe which you can vary.

SERVES 4

4 tomatoes, finely chopped
1 onion, preferably purple, peeled and finely chopped
2 tablespoons red wine vinegar
4 tablespoons chopped coriander
1 green chili, de-seeded and very finely sliced
salt and freshly ground black pepper

Put the chopped tomatoes and onion in a bowl with the vinegar, chopped coriander and chili. Season with salt and pepper to taste. Stir and leave to stand for 10 minutes (or longer) to allow the combined flavors to develop. Check the seasoning and serve.

Variations

A little crushed garlic can be added. Chopped avocado, mango or cucumber make good additions, too. You can substitute lime or lemon juice for some or all of the vinegar, plus a little of the grated rind. Try using different herbs such as fresh mint, flat-leaf parsley, lovage or thyme; add some capers or finely chopped sundried tomatoes – the possibilities are endless.

Tomato Salsa

SAVORY COCONUT SAUCE

A delicately flavored, golden sauce. Serve it with steamed vegetables and brown rice, for a simple meal, or heat halved hard–boiled eggs in it for a delicious egg curry.

SERVES 4

4 ounces desiccated coconut
2½ cups water
1 onion, peeled and chopped
2 tablespoons butter or vegan margarine
1 teaspoon turmeric
1 teaspoon grated fresh ginger
1 garlic clove, crushed
½ cinnamon stick or a pinch of ground cinnamon
salt and freshly ground black pepper
a little sugar
a few drops of lemon juice (optional)

1 Put the coconut into a saucepan with the water. Bring to a boil, then remove from the heat, cover and leave to stand in the saucepan for 10 minutes.

2 Meanwhile, sauté the onion in the butter or vegan margarine in a medium saucepan for 5 minutes. Add the turmeric, ginger, garlic and cinnamon, and sauté gently for a further 5 minutes.

3 Strain the coconut mixture into the onion mixture, pressing as much liquid through as you can. Discard the coconut in the sieve.

4 Remove the cinnamon stick, then purée the mixture in a blender or food processor. Return the sauce to the rinsed-out pan, season to taste with salt, pepper and a little sugar, and add the lemon juice to sharpen if necessary.

MENU
Quick and Easy Supper

SERVES 4

Fusille Colbuco with Eggplant and
Wine Sauce
255
Parmesan Cheese
Endive, Watercress and Walnut Salad
161

Quick Cherry and Lime Cheesecake
288

This is a meal which you can whizz up on the spur of the moment, assuming you have some fresh salad vegetables in the fridge and the ingredients for the Quick Cherry and Lime Cheesecake. Otherwise, serve the pasta with some frozen vegetables which, hopefully, you have in the freezer, and offer fresh fruit or biscuits and cheese instead of a dessert, if you have them available.

First make the cheesecake, then while that is chilling prepare the Eggplant and Wine Sauce. While that cooks, wash the salad, make a dressing and, when the sauce is almost done, cook the pasta. Serve with a chilled lager, or a wine with some body, to support all the flavors of the sauce: perhaps an Italian red – a Chianti, Barolo or Barbaresco – or a good-value Cabernet Sauvignon or Zinfandel.

Accompanying Vegetables

These recipes for accompanying vegetable dishes are the ones I find the most practical and useful. Some, such as Red Cabbage Casserole (below), are labor-saving because they can be cooked slowly and add moisture to a main dish, eliminating the need for a separate sauce. Many also add a bright splash of color, enhancing the look of the meal. Sometimes a simply cooked accompanying vegetable is best, especially if the main course is vegetable-based, and you will find some recipes for these in this section, and further ideas in the Ingredients section (p. 32), under individual vegetables.

Quantities for Vegetables

It's difficult to give exact quantities, because these depend on what else you're serving at the meal – whether there's another vegetable, for instance, and the type of main dish – and how much you like vegetables! As a general rule, allow 1–1½ cups per person. I'm quite greedy with vegetables, because my favorite way of staying slim is to have lots of vegetables and just a small amount of the main course.

[V] ## WILTED SPINACH [V]

Cooking tender young spinach in a little olive oil until it is just wilted ensures a bright-green result, half way between a salad and fully cooked spinach. It can be served hot or simply warm.

SERVES 4

2 tablespoons olive oil
1 pound tender spinach, washed, tough stems
   removed
salt and freshly ground black pepper

1 Heat a quarter of the oil in a large saucepan. Add a quarter of the spinach.

Stir-fry for a few seconds, until it has wilted, then remove it from the saucepan and place in a bowl. Warm the bowl in the oven first if you are serving it hot.
2 Repeat in batches with the remaining spinach and oil. Season with salt and pepper and serve immediately.

[V] ## RED CABBAGE CASSEROLE [V]

A useful dish, because it can cook away gently, and the result is moist enough to stand in for both a vegetable and a sauce.

SERVES 4–6

1 red cabbage, about 2¼ pounds, cored and
   shredded
1 large onion, peeled and chopped
2 tablespoons oil
2 tablespoons lemon juice
salt and freshly ground black pepper
a little sugar

1 Put the cabbage into a large saucepan, cover with water and bring to a boil, then drain thoroughly.
2 Meanwhile, sauté the onion in the oil in a large saucepan for 5 minutes, then add the cabbage, cover and cook very gently for 45–60 minutes, until the cabbage is very tender, stirring occasionally.
3 Add the lemon juice and salt, pepper and sugar to taste.

[V] # SPRING VEGETABLE BRAISE [V]

This is a particularly good way to cook a colorful selection of
tender young vegetables, but this method can be used throughout
the year for different mixtures, according to what is in season.

SERVES 4

6 tablespoons olive oil
6 tablespoons water
pared rind of ½ lemon
a good sprig each of parsley and thyme
1 pound tender young carrots, scraped and
    halved or quartered if large
1 pound tender young turnips, scrubbed and
    halved or quartered if necessary
½ pound snow peas, trimmed
½ pound fava beans (shelled weight)
salt and freshly ground black pepper
2–3 tablespoons chopped parsley

1 Put the oil into a large saucepan with
the water, lemon rind, parsley and thyme
and bring to a boil.
2 Add the carrots and turnips; cover and
simmer gently for 5–10 minutes, until
just tender.
3 Meanwhile, blanch the snow peas by
plunging them into a saucepan of boiling
water and boiling for 1 minute. Drain
and refresh under cold running water, to
preserve the color.
4 Add the beans and snow peas to the
carrot mixture and cook for a further 2–3
minutes, until heated through.
5 Season with salt and pepper. Serve
sprinkled with parsley.

Spring Vegetable Braise

[V] # STIR-FRIED CARROTS WITH
WATERCRESS AND SESAME SEEDS [V]

A quick vegetable dish, excellent with Japanese or Chinese meals.

SERVES 2–4

2 teaspoons oil
4 scallions, trimmed and sliced
4 medium carrots, scraped and cut into
    matchsticks
1 bunch watercress, tough stems removed
1 tablespoon soy sauce
salt
TO GARNISH
1–2 tablespoons sesame seeds

1 Heat the oil in a wok or saucepan, then
add the onions and carrots and stir-fry
over high heat for 2 minutes.
2 Add the watercress, stir-fry for 1–2
minutes, then cook gently for a further
3–4 minutes, stirring from time to time.
3 Stir in the soy sauce and a little salt,
then sprinkle the vegetables with sesame
seeds and serve immediately.

V   # BRAISED CELERY HEARTS   V

Braised vegetables are cooked slowly with a little liquid and flavoring ingredients. Sometimes the vegetables are lightly browned in fat before the liquid is added. Braising suits bulb vegetables such as celery, leeks and fennel particularly well.

SERVES 4

TURNING CARROTS

1 Cut carrots into rectangles about 2 inches long

2 Round off the corners with a sharp knife, to make a barrel shape

4 celery hearts, trimmed to about 5–6 inches
1 onion, peeled and chopped
2 carrots, scraped and diced
1 bouquet garni, including a piece of lemon peel
salt and freshly ground black pepper
TO GARNISH
chopped parsley

1 Wash the celery thoroughly, using a bottle brush, if necessary, to clean the inside.
2 Put the celery into a large saucepan, cover with water, bring to a boil, then boil for 10 minutes. Drain well, saving the water.
3 Cover the base of a large, heavy-bottomed saucepan with the onion and carrot, then place the celery on top. Add the bouquet garni, season to taste with salt and pepper, then pour in enough of the reserved cooking water to cover.
4 Bring to a boil, then simmer, with a lid on the pan, until the celery is very tender – 45–60 minutes.
5 Remove the celery from the saucepan with a slotted spoon and put it into a warmed shallow serving dish.
6 If the liquid has reduced to a sauce-like consistency, strain this over the celery. If not, boil it vigorously for a minute or two to reduce it, then strain it over the celery.
7 Sprinkle the celery with parsley and serve immediately.

Variation
BRAISED FENNEL
Make this in the same way as Braised Celery Hearts, but cut the fennel bulbs in half and instead of parboiling, sauté them in a little olive oil for about 10 minutes in a covered pan. Turn the fennel pieces from time to time during the cooking, allowing them to brown evenly on all sides.

V   # GLAZED CARROTS   V

For a special effect and a professional finish, the carrots can be "turned." I do this sometimes when I feel like being impressive, but normally I cut them into rings or sticks. They are particularly delicious with savory nut dishes.

SERVES 4

2 pounds carrots, peeled or scraped and sliced into sticks or rings
2 tablespoons butter or vegan margarine
salt and freshly ground black pepper
2 tablespoons white or soft light brown sugar
TO GARNISH
2 tablespoons chopped parsley

1 Put the prepared carrots into a large saucepan, cover them with cold water and bring the water to a boil.
2 Half-cover the saucepan, and leave the carrots to simmer gently until just tender – 8–15 minutes.
3 Drain the carrots, then return them to the pan with the butter or vegan margarine and salt and pepper. Cook over gentle heat until the butter or vegan margarine has melted, shaking the pan to coat all the carrots in butter or margarine.

Glazed Carrots (p. 182); Peas Cooked in the French Style

4 Sprinkle on the sugar, mixing gently over the heat until all the sugar has melted and the carrots are shining with glaze. Sprinkle the chopped parsley over the top and serve immediately.

Variation

GLAZED TURNIPS

Cook as described, using whole baby turnips if you can get them, otherwise use sliced or "turned" turnips.

Ⓥ PEAS COOKED IN THE FRENCH STYLE Ⓥ

This is a wonderful way to make frozen peas (or fresh peas, when you can get young, tender ones) taste really good.

SERVES 4

1 small bunch scallions, trimmed and chopped
2 tablespoons butter or vegan margarine
outer leaves from 1 lettuce, washed and
  roughly shredded
1–1½ cups frozen peas or shelled fresh peas
½ teaspoon sugar
salt and freshly ground black pepper
2–3 mint sprigs, when available

1 Sauté the scallions in half the butter or vegan margarine in a medium saucepan for 2–3 minutes on medium heat.

2 Add the lettuce and peas. Sprinkle with the sugar and salt and pepper to taste.

3 Dot with the remaining butter or vegan margarine, and, if you are using the sprigs of mint, place them on top, then cover.

4 Cook over gentle heat for 10–15 minutes, until the peas are tender.

5 Check the seasoning and remove the mint. Serve the cooked peas immediately, with the shredded lettuce (my preference) or without.

JULIENNE OF ROOT VEGETABLES

This mixture of orange carrots, yellow rutabaga and white turnips works well, but you could use just two of these vegetables, or different ones. Some kohlrabi makes a pleasant addition.

SERVES 4

CUTTING JULIENNE SLICES

1 Cut rounded edges off root vegetables so that they are rectangular in shape

2 Cut into thin slices one way, then the other way, to make matchsticks

¾ pound carrots, scraped
½ pound turnips, peeled
½ pound rutabaga, peeled
1 tablespoon butter or vegan margarine
salt and freshly ground black pepper
TO GARNISH
1–2 tablespoons chopped parsley

1 Cut the vegetables into julienne strips, then put them into a saucepan, cover with cold water and bring to a boil.
2 Half-cover the pan and cook gently until the vegetables are just tender – about 10 minutes, depending on how thinly you cut them.
3 Drain, saving the water, which makes particularly good stock, then return the vegetables to the pan and add the butter or vegan margarine. Season to taste with the salt and pepper, sprinkle with the chopped parsley and serve.

Variations
JULIENNE BUNDLES
Keep the vegetables separate during cooking. Soften a thin strip of leek by dipping in boiling water for 1–2 minutes. Serve the vegetables in bundles tied with the blanched leek strip.

JULIENNE OF CARROTS
This is very good made with carrots alone, especially when you want to bring a splash of bright color to a meal. A pinch or two of aniseed, caraway or dill gives a pleasant, unusual flavor to this vegetable dish.

Soy Sauce

This is a richly flavored, salty and slightly sweet liquid which has been used in China and Japan for centuries and is useful for adding both flavor and color to stews, casseroles, sauces and marinades, as well as for flavoring stir-fries, and as a dip for tempura. Choose a naturally fermented soy sauce without added caramel. Tamari has the strongest flavor and the darkest color; shoyu is lighter; the difference between these in cooking terms can be compared to that between red and white wine, though they can really be used interchangeably in most recipes.

CHINESE-STYLE MUSHROOMS

This simple dish is pleasant with plain boiled rice and Roasted Marinated Tofu with Satay Sauce (p. 231).

SERVES 4

½ pound small button mushrooms, wiped
1 tablespoon olive oil
1 teaspoon cornstarch
3 tablespoons soy sauce
TO GARNISH (OPTIONAL)
roughly chopped scallions

1 Sauté the mushrooms quickly in the olive oil in a small saucepan for 2–3 minutes, over high heat, until just tender.
2 Blend the cornstarch and soy sauce. Add to the mushrooms, and stir for 1–2 minutes, until thickened. Garnish with the chopped scallions, if using, and serve immediately.

GOLDEN SPICED CAULIFLOWER

Ⅴ   Ⅴ

A beautiful golden dish, one of my favorite ways of preparing cauliflower. Some chopped fresh coriander (or parsley) is the perfect finishing touch, but it's also very good without.

SERVES 4

1 onion, peeled and chopped
2 tablespoons oil
1 garlic clove, crushed
½ teaspoon turmeric
1 teaspoon ground coriander
2 cardamom pods
1 small cauliflower, divided into florets
¼ cup (generous) water
salt and freshly ground black pepper
TO GARNISH
sprig of mint

1 Sauté the onion in the oil in a medium saucepan for 8 minutes, then add the garlic, turmeric, coriander and cardamom. Stir over the heat for a further 2–3 minutes.
2 Add the cauliflower, turning it gently with a spoon to coat with the onion and spice mixture, then add the water and some salt and pepper. Bring the mixture to a boil.
3 Cover and leave to cook gently for about 15 minutes, until the cauliflower is just tender. Shake the pan from time to time to prevent sticking and ensure even cooking.
4 Check the seasoning, then garnish with a sprig of mint and serve the cauliflower immediately.

Variations
SPICED POTATOES
For this excellent variation, use 2 pounds peeled potatoes, cut into ½-inch dice. Make exactly as described, but do cook it gently and keep an eye on the pan, to prevent sticking. Most of the liquid should have been absorbed by the time the potatoes are cooked – 8–10 minutes – leaving them bathed in just a little golden, spicy sauce. The chopped fresh coriander is particularly good with potatoes cooked this way, but parsley can be used if coriander is unavailable.

SPICED ROOT VEGETABLES
A delicious winter variation. Use 2 pounds peeled root vegetables cut into ½-inch dice. A mixture of root vegetables can be used: rutabaga, carrots, turnips, parsnips, as well as sliced onions and celery, as available. Make as described for the Spiced Potatoes variation. This makes a good accompaniment to a mild-flavored dish and goes well with nut or lentil burgers.

Okra with Cumin and Coriander (p. 186); Golden Spiced Cauliflower

PEPERONATA

For this delicious Italian pepper stew, you can use all red peppers,
or a mixture of red, yellow and green peppers, which gives a
particularly attractive result.

SERVES 4

Reheating Vegetables in the Microwave

Cook the vegetables in the usual way until they are slightly underdone. Then drain, refresh under cold water and drain again well. Place in a shallow serving dish, dot with butter if you like, cover with a plate and keep in a cool place until needed. Then microwave on full power for a few minutes (the time will depend on the quantity of vegetables) until piping hot. Serve at once. It can be convenient to reheat vegetables in the microwave in this way when you're cooking for a dinner party and want to keep last-minute preparations to the minimum.

1 large onion, peeled and chopped
1 tablespoon butter or vegan margarine
1 tablespoon olive oil
2 large red peppers
2 large yellow peppers
2 large green peppers
1 large garlic clove, crushed
1 pound tomatoes, peeled and chopped
salt and freshly ground black pepper
TO GARNISH
1–2 tablespoons chopped parsley

1 Sauté the onion in the butter or vegan margarine and the oil in a large saucepan for 10 minutes, allowing the onion to brown lightly.
2 Meanwhile, deseed the peppers and cut them into strips, then add them to the onion. Cover and cook gently for 10–15 minutes.
3 Add the garlic and tomatoes, then cover and cook for a further 40 minutes or so, until the peppers are very tender and soft.
4 Season to taste with salt and pepper, sprinkle with chopped parsley and serve. Peperonata reheats well, or is excellent served cold.

OKRA WITH CUMIN AND CORIANDER

This lightly spiced dish can be made in advance and then reheated.

**SERVES 2, OR 4, WITH OTHER DISHES, AS PART OF A
CURRY MEAL**

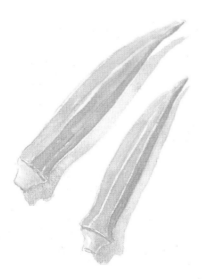

1 onion, peeled and chopped
2 tablespoons oil
½ pound okra, washed and trimmed
1 teaspoon salt
1 teaspoon whole cumin seeds
1 tablespoon ground coriander
1 cup (scant) water
2 tomatoes, chopped
salt and freshly ground black pepper
TO GARNISH
1–2 tablespoons chopped fresh coriander

1 Sauté the onion in the oil in a medium saucepan for 5 minutes, then add the okra, salt, cumin seeds and ground coriander. Mix well, then cook gently, uncovered, for 5 minutes.
2 Add the water; then simmer, un-covered, for 20 minutes, until the okra is tender and most of the water has been absorbed. Shake the pan or stir from time to time to prevent sticking.

3 Add the tomatoes, check the season-ing, and sprinkle with the chopped fresh coriander. Serve hot or warm. (It's also pleasant cold, garnished with a slice of lemon and chopped parsley.)

Variations
SPICED GREEN BEANS
This is also a good way to serve green beans, especially if you grow them and are getting tired of them while they're still producing prolifically! Trim and slice the beans in the usual way (p. 61), then cook as described.

SPICED EGGPLANT
Another variation which works well and makes a useful side dish for serving with curries. Dice and salt (p. 73) a medium-sized eggplant and sauté with the onion for 10 minutes before adding the tomatoes.

[V]   # RATATOUILLE   [V]

This delicious Provençal vegetable mixture is good with cooked
brown rice or crusty bread and a crisp salad. If you're serving it with rice,
put this on to cook before you start making the ratatouille.

SERVES 4

3 tablespoons olive oil
2 large onions, peeled and chopped
3 large red peppers, deseeded and sliced
3 garlic cloves, crushed
1 pound zucchini, cut into even-sized pieces
1 pound eggplant, diced
1½ pounds tomatoes, peeled and chopped
salt and freshly ground black pepper
TO GARNISH
chopped parsley

1 Heat the oil in a large saucepan and
sauté the onions and peppers gently for
5 minutes.
2 Add the garlic, the zucchini and the
eggplant. Stir gently, then cover and
cook over a low heat for about 25 minutes, until all the vegetables are tender.
3 Add the tomatoes, stir gently and
cook, uncovered, for about 5 minutes, to
heat through. Season to taste with salt
and pepper and sprinkle with parsley.
Serve hot or cold.

Flavoring Vegetarian Dishes

You can introduce strong, almost
"meaty" flavors by using yeast
extracts and soy preparations such as
miso and soy sauces. Or – and I
must admit that this is my own
preference – you can concentrate on
the assets of the vegetarian diet,
which are the fresh flavors of the
vegetables, nuts and grains, and
accent these by joyous use of fresh
herbs, chopped and in bouquets
garnis; citrus rinds and juices;
good-quality salt and freshly ground
black pepper; the judicious – and
sometimes generous – use of spices;
the use of wine.

[V]   # LEEK AND PEAR PURÉE   [V]

This is particularly good with savory legume and nut dishes.

SERVES 4–6

1 pound leeks, trimmed, cleaned and sliced
1 pound pears, peeled, cored and sliced
1¼ cups water
4 unpeeled garlic cloves
2 tablespoons butter or vegan margarine,
    softened
salt and freshly ground black pepper

1 Put the leeks and pears into a large
saucepan with the water and whole garlic
cloves. Boil for about 15 minutes, until
tender.
2 Remove the garlic cloves and pop
them out of their skins; put them into a
blender or food processor with the leeks,
pears and cooking liquid, and blend until
smooth.
3 Reheat the mixture gently and stir in
the butter or vegan margarine. Season to
taste with salt and pepper.

Variations
CARROT, APPLE AND CORIANDER PURÉE
Make as described, using carrots instead

of leeks and apples instead of pears,
and a medium onion, peeled and sliced.
Add 1 tablespoon crushed coriander
seeds, tied in a piece of cheesecloth.
Remove this, squeezing it well to extract
all the flavor, before puréeing. Garnish
with fresh chopped coriander, if available, or chopped parsley.

PUMPKIN AND GINGER PURÉE
Replace the leeks and pears with 2 pounds
pumpkin or winter squash (weighed
without skin and seeds). Cook the squash
with the water as described and a walnut-
sized piece of ginger, grated.

CARROT AND RUTABAGA PURÉE
Replace the apples with rutabaga, peeled
and cut into even-sized pieces. Some
freshly grated nutmeg and a pinch of a
warm spice, such as cinnamon, allspice
or ground cloves, are good with this, or
2–3 tablespoons chopped parsley.

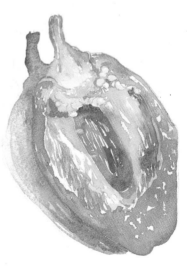

Potato and Almond Croquettes; Carrot Purée (p. 189)

Ⅴ   POTATO AND ALMOND CROQUETTES   Ⅴ

These croquettes make a good vegetarian cooked breakfast, served with broiled tomatoes and mushrooms. For a light meal, serve them with Sweet Carrot and Fennel Salad (p. 162); or with Mushrooms in Cream (p. 79) and a green vegetable.

SERVES 4

4 large potatoes, peeled and cut into
*   even-sized pieces*
1 tablespoon butter or vegan margarine
2–3 tablespoons milk or soy milk
¾ cup (generous) slivered almonds
3 tablespoons chopped parsley
salt and freshly ground black pepper
whole-wheat flour or ground almonds for
*   coating*
oil for shallow frying

TO GARNISH
lovage sprigs

1 Boil the potatoes in water to cover until they are tender – about 20 minutes.

2 Drain the potatoes, then dry them in the pan over low heat for 1–2 minutes.

3 Mash the potatoes with the butter or vegan margarine and enough milk or soy milk to give a creamy consistency.

4 Stir in the slivered almonds and parsley, and season with salt and pepper.

5 Form into 8 croquettes, then coat with whole-wheat flour or ground almonds.

6 Shallow-fry in a little hot oil in a frying pan until the undersides are crisp, then turn the croquettes and fry on the other side until crisp.

7 Drain on paper towels. Serve immediately, garnished with lovage.

[V]   # POTATO PURÉE   [V]

This is really a way of saying very light, smooth mashed potatoes, perhaps made a bit moister than you normally would. It's one of my favorite ways of serving potatoes, very useful because it is not only delicious but it adds some moisture to the meal, often eliminating the need for extra sauces.

SERVES 4

1½ pounds potatoes, peeled and cut into
   even-sized pieces
½ cup (generous) milk or soy milk
salt and freshly ground black pepper
1–2 tablespoons butter or vegan margarine
TO GARNISH
chopped parsley

1 Put the potatoes into a large saucepan, cover with cold water and bring to a boil. Boil, half-covered, for about 15 minutes, until just tender.
2 Drain the potatoes, and either return to the pan and mash very thoroughly with a potato masher, or, for best results, pass the potatoes through a food mill.
3 Put the puréed potato back into the saucepan. Heat the milk or soy milk in another saucepan and, when it comes to a boil, add it gradually to the potatoes, beating all the time. The potatoes will become fluffy and whiter and should be the consistency of whipped cream.
4 Season to taste with salt and pepper. If you are serving the potatoes right away, beat in the butter or vegan margarine; if not, keep the potatoes warm by standing the saucepan in an outer pan of boiling water; or transfer the potatoes to another container standing in a saucepan of water. Then beat in the butter or vegan margarine and sprinkle with chopped parsley just before serving.

Variations
POTATO PURÉE WITH OLIVE OIL
Replace the butter or margarine with 2–3 tablespoons olive oil.

POTATO AND CELERIAC PURÉE WITH PISTACHIOS
Replace ½ pound of the potatoes with celeriac, peeled, cut into even-sized pieces and cooked with the potatoes. Garnish with a scattering of chopped shelled pistachio nuts.

CARROT PURÉE
Replace the potatoes with the same amount of carrots. Cook until tender, then drain. Use some of the cooking water instead of some of the milk, if you wish. Garnish with chopped parsley.

[V]   # RÖSTI   [V]

This delicious crisp golden potato cake from Switzerland is quick and easy to make.

SERVES 4

¼ cup oil
1 pound potatoes, scrubbed or peeled, then
   coarsely grated
salt

1 Heat the oil in a large frying pan with a lid, add the potatoes and salt. Press down.
2 Cook the potatoes gently, covered, until they are browned on the bottom.
3 Turn the rösti over, either with a spatula, or by turning it out onto a plate then sliding it back into the frying pan.
4 Cook until the second side is browned and crisp. Serve immediately.

MENU
Winter Brunch for Eight

Millet Pilaf with Nuts and Raisins
245
Rösti
Illustrated on p. 191

Scrambled Eggs
107

Waffles with Clear Honey
298
Dried Fruit Compote
Illustrated on p. 14
102

BAKED POTATOES

Baked potatoes make one of the easiest and most economical dishes. Simply scrub one or two large potatoes per person, prick and bake at 450°F for 1–1½ hours, until the potatoes feel soft when squeezed and the skins are crisp. Then split open and serve with butter and grated cheese, or some cottage cheese or sour cream or plain yogurt, or with one of the following toppings.

Accompanying Vegetables as Main Courses

Some accompanying vegetables make excellent main courses if served with extras such as cooked brown rice, warm rolls, garlic bread, hot cooked pasta or a potato dish. Some suggestions are:

Spring Vegetable Braise (p. 181) with wedges of hard-boiled egg and new potatoes, or with warm crusty bread

Red Cabbage Casserole (p. 180) with Baked Potatoes (right) and sour cream, or with Gratin Dauphinois (below right)

Stir-fried Carrots with Watercress and Sesame Seeds (p. 181) with Chinese-Style Mushrooms (p. 184) and Sweet Vinegared Rice (p. 241)

Toppings for Baked Potatoes

CREAMY MUSHROOMS

Top the potatoes with Mushroom Sauce (p. 174).

CREAMED CORN

Heat ½ cup frozen corn kernels in ¼ cup cream, dairy or vegan, stirring, until the corn is hot, then season to taste with salt and pepper.

CHILI-TOMATO-CHEESE

A non-vegan topping. Sauté a small, finely chopped onion in 1 tablespoon butter for about 10 minutes, until soft but not browned. Then add one 8-ounce can tomatoes, mashing them a bit as you put them in, and a pinch of chili powder and 1 cup grated cheese. Stir gently over the heat until the cheese has melted and the mixture is hot.

AVOCADO

Top with chopped ripe avocado tossed in lemon juice, salt and pepper.

SOUR CREAM AND CHIVES

Add 2 tablespoons snipped chives to ½ cup sour cream for this excellent non-vegan topping. Mix the chives and cream together gently, season to taste with salt and pepper, and spoon over the hot potatoes.

Braised Celery Hearts (p. 182) with Cheese Sauce (p. 175) and crusty bread

Ratatouille (p. 187) with hot cooked brown rice and a lettuce and fresh herb salad

Baked Potatoes (p. 190) with Technicolor Cabbage Salad (p. 162)

Stuffed Baked Potatoes (p. 191) with Favorite Coleslaw (p. 161)

Rösti (p. 189) or Hashed Brown Potatoes (p. 191) with Apple Sauce (p. 84) and Carrot, Fennel and Red Pepper Salad (p. 162)

GRATIN DAUPHINOIS

A delectable dish for a special occasion. Keep the other vegetables in the meal fairly simple.

SERVES 6

3 tablespoons butter
1½ pounds potatoes, peeled and sliced as thinly as possible
salt and freshly ground black pepper
freshly grated nutmeg (optional)
1 large garlic clove, crushed
½ cup (generous) heavy cream

1 Preheat the oven to 325°F. Use half the butter to grease a shallow ovenproof dish generously.
2 Put the potato slices into a colander and rinse well under cold running water; drain and dry on paper towels.
3 Layer the potato slices in the prepared dish, seasoning with salt, pepper and nutmeg, if using, and a smear of crushed garlic between each layer.
4 Pour the cream evenly over the top of the potatoes and dot with the rest of the butter.
5 Bake, uncovered, for 1½–2 hours, until the potatoes feel tender when pierced with the point of a knife.

V # HASHED BROWN POTATOES V

This classic way with fried potatoes gives a particularly savory result at breakfast.

SERVES 2–4

¼ cup oil
1 pound potatoes, scrubbed or peeled and
    diced, cooked or uncooked
1 small onion, finely chopped (optional)
salt and freshly ground black pepper

1 Heat the oil in a large frying pan with a lid, then add the potatoes with the onion, if used, and press down with a spatula.
2 If the potatoes are raw, cook them over gentle heat, covered, until they are tender, then turn up the heat to brown them.
3 Fry cooked potatoes over moderate heat until golden-brown underneath. Press them down into the oil several times with a spatula.
4 Divide the potatoes in the middle and turn each half over. When they are golden-brown and crisp, drain on paper towels. Season and serve immediately.

Clockwise from top: Hashed Brown Potatoes; Rösti (p. 189); Gratin Dauphinois (p. 190)

V # STUFFED BAKED POTATOES V

Serve these with some salad, such as Technicolor Cabbage Salad (p. 162) or Sweet Carrot and Fennel Salad (p. 162).

1–2 large potatoes per person
a little butter and milk per person
¼–½ cup grated cheese per person
salt and freshly ground black pepper
2–3 tablespoons chopped fresh herbs

1 Scrub and prick the potatoes, then bake them at 450°F for 1–1½ hours until the skins are crisp and the potatoes feel tender inside when squeezed.
2 Halve the potatoes and scoop out the insides, being careful not to tear the skin. Place the skins on a baking sheet. Mash the scooped-out potato with a little butter and milk and half the cheese. Season to taste with salt and pepper.
3 Spoon the mixture back into the potato skins, sprinkle with the remaining cheese and return the potatoes to the oven for about 20 minutes, until golden-brown and crisp.

Vegan Variation
HERBED BAKED
POTATOES
Omit the cheese, replace the butter with vegan margarine and use plenty of herbs. Season well with salt and pepper.

Main Vegetable Dishes

Vegetables can be made into some filling and tempting main courses, ranging from simple homely dishes like Vegetable Hotpot (p. 200), to exquisite stuffed vegetables, one of my favorite main courses for a special meal. Other particularly popular dishes include vegetable kebabs and vegetable tempura, which, served with rice, make main courses that appeal — especially to non-vegetarians. Although some of the stuffed vegetables are a bit complicated to make, other recipes in this section, such as the Sweet-and-Sour Vegetable Stir-Fry (p. 199) and the Potato and Cheese Layer (p. 200), are particularly easy, good for midweek and family cooking, when time presses.

Ⓥ
STUFFED EGGPLANTS À LA PROVENÇALE
Ⓥ

Served on a bed of cooked rice, potato purée or cooked noodles, and accompanied by a green salad, these stuffed eggplants make a delicious main course.

SERVES 4

2 eggplants, total weight about 1 pound
salt
olive oil
1 large onion, peeled and chopped
4 tomatoes, peeled and chopped
2 garlic cloves, crushed
2 tablespoons chopped parsley
freshly ground black pepper
¼ cup fresh whole-wheat breadcrumbs
a little butter or vegan margarine

SCOOPING OUT AN EGGPLANT

Cut around the edge of the eggplant, and make crisscross cuts over the surface. Salt, drain and rinse (p. 73), then scoop out the flesh

1 Remove the stalks from the eggplants and cut them in half lengthways. Make cuts across the flesh, without piercing the skin, then salt, drain and rinse as described on p. 73.

2 Scoop the flesh out of the skins and chop the flesh. Be careful not to tear the skins, and set them aside.

3 Preheat the oven to 400°F.

4 Heat a little oil in a large saucepan and sauté the eggplant skins for about 3 minutes on both sides. Remove from the pan, place in a shallow ovenproof dish and set aside.

5 Next sauté the onion and eggplant flesh for 7 minutes, adding a little more oil if necessary. Add the tomatoes and garlic and sauté for a further 3 minutes, then mix in the parsley and season to taste with salt and pepper.

6 Spoon the mixture into the eggplant skins, sprinkle with the crumbs, dot with butter or vegan margarine and bake for 20–30 minutes, until the eggplant skins are tender and the filling mixture is browned on top.

MENU

Early-Autumn Lunch for Four

Roasted Hazelnut Soup
Illustrated on p. 136
135
Quick Whole-Wheat Rolls
328

Stuffed Eggplants à la Provençale

Fresh Tomato Sauce
170
Potato Purée
189
Buttered Spinach
55

Pear Sorbet
282

Ⅴ ZUCCHINI WITH CARROT, GINGER Ⅴ AND ALMOND STUFFING

Light and delicately spiced, these zucchini are good with a green
salad and a Vegan Yogurt and Herb Dressing (p. 156).

SERVES 4

1 large onion, peeled and chopped
2 tablespoons olive oil
4 medium zucchini, total weight about 1½
  pounds
1 garlic clove, crushed
4 medium carrots, scraped and finely diced
¾ teaspoon grated fresh ginger
⅔ cup slivered almonds
salt
freshly ground black pepper

1 Preheat the oven to 375°F.
2 Sauté the onion in the oil in a medium saucepan for 5 minutes.
3 Meanwhile, halve the zucchini lengthways and scoop out as much of the centers as you can, to make a good cavity for stuffing.
4 Chop the scooped-out zucchini and add it to the onion along with the garlic, carrot and ginger. Cover and sauté gently for about 10 minutes, until the vegetables are soft.

5 Remove from the heat and add the almonds and salt and pepper to taste.
6 Place the zucchini skins in a greased shallow casserole and fill them with the carrot mixture. (If the zucchini are long, they can be cut in halves or thirds.)
7 Cover with foil and bake for about 40 minutes, until the zucchini are tender. Serve immediately.

Variation
ZUCCHINI WITH COTTAGE CHEESE AND ALMOND STUFFING
For this variation, which is good served on a base of stir-fried shredded Chinese cabbage, replace the carrots with 1½ cups cottage cheese or ricotta cheese. Flavor with fresh ginger as suggested, or with 1–2 teaspoons grated lemon rind and a few drops of lemon juice. 1–2 tablespoons chopped parsley or chives can also be added.

PREPARING A
ZUCCHINI FOR
STUFFING

Cut in half lengthways and scoop
out the seeds and pulp to leave a
cavity for stuffing

Baked Stuffed Avocado (p. 196);
Stuffed Peppers (p. 194); Zucchini with
Carrot, Ginger and Almond Stuffing

Ⓥ Zucchini with Hazelnut Stuffing Ⓥ and Apple Sauce

This is a pleasant blend of flavors. Serve as a main course with crisp roast potatoes and one or two cooked vegetables, such as green beans and carrots. A Vegetarian Gravy (p. 172) can be served with it as well as the apple sauce.

SERVES 4–6

1 large, overgrown zucchini, weighing about 2¼ pounds
2 large onions, peeled and chopped
4 tablespoons butter or vegan margarine
½ cup hazelnuts, roasted, peeled and grated
1⅓ cups fresh whole-wheat breadcrumbs
2–3 tablespoons chopped fresh sage
salt
freshly ground black pepper
a little extra butter or vegan margarine for greasing
1 quantity Apple Sauce (p. 84)

1 Preheat the oven to 400°F.
2 Cut the stalk off the zucchini, then peel the zucchini, keeping it whole. Cut a lengthwise slice off one end, and, using a spoon, carefully scoop out the seeds. This will leave a cavity for stuffing.
3 Sauté the onions in the butter or vegan margarine for 10 minutes, until soft, then add the hazelnuts, breadcrumbs, sage and salt and pepper to taste. Push the mixture into the zucchini, then replace the sliced-off end, holding it in place with toothpicks or small skewers.
4 Wrap the zucchini completely in aluminum foil and place in a baking pan.
5 Bake for about 1 hour, until the zucchini is tender when pierced with a skewer. Remove the aluminum foil and serve, cut into slices, with Apple Sauce.

SCOOPING OUT A ZUCCHINI

Cut a thin slice off the stalk end, then scoop out the seeds and pulp; replace the slice after stuffing, holding it in place with toothpicks or small skewers.

DESEEDING A PEPPER

Halve the pepper, cut out the white membranes, then rinse away the seeds

Ⓥ Stuffed Peppers Ⓥ

Red, green or yellow peppers can be used for this, either 6 of one type, or a mixture, for a multicolored dish. I think a puréed vegetable, particularly potatoes, or buttered noodles with poppy seeds, and a simple green salad of cucumber or lettuce goes well with this dish.

SERVES 6

SCOOPING OUT A TOMATO

Slice the top off the tomato and scoop out the flesh with a teaspoon

1 large onion, peeled and finely chopped
¼ cup olive oil
2 garlic cloves, crushed
2 large tomatoes, peeled and chopped
1¼ cups long-grain brown rice
1 teaspoon dried oregano
2½ cups water
salt and freshly ground black pepper
6 peppers with a good, squarish shape
2 tablespoons chopped parsley
a little extra oil, for greasing

1 Sauté the onion in the oil in a medium heavy-bottomed saucepan, then add the garlic, tomatoes and rice, and cook gently, stirring often, for a further 3–4 minutes until the onion is soft.
2 Add the oregano, water and a teaspoon of salt. Bring to a boil, then cover the saucepan tightly and let cook very gently for 45 minutes.
3 Meanwhile, cut the peppers in half lengthways and scoop out the seeds. Parboil the peppers in 1 inch of water for

5 minutes, then drain them and dry on paper towels.

4 Preheat the oven to 350°F. Season the rice mixture with pepper and more salt if necessary, and stir in the chopped parsley, then spoon this mixture into the pepper halves.

5 Stand the peppers in a lightly oiled casserole. Bake for 25–30 minutes, until the peppers feel tender when pierced with a skewer.

Variations

The stuffing mixture can be varied in many ways. Try adding small quantities of tasty vegetables such as finely chopped mushrooms or celery; add grated cheese for non-vegan versions. For a Middle Eastern flavor, replace the oregano with 1 teaspoon ground cinnamon or allspice and add ¼ cup each of chopped dried apricots, currants and pine nuts or cashew nuts to the mixture.

Tomatoes with Zucchini and Corn Stuffing

Ⓥ TOMATOES WITH SPICY STUFFING Ⓥ

Beefsteak tomatoes lend themselves to many different stuffings. One of my favorites is this spicy potato mixture. Serve these tomatoes with plain or spiced brown rice (p. 241) and a moist side dish, such as Okra with Cumin and Coriander (p. 186) or Wilted Spinach (p. 180).

SERVES 4

4 large beefsteak tomatoes
salt and freshly ground black pepper
1 large onion, peeled and chopped
¼ cup oil
1 pound potatoes, peeled and cut into
*   ¼-inch dice*
2 garlic cloves, crushed
2 teaspoons cumin seeds
½ teaspoon turmeric
2 tablespoons roughly chopped coriander
salt and freshly ground black pepper
butter for greasing
TO GARNISH
coriander sprigs

1 Cut off and reserve the tops of the tomatoes, then scoop out the pulp. Chop the pulp, season with salt and pepper, then put it into the base of a lightly greased shallow ovenproof dish large enough to hold all the tomatoes.

2 Sprinkle the inside of each tomato with salt, then turn them upside down on a paper towel to drain. Preheat the oven to 400°F.

3 Next, make the stuffing. Sauté the onion in the oil in a frying pan for 5 minutes, then add the potato and garlic.

4 Cook gently for 10 minutes, then add the spices and coriander. Cook for a further 4–5 minutes, until the potato is just tender. Season to taste with salt and pepper.

5 Spoon the potato mixture into the tomatoes. Stand the tomatoes in the dish on top of the tomato pulp, replace their sliced-off tops, and bake for 15–20 minutes, until the tomatoes are just tender. Garnish with the coriander sprigs and serve immediately.

Variations
TOMATOES WITH HERB STUFFING

This variation has a Provençal flavor. Prepare the tomatoes as described. For the filling, use the Herb Stuffing mixture on p. 239. Bake as described. These tomatoes are good served on a base of potato purée, accompanied by a lightly cooked vegetable, such as green beans, or a green salad.

TOMATOES WITH ZUCCHINI AND CORN STUFFING

Replace the potatoes with ½ pound zucchini cut into ¼-inch dice, and 1 cup fresh or frozen corn. Omit the spices and add 2 tablespoons roughly chopped parsley and a pinch of chili powder, if you wish.

MENU
Meal with a Provençale Flavor

Vegetables à la Grecque
150
with Crusty Bread

Tomatoes with Herb Stuffing

Rice or Potatoes Mashed with Olive Oil
189
Green Salad

Tarte au Citron
291

BAKED STUFFED AVOCADOS

Hot stuffed avocados make an easy and luxurious meal. Serve with Sauce Soubise (p. 173) and lemony carrots, or on a base of cooked rice or puréed carrot or potato.

SERVES 4

1 onion, peeled and chopped
1 tablespoon butter or vegan margarine
2 large ripe avocados, halved and pits removed
1 cup Brazil nuts, chopped
1 cup diced Gruyère cheese
1/4 cup grated Parmesan cheese
2 tablespoons chopped parsley
2 tablespoons sherry
salt
freshly ground black pepper

1 Preheat the oven to 400°F.
2 Sauté the onion in the butter or vegan margarine for 10 minutes, until soft but not browned.
3 Meanwhile, scoop the flesh out of the avocado skins with a spoon, taking care not to damage the skins. Dice the flesh.
4 Add the sauteed onion to the avocado flesh, together with the Brazil nuts, cheeses, parsley and sherry. Season to taste with salt and pepper.
5 Heap the mixture back into the avocado skins, place them in a shallow ovenproof dish and bake for 10–15 minutes. Serve immediately.

Stuffed Vegetable Platter

A selection of 3 or 4 different types of stuffed vegetables arranged on a base of saffron rice makes a stunning centerpiece for a special meal. Choose small vegetables, so that everyone can have several types, and arrange them attractively on a base of saffron rice on two large, flat serving dishes. This is a slightly fiddly meal to make, but the work can be done well in advance, and a cold sauce or dip, such as Tapenade (p. 146), or Yogurt and Herb Dressing (p. 156), and a green salad, are all the accompaniments needed. This selection would serve 6:

☐ 3 small Stuffed Eggplants à la Provençale (p. 192), using 1/2 stuffing ingredients
☐ 2 Zucchini with Carrot, Ginger and Almond Stuffing (p. 193), using 1/2 stuffing ingredients, and halved to give 8 portions
☐ 6 large (but not "beefsteak") tomatoes filled with 1 quantity Herb Stuffing (p. 239)
☐ 6 flat mushrooms stuffed with Fava Bean Dip as described on p. 61
☐ Double quantity Saffron Rice (p. 241)

Filling for Crepes

Golden Spiced Cauliflower (p. 185)
Red Cabbage Casserole (p. 180)
Ratatouille (p. 187)
Peperonata (p. 186)
Creamed White Beans (p. 206)
Avocada and Red Pepper Salasa (p. 176)
Mushrooms – or Wild Mushrooms – in Cream (p. 79)
Glazed Carrots (p. 182)
Okra with Cumin and Coriander (p. 186)
Spring Vegetable Braise (p. 181)

LITTLE CARROT AND CARDAMOM TIMBALES

Served warm or cold, these pretty orange timbales, delicately flavored with cardamom, make an excellent first course.

SERVES 6

1 tablespoon butter, plus extra for greasing
1–2 tablespoons grated Parmesan cheese
1/2 pound carrots, sliced
4–5 cardamom pods
2 eggs
2 egg yolks
2/3 cup light cream
1/4 cup thick cream
salt and freshly ground black pepper
TO SERVE
dill leaves
Lemon Vinaigrette (p. 154)

1 Preheat the oven to 325°F. Line the bases of six 2/3-cup dariole molds with circles of wax paper, then grease generously with soft butter and sprinkle with dry grated Parmesan cheese.
2 Boil or steam the carrots until tender – about 15 minutes – then drain. Crush the cardamom and discard the pods.
3 Put the carrots into a food processor with the butter and cardamom and blend to a smooth purée. Allow to cool slightly, then add the eggs, egg yolks and both creams and blend again to combine. Season with salt and pepper.
4 Pour the mixture into the darioles, then stand these in a baking pan. Pour very hot water into the pan around the darioles, to come half way up their sides.
5 Bake for 30–35 minutes, or until the mixture is firm to the touch and a skewer inserted into the center comes out clean.
6 Let them cool slightly – or completely if you want to serve them cold – then loosen the sides with the blade of a knife and turn each timbale out on to a small plate. Decorate with dill leaves and pour a little vinaigrette around each timbale.

CREPES STUFFED WITH ASPARAGUS AND COTTAGE CHEESE

Serve this summery main course with baby carrots and new potatoes. Begin the meal with a chilled soup.

SERVES 4–6

1½ pounds fresh asparagus, trimmed,
    washed and cooked as described on p. 63,
    or 1 pound frozen asparagus, cooked
1 pound cottage cheese
finely grated rind of 1 lemon
salt and freshly ground black pepper
FOR THE BATTER
1 cup (scant) unbleached white flour
½ teaspoon salt
2 eggs
1 tablespoon olive oil or melted butter
½ cup (generous) milk
½ cup (generous) water
TO FINISH
1¼ cups light cream
TO GARNISH
lemon twists
asparagus spears

Crêpes Stuffed with Asparagus and Cream Cheese

1 First make the filling: cut the asparagus into 1-inch lengths, then mix with the cottage cheese and lemon rind and season to taste with salt and pepper.
2 Next make the crêpe batter: either put all the ingredients into a blender or food processor and whizz until smooth, or put the flour into a bowl with the salt, make a well in the center and add the eggs, oil or butter and a little of the liquid. Beat until smooth, then gradually add the rest of the liquid.
3 Preheat the oven to 350°F.
4 Use the crêpe batter to make about 12 thin crêpes as described on p. 299.
5 Put a little of the asparagus mixture in the middle of each crepe, dividing it evenly among them. Roll the crêpes up and place them side by side in a shallow casserole.
6 Pour the cream over the top of the crêpes. Cover tightly with foil and bake for 20–30 minutes, until heated through. Remove the foil and garnish the crêpes with lemon twists and asparagus spears before serving.

Variations

VEGAN CRÊPES

For vegan crêpes, mix 1 cup (scant) chick pea flour (p. 41) with 1¾ cup cold water and ½ teaspoon salt. Cook the crêpes as described, using enough oil to prevent them from sticking; these crêpes need more fat than egg-based ones, but are excellent. Use Sauce Soubise (p. 173) instead of the cottage cheese, and non-dairy cream instead of the single cream.

CRÊPES WITH COTTAGE CHEESE AND MUSHROOMS

Use 1 pound sliced button mushrooms instead of the asparagus. Sauté in 2 tablespoons butter for 2–3 minutes, until just tender. Mix the mushrooms with the cottage cheese, omitting the lemon rind.

Colored Crêpes

The basic crêpe batter can be colored with saffron, turmeric, or vegetable purées; served with contrasting fillings, some attractive color effects can be created.

For pale green crêpes, add 2 tablespoons spinach purée to the batter; try this with a vivid red filling such as Ratatouille (p. 187) or Peperonata (p. 186).

To make pale yellow crêpes, soak a few strands of saffron in the milk before making the batter, or add ½–1 teaspoon turmeric. The turmeric version is good with a spicy vegetable filling such as Okra with Cumin and Coriander (p. 186).

VEGETABLE TEMPURA WITH DIPPING SAUCE

SERVES 4

Serving Ideas for Vegetable Tempura

A basket of these crisp mixed vegetable fritters looks appetizing and makes a delicious meal. Serve them with Sweet Vinegared Rice (p. 241), and follow with fresh lichees, for a meal with a Japanese flavor. All the main preparation can be done in advance, leaving only the frying to be completed just before eating.

½ pound eggplant, cut into ½-inch cubes
2 large carrots, scraped and cut into strips
8 medium mushroom caps, wiped
1 green pepper, deseeded and cut into strips
½ cauliflower, broken into florets, larger ones halved or quartered
FOR THE DIPPING SAUCE
¼ cup mirin (p. 308)
½ cup (generous) soy sauce
1 teaspoon grated fresh ginger
FOR THE BATTER
2 large eggs
1¼ cups water
1¾ cups unbleached white flour
1 teaspoon salt
oil for deep frying
TO GARNISH
julienne strips of carrot, fresh ginger and pepper

1 First make the dipping sauce. Bring the mirin to a boil in a small saucepan.
2 Remove from the heat and add the soy sauce and ginger. Pour the dipping sauce into 4 small bowls.
3 Make the batter: break the eggs into a bowl and beat them gently until just

broken up but not foamy.
4 Mix in the water, then sift in the flour and salt; mix lightly until combined. Don't worry if there are one or two lumps.
5 Have all the vegetables prepared and in separate piles ready for coating in batter.
6 Heat a deep fryer, half-filled with vegetable oil, to 350°F, or when bubbles form on a chopstick dipped into the hot oil.
7 Dip the eggplant into the batter, then put into the hot oil. Do not put in more than a single layer at a time.
8 After about 2 minutes turn the pieces over and fry the other side for a further 2 minutes, until light golden-brown.
9 Remove from the oil and place on paper towels. Keep the eggplant fritters warm while you fry the rest of the vegetables in the same way.
10 As soon as all the vegetables are done, serve them on 4 heated plates or in baskets lined with paper napkins, garnished with strips of carrot, ginger and pepper. Serve with the small bowls of dipping sauce.

[V] # EGGPLANT FRITTERS IN CHICK PEA BATTER [V]

Serve these fritters with potatoes and a green vegetable, and follow with a substantial dessert, such as Rose Cheesecake (p. 289).

SERVES 4

2 medium eggplants
oil for shallow frying
FOR THE BATTER
1 cup chick pea flour
½ teaspoon salt
¾ cup cold water
TO SERVE
lemon slices

Sour Cream or Yogurt and Herb Dressing (p. 156)

1 Cut the eggplants lengthways into ¼-inch slices, place in a colander, and salt, as described on p. 73.
2 Rinse the eggplant slices under cold water; pat dry on paper towels.

3 To make the batter, mix the chick pea flour and salt with the water until the mixture is completely smooth and thick.
4 Dip the eggplant slices in the batter, then fry on both sides in hot shallow oil.

5 Drain on paper towels. Keep the first batch warm while you fry the rest, then serve at once, garnished with lemon slices and accompanied by Sour Cream or Yogurt and Herb Dressing.

[V]

SWEET-AND-SOUR VEGETABLE STIR-FRY WITH ALMONDS

[V]

A delicious mixture of sweet and sour flavors with the crunch and nourishment of almonds. If you are planning to serve this with cooked brown rice (which goes very well with it), put the rice on to cook well in advance, as the stir-fry is very quick to make, and the rice takes 45 minutes. It's also very good cold, as a salad or first course.

SERVES 4

1 large red pepper, deseeded
1 large green pepper, deseeded
1 medium zucchini
3–4 celery stalks
1 bunch scallions
½ pound button mushrooms, wiped
½ cup olive oil
1 cup blanched almonds
FOR THE SWEET-AND-SOUR DRESSING
2 garlic cloves, crushed
¼ cup grated fresh ginger
¼ cup soy sauce
¼ cup lemon juice
1 tablespoon wine vinegar
2 tablespoons clear honey

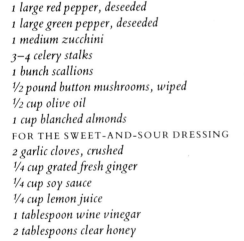

1 Cut the peppers, zucchini and celery into 2-inch matchsticks. Trim the scallions so that there is about 1 inch of the green part left. Slice the button mushrooms.
2 Next make the sweet-and-sour dressing: blend all the ingredients in a blender or food processor, or mix them in a bowl.
3 Make the stir-fry just before you want to eat: it only takes a few minutes to cook. Heat the oil in a wok or large saucepan, then put in the vegetables and stir-fry over high heat for 2 minutes, until they are beginning to soften.
4 Add the almonds and the sweet-and-sour mixture and stir-fry for a further 1–2 minutes, to heat through.

MENU

Dieters' Lunch

Carrot and Ginger Soup
129

Sweet and Sour Vegetable Stir-Fry with Almonds

Fresh Ripe Figs or Peaches

Sweet-and-Sour Vegetable Stir-Fry with Almonds

Quick Main Courses

Creamed White Beans with Potato Pancakes and Broiled Yellow Pepper Strips (p. 206) is quick to make if you use canned beans; Lentil Dal (p. 209) and Spinach Dal (p. 211) are also speedy and good served simply with rice or bread and a salad or with Spiced Potatoes (p. 185) or Golden Spiced Cauliflower (p. 185) for more of a meal. Satay Sauce (p. 238) makes any lightly cooked vegetables into a quick and satisfying meal. Many egg and cheese dishes are quick, especially the Frittata of Summer Vegetables (p. 223), Pipérade (p. 213), Cheese Fondue (p. 230), Halloumi with Parsley and Lemon Sauce (p. 226) and any of the omelettes (pp. 220 and 221).

Nut Burgers (p. 232), Risotto (p. 244) – especially the microwave variation – Millet Pilaf with Nuts and Raisins (p. 245) and Bulgur Wheat Pilaf with Red Peppers and Feta Cheese (p. 242) are fast to make too, as are many pasta dishes, especially Fusille Verde with Mushrooms and Cream (p. 251), Tagliatelle with Gorgonzola and Walnuts (p. 250), Tagliatelle Verde with Lentil Sauce (p. 252)

Quick Spring Onion and Fresh Herb Flan (p. 266) is a speedy pastry dish, and Sweet and Sour Vegetable Stir-Fry with Almonds (p. 199) is a quick vegetable mixture.

POTATO AND CHEESE LAYER

This is very quick and easy to make and popular with children; you need to allow time for it to bake slowly in the oven. It's nice with a plainly cooked green vegetable or some watercress.

SERVES 2–4 AS A MAIN COURSE

2–3 tablespoons butter
2 large potatoes, peeled and thinly sliced
2 onions, peeled and thinly sliced
1 cup grated Cheddar cheese
salt and freshly ground black pepper
¼ cup milk or soy milk
TO GARNISH
parsley sprigs
tomato slices

1 Preheat the oven to 325°F. Grease a shallow casserole well with 1 tablespoon of the butter.

2 Put a layer of potatoes in the bottom of the dish, then a thin layer of onion slices, a little grated cheese, then season with salt and pepper.

3 Continue in layers like this until all the ingredients are used, ending with a layer of potato slices. Pour the milk over the top and dot the remaining butter over the top.

4 Bake for about 1½ hours, until the potato feels tender when pierced with a sharp knife or skewer. Garnish with parsley sprigs and tomato slices.

[V] # VEGETABLE HOTPOT [V]

Serve this family dish with lightly cooked broccoli and perhaps Vegetarian Gravy (p. 172).

SERVES 4

one 14-ounce can chopped tomatoes
1 cup walnuts, chopped
1 tablespoon dried oregano
salt
freshly ground black pepper
4 large potatoes, peeled, cut into ¼-inch slices, parboiled for 4 minutes, then drained
2 green peppers, deseeded and sliced
2 onions, peeled and sliced
1 tablespoon olive oil
butter for greasing
TO GARNISH
parsley sprigs

1 Preheat the oven to 400°F. Grease a deep casserole with a little butter.
2 Mix together the tomatoes, walnuts and oregano. Season with salt and pepper.
3 Put a layer of potato slices in the casserole, followed by a layer of pepper, a layer of onion slices and then some of the tomato and walnut mixture.
4 Continue in this way until all the ingredients are used, ending with potato. Drizzle the olive oil on top.
5 Cover with foil and bake for 1 hour, removing the foil for the last 20 minutes, to brown the top. Garnish with parsley.

Variation

VEGETABLE-CHEESE HOTPOT
For a richer, non-vegan version, add 2 cups grated cheese, layering it with the rest of the ingredients.

Ⅴ VEGETABLE KEBABS WITH ROSEMARY Ⅴ

Marinating the vegetables for several hours allows them to absorb the flavors. Serve with Mixed Rice (p. 246) or Rice Salad with Fruit and Nuts (p. 158).

SERVES 6

12 small button mushrooms, wiped
½ pound firm tofu, cut into ½-inch cubes
½ pound firm tofu or Halloumi cheese, cubed
1 small red pepper, deseeded and cut into strips about 1 inch long and ½ inch wide
12 miniature corn
3 small zucchini, total weight about ¾ pound, cut into slices ½ inch thick
12 cherry tomatoes
six 8–10-inch rosemary sprigs, leaves scraped off the lower part, or 6 kebab skewers

FOR THE MARINADE
1 teaspoon mustard powder
1 garlic clove, crushed
2 tablespoons clear honey
2 tablespoons soy sauce
2 tablespoons olive oil
1 teaspoon salt
freshly ground black pepper

1 Thread vegetables and tofu or cheese on to the rosemary sprigs or skewers, putting on first a mushroom, then tofu or cheese followed by some red pepper, corn, zucchini and a cherry tomato.

2 Continue in this way until all the rosemary sprigs or skewers are full.

3 To make the marinade, mix together the mustard, garlic and honey, then gradually stir in the other ingredients.

4 Lay the kebabs on a nonmetal tray, plastic container, large plate or casserole big enough for them to lie flat.

5 Spoon the marinade over them, turning them to make sure that all the vegetables are coated.

6 Let the kebabs marinate for at least 1 hour, preferably for several hours, spooning the marinade over them occasionally.

7 Cook the kebabs under a hot broiler or on the grille of a barbecue for 10–15 minutes, until the vegetables are tender, turning the skewers so that the vegetables cook evenly.

8 Pour the remaining marinade into a small pitcher and serve separately.

Variation
All kinds of vegetables, cut into suitably sized pieces – eggplant cubes or cauliflower florets, for instance – can be used for Vegetable Kebabs, and the tofu or Halloumi cheese can be replaced by sietan, other firm cheeses or extra vegetables such as slices of onion.

Vegetable Hotpot (p. 200); Spinach Gnocchi (p. 203)

Ⅴ # VEGETABLE CURRY Ⅴ

This curry is delicious served with plain or spiced rice and, if there's any left over, it tastes even better the next day. Vary the vegetables according to your preferences and what is available. When preparing the vegetables, cut quicker-cooking ones into larger pieces than ones that take longer to cook, so they will all be done at the same time.

SERVES 4

1 onion, peeled
walnut-sized piece of fresh ginger
2 garlic cloves, peeled
2 tablespoons ground nut oil
2 teaspoons each ground coriander and cumin
1 teaspoon each ground turmeric, fenugreek and cinnamon
3 pounds mixed vegetables, such as carrots, potatoes, cauliflower and green beans, trimmed and peeled as necessary, then cut into pieces
3¾ cups water or Light Vegetable Stock (p. 129)
salt and freshly ground black pepper
TO GARNISH
chopped coriander

1 Cut the onion and unpeeled ginger into chunks and put into a blender or food processor with the garlic. Whizz to a purée.
2 Heat the oil in a large saucepan and put in the onion mixture. Cook gently for 5 minutes, then stir in the spices and cook for a minute or two longer.
3 Add the vegetables to the pan and stir over the heat until they are well coated.
4 Add the water or vegetable stock and 2 teaspoons of salt. Bring to the boil, then simmer for about 30 minutes or until all the vegetables are tender and the liquid has reduced and thickened slightly.
5 Check the seasoning then serve garnished with chopped coriander.

EGGPLANT PARMIGIANA

This makes an excellent supper, especially when accompanied by some red wine. Serve it with a green salad and some crusty bread, and follow with fresh fruit or a dish of homemade cookies.

SERVES 4

2 pounds eggplant
salt
olive oil for frying
2 large onions, peeled and finely chopped
2 garlic cloves, crushed
one 14-ounce can chopped tomatoes
½ pound cheese, preferably mozzarella, thinly sliced
6 tablespoons grated Parmesan cheese
freshly ground black pepper

1 Cut the eggplant into ¼-inch circles. Salt, drain and rinse the eggplant slices as described on p. 73.
2 Preheat the oven to 400°F

3 Heat a little olive oil in a large saucepan and saute the onion and garlic over medium heat for 10 minutes.
4 Remove the onion mixture with a slotted spoon to a plate, add the eggplant slices to the pan and sauté until crisp and lightly browned, adding more oil if necessary.
5 Layer the eggplant, onion, tomatoes and sliced cheese in an ovenproof dish, sprinkling some Parmesan cheese and salt and pepper between the layers and ending with a layer of Parmesan.
6 Bake, uncovered, for 40–60 minutes, until the eggplant is tender.

Side Dishes for Curries

Any of these, served in small wooden bowls or ramekins, make attractive accompaniments to curries and spiced rice dishes:

Roasted peanuts or cashew nuts
Macadamia nuts
Sliced tomatoes
Mango chutney or pickle
Sweet Spiced Apricot Chutney (p. 342)
Lime pickle
Sliced banana
Desiccated coconut
Sliced cucumber in plain yogurt
Nuts and raisins
Chopped celery and red pepper
Diced apple

Olive Oil

Perhaps the most delicious oil, made by pressing ripe olives. The oil is extracted by centrifugal force to give pure, pale green-gold "first pressing" cold-pressed oil. The pulp is then pressed again, under heat, to yield more virgin oil. "Virgin" on the label means that the oil has not been chemically treated to keep its natural acidity at a safe level. There are several permitted categories of virgin oil:

EXTRA-VIRGIN Must be under 1 percent acidity
SOPRAFINO OR EXTRA-FINE VIRGIN Can be up to 1.5 percent acidity
FINE VIRGIN Can have less than 3 percent acidity
VIRGIN Can have up to 4 percent acidity

These categories are often grouped into just two: extra-virgin, below 1 percent acidity, and virgin, below 4 percent acidity.

SPINACH GNOCCHI

Vegetable Curry (p. 202) with Spiced Rice (p. 241) and Chapatti (p. 331)

Serve the gnocchi with a colorful Italian-style salad for a light main course.

SERVES 4

1½ pounds fresh spinach, cooked, drained
    and chopped, or 1 pound frozen chopped
    spinach, thawed
½ pound mozzarella, grated, or other
    skim-milk soft white cheese
1½ cups flour
1 cup grated Parmesan cheese
2 eggs, beaten
salt and freshly ground black pepper
freshly grated nutmeg
extra flour for coating
a little butter
TO SERVE
grated Parmesan cheese

1 Drain the spinach, then purée it in a blender or food processor. Put the purée into a saucepan and dry it over the heat for a minute. Remove from the heat.
2 In a bowl, mix together the mozzarella cheese, flour, Parmesan cheese, eggs, and spinach. Season with salt, pepper and nutmeg. If the mixture is very soft, put it into the refrigerator to firm up for

about 30 minutes.
3 Roll heaped teaspoons of the mixture in a little flour. (All this can be done in advance.)
4 To cook the gnocchi, first heat the oven to low, to keep the gnocchi warm as they're ready. Half-fill a large saucepan with lightly salted water and bring just to a boil.
5 Drop 6–8 gnocchi into the water and let them simmer very gently for about 5–10 minutes, until they float to the surface.
6 Make sure the water does not get beyond a bare simmer, and remove the gnocchi as soon as they are ready, or they may fall apart.
7 Drain the gnocchi well, then put them into a warmed serving dish, dot with a little butter and keep them warm while you cook another batch.
8 When all the gnocchi are done, sprinkle with grated Parmesan cheese and serve immediately.

MENU

Family Lunch

SERVES 4–6

Tomato Soup with Basil
130

Garlic Bread
137

Cheese and Parsley Fritters
with Parsley Sauce
217 and 175

French-Fried Potatoes
71

Green Beans

Fresh Fruit Salad
286

This is a warming lunch for a chilly winter Saturday, when everyone needs cheering up. Most children, in my experience, like this homemade tomato soup and they usually adore garlic bread, too. (If some don't like garlic, leave this out when you butter one end of the loaf.) The Cheese and Parsley Fritters are another winner, but get organized in advance for this, as the mixture has to get completely cold before cutting; make it the evening before, or first thing in the morning. Since this is a day for spoiling the family, I've suggested French-fried potatoes and green beans to go with the fritters, with a fresh fruit salad for dessert to balance the richness.

To drink, I suggest a sparkling fruit cup made from mixed apple and orange juices and soda water; or, if you feel like something alcoholic for the grown-ups, I'd go Italian, with either a chilled white Soave or a red wine – a Chianti, perhaps.

Beans, Peas and Lentils

I know that some people are put off using legumes – dried beans, peas and lentils – because of the need to soak and cook them in advance. All the recipes in this section can either be made from quick-cooking legumes which do not need soaking first, or from canned ones, which I find excellent. However, the most economical way is to buy dried legumes and soak and cook them yourself, and all the information about this is to be found in the Ingredients section of the book (p. 40) along with more ideas for using the various types. Once cooked, beans and lentils can be made into a range of excellent main dishes, from colorful casseroles to savory bakes, loaves and burgers.

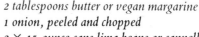

☑ CREAMED WHITE BEANS WITH ☑
POTATO PANCAKES AND BROILED
YELLOW PEPPER STRIPS

SERVES 4

2 tablespoons butter or vegan margarine
1 onion, peeled and chopped
2 × 15-ounce cans lima beans or cannellini beans, or 1 cup dried beans, soaked, cooked and drained (p. 40), cooking liquid reserved
salt and coarsely ground black pepper
2 large yellow peppers, quartered
FOR THE POTATO PANCAKES
olive oil for frying
1 pound potatoes, peeled and coarsely grated

1 Melt the butter in a saucepan, add the onion, then cover and cook for 10 minutes, until soft and golden but not browned.

2 Add the beans, together with 1¼ cups of their liquid. Simmer gently, un-covered, until the beans are very soft and the liquid has reduced to a buttery glaze. Mash the beans or purée in a blender or food processor, then season with salt.

3 Meanwhile, place the peppers under a hot broiler until the skin has blistered and blackened in places, turning them as necessary. Cool, then remove the skin and seeds under cold running water, and cut the peppers into strips.

4 Put the bean purée in a shallow baking dish and arrange the pepper strips on top. Keep warm while you make the potato pancakes.

5 Heat a thin film of oil in a non-stick frying pan. Season the grated potatoes with salt, then divide the mixture into 8 portions and put 2 or more in the frying pan, depending on size. Press down with a pancake turner. Fry until golden brown and crisp on one side, then turn the pancakes over and cook the other side: they will take about 5 minutes in all. Drain them on paper towels and keep them warm while you cook the remaining pancakes.

6 Arrange the pancakes around the edge of the baking dish, sprinkle some coarsely ground black pepper over the bean purée and serve.

Variation
CREAMED RED BEANS WITH
POTATO PANCAKES AND BROILED
RED PEPPER STRIPS
Use red beans instead of white and red pepper instead of yellow. Add some chili powder to the beans.

LENTILS AND MUSHROOMS AU GRATIN

In this recipe, lentils are made into a thick sauce, poured over mushrooms, topped with crumbs and cheese and baked until crisp and browned. Serve with a lightly cooked green vegetable such as cabbage or broccoli.

SERVES 4

1 cup dried split red lentils
2½ cups water
1 large onion, peeled and finely chopped
4 tablespoons butter
finely grated rind and juice of ½ lemon
1 teaspoon yeast extract
salt and freshly ground black pepper
¼ pound mushrooms, washed and sliced
⅔ cup fresh whole-wheat breadcrumbs
½ cup grated Cheddar cheese

1 Put the lentils and water into a medium saucepan and simmer very gently, uncovered, until the lentils are tender and all the liquid is absorbed. This should take about 20 minutes.
2 Preheat the oven to 350°F.
3 Sauté the onion in half the butter for 10 minutes until soft and lightly browned.
4 Add the onion to the lentils, together with the lemon rind and juice, yeast extract and salt and pepper to taste. Purée in a blender or food processor, or beat well with a wooden spoon, to make a thick purée.
5 Sauté the mushrooms in the remaining butter for 2–3 minutes, then put them into a shallow ovenproof dish and pour the lentil mixture on top. Sprinkle with the breadcrumbs and the grated cheese.
6 Bake for 40–45 minutes, until golden and crisp on top and hot and bubbly underneath.

Variation

LEEKS AND LENTILS AU GRATIN

Make the lentil sauce exactly as described. Replace the mushrooms with 2¼ pounds leeks, cleaned, cut into 1-inch lengths, boiled until tender, then drained.

PEASE PUDDING

This is traditionally served as an accompaniment to meat.

SERVES 4

1 pound dried yellow split peas
2 large onions, peeled and chopped
4 tablespoons butter
2 teaspoons fennel seeds
2 eggs (optional)
salt and freshly ground black pepper

1 Put the split peas into a saucepan, cover with water and cook gently until soft – this takes about 30 minutes or so. Drain.
2 Preheat the oven to 350°F. (Or, if you're roasting potatoes at a higher temperature, put the pease pudding in the oven on a low shelf – the temperature isn't crucial.)
3 Sauté the onions in the butter for 8 minutes, then add the fennel seeds, stir for 1–2 minutes, then add the split peas and the eggs, if you're using these. Season with salt and pepper.
4 Spoon the mixture into a lightly greased, fairly shallow ovenproof dish and bake for 50–60 minutes, until browned on top.

Yeast Extract

A sticky dark brown paste made from brewers' yeast, and often fortified by other vitamins (such as B12), yeast extracts are highly nutritious and are useful for giving a savory flavor to casseroles, sauces, gravy, nut roasts and other dishes, and also as a spread for bread. Use with a light touch; add a little at a time.

Sprouting Legumes

Most whole legumes, with the exception of red kidney beans, can be sprouted, and make a delicious, crunchy and highly nutritious addition to salads and stir-fries.

To sprout legumes, put 2 heaping tablespoons of your chosen variety into a quart jar. Cover the legumes with cold water and leave overnight. Next day fix a piece of gauze over the top, securing with a rubber band. Pour the soaking water out through the gauze, then, again without removing the gauze, fill the jar with cold water, shake, and pour it out. Leave the jar on its side for 2–4 days until the legumes have sprouted, repeating the rinsing at least twice a day. Once sprouted, the legumes can be stored in a plastic bag in the refrigerator.

V

VEGETARIAN CHILI

V

A tasty, substantial dish which has been responsible for more than one male convert to vegetarianism. Serve with hot brown rice or baked potatoes with sour cream and chives, and a green salad.

SERVES 4

1 tablespoon olive oil
1 onion, peeled and chopped
1 red pepper, deseeded and chopped
1–2 garlic cloves, crushed
one 14-ounce can tomatoes
1 cup dried red kidney beans, soaked, cooked
    and drained (p. 40), or two 15-ounce cans
    red kidney beans
½ cup dried whole green lentils, simmered in
    plenty of water for 40–45 minutes, until
    tender
1 teaspoon mild paprika
1–2 tablespoons chili powder
salt and freshly ground black pepper
a little sugar
TO GARNISH
coriander sprig

1 Heat the oil in a large saucepan and sauté the onion and pepper for 10 minutes. Add the garlic and cook for 1–2 minutes, then add the tomatoes.
2 Drain the beans and lentils, reserving liquid. Add both to the tomato mixture, along with the paprika and chili powder.
3 Simmer for 15 minutes, adding the bean water as needed for consistency. Season, add sugar, garnish and serve.

V

FELAFEL

V

This is the traditional Israeli recipe for these crisp, tasty rissoles, made with soaked but uncooked chick peas. You need a food processor with a good sharp blade to purée the chick peas. The resulting crisp felafel are excellent served with salad and some tahini dip or dressing; they can also be stuffed into pita pockets for a substantial snack meal.

MAKES ABOUT 22

Serving Ideas for Felafel

These crisp, tasty little savory balls make a filling and delicious snack, served in a pocket of pita bread with salads and any spicy relishes you fancy. Or the felafel are good served with a salad and a Yogurt and Herb Dressing (p. 156), Mayonnaise (p. 155), or Tahini Dressing (p. 155).

1½ cups dried chick peas
⅔ cup fresh parsley, thick stalks removed
1 garlic clove, peeled and roughly sliced
1 onion, peeled and cut into chunks
1 teaspoon each of ground coriander, ground
    cumin and rock salt
ground nut or canola oil for deep-frying

1 Cover the chick peas generously with cold water and leave to soak for 24 hours.
2 Drain and rinse the chick peas. Put them into a food processor with the parsley, garlic, onion, spices and salt. Blend to a grainy paste that holds together. If the mixture is on the wet side, chill in the refrigerator for an hour or so.
3 Heat the oil in a saucepan or deep fryer until it forms bubbles around the end of a wooden chopstick dipped into it. Form pieces of the mixture into walnut-sized balls, then flatten them a bit.
4 Put the chick pea patties into the oil, three or four at a time. Fry them for 2–3 minutes, until crisp and brown. Drain on paper towels and keep warm.
5 Use immediately, or freeze them by putting the cooked felafel on a tray and freezing until firm, then putting them into a plastic container. Microwave or broil them straight from the freezer.

Vegetarian Chili (p. 208); Felafel in Pita Pockets (p. 208)

LENTIL DAL

Dal is usually served as an accompaniment to curries or spiced rice dishes, spooned or poured over the top, adding extra flavor.

SERVES 4

1 cup dried split red lentils
1 onion, peeled and chopped
1 large garlic clove, crushed
1 bay leaf
1 whole fresh green chili
1-inch piece fresh ginger, peeled and grated
½ teaspoon turmeric
2 teaspoons each ground cumin and ground coriander
1–2 teaspoons salt
¼ cup coconut cream
1 tablespoon lemon juice
TO GARNISH
fresh mint leaves

1 Put the lentils into a saucepan with enough cold water to come ½ inch above them, and add the chopped onion, garlic, bay leaf, whole chili, ginger and turmeric.

2 Cook gently, half-covered, for about 20 minutes, until the lentils are soft, stirring occasionally and adding a little more water if necessary to prevent the lentils from sticking. The final mixture should be quite runny, like a purée, but not watery.

3 Stir in the cumin, coriander and salt to taste. If possible, leave to stand, covered, for 20–30 minutes, to allow the flavors to blend.

4 Discard the bay leaf and chili and stir in the coconut cream. Reheat gently, stirring, until the coconut has melted. Add the lemon juice, check the seasoning and serve the lentil dal, garnished with a few fresh mint leaves.

Serving Ideas for Lentil Dal

I also like dal as a main dish, poured over lightly cooked vegetables and served with mango chutney and lime pickle, or with some plain boiled rice and some wedges of hard-boiled egg. It's also good served with the Spiced Potatoes on p. 185, with a side dish of tomato and onion salad. It depends how hungry you're feeling!

V   SPICY LENTIL BURGERS   V

Lightly spiced, moist and delicious, these burgers can be
served in soft whole-wheat burger buns, with salad and a yogurt
and herb sauce or mayonnaise, or with cooked vegetables and a
savory sauce. The burgers freeze well and can
be cooked frozen.

SERVES 4

Oils for Cooking

CANOLA OIL   The high level of
monounsaturates (along with useful
amounts of polyunsaturates and the
lowest level of saturates of any oil)
makes this another useful oil for
general cooking.

CORN OIL   Made from the kernels
of maize, this is a bland oil, high in
polyunsaturates. It is healthiest
when cold pressed, for recipes like
mayonnaise in which it is not heated.

GRAPE SEED OIL   Made from the
seeds of grapes, this is a light oil,
high in polyunsaturates.

GROUND NUT OIL   A useful all-
round oil, fairly low in
polyunsaturates but stable when
heated, so a healthy oil for cooking.

SAFFLOWER OIL   Made from the
seeds of the safflower (a relative of
the sunflower), this is one of the
most nutritious oils, rich in
polyunsaturates, and cold-pressed
safflower oil can be mixed with olive
oil to increase the polyunsaturates.
Safflower oil has rather a strong
flavor which limits its uses.

SESAME OIL   An oil which keeps
well and is fairly high in polyunsaturates, this oil is made from
roasted sesame seeds and has a strong,
distinctive flavor. It is much used in
Chinese and Asian cooking.

SOYBEAN OIL   A good, mild-
flavored oil made from soybeans and
rich in polyunsaturates. Reasonably
priced, stable when heated and
useful for most cooking, including
cakes and pastries.

SUNFLOWER OIL   High in the
valuable linoleic acid, and in
polyunsaturates generally.
Healthiest when cold pressed, in
dishes that do not require cooking.

2 large onions, peeled and finely chopped
2 carrots, scraped and finely chopped
1 celery stalk, finely chopped
2 tablespoons olive oil
1 large garlic clove, crushed
*1 cup dried green or brown lentils, cooked
    until tender, and well drained (p. 40)*
½ teaspoon ground cumin
½ teaspoon ground coriander
6 tablespoons chopped parsley
1 tablespoon lemon juice
salt and freshly ground black pepper
unbleached white flour for coating
oil for shallow frying
TO GARNISH
watercress
tomato slices

1 Sauté the onion, carrot and celery in
the oil in a large saucepan for 10 minutes
until soft and lightly browned, stirring
from time to time.
2 Add the garlic, lentils, cumin, coriander, parsley and lemon juice. Mash by
hand, or purée roughly in a food processor or blender, until the mixture holds
together. Season with salt and pepper.
3 With floured hands, shape the mixture
into 10–12 flat burgers, using a palette
knife. Coat the burgers with flour.
4 Sauté the burgers in a little oil until
crisp and browned, turning them over
carefully to cook the second side.
5 Drain on paper towels and serve garnished with watercress and tomato.

V   LENTIL SHEPHERD'S PIE   V

This can be prepared in advance, ready for cooking, and only
needs a quickly cooked vegetable, such as Brussels sprouts or
carrots, to go with it.

SERVES 4

1 cup dried green or brown lentils
4 tablespoons butter or vegan margarine
2 large onions, peeled and thinly sliced
1 garlic clove, crushed
1 teaspoon dried herbs de Provence
one 15-ounce can tomatoes, chopped
2 tablespoons soy sauce
2–3 tablespoons chopped parsley
salt and freshly ground black pepper
1½ pounds potatoes, cooked and mashed
a little extra butter or vegan margarine

1 Put the lentils into a large saucepan,
cover with water and boil gently until
tender – about 45 minutes. Drain.
2 Preheat the oven to 400°F. Use half the

butter or vegan margarine to grease a
shallow ovenproof dish.
3 Sauté the onions in the remaining
butter or vegan margarine in a large
saucepan for 10 minutes.
4 Add the garlic, mixed herbs, tomatoes, soy sauce, lentils, parsley and salt
and pepper to taste.
5 Spoon the mixture into the dish.
Spread the mashed potatoes evenly over
the top, drawing the prongs of the fork
over the surface to make ridges. Dot the
whole surface with a little butter or vegan
margarine.
6 Bake the pie for 45 minutes, until the
potato topping is golden-brown.

V MIDDLE EASTERN CHICK PEA STEW V

SERVES 4

2 pounds eggplant
salt
2 large onions, peeled and chopped
1/4 cup olive oil
2 garlic cloves, crushed
one 15-ounce can tomatoes
1/2 cup dried chick peas, soaked, cooked and drained, or one 15-ounce can chick peas, drained
freshly ground black pepper
TO GARNISH
fresh mint leaves

1 Cut the eggplant into 1/2-inch dice, sprinkle with salt, place in a colander, put a weight on top and leave for 30 minutes.
2 Rinse the eggplant and gently squeeze out as much liquid as you can.
3 Preheat the oven to 400°F.
4 Sauté the onion in half the oil in a large saucepan for 10 minutes. Remove with a slotted spoon, and sauté the eggplant pieces in the remaining oil until crisp and lightly browned. Drain on paper towels.
5 Put the eggplant and onion into an ovenproof dish, then add the garlic, tomatoes, chick peas and salt and pepper. Mix well, cover, and bake for 40–60 minutes. Garnish with fresh mint leaves.

Middle Eastern Chick Pea Stew

V SPINACH DAL V

Quick to make and packed with iron, this is good served with plainly cooked rice, warm nan and a tomato salsa (p. 177).

SERVES 2–3

1 tablespoon oil
1 onion, peeled and finely chopped
1 garlic clove, crushed
1 dried red chili, crumbled
1 teaspoon cumin seeds
1 teaspoon ground coriander
1/4 teaspoon ground turmeric
2/3 cup split red lentils
2 1/2 cups water
1/2 pound tender spinach, washed
1–2 tablespoons lemon juice
salt and freshly ground black pepper

1 Heat the oil in a large saucepan and put in the onions; let them cook gently, covered, for 10 minutes.
2 Add the garlic, crumbled chili and spices. Cook for 1 minute, stirring, then add the lentils. Stir well, then add the water. Bring to a boil then simmer, uncovered, for 30 minutes, until soft.
3 Add the spinach to the pan and cook for about 10 minutes, or until the spinach is tender: it will shrink considerably and blend with the lentils.
4 Add lemon juice, season, then serve.

Fruit with Legumes

The flavor of fruit complements legumes well and a number of traditional recipes, especially in Germany, Scandinavia, and Russia, feature this.

Try the Savory Lentil Loaf (p. 213) with Cranberry Sauce as a change from apple; Pease Pudding (p. 207) with Apple Sauce or Leek and Pear Purée (p. 187); Spicy Lentil Burgers (p. 210) with sliced pineapple or mango; sultanas added to Middle Eastern Chick Pea Stew (p. 211).

Egg and Cheese Dishes

Eggs and cheese are useful protein foods for lacto-vegetarians and can be made into some particularly pleasant dishes such as fondues (p. 217), soufflés (p. 222), roulades (p. 224) and gnocchi (p. 227). Served with lightly cooked vegetables or a fresh salad, there is no reason why cheese and egg dishes, although relatively high in fat, should not feature in the main meals of a healthy diet. Aim to achieve a good balance by serving bean, pasta, cereal or nut dishes frequently on other days, and by keeping your other meals of the day low in fat. Then you can enjoy these tasty and time-saving dishes with a clear conscience!

Reducing the Calories in Cheese

If you want to cut down on the calories in a cheese dish, try using small quantities of a strongly flavored cheese such as an aged farmhouse Cheddar or Parmesan. Personally I prefer following this course of action to using the reduced-fat cheeses which are now available. I would rather have half or two-thirds the quantity of a traditionally produced cheese with a really good flavor and texture.

SPINACH OMELETTE WITH RAISINS AND PINE NUTS

You need to use tender spinach for this recipe, and if it's tender enough, you won't need to remove the stems. It makes a good quick dinner, served with a salad and perhaps a yogurty sauce or mayonnaise.

SERVES 2

2 tablespoons olive oil
½ pound tender leaf spinach, washed
¼ cup raisins
¼ cup pine nuts
salt and freshly ground black pepper
2 eggs, beaten
½ cup grated Parmesan cheese

1 Heat the oil in a frying pan, then put in the spinach and stir-fry over the heat for 2–3 minutes, until tender. Heat the broiler.
2 Add the raisins and pine nuts, season with a little salt and pepper then spread the mixture over the frying pan so that it covers the base evenly and completely.
3 Season the beaten eggs then pour them into the pan, moving the spinach so that they run right down to the bottom.
4 Cook gently for a minute or two, until the base of the omelette is set and lightly browned.
5 Sprinkle the Parmesan cheese evenly over the top; then pop the frying pan under the broiler and leave for another minute or two to set and brown the top. Serve at once, cut in half or thick wedges.

MENU

Quick Easy Supper

Charentais Melon Halves

Spinach Omelette with Raisins and Pine Nuts

Crusty Wholewheat Stick

Tomato Salad
73

Fresh Figs, Assorted Yogurts, Fromage Frais

OMELETTE CANNELLONI

In this recipe thin omelettes are wrapped around a tasty filling of spinach and ricotta cheese and topped with a tomato sauce. It's good served as a first course, or as a main course with a salad.

SERVES 4

1 pound tender spinach
½ pound ricotta cheese
¾ cup Parmesan cheese, freshly grated
salt and freshly ground black pepper

freshly grated nutmeg
4 eggs
a little olive oil
1 quantity Italian Tomato Sauce (p. 171)

1 Preheat the oven to 350°F.
2 Wash the spinach, then put it in a saucepan with just the water clinging to its leaves. Cover and cook for 3–4 minutes or until tender. Drain well and chop finely.
3 Add the ricotta cheese and half the Parmesan cheese to the spinach. Mix well and season with salt, pepper and nutmeg.
4 Whisk the eggs with a tablespoon of water and some salt and pepper. Brush a small frying pan generously with olive oil and heat. Pour in a little of the beaten egg – just enough to make a thin, crêpe-like omelette – and cook for a few sec-

onds until it is set. Transfer it to a plate with a spatula. Repeat the process to make 7 more omelettes, adding a little more oil to the frying pan as necessary.
5 Put some of the spinach mixture down the center of each omelette and roll up like a pancake. Place in a shallow baking dish.
6 Pour some of the tomato sauce over the rolled omelettes, without covering them completely. Sprinkle with the rest of the grated Parmesan and bake for 20–30 minutes, to heat through and brown the top. Heat any remaining sauce and serve with the cannelloni.

Basic Egg Cookery

For simple, basic ways of cooking eggs – boiling, scrambling, poaching and frying – see the Ingredients section (p. 107).

Hard-boiled Eggs

The best egg for hard-boiling is several days old. A newly laid egg is difficult to peel because the white sticks so firmly to the shell.

PIPÉRADE

This French version of scrambled eggs with vegetables makes a delicious and economical supper dish in the late summer when tomatoes and peppers are cheap. It's an excellent dish for one person: just halve the ingredients.

SERVES 2

1 large onion, peeled and chopped
2 tablespoons butter
1 large green pepper, deseeded and chopped
1 pound tomatoes, peeled and chopped
1–2 garlic cloves, crushed
4 eggs, beaten
salt and freshly ground black pepper
TO GARNISH
lovage sprig
TO SERVE
hot, crusty rolls or fingers of hot whole-wheat toast

1 Sauté the onion in the butter for 10 minutes, until soft but not browned.
2 Add the green pepper, tomatoes and garlic and cook gently, uncovered, for a further 15–20 minutes, until the vegetables are soft but not mushy, stirring from time to time.
3 Strain in the beaten eggs and stir gently until they begin to set. Remove from the heat (the eggs will continue to cook in their own heat).
4 Season with salt and pepper, garnish with lovage and serve with the crusty rolls or fingers of toast.

Spinach Omelette with Raisins and Pine Nuts (p. 214); Omelette Cannelloni

GRUYÈRE PROFITEROLES STUFFED WITH FENNEL, WITH GREEN PEA SAUCE

These puffy golden profiteroles with their creamy fennel filling and
green pea sauce make an excellent main course for a spring meal.
The Gruyère mixture, filling and sauce can all be made in advance,
so that all you have to do before the meal is bake and fill the profiteroles.

MAKES 8

¼ pound Gruyère cheese, grated
1 quantity Choux Pastry (p. 271)
1 small fennel bulb
scant 1 cup medium-fat soft cheese
salt and freshly ground black pepper
FOR THE SAUCE
1 tablespoon butter
1 shallot, peeled and chopped
2 ounces potato, peeled and cut into ¼-inch
   dice
1 cup frozen peas
2 sprigs of mint
⅔ cup water

*Gruyère Profiteroles Stuffed with
Fennel, with Green Pea Sauce*

1 Preheat the oven to 400°F. Grease a
cookie sheet, then dampen it under cold
water (if you do this, the steam created in
the oven helps the pastry to rise).
2 Add two-thirds of the grated cheese to
the choux pastry dough and mix well.
Put spoonfuls of the mixture well apart
on the cookie sheet and sprinkle with the
rest of the cheese, then bake in the oven
for 30 minutes, until well risen and
golden brown. Meanwhile make the
sauce and the filling.
3 For the sauce, melt the butter in a
medium saucepan, add the shallot and
potato, then cover and cook gently without browning for 10 minutes. Add the
peas, mint and water, bring to a boil and
simmer for 4–5 minutes, until the potato
is tender. Remove the mint.
4 Purée the sauce in a blender or food
processor, adding more water if necessary, until it is the consistency of light
cream. Season to taste.
5 For the filling, trim the fennel, removing any tough parts, and chop finely. Mix
with the soft cheese and season.
6 When the profiteroles are done, immediately pierce them with a knife to let
out the steam. They can be served hot or
warm. Slit them open and fill with the
fennel mixture, then either serve on a
pool of sauce or hand the sauce round
separately.

Variation
GRUYÈRE PROFITEROLES WITH
GARLIC AND RED PEPPER SAUCE
Use 1–2 crushed garlic cloves instead of
the fennel and one red pepper, deseeded
and chopped, instead of the peas. Fry the
pepper with the shallot and potato. Add
the water, simmer until the vegetables
are tender. Omit the mint.

SWISS CHEESE FONDUE

Cheese fondue makes an excellent, cozy supper for 2–4 people. It's best made in a heavy-bottomed saucepan or casserole which can be brought to the table and set on a fondue burner.

SERVES 4

1 garlic clove, halved
1 ¼ cups dry white wine or hard cider
3 ½ cups grated Gruyère or Edam cheese
1 tablespoon cornstarch
2 tablespoons kirsch or gin (optional)
2 teaspoons lemon juice
salt and freshly ground black pepper
freshly grated nutmeg
TO SERVE
1–2 loaves French or Italian bread, white or
*   whole-wheat, cut into bite-sized cubes*

1 Rub the garlic around the inside of a medium saucepan, then discard.
2 Put all but ¼ cup of the wine or cider into the saucepan and bring just to a boil, then add the cheese and stir over gentle heat until melted.
3 Mix the cornstarch with the remaining wine or cider and the kirsch or gin. Pour this into the cheese mixture, stirring until slightly thickened.
4 Remove from the heat and add the lemon juice. Season to taste with salt, pepper and nutmeg. Put the warmed bread cubes into 1 or 2 baskets, mixing up the white and whole-wheat if using both types.
5 Place the pan of fondue in the center of the table, and use long forks to spear pieces of warm bread and dip them into the cheese fondue.

Oils for Cooking

Some oils and fats are chemically more stable than others (and therefore better for health) when heated and so are better for cooking. These include butter, clarified butter and ghee, and of the oils, olive and peanut oil.

Almost-instant Cheese Fondue

Cheese fondue is an excellent emergency meal. Keep a bag of grated cheese and a couple of loaves of French or Italian bread in the freezer, and a bottle of hard cider or white wine in the cupboard, and you can whip up a cheese fondue in minutes.

CHEESE AND PARSLEY FRITTERS

Children love these served with Parsley Sauce (p. 175), French-fried potatoes (if allowed!), and a lightly cooked vegetable.

SERVES 4

2 ½ cups milk
1 small onion, peeled and stuck with 1 clove
1 bay leaf
½ cup semolina
1 cup grated Cheddar cheese
1–2 tablespoons chopped parsley
good pinch cayenne pepper
salt and freshly ground black pepper
1 large egg, beaten with 1 tablespoon water
dried breadcrumbs for coating
oil for shallow frying
TO GARNISH
lemon slices
parsley sprigs

1 Bring the milk, onion and bay leaf to a boil in a large saucepan.
2 Remove from the heat, cover and leave to infuse for 10–15 minutes.
3 Remove and discard the onion and bay leaf. Return the milk to a boil, then gradually sprinkle the semolina over the top, stirring all the time.
4 Simmer for about 5 minutes, stirring often, to cook the semolina, then remove from the heat and beat in the cheese, parsley, cayenne pepper and salt and pepper.
5 Spread the mixture out to a depth of about ½ inch on an oiled plate or baking sheet. Smooth the surface and allow to cool completely.
6 Cut the mixture into squares or triangles. Dip first into beaten egg, then dried breadcrumbs, to coat thoroughly. Shallow-fry in hot oil until crisp on both sides, then drain the fritters well on paper towels.
7 Garnish with lemon slices and parsley sprigs and serve immediately.

Cooking Cheese

Certain cheeses, mainly the hard and semihard types, are best for cooking, because they melt well without becoming tough or stringy. Sometimes a particular type is best, in which case I have suggested this in the recipe; where no type is specified, use a reasonably priced Cheddar or Cheddar-type cheese.

YEAST PIZZA

SERVES 4

3½ cups plain 85% whole-wheat flour
1 package active dried yeast
½ teaspoon salt
about ¾ cup warm water
2 tablespoons oil
FOR THE TOPPING
2 large onions, peeled and chopped
oil
¼ cup tomato paste
1 garlic clove, crushed
salt and freshly ground black pepper
1⅓ cups washed and sliced mushrooms, or 1
* green pepper, deseeded and sliced*
1 cup sliced mozzarella cheese
a few black olives
a little dried oregano

Yeast

Dried yeast, quick-rising yeast (which you add straight to the flour without mixing with water) and fresh yeast are all interchangeable.

Allow 1 ounce fresh yeast or ½ ounce (1 tablespoon) dried yeast to 31 pounds flour. For quick-rising yeast, follow directions on the package.

It is essential that the yeast, whether fresh or dried, is in good condition. Buy from a shop with a quick turnover and store carefully.

Fresh yeast will keep in an airtight jar in a cool place for up to a week. It should be pale beige in color with no dark specks and look moist but not damp; it should feel cool to the touch and break cleanly and easily when crumbled. It should have a sweet, fresh smell. Dried yeast does not last forever. If it smells "winey" and does not froth up vigorously when mixed with water and sugar, it is not working properly. Throw it away; if you use it, you will only waste your time and ingredients.

Although yeast likes warmth, too much heat kills it. So don't let it get too hot at any stage.

Fancy Pizza (p. 218)

1 First make the dough. Put the flour, yeast, salt, water and oil into a large mixing bowl and mix to a dough.
2 Turn the dough out onto a lightly floured work surface and knead for 5 minutes until smooth and silky.
3 Put the dough into a large bowl, cover with a damp cloth and leave until doubled in size.
4 Punch down the dough, divide it between two well-greased 8-inch pie pans or one 12-inch one, or press it into a 12-inch circle on a baking sheet. Leave in a warm place while you make the topping.
5 To make the topping, sauté the onion in 2 tablespoons oil for 10 minutes, until soft and lightly colored, then remove from the heat and stir in the tomato paste and garlic and season to taste with salt and pepper.
6 Preheat the oven to 500°F.
7 Flatten the dough with your hands, pressing it well into the pans and up the sides a little, or raising the edge of the dough circle slightly.
8 Spread the tomato mixture on top of the dough, then arrange the mushrooms or green pepper, cheese slices and olives on top.
9 Drizzle a little oil over the top and sprinkle with oregano. Leave in a warm place for 15–20 minutes, for the dough to prove, then bake for 15–20 minutes, until the pizza is puffed up and golden-brown on top.

Variations
QUICK SCONE PIZZA
Make the scone mixture (p. 326), adding ½ cup grated cheese before putting in the liquid. Use ½ cup milk or soy milk and omit the egg. Roll out the dough and make the topping as described above. Bake the pizza immediately, at 425°F, for 20–25 minutes, or until the top of the pizza is golden brown.

KALEIDOSCOPE PIZZA
Using a knife, gently score the top of the pizza into six sections. Fill each section with a different-colored topping, for instance, cooked and drained corn kernels, sliced tomatoes, lightly sautéed onion rings, lightly sauteed green pepper, sliced and sautéed mushrooms, lightly steamed sliced zucchini. Sprinkle with a little grated cheese and oil, then bake as described.

PEPPER PIZZA
Divide the pizza as described above, making six or eight sections. Fill the sections with different-colored peppers, deseeded, chopped and lightly sautéed. Use as many different colors as you can find: green, red, yellow and black, sautéing them separately to keep the colors clear. Sprinkle with cheese and bake as described.

FANCY PIZZA
For this pretty variation, arrange pepper slices in the center, then a circle of sliced button mushrooms, a circle of cooked corn kernels and one of black olives and an outer circle of sliced mozzarella cheese. Cover the pizza with foil. Bake for 10 minutes, then uncover for the remaining baking time. Garnish the pizza with parsley sprigs or basil leaves.

OMELETTE

SERVES 1

Making Omelette Rolls

These make a pleasant savory appetizer and look attractive as part of a selection of canapés. Make a 1-egg omelette, keeping it flat. Spread thinly with a colored filling such as spinach or tomato paste, Black Olive Pâté (p. 258) or Mushroom and Herb Terrine (p. 146), roll up like a jelly roll, then cut into ¼-inch slices.

Omelette Fillings

Allow about 2 heaping tablespoons filling for an omelette to serve 1 person. Have the filling warmed and ready when you start to make the omelette. Here are some ideas for fillings:

- ☐ Fines herbes: chopped fresh parsley, chives and chervil
- ☐ Peeled, deseeded (if you like), chopped tomato, heated through – a little chopped fresh basil is good with this
- ☐ Cooked, chopped asparagus; reserve an asparagus tip to garnish
- ☐ Sliced button mushrooms sautéed in butter
- ☐ Black Olive Pâté, spooned thinly (p. 258)
- ☐ Finely chopped scallion, lightly sautéed in butter, or used raw
- ☐ Watercress, lightly sautéed in butter to soften
- ☐ 4–6 tablespoons very finely grated cheese, half added to the eggs before cooking, then the remainder sprinkled on top before rolling the omelette

2–3 eggs
salt and freshly ground black pepper
½ tablespoon butter

1 Crack the eggs into a bowl, season with salt and pepper, and beat lightly, just to combine.
2 Put a 5–6-inch nonstick frying pan over a moderate to high heat and add the butter. When it has melted and the froth has subsided, pour in the eggs.
3 Stir the eggs gently with a fork, and as the bottom begins to set draw the cooked portions back with a spatula and tip the pan to allow the unset egg to run onto the hot pan.
4 When the omelette is almost set – remember it will go on cooking in its own heat – arrange your chosen filling on top of it.
5 To fold the omelette and turn it out of the frying pan in one movement, hold the frying pan up by its handle at right angles to a warmed plate.
6 Using the spatula, roll the top third of the omelette down, and at the same time tip the frying pan over the plate, so that the omelette rolls and comes out of the pan on to the plate, fold side down, at the same time. Serve immediately.

ROLLING AN OMELETTE

1 Flip over the top third of the omelette

2 Holding the handle of the pan uppermost, tip the omelette onto a warmed plate, allowing it to roll over itself as it comes out of the pan

FRITTATA OF SUMMER VEGETABLES

A frittata, the Italian version of a thick, flat, savory omelette, is very quick to make, attractive to look at and good to eat. Try it with some crusty bread, a green salad and a glass of chilled wine. The vegetables can be varied according to what is available; tender fava beans make a good addition in summer.

SERVES 2

2 tablespoons olive oil
1½ pound tender young vegetables, such as baby carrots, zucchini, fennel and eggplant, trimmed and finely sliced
salt and freshly ground black pepper
4 eggs

⅓ cup Parmesan cheese, grated
2 tablespoons chopped parsley

1 Heat an 8-inch frying pan over a moderate heat, then add the oil. When the oil is hot, add the vegetables and cook gently

for about 10 minutes, stirring from time to time. Season to taste.

2 Whisk the eggs lightly, add the cheese and season with a little salt and pepper – you won't need much salt as the Parmesan is quite salty.

3 Pour the egg mixture into the pan and move the vegetables gently with a spatula to let the egg run down evenly through the layers. After a few minutes, when the bottom of the frittata is set and golden brown, put the frying pan under the broiler and leave for a further minute or two to set the top.

4 Sprinkle parsley over the top. Serve at once, cut in half or in thick wedges.

SOUFFLÉ OMELETTE

A soufflé omelette can be savory or sweet. Serve a savory one with a simple salad, such as watercress, for a quick main course, and a sweet one with Apricot Jam Filling, or one of the other suggestions on the right.

SERVES 1

2 eggs, separated
2 tablespoons cold water
salt and freshly ground black pepper, for a
    savory omelette
1 tablespoon butter

1 Preheat the broiler.

2 Put the egg yolks into a fairly large bowl with the water. Season lightly with salt and pepper, for a savory omelette.

3 In another bowl, whisk the egg whites until they form soft peaks.

4 Gently fold the egg whites into the egg yolks and water mixture.

5 Heat the butter in a small nonstick frying pan, swirling the pan so that the butter coats the sides as well as the base. Then pour in the egg mixture. Cook over a moderate heat until the omelette is golden-brown underneath.

6 Put the pan under the broiler to cook and brown the top of the omelette, but don't let it get too firm.

7 Cut across the surface of the omelette at right angles to the frying-pan handle and insert the filling, if using, then fold the omelette in half and lift it gently onto a serving plate.

Separating Eggs

Crack the egg by tapping it sharply against the edge of a bowl or other hard surface, then, holding the egg over a bowl, carefully prise apart the two halves. Tip the white from the half of the shell that does not contain the yolk into a bowl, then tip the yolk into this empty half shell, allowing the white surrounding it to drip into the bowl. Transfer the egg yolk between the two shells until it is separated from as much of the egg white as possible.

Sweet Fillings for Soufflé Omelettes

☐ 2 tablespoons raisins, soaked in rum for 30 minutes
☐ Canned black cherries, heated through, with a little kirsch added
☐ Apricot jam, warmed with a little
☐ water, a few slivered almonds, a dash of Grand Marnier
☐ Any good reduced-sugar
☐ preserve, warmed through
☐ A little preserved ginger in syrup

DEEP-FRIED CAMEMBERT

The crisp coating makes a delightful contrast with the hot, runny cheese inside. Serve with a fresh salad and mango or apricot chutney.

SERVES 2–3

1 box of Camembert, containing 6 individual
    triangles; chilled in the refrigerator
1 egg, beaten with 1 tablespoon water
dried breadcrumbs or wheat germ for coating
oil for deep frying

1 Dip the Camembert triangles, with the rind, into the egg, then into the crumbs or wheat germ, to coat well. Chill in the refrigerator while you heat the oil for deep frying.

2 Pour oil into a deep fryer, filling it no more than one-third full. Heat the oil to 375°F, or when a small cube of stale bread sizzles as soon as it is dropped into the oil and becomes golden-brown in 30 seconds.

3 Put in the pieces of Camembert and fry for 4–5 minutes, until crisp and golden-brown. Remove them with a slotted spoon and drain on paper towels. Serve immediately.

Deep-frying

Use a deep, heavy pan, so that by the time the food has been put in the oil will not come further than half way up the pan. The fat is hot enough if a small cube of bread sizzles and rises immediately it is dropped into it or when bubbles form immediately around a wooden chopstick dipped in the oil.

Make sure the food is dry before putting it into the oil, to avoid spluttering; after frying, drain well on crumpled kitchen paper.

CHEESE SOUFFLÉ

In spite of its reputation, a soufflé is very easy to make, and is an excellent dish if you have to rustle up something good on the spur of the moment. This soufflé is light but filling and serves 4 people generously. Serve with a green salad or a tomato salad.

SERVES 4

Small Soufflés

You can make individual soufflés, an excellent first course or light lunch, by baking either the Cheese Soufflé mixture (right) or the Little Twice-Baked Soufflés (p. 223) in 4 ramekins for 15–20 minutes and serving immediately.

For soufflé tomatoes, bake the mixture in 4 hollowed-out and seasoned "beefsteak" tomatoes.

The basic quantities can be halved to make a soufflé for 2 people; it will take about 30 minutes to cook.

To make a soufflé for 1 person, follow the method given, using a quarter of all the ingredients and baking for 15–20 minutes.

*Little Twice-Baked Soufflés (p. 223);
Frittata of Summer Vegetables (p. 220)*

4 tablespoons butter
2 tablespoons unbleached white flour
1 cup milk
*1¼ cups grated cheese, including some
   Gruyère*
4 eggs, separated
salt and freshly ground black pepper
extra butter for greasing
buttered breadcrumbs for coating

1 Preheat the oven to 375°F.
2 Grease a 4½-cup soufflé dish or straight-sided casserole generously with butter and press the buttered breadcrumbs into it, to give the finished soufflé a crisp coating.
3 Melt the 4 tablespoons butter in a medium saucepan and stir in the flour. Cook for 2–3 minutes, until frothy, then add the milk and stir over the heat until thickened.
4 Remove the saucepan from the heat and beat in the cheese. Let the pan cool until you can put your hand against it, then beat in the egg yolks and salt and pepper.
5 Whisk the whites until they form stiff peaks. Stir a couple of tablespoons of egg white into the cheese mixture to lighten it. Using a metal spoon, gently fold in the rest of the egg whites, until none is visible.
6 Turn the mixture into the prepared dish. Bake for about 40 minutes, until the soufflé is puffed up and doesn't wobble when shaken slightly, and a skewer inserted into the center comes out clean. Serve immediately.

Variations

ZUCCHINI SOUFFLÉ

For this pretty, green-flecked version, stir 1½ cups grated raw zucchini into the soufflé mixture before beating in the egg yolks.

ASPARAGUS SOUFFLÉ

Mix 1⅓ cups cooked asparagus, cut into 1-inch lengths, into the mixture before adding the egg whites.

LEEK SOUFFLÉ

Use either 2 cups finely shredded raw leek (including some of the green), or ½ pound cooked thin leeks, cut into 1-inch lengths. Add the leeks to the soufflé mixture after the egg yolks.

MUSHROOM SOUFFLÉ

Add ½ pound mushrooms, sliced and sautéed until no liquid remains, to the mixture after adding the egg yolks.

LITTLE TWICE-BAKED SOUFFLÉS

Twice-baked soufflés take all the worry out of soufflé-making because you cook them at a convenient time, then let them get cold. Just before you want to eat them, turn them out of their containers and reheat in the oven. They will be risen and golden with a lovely crisp outside. Served as a first course or a main course, with a good contrasting sauce such as tomato and red pepper, vegetables such as broccoli, snow peas or French beans and, perhaps, new potatoes.

MAKES 6

butter for greasing
dry grated Parmesan cheese for dusting
¼ cup farmer's cheese
1⅓ cups Gruyère cheese, grated
4 eggs, separated
⅔ cup light cream
salt and freshly ground black pepper
⅔ cup Parmesan cheese, grated

1 Preheat the oven to 400°F. Grease 6 ovenproof cups, ramekins or individual baking dishes with butter, then dust with dry grated Parmesan cheese.
2 Put the farmer's cheese into a bowl with the grated Gruyère, egg yolks, cream and a little salt and pepper and mix together well.
3 Whisk the egg whites until they are stiff but not so dry that you can slice them. Stir 2 tablespoons of the whisked egg whites into the cheese mixture, then gently fold in the rest with a metal spoon.
4 Pour the mixture into the prepared containers and stand them in a baking pan, then pour in almost-boiling water to come half way up the sides of the containers.

5 Put the soufflés into the oven and bake until they are risen and a skewer inserted in the center comes out clean – about 15–20 minutes. Leave the soufflés to cool in their containers – they will probably sink a good deal.
6 To re-heat the soufflés, preheat the oven to 425°F. Turn out the soufflés and put them, baked side uppermost, into a shallow baking dish. Sprinkle with the grated Parmesan cheese and bake for about 15 minutes, until risen, heated through and golden brown. Serve from the dish.

Variations

LITTLE TWICE-BAKED STILTON SOUFFLÉS

Make as described but use 1⅓ cups of grated Stilton cheese instead of the Gruyère for this rich-tasting, tangy variation.

LITTLE TWICE-BAKED GRUYÈRE AND HERB SOUFFLÉS

Add 1–2 crushed garlic cloves and 2 tablespoons chopped fresh herbs to the farmer's cheese.

MENU

Early Summer Celebration

Asparagus with Orange Vinaigrette
144

Little Twice-baked Soufflés
(surrounded by baby carrots, cooked spinach, snowpeas, cherry tomatoes, fava beans, young whole turnips)

Chocolate Torte
279
with Fresh Strawberries

Soufflé Tips

A soufflé can be completely prepared for baking, covered in plastic wrap and kept in the refrigerator for several hours before cooking. Let it stand at room temperature for 30 minutes or so before putting it into the oven.

If the soufflé is ready before you are, leave it in the oven with the heat turned off: it will stay risen for several minutes, though it's best eaten as soon as it's done.

ROLLING A ROULADE

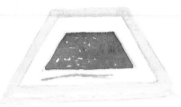

1 Place the cooked roulade on a piece of wax paper on top of a dampened clean dishtowel; remove aluminum foil and trim edges

2 Spread the filling on top of the roulade and roll up like a jelly roll, removing the wax paper as you do so

GRUYÈRE ROULADE WITH WILD MUSHROOMS

SERVES 6

butter for greasing
dry grated Parmesan cheese for preparing the
pan
¼ cup farmer's cheese
1⅓ cups grated Gruyère cheese
4 eggs, separated
⅔ cup light cream
salt and freshly ground black pepper
½ cup Parmesan cheese, grated
FOR THE FILLING
1 quantity Wild Mushrooms in Cream
(p. 79)

1 Preheat the oven to 400°F. Line a 9 × 13-inch jelly roll pan with wax paper. Grease the paper lightly and sprinkle with dry Parmesan cheese.
2 Put the farmer's cheese into a bowl with the grated Gruyère cheese, egg yolks, cream and a little salt and pepper and mix well.
3 Whisk the egg whites until they are stiff but not so dry that you can slice them. Stir 2 tablespoons of the whisked egg white into the cheese mixture to lighten it, then fold in the rest gently with a metal spoon.
4 Pour the mixture into the pan, spreading it gently to the edges. Bake for 12–15 minutes, until firm to the touch.
5 While the roulade is cooking spread out a piece of wax paper large enough to take the roulade and sprinkle the surface with the grated Parmesan. Reheat the filling mixture.
6 Turn the roulade out onto the paper and strip the lining paper from the roulade. Spread the mushrooms in cream on top, to within ½ inch of the edges.
7 Starting from one of the long edges, roll up the roulade like a jelly roll. Transfer it to a serving dish and serve immediately, or use an ovenproof serving dish, cover the roulade with foil and reheat in the oven for about 20 minutes before serving.

SPINACH ROULADE WITH RICOTTA CHEESE AND PINK PEPPERCORNS

SERVES 4–6

4–6 tablespoons grated Parmesan cheese
2 pounds fresh spinach, or 1 pound frozen
spinach, cooked and drained
2 tablespoons butter
4 eggs, separated
salt and freshly ground black pepper
freshly grated nutmeg
1 cup ricotta cheese
1–2 tablespoons pink peppercorns
butter for greasing
TO GARNISH
radicchio leaves
chicory leaves
pink peppercorns

1 Preheat the oven to 375°F.
2 Line a 9½ × 13-inch jelly roll pan or lasagne pan with aluminum foil, grease generously with butter and sprinkle with half the Parmesan cheese.
3 Using your hands, squeeze as much water as you can from the cooked and drained fresh or frozen spinach, then chop it.
4 Put the spinach in a saucepan with the butter and cook gently until heated through. Remove the saucepan from the heat and add the egg yolks, mixing them in thoroughly.
5 Beat the egg whites until stiff but not

Spinach Roulade with Cottage Cheese and Pink Peppercorns (p. 224)

dry and fold them into the spinach. Season the mixture with salt, pepper and nutmeg.

6 Spoon the soufflé mixture into the pan, easing it into the corners, and level gently with the back of the spoon.

7 Bake for about 15–20 minutes, until the roulade is puffed up, golden-brown and set in the middle.

8 Have ready a dampened clean dishtowel spread with a large piece of wax paper sprinkled with the rest of the Parmesan cheese.

9 Turn the roulade out onto the paper and carefully strip the aluminum foil off the roulade. Allow to cool completely if you're serving the roulade cold.

10 Spread the ricotta cheese evenly over the roulade and sprinkle with the peppercorns.

11 Gently roll up the roulade, from one of the long edges. Trim the ends with a sharp serrated knife.

12 If serving the roulade cold, put it on a serving plate. If serving hot, lift the roulade onto a flat ovenproof dish and put into the oven for 5–10 minutes to heat it through. Serve immediately, garnished with radicchio and chicory leaves and a few pink peppercorns.

SAVORY OLIVE MUSHROOM CAKE

This recipe was given to me by a French friend and I love the combination of flavors. If you haven't any leftover white wine, water will do, but the wine gives a subtle, fruity savor. Serve cut into thick wedges, like a cake, with a green salad dressed with walnut oil, and a glass of full-bodied white wine, such as a Chablis or robust Chardonnay.

SERVES 4

2 cups (generous) self-rising 85% whole-wheat flour
a pinch of salt
4 eggs
½ cup (generous) white wine
¼ cup olive oil
2 cups sliced pitted green olives
2 cups sliced mushrooms
1½ cups grated cheese
butter for greasing
TO GARNISH
chicory leaves
watercress

1 Preheat the oven to 500°F. Grease an 8-inch cake pan or a 2-pound loaf pan.
2 Put the flour and salt into a mixing bowl and break in the eggs. Add the wine and oil. Mix until smooth, then stir in the olives, mushrooms and cheese.
3 Spoon the mixture into the prepared pan. Bake for 10 minutes, then turn down the oven to 375°F and bake for a further 40–50 minutes, until the cake is firm, golden-brown and shrunk from the sides of the pan. Garnish with chicory and watercress and serve immediately.

HALLOUMI WITH PARSLEY AND LEMON SAUCE

This delicious quick dish can be served as a light main course with vegetables or as a first course.

SERVES 4

2 packages of Halloumi cheese
a little olive oil
FOR THE SAUCE
1 cup parsley, tough stems removed
1 garlic clove, peeled
juice of 1 lemon
6 tablespoons olive oil
salt and freshly ground black pepper
TO GARNISH (OPTIONAL)
lemon slices

1 Drain the Halloumi cheese and pat it dry with paper towels, then cut it into thin slices.
2 Make the sauce: chop the parsley finely by hand or in a food processor. Add the garlic, lemon juice and oil, whisking well to make a dressing. It will thicken a little as the oil and lemon juice emulsify. Season with salt and pepper.
3 Fry the slices of cheese in a little hot olive oil for a few seconds on each side, until golden brown. Drain them on paper towels. You will probably have to fry the cheese in 2 batches, so keep one batch warm in a low oven while you do the rest.
4 Serve the cheese slices with the parsley and lemon sauce, garnished with lemon slices, if desired.

Opposite page:
Brie Parcels with Cranberry Sauce; Halloumi with Parsley and Lemon Sauce (p. 226)

BRIE PARCELS WITH CRANBERRY SAUCE

Hot, melting cheese encased in crisp pastry makes a delicious main course. Other cheeses can be used instead of Brie; individual goat's cheese rounds are particularly good.

SERVES 4

½ pound package phyllo pastry
6 tablespoons butter, melted
¾ pound Brie, not too ripe
1 quantity Cranberry Sauce (p. 174)

1 Preheat the oven to 375°F.
2 Lay 2 sheets of phyllo on a board, overlapping them by about 2 inches to make one large sheet. Brush with melted butter, then put 2 more overlapping sheets on top and brush them with more butter.
3 Divide the Brie into 4 equal portions. Put one near the top left-hand corner of the pastry and fold the pastry over to cover the cheese. Fold in the sides and continue to roll over the pastry until the Brie is loosely but thoroughly wrapped in a neat parcel. It is important that the Brie is well wrapped to prevent it oozing out as it cooks. Decorate with phyllo strips, cut from a separate sheet and scrunched on top of the parcel.
4 Brush the parcel with melted butter and place on a cookie sheet. Repeat with the remaining cheese and pastry to make 3 more parcels.
5 Bake the parcels for 15–20 minutes, until golden brown and crisp. Serve at once, with the cranberry sauce.

Variation
CAMEMBERT PARCELS WITH CRANBERRY SAUCE
Use Camembert to fill the parcels, instead of Brie.

MENU
Midsummer Wedding

SERVES 30

Pink Potato Salad
166

Asparagus Boats
263

Gruyère Roulade with Avocado Filling
224

Green Salad
54

Technicolor Cabbage Salad
162

Profiteroles
314

All the main preparation for this wedding buffet, with its pink theme, can be done in advance. Make the pastry cases (as thin as you can!) for the Asparagus Boats up to 4 weeks in advance and freeze. Fill them the day before the wedding, then warm them in the oven before serving.

Fill the roulade, assemble the salads and finish the profiteroles on the morning of the wedding. If you are a member of the bridal party, you will need a reliable friend to take over from you on the day, and mastermind the operation, together with someone to see to all the drinks and others to serve the food.

Phone around to local catering firms well in advance to rent linen, plates, flat serving dishes, cups and saucers, cutlery. Rent glasses for wine and champagne from the store where you order these. Drink champagne throughout the wedding if your budget can stand it; otherwise welcome guests with a medium-dry white wine, such as a Vouvray, which you can then drink throughout the meal. Then, for the toast, pink champagne!

Nut Dishes

Nuts are one of the most nutritious ingredients and can also be one of the most tasty, forming the basis of some excellent recipes. I particularly like both a good nut roast and the "dreaded nut cutlet," which can be moist, full of flavor and a real pleasure to eat. They are good served with some of the sauces and accompaniments generally reserved for meat: tasty Vegetarian Gravy (p. 172), for instance, or Apple or Gooseberry Sauce (p. 84), Horseradish Sauce (p. 124) or, for that Christmas pièce de résistance, Bread Sauce (p. 175) and Cranberry Sauce (p. 174).

Ⅴ ROASTED VEGETABLES WITH PEPPER AND ALMOND SAUCE Ⅴ

Nuts and seeds make natural thickeners for sauces and are used in this way in many parts of the world. The inspiration for this sauce is romesco sauce from Spain. You can vary the root vegetables according to your own preferences and what is available.

SERVES 4

¾ pound parsnips
¾ pound large carrots
¾ pound red onions
1 pound new potatoes, scrubbed
2 tablespoons butter
2 tablespoons olive oil
salt and freshly ground black pepper
FOR THE SAUCE
2 tablespoons olive oil
1 onion, peeled and chopped
2 red peppers, de-seeded and chopped
1 dried red chili
¼ pound almonds, blanched
1–2 garlic cloves, peeled
juice of 1 lemon
2–3 teaspoons balsamic vinegar

1 Set the oven to 400°F. Bring a large pan of water to the boil.
2 Scrub, scrape or peel the parsnips and carrots, depending on their condition, then cut into even-sized wedges so that they are about the same size as the potatoes. Trim the tops of the onions, peel off the outer skin without removing the root, then cut them into quarters, still leaving the root to hold them together.
3 Put the butter and olive oil into a roasting pan and put it into the oven to heat up; meanwhile, boil the vegetables in the pan of water for 5 minutes.
4 Drain the vegetables and add them to the sizzling hot fat, then return the roasting pan to the oven and roast for about 45–50 minutes, or until golden brown.
5 Meanwhile, make the sauce. Heat the oil in a pan and add the onion, red peppers and chili. Cover and cook gently for 15 minutes, stirring from time to time.
6 Spread the almonds out on a cookie sheet and toast them in the oven for 5–8 minutes, until golden brown. Keep your eye on them as they can burn easily.
7 Put the almonds into a blender or food processor with the red pepper mixture and the garlic. Blend to a thick purée, then add the lemon juice, a little at a time, the balsamic vinegar and salt and pepper to taste. Give it a final blend, then transfer to a bowl for serving.
8 Put the roasted vegetables on plates or a large platter and serve with the sauce.

ROASTED MARINATED TOFU WITH SATAY SAUCE

☑   ☑

Soaking the tofu in a tasty marinade and then roasting it gives a good flavor and pleasantly crisp texture. The satay sauce contrasts well, and the two together are packed with protein and other nutrients. Serve it with plain boiled brown rice and some scallion tassels, or a carrot, scallion and red pepper salad, for a healthy and well-balanced meal.

SERVES 4

2 × 10-ounce packages firm tofu, drained and cut into cubes
FOR THE MARINADE
2 garlic cloves, crushed
4 tablespoons soy sauce
4 tablespoons medium or sweet sherry
2 tablespoons rice vinegar or white vinegar
FOR THE SATAY SAUCE
4 slightly rounded tablespoons smooth peanut butter
2/3 cup water
4 garlic cloves, crushed
1/2 cup coconut cream
TO GARNISH (OPTIONAL)
scallion tassels

1 Put the tofu on a shallow plate. Mix together all the ingredients for the marinade and pour it over the tofu. Stir gently, then leave for at least 2 hours. Preheat the oven to 400°F.
2 Drain the tofu, reserving the marinade. Arrange the tofu on a cookie sheet in a single layer and roast near the top of the oven for 25–30 minutes, until it is well browned and fairly crisp.
3 Meanwhile, make the satay sauce. Put the peanut butter, garlic and water into a small saucepan with the reserved marinade and heat gently, stirring until smooth. Stir in the coconut cream, cut into small pieces. Season with salt.
4 Serve the tofu with the sauce and scallion tassels, if wished.

Variation
ROASTED MARINATED SMOKED TOFU WITH HAZELNUT SAUCE
Replace the plain tofu with smoked, and the peanut butter with 1/2 a cup of skinned, toasted, then finely ground hazelnuts. Put the ground hazelnuts into the water with the garlic and reserved marinade and heat gently before adding the coconut cream.

Making Scallion Tassels

1 Cut off the root end, making sure the layers are free, and trim off most of the green.
2 Cut down from each end to within about 1/2 inch of the center.
3 Give the scallion a half turn and cut again in the same way.
4 Put into cold water for 30–60 minutes to curl.

Roasted Marinated Tofu with Satay Sauce; Roasted Vegetables with Pepper and Almond Sauce (p. 230)

Nut Burgers with Red Onion Confit;
Creamy Nut Korma (p. 235)

V   # NUT BURGERS WITH RED ONION   V
CONFIT

This makes a large quantity but the burgers freeze well and can be
fried from frozen. The confit can be made well ahead.

MAKES 12

2 onions, peeled and chopped
2 celery sticks, finely chopped
1/2 cup butter or vegan margarine
2 teaspoons mixed dried herbs
2 tablespoons whole-wheat flour
1 1/4 cups Light Vegetable Stock (p. 129)
2 tablespoons soy sauce
2 teaspoons yeast extract
1 pound mixed nuts, including cashews, grated
1 1/3 cups fresh whole-wheat breadcrumbs
salt and freshly ground black pepper
dried breadcrumbs to coat
oil for shallow frying
FOR THE CONFIT
2 tablespoons olive oil
1 pound red onions, peeled and chopped
1 1/4 cups red wine
1/4 cup sugar
1/4 cup red wine vinegar
salt and coarsely ground black pepper

1 Fry the onions and celery in the butter
or margarine for 10 minutes, browning
them lightly. Stir in the herbs and flour
and cook for a further 1–2 minutes.
2 Add the stock and stir until thickened,
then add the soy sauce, yeast extract,
nuts, breadcrumbs and salt and pepper.
3 When cool, form into 12 flat burgers
1/2 inch thick. Coat with breadcrumbs.
4 Fry in a very little oil for about
3 minutes on each side, until browned
and crisp. Drain on paper towels.
5 To make the confit, heat the oil in a
medium saucepan and put in the onions.
Cover and cook gently for 10 minutes,
stirring occasionally, then add the wine,
sugar and vinegar. Bring to the boil, then
simmer gently, uncovered, for 45–60
minutes, or until the onion is tender and
the mixture syrupy; season. Serve warm.

CHESTNUT ROAST

A pleasant roast for a chilly winter day, and a traditional Christmas main course for many vegetarians.

SERVES 4–6

2 tablespoons butter
1 large onion, peeled and chopped
2 celery stalks, finely chopped
2 pounds chestnuts, peeled and cooked (yields
   about 1½ pounds); or three 15-ounce cans
   whole chestnuts, or about ½ pound dried
   chestnuts, soaked and cooked
2 tablespoons chopped parsley
2 tablespoons lemon juice
1 garlic clove, crushed
a few fresh whole-wheat breadcrumbs
   (optional)
salt and freshly ground black pepper
¼ cup oil
dried breadcrumbs for coating

1 Melt the butter and sauté the onion and celery over moderate heat for 10 minutes until soft but not brown. Transfer to a large bowl. Drain the chestnuts and add to the bowl. Mix these ingredients together well.

2 Mash the chestnuts, onion and celery, then mix into the bowl the chopped parsley, lemon juice and garlic.

3 The mixture should be soft but firm enough to form into a roll, so add a few whole-wheat breadcrumbs, if necessary, especially if you're using canned chestnuts. Season the mixture with salt and pepper to taste.

4 Preheat the oven to 400°F. Pour a little of the oil into a roasting pan and put into the oven to heat.

5 Form the chestnut mixture into a roll about 8 inches long, pressing it together carefully, then coat it well with the dried breadcrumbs.

6 Put the chestnut roll into the roasting pan and carefully turn it so that it is coated with hot oil.

7 Bake for 45 minutes, until it is crisp on the outside, spooning a little more of the oil over the roll from time to time during the cooking. Serve the Chestnut Roast cut into slices.

MENU

Christmas Menu

Warm Salad of Oyster
Mushrooms
163

Chestnut Roast

Sauce Soubise
173
Red Cabbage Casserole
180
Braised Celery Hearts
182

Ginger Trifle
285

PEELING CHESTNUTS

1 Place chestnut flat side down on a board and make a cut in the pointed end

2 Boil or bake the chestnuts in a hot oven for 10–20 minutes until the cuts open

3 Strip the skins off the chestnuts using a small, sharp, pointed knife

---

SHAPING NUT OR LENTIL BURGERS

1 Flatten burgers and give them a professional look by tapping them firmly on top and around the sides with a palette knife

2 Press them together firmly, which will help the nut or lentil burgers to remain intact when you fry them

Making Breadcrumbs

Bread that is a day or two old is best for these. Cut off the crusts and crumble the bread between your fingers, or pop chunks of bread into a food processor or blender and whizz for a moment or two. If you have a freezer, it's easy to make any leftover pieces of bread into crumbs and freeze them in a plastic bag. The breadcrumbs can be used straight from the freezer.

Alternatively, you can dry out slices of bread in the bottom of the oven while something else is cooking, or in a microwave (they only take about 5 minutes). Then crush them with a rolling pin. It's useful to have both fresh and dried breadcrumbs available.

CROUSTADE OF MUSHROOMS

This is an updated version of my most popular recipe, which I invented for one of my first dinner parties, and which first appeared in my second book, *Not Just a Load of Old Lentils*.

SERVES 4–6

⅔ cup almonds, or other nuts, slivered in a food processor
1 cup fresh whole-wheat breadcrumbs
½ cup ground almonds or other finely ground nuts
1 small onion, peeled and grated
1 garlic clove, crushed
7 tablespoons butter, softened
salt and freshly ground black pepper
1 pound mushrooms, washed and sliced
1¼ cups sour cream
freshly grated nutmeg
paprika

Croustade of Mushrooms

1 Preheat the oven to 350°F.
2 Reserve a few of the slivered almonds for garnishing. Mix together the breadcrumbs, ground and remaining slivered almonds, or other nuts, onion, garlic and 6 tablespoons of the softened butter. Season well with salt and pepper. The mixture should hold together like a crumbly pastry.
3 Press the mixture into the base of an 8-inch loose-bottomed tart pan. Bake for 20 minutes, until golden-brown and crisp.
4 Meanwhile, sauté the mushrooms in the remaining butter for 15–20 minutes, until all the liquid has evaporated. Season with salt and pepper.
5 Spoon the mushrooms on top of the croustade. Stir the sour cream with a fork, season with salt, pepper and nutmeg, then swirl about half the sour cream on top of the mushrooms, so that some show through the cream. Sprinkle with paprika.
6 Return the croustade to the oven for 10–15 minutes, to heat through, then remove from the pan and serve on a warmed plate. Scatter reserved slivered almonds over the top. Serve the rest of the sour cream separately, in a small bowl or pitcher.

Variations

VEGAN CROUSTADE OF MUSHROOMS
Use vegan margarine instead of butter, and nondairy cream or yogurt instead of sour cream.

CROUSTADE OF LEEKS
Replace the mushrooms with 1 pound cleaned and sliced leeks. Cook the leeks in a little lightly salted boiling water for about 10 minutes, then drain well and add the sour cream and seasoning.

CREAMY NUT KORMA

In this delicately spiced dish, ground almonds and coconut cream
are used to thicken the sauce.

SERVES 4

2 tablespoons oil
1 onion, peeled and chopped
2 garlic cloves, crushed
1-inch piece of fresh ginger
8–10 cardamom pods
1/2 teaspoon turmeric
1 teaspoon ground cumin
1 teaspoon ground coriander
1/2 cup coconut cream
2 cups water
3/4 cup ground almonds
1–2 tablespoons lemon juice
salt and freshly ground black pepper
florets from 1 medium cauliflower
8 ounces fine green beans, trimmed and
   halved
8 ounces carrots, scraped and thinly sliced
2–4 tablespoons chopped coriander

1 Heat the oil in a large saucepan, then add the onion, cover and cook gently for 7 minutes. Stir in the garlic.

2 Grate the unpeeled ginger and crush the cardamom pods with the end of a rolling pin or a mortar and pestle. Stir into the pan with the turmeric, cumin and coriander. Leave to cook gently for 1 minute.

3 Slice the coconut cream with a sharp knife so that it breaks up into flakes. Add to the pan with the water and bring to the boil. Stir, then leave to melt.

4 Add the ground almonds and cook for a minute or two. Now you can purée the mixture in a blender or food processor if you wish, or leave it as it is. Add lemon juice, salt and pepper to taste. Keep warm.

5 Cook the vegetables in a large pan of boiling water for 3–4 minutes or until just tender. Drain, then return them to the pan and add the spice mixture. Check the seasoning and reheat gently. Sprinkle with coriander and serve.

QUICK SAVORY NUT LOAF

This easy-to-make loaf is good served hot or cold.

SERVES 4

4 tablespoons butter or vegan margarine
2 large onions, peeled and finely chopped
1 teaspoon dried thyme
1 tablespoon whole-wheat flour
1/2 cup (generous) water
1 cup cashew nuts, fairly finely ground
1 cup hazelnuts, fairly finely ground
1 1/3 cups dried whole-wheat breadcrumbs
1 tablespoon lemon juice
salt and freshly ground black pepper
dried breadcrumbs for coating
1/2 cup oil for roasting

1 Preheat the oven to 400°F.
2 Melt the butter or vegan margarine in a large saucepan and sauté the onions

gently for 10 minutes, until tender.
3 Add the thyme and flour; stir for 1–2 minutes, then add the water and stir until thickened.
4 Remove from the heat, add the nuts, breadcrumbs, lemon juice and salt and pepper to taste. Mix well. Form into a loaf shape and coat in dried crumbs. Heat the oil in a small roasting pan in the oven until smoking hot. Put the nut loaf in the pan and baste with the oil.
5 Bake for 35–40 minutes.
6 Remove from the pan. Serve immediately, cut into thick slices, or leave to cool to room temperature before refrigerating, if you want to serve it cold.

MENU
Warming Family Supper

Quick Savory Nut Roast

Baked Potatoes
190
Steamed Broccoli
Vegetarian Gravy
172
or Italian Tomato Sauce
171

Fresh Fruit
or
Pancakes with Lemon and Honey
299

Serving Nut or Lentil Roast

It's useful to make enough nut or lentil roast for one serving hot and one cold. Sliced cold nut roast is delicious with salad and any of the following

☐ Mayonnaise with Green Peppercorns (p. 155)
☐ Mango Chutney Mayonnaise (p. 155) or Cranberry Sauce (p. 174)
☐ Sliced Fresh Mango
☐ Yogurt and Herb Dressing (p. 156)

⟨V⟩ BRAZIL NUT ROAST EN CROÛTE ⟨V⟩

MENU

Late Summer Supper for Friends

Chilled Lettuce Soup

130

Brazil Nut Roast en Croûte
Illustrated on p. 318

Horseradish Sauce
124
Potato Purée
189
Carrot Purée
189
French Beans

Little Coffee Custards
278

Salts

Salt, or sodium chloride, has been used as a flavoring and food-preservative since Neolithic times. It is available in various forms:

SEA SALT Sometimes called "gros sel," sea salt is evaporated naturally in bays and enclosures or from salt marshes. It contains traces of minerals, including iodine. Most cooks agree that there is nothing to touch sea salt from the point of view of flavor. Sea salt is available as coarse granules for use in a grinder, or as fine grains or flakes.

ROCK SALT This salt is mined from the deposits made by ancient seas. It is sold in various degrees of coarseness.

TABLE SALT, BLOCK SALT and KITCHEN SALT These are produced from rock salt. Iodine is sometimes added to table salt to make iodized salt. This is a useful way of adding essential iodine to the diet in parts of the country where it is not present in the soil (and thus in the vegetables). Flavored salts, such as onion salt, garlic salt and celery salt, are made from table salt with dried and powdered onion, garlic or celery seed added.

SERVES 8

1 quantity Flaky Pastry made with white flour (p. 268) or 1 pound frozen puff pastry
beaten egg to glaze (optional)
FOR THE NUT ROAST
2 large onions, peeled and chopped
4 tablespoons butter or vegan margarine
3¼ cups Brazil nuts, finely ground
2⅔ cups fresh fine breadcrumbs
½ teaspoon dried thyme
3 tablespoons lemon juice
2 eggs (optional)
a good pinch each of grated nutmeg, ground cloves and ground cinnamon
salt and freshly ground black pepper
FOR THE STUFFING
2⅔ cups fresh fine white breadcrumbs
¼ cup chopped parsley
grated rind of 1 lemon
1 tablespoon lemon juice
1 teaspoon each dried thyme and marjoram
1 tablespoon grated onion
6 tablespoons butter or vegan margarine
TO GARNISH
8 clementine halves filled with cranberries
thyme sprigs

1 Preheat the oven to 400°F.
2 To make the nut roast, sauté the onion in the butter or vegan margarine for 10 minutes, until soft but not browned.
3 Remove from the heat and add the rest of the nut roast ingredients. Season.
4 Make the stuffing by mixing all the ingredients together into a soft mixture that holds together. Season.
5 Roll out the pastry on a floured board to a 12 × 14-inch rectangle.
6 Form the stuffing into a sausage about 10 inches long and place down the middle of the pastry. Pile the nut roast mixture all over the stuffing, covering it.
7 Fold the ends of the pastry up to enclose the nut mixture completely. Tuck in the ends, then place on a damp baking sheet, join side down. Mark a lattice design on the top.
8 Make one or two steam holes, decorate with pastry trimmings, and brush with beaten egg, if using. Bake for 30 minutes, until crisp. Garnish with clementine halves filled with cranberries and thyme sprigs.

PREPARING NUT ROAST EN CROÛTE

1 Put the stuffing in the center of the pastry

2 Cover the stuffing with the nut mixture

3 Fold up the sides of the pastry, to enclose the nut mixture

4 Place on a baking sheet, seam side down

PINE NUT ROULADE WITH ASPARAGUS HOLLANDAISE FILLING

This dish, which I've developed from a recipe invented by Michael Smith, is very rich. It is wonderful for a celebration summer meal and can be made a few hours in advance and reheated just before serving. Serve with new potatoes, snow peas and baby carrots.

SERVES 6

4 large eggs
salt and freshly ground black pepper
2 cups pine nuts, lightly crushed
a little butter and oil for greasing
FOR THE FILLING
1 quantity Quick Hollandaise Sauce
    (p. 176)
1 pound fresh young asparagus, lightly
    cooked, tips only
12 quails' eggs, hard-boiled, shelled and
    halved
2 tablespoons snipped chives

1 Preheat the oven to 400°F. Line a 13 × 9-inch baking pan with buttered aluminum foil, letting it extend 2 inches above the edge of the pan and snipping diagonally into the corners (p. 230).
2 Whisk the eggs with salt and pepper until thick, fold in half the pine nuts and pour into the pan, spreading the mixture evenly into the corners.
3 Bake in the upper third of the oven for 6–8 minutes, until firm in the middle.
4 Put a clean dishtowel, wrung out in cold water, on a flat surface. Cover with a piece of wax paper spread evenly with the remaining pine nuts. Invert the roulade onto the pine nuts and remove the aluminum foil.
5 Spread the roulade with all but 2 tablespoons of the hollandaise sauce. Arrange the asparagus tips (reserving 6 for the garnish), quail's eggs (reserving 3 halves) and chives on top.
6 Carefully roll up the roulade by folding one long side into the center and the other on top. Place a large oiled piece of aluminum foil on top and turn the roulade upside down. Carefully slide a baking sheet underneath the roulade and remove the cloth.

7 Reheat, either immediately or when required, still wrapped in foil, at 375°F, for 15–20 minutes.
8 Remove the foil and transfer the roulade to a heated oval or oblong serving plate. Spoon the reserved sauce down the center and arrange the reserved asparagus tips and quail's eggs on top. Serve immediately.

Variations

ROASTED CASHEW NUT ROULADE WITH WILD MUSHROOM FILLING

Make as described, using roasted cashew nuts instead of pine nuts, and Wild Mushrooms in Cream (p. 272) for the filling, instead of the asparagus and hollandaise sauce. Use the quail's eggs, or not, as you like, and garnish with sautéed mushrooms and roasted cashew nuts.

PECAN NUT ROULADE WITH RATATOUILLE FILLING

A less rich but still very tasty version. Use pecan nuts instead of pine nuts, and replace the asparagus and hollandaise sauce with Ratatouille (p. 187). Use the quail's eggs or not, as you like, and garnish the roulade with parsley sprigs and pepper rings.

HAZELNUT ROULADE WITH LEEK FILLING

Use roasted hazelnuts (p. 37) instead of the pine nuts, 1 pound cleaned and sliced leeks, cooked in a little boiling water until tender, and well drained, instead of the asparagus, and 1¼ cups sour cream instead of the hollandaise sauce.

Salt Substitutes

Various substitutes for salt are available, some based on potassium chloride instead of sodium chloride, others consisting of mixtures of herbs and other seasonings. These are certainly worth a try, though none of them are very satisfactory, in my opinion – personally I'd rather use just a little sea salt with other flavorings such as fresh herbs, sea vegetables and lemon juice, than one of the substitutes. If you have a heart condition, or are on a potassium-restricted diet, you should get your doctor's advice before using a potassium-based salt.

Gomasio

A mixture of roasted sesame seeds and salt, much used in Japan. To make gomasio, put ten parts sesame seeds and one part sea salt into a frying pan and heat gently, stirring, for a few minutes, until the sesame seeds smell roasted, turn a darker brown and one or two start to "pop." Then remove from the heat and grind to a fairly fine powder in a coffee grinder. Store in an airtight jar. Use in cooking or at the table instead of salt. This is a useful way of reducing salt intake as well as adding a savory flavor.

Nut Milk Made with Blanched Almonds

Making Nut Milks

You can make some delicious milks from nuts, far superior in flavor, I think, to cow's milk. All you do is whizz up a few cashew nuts or freshly blanched almonds with some water in a blender. You can make the mixture thick, like cream, or thin and delicate. I find 3 or 4 tablespoons blanched almonds (about 30 nuts) to a tumbler of water makes a good consistency for drinking. You can drink it as is, or strain it.

For a fruit and nut drink, which makes a reviving and sustaining lunch or evening meal when you don't feel like eating anything else, try whizzing up a peeled banana or a few strawberries or raspberries with the almonds and water. This is especially good – like a thick milk shake – when made with a fruit which you've chilled in the freezer for a few hours beforehand.

V # GADO GADO V

The combination of very lightly cooked vegetables, served cold, with a peanut sauce, is unusual and delicious.

SERVES 4

2 large potatoes, boiled in their skins
3 carrots, scraped and cut into matchsticks
½ small cabbage, sliced
½ pound beansprouts
½ pound green beans, topped, tailed and halved
packet of watercress, washed
2 hard-boiled eggs, peeled and quartered (optional)
scallion tassels (p. 231)
FOR THE SATAY SAUCE
4 rounded tablespoons smooth peanut butter
⅔ cup water
4 garlic cloves, crushed
½ cup coconut cream
salt

1 Skin and slice the boiled potatoes. Cook the carrots in a pan of boiling water until they are just tender, then drain and refresh them under cold water. Drain well. Repeat this process with the cabbage, beansprouts and beans, cooking them separately but using the same water. The beansprouts will only take about 30 seconds; the other vegetables will take longer, but don't let them get soggy. Leave the vegetables to cool.
2 To make the satay sauce, put the peanut butter into a small saucepan with the water and garlic and heat gently, stirring, until smooth. Stir in the coconut cream, cut into small pieces. Season with salt. Cool.
3 Put a base of watercress on a serving platter, then arrange the vegetables, and the hard-boiled eggs if you are using them, on top. Decorate with the scallion tassels and serve with the sauce.

CORN FRITTERS

These fritters make a good light breakfast or supper dish, perhaps accompanied by some broiled tomatoes and lightly sautéed mushrooms. Or they can be served as an accompaniment to a nut roast with Potato Purée (p. 189) and Cranberry Sauce (p. 174).

SERVES 2–3 AS A MAIN COURSE, 4–6 AS AN ACCOMPANIMENT

1 cup frozen corn kernels, or fresh ones scraped from the cob, lightly cooked and drained
½ cup chopped almonds
1 egg, separated
3 tablespoons whole-wheat flour
salt and freshly ground black pepper
oil for shallow frying

1 Put the cooked corn into a bowl with the chopped almonds, egg yolk and flour. Mix well and season to taste with salt and pepper.
2 Whisk the egg white until it stands in stiff peaks, then gently fold into the corn mixture.
3 Heat a little oil in a frying pan, then drop tablespoons of the corn mixture into the oil and fry them on both sides until crisp.
4 Drain the fritters on paper towels. Put the first batch into a warm oven while you fry the rest, then serve them immediately.

Variation
VEGAN FRITTERS
Make the batter using 1 cup chick pea flour, ½ teaspoon salt and 1 cup water. Put the flour and salt into a bowl and mix in the water to make a coating batter. Stir in the corn.

WHITE NUT ROAST WITH HERB STUFFING

I like to serve this at Christmas with all the traditional accompaniments, including Bread Sauce (p. 175), Cranberry Sauce (p. 174) and Vegetarian Gravy (p. 172).

SERVES 8–10

1 large onion, peeled and chopped
4 tablespoons butter
1 teaspoon dried thyme
1 tablespoon unbleached white flour
1¼ cups milk
1¾ cups mixed white nuts, finely ground:
*   use cashew nuts, blanched almonds and*
*   pine nuts*
1⅓ cups fresh white breadcrumbs
salt and freshly ground black pepper
freshly grated nutmeg
2 egg whites
a little extra butter for greasing
3–4 tablespoons dried breadcrumbs for coating
FOR THE HERB STUFFING
2 cups fresh white breadcrumbs
¼ pound (1 stick) butter
¼ cup chopped parsley
grated rind of ½ lemon
2 tablespoons grated onion
1 teaspoon each dried marjoram and thyme
2 egg yolks
TO GARNISH
lemon slices
parsley sprigs

1 Preheat the oven to 375°F.
2 Grease a 2-pound loaf pan with butter and line with a strip of buttered aluminum foil to cover the base of the pan and extend up the narrow sides. Sprinkle with dried breadcrumbs.
3 Sauté the onion in the 4 tablespoons butter for 10 minutes until soft. Add the thyme and flour and cook for a minute or two, then add the milk and stir until thickened.
4 Remove from the heat and add the nuts and breadcrumbs. Season generously with salt, pepper and nutmeg.
5 Beat the egg whites until stiff but not dry, then fold in.
6 Make the stuffing by thoroughly mixing all the ingredients together and sea-soning to taste with salt and pepper.
7 Spoon half the nut mixture into the prepared pan in an even layer.
8 With your hands, form the stuffing into a flat layer which will fit over the top of the nut mixture; put into the pan on top of the layer of nut mixture.
9 Cover the stuffing with the rest of the nut mixture.

White Nut Roast with Herb Stuffing

10 Level the top, cover with buttered foil, and bake for 1–1¼ hours, until firm in the center. (Remove the foil for the last 15 minutes of cooking time to allow the top to brown.)
11 Let the loaf stand for 4–5 minutes, then slip a knife around the edges and invert it on to a warmed serving dish. Garnish with the lemon slices and parsley sprigs.

Grain Dishes

*Nutritious, high-fiber protein food, grains can be made into some particularly
healthy dishes, excellent for alternating with richer ones, perhaps those based
on cheese and eggs, for creating a balanced diet. Most grain dishes are also
quick and easy to make, thus being excellent midweek standbys; in addition,
leftovers can often be made into croquettes or used to stuff peppers or large
tomatoes, saving time another day. Try experimenting with some of the
more unusual grains; you'll find full details of basic cooking in the
Ingredients section (p. 44).*

[V] WILD RICE AND CHESTNUTS [V]

SERVES 4

½ ounce dried porcini mushrooms
3¾ cups boiling water
1 large onion, peeled and sliced
1 tablespoon olive or ground nut oil
2 garlic cloves, crushed
2 celery stalks, sliced
1 cup brown rice
⅓ cup wild rice
¼ pound dried chestnuts
lemon juice, salt and pepper to taste
chopped fresh parsley

1 Put the porcini into a measuring jug
and fill with the boiling water. Leave on
one side to soak.

2 Sauté the onion in the oil in a large
saucepan for 5 minutes, then add garlic
and celery and cook for 5 minutes more.

3 Wash the brown rice, wild rice and
chestnuts together in a strainer then add
to the pan. Strain in the water from the
jug. Roughly chop the porcini and add
them to the pan, too.

4 Bring to a boil, then cover and simmer
gently for about 1 hour, until all the water
is absorbed and the chestnuts are tender.

5 Season with lemon juice, salt and pepper, top with a little chopped parsley.

[V] POLENTA [V]

SERVES 4

Cooking Polenta

Polenta – finely milled corn – is
made into a kind of oatmeal which
can either be served straight from
the pan, or it can be pressed flat,
allowed to cool, then broiled, baked
or fried until it is crisp. It's good
accompanied with a tasty sauce such
as Italian Tomato (p. 171). I also
like it served with mayonnaise,
perhaps enlivened with some green
peppercorns.

2 cups polenta
3¾ cups water
salt and freshly ground black pepper
olive oil
TO SERVE
Italian Tomato Sauce (p. 171)
lemon wedges

1 Put the polenta into a medium saucepan and mix to a smooth paste with the
water. Then put the pan on a gentle heat
and stir until the mixture comes to the
boil, and is thick and smooth.

2 Let the polenta cook gently until it is
very thick and comes away from the sides
of the pan – about 30 minutes. Season
with plenty of salt and pepper.

3 Spread the mixture out on a flat plate or
cookie sheet, to a depth of just under ½
inch, then leave it to get cold.

4 Just before you want to serve the polenta, cut it into slices. Fry them in a little
hot olive oil in a frying pan until crisp on
both sides; drain on paper towels.

5 Serve with tomato sauce and lemon
wedges.

V ⬛ # SAFFRON RICE V ⬛

SERVES 4

1 ¼ cups long-grain brown rice
2 ½ cups water
1 teaspoon salt
good pinch of saffron strands

1 Wash the rice, drain and dry on paper towels.
2 Put the rice into a heavy-bottomed saucepan with the water, salt and saffron.
3 Bring to a boil, then cover and turn the heat down as low as possible.
4 Cook the rice for 40–45 minutes, until it is tender and all the water is absorbed.
5 The rice will improve if you can allow it to stand off the heat, but still covered, for a further 5 minutes. Fluff the rice by stirring gently with a fork.

Variations

SWEET VINEGARED RICE
Sweet Vinegared Rice is used to make Sushi (p. 142), and I like to serve it with Japanese vegetable dishes too. Make rice as described, above, using short-grain rice. Put a piece of kombu (wiped with a damp cloth), if available, in the saucepan with the rice and water. When the water comes to a boil, remove the kombu. This flavors the rice delicately. When the rice is cooked, add 2 teaspoons sugar which have been dissolved in 4 tablespoons rice vinegar. Mix gently.

RICE WITH WILD RICE
Wild rice is very expensive, but the addition of a little to brown rice makes it extra special. The dark brown grains of wild rice look attractive against the paler brown rice. Make as described, adding ⅓ cup wild rice and increasing the amount of water to 3 cups (generous).

V ⬛ # SPICED RICE V ⬛

This delicately flavored golden rice is a good accompaniment for curries, spiced vegetable mixtures and stuffed vegetables.

SERVES 4

1 ¼ cups brown rice
1 ½ tablespoons oil
¾ teaspoon turmeric
3 cloves
1 bay leaf
2 ½ cups water
salt and freshly ground black pepper

1 Wash, drain and dry the rice. Heat the oil in a medium-sized saucepan, then add the rice and sauté without browning, stirring, for 3–4 minutes.
2 Stir in the turmeric, cloves and bay leaf. Cook for a few seconds longer, then pour in the water and add some salt and pepper.
3 Bring to a boil, then put a lid on the saucepan and turn the heat down as low as possible. Cook the rice undisturbed for about 40–45 minutes, until the grains are tender and all the water has been absorbed.
4 Fluff the rice by stirring gently with a fork to separate the grains.

Vinegar

One of the earliest flavoring ingedients of all, vinegar is made by souring wine, beer or cider. It contains 4%–6% acetic acid.

MALT VINEGAR Dark brown in color and made from beer, it has a strong flavor which is too harsh for most cooking purposes, though it is good for some chutneys and pickles.

WINE VINEGAR Made from both red and white wine, by the slow Orléans method, it has a delicate flavor and makes a delicious dressing. Look for the word 'Orléans' on the bottle.

BALSAMIC VINEGAR Deliciously sweet, mellow vinegar made from grape juice that has been cooked down before long fermentation in wooden barrels. Buy the most expensive you can afford.

RICE VINEGAR Made from rice wine. Used widely in the Far East.

CIDER VINEGAR Made from cider, has many health-giving properties associated with it. It can be used for salad dressings and complements fruity mixtures.

DISTILLED VINEGAR Malt vinegar which has been distilled so it is clear and contains up to 12% acetic acid. It is used for pickling.

FLAVORED VINEGARS Many different kinds of flavored vinegar can be bought, such as tarragon, raspberry, garlic, chilli, rose and violet. These are fun to experiment with, and you can easily make them by adding flavoring ingredients – such as sprigs of tarragon – to a bottle of wine vinegar.

Bulgur Wheat Pilaf with Red Peppers and Feta Cheese; Baked Lemony Rice with Yellow Peppers (p. 243)

MENU

Middle Eastern Summer Garden Supper

Fava Bean Dip with Mint
146

Felafel
208
Yogurt and Herb Dressing
156

Bulgur Wheat Pilaf with Red Peppers and Feta Cheese

Spinach Omelette with Raisins and Pine Nuts
214
Tomato Salsa
177

Ⅴ # BULGUR WHEAT PILAF WITH RED PEPPERS AND FETA CHEESE Ⅴ

SERVES 4–6

2 red peppers, halved
2 tablespoons olive oil
1 onion, peeled and chopped
1 garlic clove, crushed
1½ cups bulgur wheat
2½ cups boiling water
a bunch of scallions, chopped
7 ounces feta cheese, diced
¼ pound green or black olives
juice of 1 lemon
salt and freshly ground black pepper
several sprigs of basil, torn

1 Place the pepper halves under a hot broiler until the skin has blistered and blackened in places. Remove from the broiler, cover with a plate and leave until cool enough to handle, then remove the skin and seeds. Slice the peppers.

2 Heat the olive oil in a saucepan, add the onion, then cover and cook gently for 10 minutes. Add the garlic and bulgur wheat and stir for a minute or two, then add the boiling water. Cover and cook gently for 10–15 minutes, until the wheat has absorbed the water and puffed up.

3 Add the peppers to the bulgur wheat, along with the scallions, cheese and olives. Stir gently over the heat so that the cheese melts slightly, then add lemon juice and season with salt and pepper to taste. Stir in the basil.

Ⅴ # VEGETARIAN PAELLA Ⅴ

In this vegetarian version of Spanish paella, the traditional fish is replaced by leeks and black olives, with peas and chopped parsley, and a good flavoring of saffron, onion and garlic. It's one of my favorite vegetarian dishes. Nuts – blanched almonds, slivered brazil nuts or whole cashew nuts – can be served separately, in a bowl. A wide shallow pan, such as a wok, a large frying pan or, best of all, a special paella pan is ideal for this, as it is roomy enough to show off the pattern of the vegetables.

SERVES 4

¼ cup olive oil
1¼ cups long-grain brown rice
1 large onion, peeled and sliced
2 large garlic cloves, crushed
good pinch of saffron strands
3 cups (generous) Light Vegetable Stock
   (p. 129) or water
thinly pared rind of ½ lemon, cut into shreds
salt and freshly ground black pepper
1 pound washed and trimmed leeks, cut into
   1-inch lengths
¼ cup frozen peas
¼–½ cup black olives
TO GARNISH
chopped parsley

1. Heat the oil in a large, deep pan. Add the long-grain brown rice and onion slices and stir until the rice is coated and begins to turn opaque.
2 Add the garlic, saffron, stock or water, lemon rind and salt and pepper. Mix well, then bring up to a boil. Mix again, to distribute the saffron coloring all through the rice.
3 Arrange the vegetables and olives attractively on top of the rice.
4 Bring to a boil. Cover with a lid or foil and simmer for 45 minutes.
5 Sprinkle with parsley and serve straight from the pan.

Tips for Cooking Rice

The test of perfect long-grain rice is for all the grains to be separate when you pick up a small handful of the cooked rice. This does not apply to rice for serving with Chinese or Japanese meals. For these, a more glutinous type of rice (p. 45) should be used, so that it clings together when cooked, making it easy to eat with chopsticks.

Ⅴ # BAKED LEMONY RICE WITH YELLOW PEPPERS Ⅴ

SERVES 4

1¼ cups brown rice
2 tablespoons olive oil
1 onion, peeled and sliced
2 garlic cloves, crushed
¼ teaspoon turmeric
2 yellow peppers, de-seeded and sliced
salt and freshly ground black pepper
2 cups boiling water
juice of 1 lemon
2–3 tablespoons chopped flat-leaf parsley
1 cup roasted cashew nuts or toasted blanched
   almonds

1 Preheat the oven to 350°F.
2 Half fill a large saucepan with water and bring to a boil. Add the rice and boil for 15 minutes, to par-cook. Drain thoroughly.
3 Meanwhile, heat the oil in a casserole, then add the onion, cover and cook for about 7 minutes. Stir in the crushed garlic and turmeric. Cook for another minute or two.
4 Add the rice, yellow peppers and some salt and pepper. Stir in the boiling water, then cover and bake in the oven for 1 hour, until the water has been absorbed and the rice is completely tender.
5 Add lemon juice to taste – it will intensify the color of the golden rice – and more salt and pepper, if necessary. Stir in the parsley and nuts and then serve.

MENU

Oven-Baked Meal for a Cold Spring Day

Baked Lemony Rice with Yellow Peppers

Baked Potatoes

Carrot and
Fennel Salad
162

Rhubarb Crumble
295

V
BIRIANI
V

Serve this tasty dish with a Dal (p. 209) and some Indian breads, such as chapatti or poppadums. I like to serve several side dishes as well, such as a cucumber salad, tomato and onion salad and some chutneys and pickles.

SERVES 6

¾ pound eggplant, cut into ½-inch dice
salt
2 cups long-grain brown rice
1 quart water
2½ teaspoons turmeric
4 tablespoons butter or vegetable ghee
1 teaspoon poppy seeds
1½ teaspoons white mustard seeds
1 teaspoon garam masala
½ teaspoon ground coriander
pinch of cayenne
freshly ground black pepper
1 red pepper, deseeded and sliced
1 onion, peeled and sliced
2 garlic cloves, crushed
butter for greasing

1 Sprinkle the eggplant with salt and allow to stand for 30 minutes, to draw out any bitter juices. Rinse and pat dry.
2 Put the rice into a heavy-bottomed saucepan with the water, 1 teaspoon salt and 2 teaspoons of the turmeric. Bring to a boil, then cover and cook very gently for 45 minutes.
3 Preheat the oven to 350°F. Grease a deep casserole.
4 Heat the butter or ghee in a saucepan, then add the poppy seeds and mustard seeds.
5 Stir for 1–2 minutes, then add the rest of the turmeric, the garam masala, coriander, cayenne and a generous grinding of black pepper. Cook for 1–2 minutes, stirring.
6 Add the eggplant, red pepper and onion. Cook gently, covered, for 7–8 minutes, then add the garlic and cook for a further 2 minutes. Taste the mixture and add more seasoning, if necessary.
7 Put one-third of the rice in a layer in the casserole. Top with half the vegetable mixture. Repeat the layers, ending with a final layer of rice.
8 Cover and bake for 30 minutes. Serve straight from the casserole.

MENU
Winter Brunch for Six

Classic Risotto

Scrambled Eggs
107
Mushrooms in Cream
79

Muffins
327
or Warm Croissants with
Assorted Preserves

Black Grapes

Coffee and Tea

CLASSIC RISOTTO

SERVES 6

¼ pound (1 stick) butter
1 onion, peeled and chopped
1 whole garlic clove
2 tablespoons finely chopped parsley
3 cups (generous) Italian arborio rice
9 cups boiling Light Vegetable Stock
 (p. 129)
salt and freshly ground black pepper
4–6 tablespoons grated Parmesan cheese
TO SERVE
extra grated Parmesan cheese

1 Melt half the butter in a large, heavy-bottomed saucepan and sauté the onion and garlic. When the onion is soft and golden, add the parsley.
2 Cook over a moderate heat for a few minutes, then discard the garlic and add the rice.
3 Sauté the rice for a few minutes, stirring constantly, then add 1 cup of the boiling stock and cook gently until absorbed.
4 Continue cooking gently, adding 1 cup of stock at a time, and stirring occasionally, for 20–30 minutes, or until the rice is tender and all the liquid has been absorbed.

5 Season to taste with salt and pepper, stir in the remaining butter and the Parmesan cheese, and leave the risotto over a low heat for a few minutes before serving.

6 Serve with plenty of extra grated Parmesan cheese on the side.

Variations

ARTICHOKE RISOTTO

Cut the leaves and hairy choke from 3 globe artichokes. Slice the bases and sauté them with the onion and garlic, then discard the garlic, add the rice and continue as described.

MUSHROOM RISOTTO

Make the risotto as described, sautéing 3 cups sliced button mushrooms along with the parsley.

ZUCCHINI RISOTTO

Add 1¾ cups sliced zucchini with the parsley.

MILLET PILAF WITH NUTS AND RAISINS

Ⅴ Ⅴ

Millet cooks quickly and makes a good pilaf that is a pleasant change from rice. It is the richest grain in both protein and iron. Serve this pilaf as a main course accompanied by a juicy tomato salad, Sweet Carrot and Fennel Salad (p. 162) or Green Bean Salad with Radicchio (p. 167).

SERVES 4

1½ cups millet
2 tablespoons oil
1 large onion, peeled and chopped
2 carrots, scraped and diced
1 garlic clove, crushed
1 walnut-sized piece of fresh ginger, grated
1-inch piece cinnamon stick
3 cups water
salt and freshly ground black pepper
⅓ cup raisins (optional)
½ cup almonds, slivered (optional)

1 First toast the millet by putting it into a large saucepan and stirring over a moderate heat for 3–4 minutes, until it begins to smell roasted and some of the grains start to pop. Remove from the heat and tip the millet onto a plate.

2 Heat the oil in the saucepan and sauté the onion for 5 minutes, then add the carrots, garlic, ginger and cinnamon, and cook for a further 5 minutes.

3 Add the toasted millet to the onion and carrot mixture. Pour in the water and season to taste with salt and pepper.

4 Bring to a boil, then cover, turn down the heat and cook very gently for 15–20 minutes, until all the water has been absorbed and the millet is tender.

5 Check the seasoning, then add the raisins and slivered almonds, if using, mixing them in lightly with a fork.

Millet Pilaf with Nuts and Raisins

Mixed Rice with Glazed Root Vegetables

$\boxed{V}$ MIXED RICE WITH GLAZED ROOT $\boxed{V}$
VEGETABLES

You can vary the mixture of vegetables in any way you like. If you wish, you may substitute for some or all of the pine nuts other ingredients, such as cooked chestnuts, which are especially delicious in winter, or some cooked and drained chick peas.

SERVES 4

Using Barley

A little barley added to a vegetable soup makes it more filling and nutritious. Pearl barley (which, though partly processed, contains more fiber than brown rice) is cooked like brown rice and can replace some or all of it in recipes for a change.

½ cup brown rice
½ cup wild rice
1½ cups water
salt and freshly ground black pepper
½ cup basmati rice
FOR THE GLAZED ROOT VEGETABLES
2 pounds mixed root vegetables, such as parsnips, carrots, turnips and rutabaga
½ cup pine nuts
3 tablespoons butter or vegan margarine
1 tablespoon olive oil
grated rind and juice of 1 lemon
2–3 tablespoons roughly chopped flat-leaf parsley

1 Cook the rice in two batches. Put the brown rice and the wild rice into a saucepan with the water and ½ teaspoon salt and bring to a boil. Cover, then turn the heat down and cook very slowly for 40 minutes, until both types of rice are tender and all the water has been absorbed.

2 Meanwhile bring plenty of water to a boil in a medium saucepan. Rinse the basmati rice in a strainer under cold water until the water runs clear, then put the rice in the boiling water and cook for about 10 minutes or until a grain feels tender when tested. Drain.

3 While the rice is cooking, peel or scrape the root vegetables as necessary and cut them into even-sized pieces. Bring half a saucepan of water to a boil, add the vegetables and cook for about 10 minutes, until they are just tender. Drain the vegetables.

4 Toast the pine nuts on a flat, ovenproof sheet under the broiler: watch them carefully as they only take a few seconds and burn easily.

5 To glaze the root vegetables, melt the butter or margarine in a large saucepan with the olive oil. Add the lemon rind and juice, then put in the drained vegetables. Cook gently for about 10 minutes, stirring often, until the vegetables are glazed and golden brown in parts. Season with salt and pepper and stir in the chopped parsley and the toasted pine nuts.

6 Mix the basmati rice with the other 2 rices, fluff with a fork and check the seasoning. Make a base of rice on a large serving dish or individual serving plates and arrange the vegetables on top.

COUSCOUS WITH SPICY CHICK PEA STEW

Couscous is quick and easy to prepare because, being precooked, it only needs soaking briefly before being heated through. The best way to do this is to put the couscous into a steamer saucepan, metal colander or sieve on top of the saucepan in which the stew is cooking; it can then absorb the flavor of the stew.

SERVES 4–5

3 cups couscous
½ teaspoon salt dissolved in 2½ cups warm water
¼ cup olive oil
2 onions, peeled and chopped
3 medium carrots, scraped and sliced
2 teaspoons each ground cinnamon, ground cumin and ground coriander
½ cup corn kernels
½ pound zucchini, diced
1⅓ cups dried chick peas, soaked, cooked until tender, then drained, or two 14-ounce cans chick peas, drained, or 1 pound frozen fava beans
1 quart water
¼ cup tomato paste
salt and freshly ground black pepper
TO GARNISH
coriander sprig

1 Spread the couscous out on a large deep plate and pour the salted water evenly over it, then rub the couscous lightly with your fingers to separate the grains. Set the plate of couscous aside.

2 Heat half the oil in a large saucepan or saucepan part of a steamer, add the onion and carrots and sauté gently for 10 minutes. Stir in the spices and cook for a further 2–3 minutes, stirring.

3 Stir in the corn, zucchini and the chick peas or fava beans, then add the water and tomato paste. Bring to a boil, then turn the heat down so that the chick pea stew simmers.

4 By now the couscous will have absorbed the water. Put it into the steamer saucepan, metal colander or sieve, breaking it up a bit with your fingers again as you do so. (If your container has large holes, you may prefer to line it with a piece of cheesecloth, to prevent the grains from falling through, but I've never found this necessary.)

5 Put the steamer, colander or sieve over the vegetable stew, cover with a lid or plate, and cook gently for 25–30 minutes.

6 Season to taste with salt and pepper. Stir the remaining olive oil into the couscous, then put the couscous and the chick pea stew on a large, warmed serving dish, garnish with the coriander and serve immediately.

MENU
Easy Summer Supper

Avocado Vinaigrette
154

Couscous with Spicy Chick Pea Stew

Green Salad
54
Tomato Salad
73

Strawberries with Cream or Thick Greek Yogurt

MENU
Vegetarian Barbecue

SERVES 6

Spicy Lentil Burgers
210

Vegetable Kebabs with Rosemary
201

Saffron Rice
241

Favorite Coleslaw
161

Baked Apples in Foil
84

Carrot Cake
306

Get the barbecue lit in good time, so that it is at the white-ash stage by the time you want to cook. I suggest that you cook the saffron rice beforehand, then keep it warm. Both the kebabs and burgers can be made in advance.

Brush the barbecue grill with oil and cook the kebabs on this for about 10–15 minutes, until the vegetables are tender, basting with the marinade. Fry the burgers for 10–15 minutes on an oiled baking sheet placed on the barbecue grill; turn them over once during cooking.

Prepare the baked apples as described on p. 84, filling them with dried fruit sprinkled with a little sherry or brandy and left overnight to marinate. Sprinkle them with a little brown sugar, dot some butter over them and wrap them in a double layer of aluminum foil. Cook on the barbecue grill for about 50 minutes, until tender.

Serve soft drinks, beer, chilled white or rosé wine or sangría. To make sangría, mix together a bottle of Spanish red wine and a bottle of lemonade, then add a glass each of brandy and port, plenty of ice and orange and lemon slices.

Pasta Dishes

Another really healthy food, pasta is popular with most people and is quick, economical and very filling. It is interesting to try different types of pasta, as I have suggested in the recipes, although you can always substitute your personal favorite or fall back on good old spaghetti if the more unusual ones are not available. A number of different pastas are identified in the Ingredients section (pp. 46–49), along with basic cooking instructions. Most of the pasta recipes in this section also make excellent first courses, if served in smaller portions, perhaps before a vegetable main course.

TAGLIATELLE WITH GORGONZOLA AND WALNUTS

Serve this quickly made, rich and delicious dish with a green salad.
If you can't get Gorgonzola, other blue cheeses such as
Roquefort can be used.

SERVES 4

MENU

*Spur-of-the-Moment
Supper for Two*

Avocado Vinaigrette
154
or Cannellini Bean Salad
with Fresh Herbs, served
with Warm Whole-Wheat
Rolls
328

**Tagliatelle with
Gorgonzola and Walnuts**
Green Salad
54

Fresh Figs, or
Honeyed Poached Pears with
Poire William Liqueur

Coffee

1 pound tagliatelle
1 tablespoon butter
salt and freshly ground black pepper
1 cup walnuts, roughly chopped
1¼ cups heavy cream
1 garlic clove, crushed
¼ pound Gorgonzola cheese,
   crumbled

1 Cook the tagliatelle in a large saucepan as described on p. 50, until *al dente*.
2 Drain immediately, then return to the still-warm pan with the butter, salt, pepper and walnuts.
3 While the tagliatelle is cooking, make the sauce. Put the cream into a small, heavy-bottomed saucepan; add the garlic and Gorgonzola and heat gently, stirring occasionally, until the cheese has melted. Season with salt and pepper.
4 Turn the pasta onto a large warmed serving dish, or individual plates, and pour the sauce into the center. Serve immediately.

☑ FUSILLI VERDE WITH MUSHROOMS ☑
AND CREAM

SERVES 4

1 pound fusilli verde
FOR THE SAUCE
1 onion, peeled and chopped
3 tablespoons butter or vegan margarine
1 garlic clove, crushed
1 pound button mushrooms, wiped and sliced
½ cup (generous) heavy or nondairy cream
salt
freshly ground black pepper
freshly grated nutmeg

1 To make the sauce, sauté the onion gently in 2 tablespoons butter or vegan margarine for 10 minutes, until softened.

2 Add the garlic and mushrooms and cook for 15–20 minutes, until all the liquid has evaporated.

3 Add the cream. Season with salt, pepper and nutmeg. Remove from the heat.

4 Cook the fusilli in a large saucepan as described on p. 50, until *al dente*.

5 Drain the pasta immediately, then return to the still-warm pan with the remaining butter, salt and pepper.

6 Quickly reheat the sauce, then tip the fusilli into a warmed serving dish, pour the sauce over the top and serve.

☑ PASTA PRIMAVERA ☑

SERVES 4

Pasta Primavera

2 tablespoons butter or vegan margarine
1 onion, peeled and finely chopped
½ pound young carrots, scraped and diced
½ pound zucchini, sliced
½ pound fresh shelled peas or snow peas
¾ pound vermicelli
2 tablespoons chopped mint
salt and freshly ground black pepper
TO GARNISH
mint sprigs

1 Melt the butter or vegan margarine in a large saucepan, then cover and sauté the onion without browning for 5 minutes.

2 Add the carrots and cook for 10 minutes, then put in the zucchini and cook for a further 5 minutes. Add the peas or snow peas and cook for 2–3 minutes.

3 Just before the vegetables are ready, cook the vermicelli in a large saucepan as described on p. 50, until *al dente*. Drain immediately, then return to the pan.

4 Add the vegetables to the vermicelli, together with the mint, salt and pepper. Mix, then serve garnished with mint.

WHOLE-WHEAT PASTA AND MUSHROOM BAKE

This is another tasty, homely dish, and like many pasta bakes, freezes well. Frozen peas go well with it, or fresh watercress.

SERVES 4

MENU

Easy Supper for Four

Pears with Piquant Cream
Dressing
148

**Whole-Wheat Pasta and
Mushroom Bake**

Illustrated on p. 256

Stir-fried Carrots with
Watercress and Sesame Seeds
181

Fresh Fruit or
Linzer Torte
293

*¼ pound small whole-wheat pasta shapes
   such as leaves or rings*
2 onions, peeled and chopped
1 tablespoon oil
¼ pound mushrooms, washed and chopped
½ pound tomatoes, peeled and chopped
1 egg, beaten
1 cup grated Cheddar cheese
freshly ground black pepper
butter for greasing
*a few whole-wheat breadcrumbs mixed with
   chopped parsley for topping*

1 Preheat the oven to 375°F. Grease an ovenproof dish.

2 Cook the pasta in a large saucepan as described on p. 50, until *al dente*. Drain.
3 While the pasta is cooking, sauté the onions in the oil for 7 minutes, then add the mushrooms and tomatoes and cook for a further 3 minutes.
4 Stir in the egg and stir over the heat for a moment or two longer until the egg begins to set. Remove from the heat and add the drained pasta, two-thirds of the cheese, and salt and pepper to taste.
5 Spoon the mixture into the dish and sprinkle crumbs and remaining cheese over the top. Bake for 25–30 minutes, until crisp and golden-brown.

Ⓥ TAGLIATELLE VERDE WITH LENTIL SAUCE Ⓥ

This is a useful dish to make when you have to rustle up a meal for a crowd unexpectedly, because it uses pantry ingredients.

SERVES 4

Tagliatelle Verde with Lentil Sauce

½–¾ pound tagliatelle verde
1 tablespoon butter or vegan margarine
FOR THE SAUCE
2 tablespoons olive oil
2 onions, peeled and chopped
2 garlic cloves, crushed
½ teaspoon ground cinnamon
1 cup dried red lentils, washed
one 15-ounce can tomatoes
2 cups water
salt and freshly ground black pepper
TO SERVE (OPTIONAL)
coriander sprigs
grated Parmesan cheese

1 To make the sauce, heat the olive oil in a large pan and sauté the onion for 10 minutes, then add the garlic, cinnamon,

lentils, tomatoes and water. Bring to a boil.

2 Reduce the heat and let the mixture simmer gently for about 20 minutes, until the lentils are tender; season to taste with salt and pepper.

3 Meanwhile, cook the tagliatelle in a large saucepan as described on p. 50, until *al dente*.

4 Drain immediately, then return to the still-warm pan with the butter or vegan margarine. Season with salt and pepper.

5 Turn the tagliatelle onto a large warmed serving dish, or individual plates, and pour the sauce into the center. Garnish with coriander and serve immediately, with grated Parmesan cheese handed separately.

Variation

TAGLIATELLE VERDE WITH LENTIL AND RED WINE SAUCE

Make as described, replacing a little of the water with red wine, say about ½ cup – or as much as you can spare! This makes an excellent supper, accompanied by a good green salad and the rest of the wine used to make the sauce.

SPAGHETTI WITH GREEN LENTIL SAUCE

This is popular with my student daughter and her friends, because it's quick to make, cheap, filling and tasty. The sauce freezes well.

SERVES 4

¾ pound spaghetti
1 tablespoon butter or vegan margarine
FOR THE SAUCE
1 cup dried whole green lentils cooked in plenty of water for 45–50 minutes, until tender, or two 14-ounce cans lentils
1 large onion, peeled and sliced
2 tablespoons oil
1 garlic clove, crushed
1 large carrot, diced
2 tablespoons tomato paste
2 tablespoons chopped parsley
salt and freshly ground black pepper
TO SERVE (OPTIONAL)
grated Parmesan or Cheddar cheese

1 To make the sauce, drain the lentils, reserving the liquid.

2 Sauté the onion in the oil in a medium saucepan for 5 minutes, allowing it to brown lightly, then add the garlic and carrot.

3 Cover the pan and cook gently for about 15 minutes, until the vegetables are tender.

4 Stir in the lentils, tomato paste, parsley, salt and pepper and a little of the reserved lentil liquid, to give a thick but moist consistency.

5 About 10 minutes before the lentil sauce is cooked, cook the spaghetti in a large saucepan as described on p. 50, until *al dente*.

6 Drain well, then return the spaghetti to the still-warm pan with the butter or vegan margarine and black pepper.

7 Check that the spaghetti and the sauce are really hot, then turn the spaghetti into a large warmed serving dish and pour the sauce on top. Offer grated Parmesan or cheddar cheese separately.

Tomato Purée

This can be bought in a can, tube or jar, and is useful for adding extra flavoring and natural thickening to tomato dishes or other savory mixtures which would be complemented by a tomato flavor. Use discreetly, as too much can give rather an acid flavor, and I find tomato purée in a tube the most useful as a little can be used at a time and the rest stored in the fridge where it will keep for several weeks. Even nicer is sun-dried tomato paste, which comes in jars and is sweet and mellow – good for a special treat.

Summer Linguine (p. 255), with an
avocado and mushroom salad

$\boxed{V}$ TAGLIONI VERDE WITH $\boxed{V}$
TOMATO SAUCE AND EGGPLANT

The green of the taglioni against the orange-red tomato sauce and
the purple tones of the eggplant give this dish a warming,
appetizing look, ideal for a quick supper on a chilly autumn day. I
like to serve it on its own, followed by a leafy salad, then a cheese
board, and, finally, perhaps a refreshing sorbet,
such as pear or blackberry.

SERVES 4

2 medium eggplants, total weight about 1
   pound
salt
8 tablespoons olive oil
1 onion, peeled and chopped
1 1/2 pounds tomatoes, peeled and chopped
freshly ground black pepper
3/4 pound taglioni verde
TO SERVE (OPTIONAL)
basil sprigs
grated Parmesan cheese

1 Slice the eggplants thinly lengthways,
then cut into strips about 2 inches long
and 1 inch wide. Salt, rinse and drain the
eggplant strips as described on p. 73.
2 Sauté the eggplant strips in 6 tablespoons of the olive oil in a medium saucepan until crisp and brown on both sides.
Remove from the pan and drain on paper
towels. Then sauté the onion in the olive
oil left in the pan for 10 minutes, without
browning. Add the tomatoes and cook
gently for 5 minutes.
3 Purée in a blender or food processor,
return to the pan and season with salt and
pepper.
4 Cook the taglioni in a large saucepan as
described on p. 50, until al dente.
5 Drain the pasta immediately, then return to the pan and add the remaining
olive oil and salt and pepper to taste.
6 Turn the taglioni onto a warmed
shallow serving dish. Pour the sauce on
top, then put the eggplant strips on top of
that. Garnish with the basil sprigs. Serve
the pasta immediately, with some grated
Parmesan cheese handed separately, if
you like.

[V] FUSILLE COLBUCO WITH EGGPLANT [V] AND WINE SAUCE

Fusille colbuco, a long spiral pasta, is particularly attractive in this
dish, but any other long type of pasta, including
spaghetti, would be good.

SERVES 4

¾ pound fusille colbuco
FOR THE SAUCE
2 medium eggplants, total weight about
    1 pound
salt
1 onion, peeled and chopped
¼ cup olive oil
1 garlic clove, crushed
1 green pepper, deseeded and chopped
½ pound tomatoes, peeled and chopped
1 tablespoon chopped fresh basil or 1 teaspoon
    dried basil
¼ cup red or white wine
freshly ground black pepper
TO GARNISH
basil sprigs
TO SERVE (OPTIONAL)
grated Parmesan cheese

1 Dice the eggplants, then salt, drain and
rinse as described on p. 73.
2 Sauté the onion in half the olive oil in a
medium saucepan for 5 minutes, without
browning, then add the eggplant, garlic,
green pepper, tomatoes, basil and wine
and cook gently for 25 minutes, until the
vegetables are soft. Season with salt and
pepper.
3 Just before the sauce is ready, cook the
fusille colbuco in a large saucepan as
described on p. 50, until *al dente*.
4 Drain immediately, then return to the
still-warm pan with the remaining olive
oil, salt and pepper.
5 Turn the pasta onto a warmed large
serving dish, or individual plates, and
pour the wine sauce on top. Garnish with
the basil sprigs and serve immediately,
with some grated Parmesan cheese
handed separately.

MENU

*Easy Autumn Supper
for Six*

**Taglioni Verde with
Tomato Sauce and
Eggplant**
254
Endive, Watercress and
Walnut Salad with Walnut
Vinaigrette
Illustrated on p. 179
161 and 154

Selection of White Cheeses
(including a cream one and
one or two goat cheeses)
Assorted Breads and
Crackers

Pear or Blackberry Sorbet
Illustrated on p. 283
282

Espresso, Filter or
Cappuccino Coffee

SUMMER LINGUINE

A perfect dish for a lazy summer's lunch in the garden, hot linguine
(or any other long slim pasta) is served here with summer
vegetables and soft melting cheese.

SERVES 4

1 pound tomatoes, peeled and sliced
1 bunch scallions, trimmed and chopped
2 garlic cloves, crushed
2–3 tablespoons fresh basil leaves
½ pound mozzarella or Brie cheese, cubed
salt and freshly ground black pepper
1 pound linguine or other long, thin pasta
2 tablespoons olive oil

1 Put the tomatoes, scallions, garlic,
basil and cheese into a serving bowl large

enough to hold the cooked pasta as well.
Season with salt and pepper.
2 Cook the linguine in a large saucepan
as described on p. 50, until *al dente*. Drain
immediately, then return to the still-
warm pan with the olive oil, salt and
pepper.
3 Mix well, then add the linguine to
the vegetables in the bowl and stir to
distribute all the ingredients. Serve
immediately.

Spinach Lasagne; Whole-Wheat Pasta and Mushroom Bake (p. 252)

SPINACH LASAGNE

This makes a big dish of particularly tasty lasagne, great for feeding a crowd, especially if accompanied by some robust red wine. A crisp green salad with fresh herbs goes well with it.

SERVES 6

1 large onion, peeled and chopped
2 tablespoons olive oil
2 garlic cloves, crushed
2 pounds cooked, fresh spinach, chopped, or
  frozen chopped spinach, thawed
2 pounds ricotta cheese
salt and freshly ground black pepper
1 quantity Italian Tomato Sauce (p. 171)
½ pound oven-ready lasagne or ¾ pound
  fresh lasagne
½ pound mozzarella cheese
butter for greasing

1 Preheat the oven to 400°F. Grease a large, shallow ovenproof dish.
2 Sauté the onion in the olive oil in a large saucepan for 10 minutes, until soft but not browned. Add the garlic, cook for a minute or two longer, then remove from the heat.
3 Squeeze any excess liquid out of the cooked or thawed spinach, then add to the onion mixture, together with the ricotta cheese, salt and plenty of freshly ground black pepper.

4 Cover the base of the dish with a thin layer of the tomato sauce, then put a layer of lasagne on top, followed by a layer of the spinach mixture. Thinly slice 1½ cups of the mozzarella cheese. Next make a layer of mozzarella cheese slices, then of tomato sauce.

5 Continue like this until all the ingredients are used up, ending with a layer of sauce. Grate the remaining cheese and arrange in 3 lines on the top.

6 Bake for 1 hour, covering the dish with foil after 40–45 minutes if the top begins to get too brown.

Variation

MIXED VEGETABLE LASAGNE

Make as described, but instead of the spinach and cheese filling use a vegetable mixture. To make this, sauté the onion in oil as described, then add the garlic and 1½ pounds each of diced carrots and sliced leeks, 1 pound of diced zucchini and 1 deseeded and chopped green pepper. Cover and sauté for about 15 minutes until tender. Layer this mixture with the lasagne, mozzarella cheese and tomato sauce.

LENTIL LASAGNE

Use a double quantity Green Lentil Sauce mixture (p. 253), layered with Italian Tomato Sauce.

MACARONI AND CHEESE

An ever-popular old favorite, with a tangy sauce. My youngest daughter always asked for this when she had a friend to a meal, and they certainly ate up enthusiastically. But I did sometimes wonder what their parents thought when they heard that their daughters had had such an apparently uninspired vegetarian dish in the home of someone who was supposed to be an expert!

SERVES 4

½ pound quick-cooking macaroni
4 tablespoons butter or vegan margarine
2 rounded tablespoons unbleached white flour
2½ cups milk
2 teaspoons Dijon mustard
1½ cups grated cheese
salt
freshly ground black pepper
1⅓ cups fresh whole-wheat breadcrumbs
a little extra butter or vegan margarine for greasing

1 Heat the broiler, or preheat the oven to 400°F. Grease a shallow flameproof dish that will fit under the broiler, if using this method for browning the macaroni and cheese.

2 Cook the macaroni in a large saucepan as described on p. 50, until *al dente*. Drain well.

3 Meanwhile, make the sauce. Melt the butter or vegan margarine in a saucepan, then add the flour; stir for 1–2 minutes over the heat, then stir in the milk, a quarter at a time, stirring well and allowing the sauce to thicken between each addition.

4 Let the sauce simmer gently for 5 minutes, then remove from the heat and add the mustard, two-thirds of the grated cheese, and salt and pepper to taste.

5 Mix together the cooked macaroni and the cheese sauce. Check the seasoning, then spoon the mixture into the dish and level the surface. Sprinkle the breadcrumbs and the remaining cheese over the top.

6 Place the dish under the preheated broiler for 5–10 minutes, or heat through in the oven for about 20 minutes, until the macaroni and cheese is hot inside and golden-brown and crisp on top.

MENU

Freezer Supper for Six

Spring Rolls with Dipping Sauce
Illustrated on p. 141
143

Mixed Vegetable Lasagne

Green Salad
54

Orange Parfait
284
or Vanilla Ice Cream
Illustrated on p. 281
280
with Raspberry Coulis
300

EGGPLANT AND PASTA CHARLOTTE

Here is pasta dressed up for a special occasion, a tasty mixture of rigatoni with tomato sauce and cheese, encased in slices of eggplant in a round mold and turned out like a cake. It's easy to do, yet always impresses. Eat as a main course, with one or two simply cooked vegetables, like green beans and baby carrots.

SERVES 6 AS A MAIN COURSE, 8 AS A STARTER

Olives

The fruit of a tree native to the Mediterranean, olives are gathered and preserved in oil or brine at various stages of development. The ones which are picked and pickled early become green olives, while the later, more mature olives become black olives. Green and black olives differ in flavor and both have their uses; green olives are also available pitted and stuffed with pimiento. They make a delicious nibble, garnish and addition to salads and savory dishes. The best way to buy olives is loose at a good delicatessen. They will keep for a couple of weeks or so in the refrigerator.

A delicious Olive Pâté can be bought in a jar or made by pitting and puréeing black olives in a blender or food processor. I think of this as the vegetarian answer to caviar and find it an attractive and piquant garnish for canapés, salads, hard-boiled and scrambled eggs; it's also excellent thinly spread on Melba Toast (p. 146) or with crusty bread.

2 medium eggplants, total weight about
   1 pound
salt
olive oil
14 ounces rigatoni
1 quantity Italian Tomato Sauce (p. 171)
6 tablespoons butter
1/2 pound mozzarella cheese, grated
1/4 cup grated Parmesan cheese
1/4 cup grated aged Cheddar cheese
1 tablespoon dried oregano
freshly ground black pepper
2 tablespoons dried breadcrumbs

1 Slice the eggplants diagonally into 1/4-inch slices. Salt, rinse and drain the eggplant slices as described on p. 73. Pat dry on paper towels.
2 Sauté the eggplant slices in a little olive oil for 2–3 minutes on each side, until soft and lightly browned. Drain well on paper towels.
3 Preheat the oven to 375°F. Brush an 8-inch round springform pan with olive oil.

4 Cook the rigatoni in a large saucepan as described on p. 50 until almost done: it should be a bit undercooked. Drain well, then return to the pan with 2 tablespoons of the tomato sauce. Mix well.
5 Melt the butter in the remaining tomato sauce; pour over the rigatoni and mix, together with the mozzarella, Parmesan and Cheddar cheeses. Add the oregano, and plenty of salt and pepper.
6 Arrange the eggplant slices over the base and sides of the prepared pan. Make sure that the slices in the base of the pan radiate attractively from the center, and that all gaps are filled.
7 Spoon the pasta mixture into the pan, press down lightly and sprinkle with the breadcrumbs. Bake for 20 minutes.
8 Allow the charlotte to stand for 15 minutes to settle, and for the flavors to develop, then slip a knife around the edges of the pan and turn the charlotte out onto a warmed serving dish.
9 Press any fallen eggplant slices back in place and serve immediately.

[V] PASTA WITH BLACK OLIVES [V]

SERVES 4

Opposite page: Eggplant and Pasta Charlotte

3/4 pound rigatoni
2 tablespoons olive oil
salt and freshly ground black pepper
1 quantity Sweet Pepper Sauce (p. 172)
1/2 cup black olives, pitted and roughly
   chopped

1 Cook the rigatoni in a large saucepan as described on p. 50, until *al dente*.

2 Drain immediately and return the rigatoni to the still-warm pan with the olive oil; season the pasta to taste with salt and black pepper.
3 While the pasta is cooking, make the sweet pepper sauce.
4 Serve the pasta on warmed plates, pour the sauce on top and sprinkle with the chopped olives.

Pastry Dishes

Favorites with most people, pastry dishes are useful for many occasions ranging from picnics and hearty family meals to dinner parties and celebrations. I use whole-wheat flour for all pastry making except puff pastry, for which I use unbleached white flour, when I make it, although for this I do often take a shortcut and use a good-quality frozen pastry, made without animal fat (check the label). Keep the high-fat pastries, such as puff, rough puff and flaky, for specials, and serve any pastry dish with low-fat accompaniments such as steamed vegetables or a lightly dressed salad, for healthy, well-balanced eating.

Fats for Pastry

Traditional fats for pastries are butter and lard. Vegetarians can use a vegetable lard, or solid white fat. I use this for some pastries, such as flaky. Otherwise I use butter, which I prefer to manufactured fats such as margarine and solid vegetable fat.

Polyunsaturated vegan margarine can be used in place of butter to make pastry. Some people use vegetable oil for shortcrust pastry, but I have never been able to make a really good, light pastry with this.

⟨V⟩ BASIC SHORTCRUST PASTRY ⟨V⟩

MAKES ½ pound

1½ cups plain 100% or 85% whole-wheat flour
½ teaspoon salt
¼ pound (1 stick) butter or vegan margarine, diced
3 tablespoons ice water

1 Put the flour into a mixing bowl with the salt and butter or vegan margarine.
2 Using your fingertips, rub the fat into the flour until the mixture resembles fine breadcrumbs.
3 Add the water and gently press the mixture together to form a dough.
4 Turn the dough onto a lightly floured board and knead lightly, pressing it into a round, square or oblong, as required, then roll it out, using a floured rolling pin and short strokes, and making sure that the pastry does not stick to the board.

5 Use as required. If you do not need the pastry immediately, wrap it in plastic wrap and leave it in the refrigerator for up to 24 hours.

Variations

CHEESE SHORTCRUST
Add ½–1 cup finely grated Cheddar cheese before you add the water.

NUT SHORTCRUST
Mix in ¼ cup grated or finely chopped nuts – almonds, walnuts, Brazil nuts or hazelnuts – before adding the water.

RICH SHORTCRUST
For this light, melt-in-the-mouth pastry, use self-rising flour and increase the fat by 2 tablespoons. You won't need any water because the extra fat will bind the dough.

Pastry Weights

By convention, the weight of pastry needed for a recipe is always given as the weight of the flour used to make it. So ½ pound pastry means pastry made from ½ pound, or 1¾ cups, flour. However, the weight stated on a package of frozen pastry is the weight of the whole amount.

LINING A TART PAN WITH PASTRY

1 Hold the pastry board at an angle of 45° at the far edge of the tart pan

2 Gently slide the pastry off the board and onto the pan, moving the pastry board back toward you as you do so

FRENCH ONION TART

This rich and delicious classic French tart makes a wonderful main course with a tomato and basil salad or a crisp green salad; or it can be served cut into thin slices, as a first course.

SERVES 4–6 AS A MAIN COURSE, 6–8 AS A STARTER

½ quantity Basic Shortcrust Pastry (p. 260)
butter for greasing
FOR THE FILLING
1 pound onions, peeled and sliced
2 tablespoons butter
½ cup light cream
1 whole egg or 2 egg yolks
salt and freshly ground black pepper
freshly grated nutmeg
TO GARNISH
chopped parsley

1 Preheat the oven to 400°F. Heat a baking sheet. Lightly grease an 8-inch tart pan or ring.
2 Roll out the pastry as thinly as possible and use to line the pan or ring. Bake blind as described on p. 266. Turn down the oven to 350°F.
3 Meanwhile, make the filling. Sauté the onions gently in the butter for 25–30 minutes, until very soft. Remove from the heat and add the cream, and egg or egg yolks, along with salt, pepper and nutmeg to taste.
4 Pour the onion mixture into the tart pan, then return the tart to the oven on the baking sheet and bake for 30–35 minutes, until the filling is set.
5 Serve warm or cold, sprinkled with a little parsley.

Variations
RATATOUILLE TART
Make as described, using a good, thick, tasty Ratatouille mixture (p. 187) instead of the onions.

SPINACH, CHEESE AND ALMOND TART
Use 1 pound fresh spinach or ½ pound frozen spinach, cooked, ¾ cup grated cheese and 1 cup toasted slivered almonds; mix with 1 egg and omit the cream or milk.

MUSTARD, TOMATO AND MOZZARELLA TART
Spread the base of the tart pan with 2 tablespoons Dijon mustard, cover with 1 pound peeled and sliced tomatoes. Arrange ¼ pound sliced mozzarella cheese on top, season, then carefully pour in the egg and cream mixture.

CAULIFLOWER, CHEDDAR CHEESE AND WALNUT TART
Use cooked florets from a small cauliflower, 1 cup grated Cheddar cheese and 1 cup chopped walnuts, instead of the onion.

WATERCRESS AND STILTON CHEESE TART
For this tangy version, use 2 eggs, 1¼ cups cream or milk, a bunch of watercress, chopped, and 1 cup grated Stilton cheese.

MUSHROOM TART
Sauté just 1 small chopped onion for 7 minutes, then add ¾ pound mushrooms, sliced, and a crushed garlic clove and sauté for about 15 minutes until all the liquid has disappeared. Add 1 tablespoon chopped parsley to the egg mixture.

LEEK AND BLACK OLIVE TART
Use 1½ pounds leeks, cooked, 2 tablespoons chopped parsley and ¼–½ cup black olives.

MENU

A Special Picnic

Mushroom Pâté with Porcini with Crusty Bread
146

French Onion Flan

Green-bean Salad with Radiccio
167

Pink Potato Salad
Illustrated on p. 165
166

Peaches

Filling a Tart Shell

If you're worried about spills, put the tart into the oven first, then fill with the egg mixture, using a pitcher.

Serving Tarts

Tarts are adaptable – they can be light and elegant, with thin, crisp pastry, or hearty and rustic, with thick pastry and a deep filling. They can be party-sized or individual.

Eminently portable and ideal for picnics or lunch boxes, a tart can also be eaten with pleasure at any meal from brunch to late-night supper, as a starter or main course.

BROCCOLI, RED PEPPER AND ALMOND TART

[V]   [V]

In this tart, bright green broccoli is covered with a light-textured sauce of red peppers and almonds and finished with a topping of roasted slivered almonds.

SERVES 4–6 AS A MAIN COURSE, 6–8 AS A STARTER

Vegan Flan Fillings

Many combinations of cooked vegetables, vegetable purées and dips can be used to make colorful and delicious non-dairy fillings. Here are some possibilities:

- Ratatouille (p. 187), made fairly thick
- Cooked leeks topped with Hummus (p. 41), thin circles of red pepper and black olives
- Golden Spiced Cauliflower (p. 185)
- Mushroom and Herb Terrine (p. 146), topped with thin slices of mushroom brushed with oil
- A thick, well-flavored purée of carrots or celeriac (p. 189), topped with lightly-fried circles of zucchini
- Broiled Peppers (p. 145)
- Fava Bean Dip with Mint (p. 146)
- Vegetables à la Grecque (p. 150)
- Warm Salad of Oyster Mushrooms (p. 163)
- Avocado and Red Pepper Salsa (p. 176)
- Glazed Root Vegetables (p. 246)

½ quantity Basic Shortcrust Pastry (p. 260)
1 pound broccoli, divided into even-sized florets, stalks removed
1 tablespoon oil
salt and freshly ground black pepper
1 quantity Red Pepper and Almond Dip (p. 146)
¼ cup slivered almonds
butter for greasing

1 Preheat the oven to 400°F. Put a baking sheet into the center of the oven, to heat up. Lightly grease an 8-inch tart pan or ring.
2 Roll out the pastry as thinly as possible and use to line the pan or ring; trim the edges. Bake blind as described on p. 266.
3 Meanwhile, cook the broccoli in 1 inch boiling water for 4–5 minutes, or until just tender. Drain and return to the pan with the oil and salt and pepper.
4 Half-fill the tart shell with the Red Pepper and Almond Dip, then arrange the broccoli on top, pressing the florets into the dip to secure them.

5 Spoon the remaining pepper and almond dip evenly over the top, making sure it runs down between the broccoli florets. Leave a few florets peeping out for color contrast. Sprinkle with the slivered almonds.
6 Return the tart to the oven on the baking sheet and bake for 25–30 minutes, until the almonds are lightly browned and the filling is heated through and looks set. Serve hot, warm, or cold.

Variations
MUSHROOM, RED PEPPER AND ALMOND TART
For this tasty variation, replace the broccoli with 1 pound button mushrooms, sliced and sautéed until all the liquid has evaporated.

SPICY VEGETABLE AND LENTIL TART
Use ½ pound cooked mixed vegetables such as carrots, potatoes and peas, and 1 quantity Lentil Dal (p. 209). Top with shredded or desiccated coconut.

Pastry quantities for tarts

Exact quantities depend on how thinly you roll your pastry and the depth of your tart pan or dish, but here is a guide:

Tart size	Quantity of flour for pastry
4 inch	½ cup
6 inch	¾ cup (generous)
7 inch	1 cup
8 inch	1¼ cups
9 inch	1⅓ cups
10 inch	1½ cups
12 inch (shallow)	2 cups

*Broccoli, Red Pepper and Almond Tart
(p. 262); Asparagus Tartlets*

ASPARAGUS TARTLETS

These tartlets – made in 4-inch tartlet pans – are perfect for a light
main course – perhaps for a late-night supper or summer garden
lunch. The little Asparagus Boats are ideal for a buffet party.

MAKES 6

*1½ quantity Basic Shortcrust Pastry
   (p. 260)
1 pound fresh asparagus, trimmed and cooked
   as described on p. 63, or 1 pound frozen
   asparagus, cooked and drained
1¼ cups light cream
2 egg yolks
salt and freshly ground black pepper
freshly grated nutmeg
butter for greasing*

1 Preheat the oven to 400°F. Put a baking
sheet into the center of the oven, to heat
up. Lightly grease six 4-inch tartlet pans.
2 Divide the pastry into 6 equal pieces.
Roll out each piece as thinly as possible
and use to line the pans; trim the edges.
Bake the tartlets blind as described on
p. 266.
3 Turn the oven down to 350°F.
4 Remove the tips from the asparagus
and chop the tender part of the stalks.
Divide the chopped asparagus and the
tips among the tartlets.
5 Whisk the cream and egg yolks
together; season to taste with salt, pepper
and grated nutmeg. Divide this mixture

between the tartlets, then put them back
into the oven on the baking sheet and
bake for about 15 minutes, until the
filling is set. Serve hot right out of the
oven, or warm.

Variations
INDIVIDUAL AVOCADO
TARTLETS
Use the diced flesh from 3 small ripe
avocados, a crushed garlic clove and 2
tablespoons lemon juice instead of the
asparagus. Make as described. These
need to be cooked just before eating, and
be careful not to overbake. If you over-
heat the avocado, it will give the tartlet a
bitter taste.

ASPARAGUS BOATS
The ingredients given above make 30
boats. Roll out the pastry, line boat-
shaped pans and bake as above. Cut the
asparagus spears into lengths to fit each
boat shape; divide among the boats, pour
in the egg mixture and bake for 8–10
minutes. Garnish each serving with a
slice of lemon and a parsley sprig.

Preparing Tarts in Advance

Filled tarts do not freeze well – they
emerge with soggy bottoms. It's
best to bake the tart shell (and be
sure to give them the hot-oil
treatment, p. 266, for superb
results), then freeze. Pack carefully.
Ideally, fill and bake just before
eating, though if you've a lot to do,
they can be cooked the night before,
then kept in a cool, airy place until
required.

☑ POTATO AND MUSHROOM TURNOVERS ☑

These turnovers are good either hot or cold and are popular for
picnics and lunch boxes. Serve with a mixed salad.

MAKES 4

SHAPING A TURNOVER

Potato and Mushroom Turnovers

*1 quantity Basic Shortcrust Pastry, Plain or
  Cheese (p. 260)*
beaten egg to glaze (optional)
FOR THE FILLING
1 onion, peeled and chopped
2 tablespoons oil
*1 large potato, peeled and cut into ¼-inch
  dice*
1 garlic clove, crushed
½ pound mushrooms, washed and chopped
1 tablespoon chopped parsley
salt and freshly ground black pepper

1 First make the filling. Sauté the onion
in the oil for 5 minutes, then add the
potato and garlic.
2 Cook gently for 10 minutes. Add the
mushrooms and cook for a further 4–5
minutes, until the vegetables are just
tender. Add the parsley and season with
salt and pepper. Cool.
3 Preheat the oven to 400°F. Divide the
pastry into 4 equal pieces; roll each piece
into a circle 6 inches in diameter.
4 Spoon a quarter of the potato mixture
onto each circle. Fold over the pastry and
press the edges together.
5 Make a couple of small steam holes in
each turnover, brush the turnovers with
beaten egg, if used, then place them on a
baking sheet and bake for 20–25 minutes,
until golden-brown.

Variations
SPICED CHICK PEA AND POTATO TURNOVERS
Make this spicy version in the same way
as the Potato and Mushroom Turnovers,
adding 1 tablespoon ground coriander
and 1 teaspoon ground cumin to the
onion, and replacing the mushrooms with
⅔ cup dried chick peas, soaked, cooked
and drained, or one 15-ounce can chick
peas, drained.

VEGETABLE TURNOVERS
Replace the mushrooms with ¾ cup
scraped and diced carrots and 1 cup
shredded leeks and a chopped peeled
tomato, added to the pan with the potatoes and sautéed until tender. Flavor with
½ teaspoon each dried oregano and basil.
Other combinations of cooked vegetables can be used, and different flavorings, such as rosemary or thyme.
Drained cooked chick peas, red kidney
beans or cannellini beans can be added to
the mixture, or some chopped nuts, such
as hazelnuts or almonds.

Savory Cheshire Cheese and Onion Pie

Simple and good, a vegetarian family favorite.

SERVES 4

1 quantity Basic Shortcrust Pastry (p. 260)
FOR THE FILLING
1½ pounds onions, peeled and sliced
1½ cups grated Cheshire cheese
salt and freshly ground black pepper
freshly grated nutmeg

1 Preheat the oven to 425°F. Put a baking sheet into the center of the oven, to heat up.
2 Parboil the onions in 1 inch lightly salted water for 5 minutes, then drain and cool.
3 Roll out just under half the pastry to fit an 8–9-inch pie plate.
4 Add the cheese to the onions; mix together and season with salt, pepper and nutmeg, then spoon on top of the pastry.
5 Roll out the remaining pastry to fit the top; press the edges together and trim. Bake for 30 minutes, until golden-brown. Serve hot.

Variations
LIMA BEAN, CHEESE AND PICKLE PIE
Make this in the same way, using ¼ pound dried lima beans, soaked, cooked and drained, or one 15-ounce can lima beans, drained, in place of one of the onions, and reducing the amount of cheese to ½ cup. Add 3 tablespoons pickle or chutney to the mixture before spooning on top of the pastry.

LEEK PIE
Wash 2 pounds leeks and cut them into pieces about 1 inch long. Cook them in 1 inch boiling water for about 10 minutes, until just tender. Drain them very well, then mix them with 1¼ cups sour cream or Béchamel Sauce (p. 175) and season with salt and pepper.

MUSHROOM AND CHESTNUT PIE
Sauté 1 large chopped onion and 2 chopped celery stalks in 2 tablespoons butter for 10 minutes, then add 2¾ cups washed and sliced mushrooms and cook for a further 2–3 minutes, or until the mushrooms are tender. Remove from the heat and add ¾–1 pound cooked chestnuts (you can use fresh cooked chestnuts, or canned whole chestnuts, or dried ones that have been soaked and cooked as described on p. 36). Add 1 tablespoon soy sauce and salt and pepper.

Mushroom Tart

SERVES 6 AS A MAIN COURSE

double quantity Basic Shortcrust Pastry (p. 260)
double quantity Mushrooms in Cream (p. 79)
butter for greasing
TO GARNISH
chopped parsley

1 Preheat the oven to 400°F. Put a baking sheet into the center of the oven to heat up. Lightly grease a 12-inch tart pan.
2 Roll out the pastry and use to line the pan; trim the edges. Bake blind as described on p. 266.
3 Spoon the mushrooms in cream into the tart shell and smooth the top. Return the tart to the oven on the baking sheet for 10–15 minutes to heat through. Sprinkle with parsley. Serve the tart hot or cold.

A Quiche By Any Other Name . . .
Strictly speaking, "quiche" refers to a light, creamy French tart, and in particular, Quiche Lorraine (which contains cream, bacon, onion and Gruyère cheese). "Flan" is the English term for a tart.

When you're handling whole-wheat pastry, which tends to be more crumbly than pastry made with white flour, it helps to roll the pastry out on a lightly floured board; then you can tip it straight from the board into your pan or dish, avoiding any breakages.

MENU
Autumn Meal for Six
Pumpkin Soup
77

Mushroom Tart
Red Cabbage Casserole
180
Potato Purée
189

Poached Pears with Cinnamon Cream
85

QUICK SCALLION AND
FRESH HERB TART

This is a light and melting tart, rather than a crisp one. It is quick
and makes a delicious lunch or supper, with a crisp, leafy salad,
such as radicchio, watercress and walnut.

SERVES 4

MAKING A REALLY
CRISP TART SHELL

I find this method of "baking blind"
better than the conventional one,
where the tart shell is weighed down
with brown paper or aluminum foil
and dried beans, because it's less
trouble and gives a crisper result.
Have a look at the tart after 5
minutes to see if the base is rising up;
if so, simply press it down gently
with the back of a fork.

1 Preheat the oven to 400°F. Lightly
grease a tart pan or ring and set on
a baking sheet.

2 Roll out the pastry and ease it into
the pan or ring. Press down, trim
edges.

3 Prick the pastry base all over.
Bake for 12–20 minutes, depending
on the size and thickness of the
pastry, until firm to a light touch
and lightly browned.

4 When the tart comes out of the
oven, have ready 2–3 tablespoons
sizzling hot oil and pour this into the
pastry shell. This will ensure that the
base of your tart will be wonderfully
crisp.

5 Next brush a little beaten egg over
the base of the tart to seal any holes
and return the tart to the oven for
3–4 minutes, until the beaten egg
glaze is thoroughly set.

½ quantity Rich Shortcrust Pastry (p. 260)
butter for greasing
FOR THE FILLING
½ cup (generous) milk, half-and-half, or
  light cream
2 eggs
3 tablespoons chopped fresh herbs
salt and freshly ground black pepper
freshly grated nutmeg
1 bunch scallions, washed, trimmed and
  chopped

1 Preheat the oven to 375°F. Put a baking
sheet into the center of the oven, to heat
up. Lightly grease an 8-inch tart pan or
ring.

2 Roll out the pastry and use to line the
pan or ring; trim the edges. Chill in the
refrigerator for a few minutes while you
make the filling.

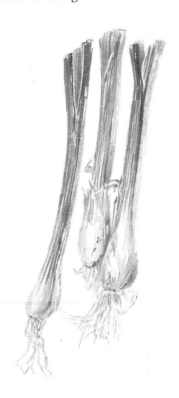

3 Whisk together the milk or cream and
the eggs. Add the herbs and salt, pepper
and nutmeg to taste. Put the scallions into
the base of the tart, then pour the egg
mixture on top.

4 Place the tart on the baking sheet and
bake for 35–40 minutes, until the filling is
set and lightly browned. Serve hot or
warm.

Variations

QUICK MUSHROOM TART
Use ¼ pound button mushrooms, thinly
sliced, instead of the scallions, and a
crushed garlic clove instead of the
chopped fresh herbs.

QUICK CORN TART
Use ¼–⅓ cup frozen corn kernels instead of the scallions and parsley.

QUICK CHEESE AND
TOMATO TART
Add ½–1 cup grated Gruyère cheese and
1 thinly sliced tomato.

QUICK MINT AND
PEA TART
Use 2 tablespoons finely chopped mint
and ¼–⅓ cup frozen peas. This mixture
is good with or without the scallions.

QUICK BEAN TART
Add ½ teaspoon prepared mustard to the
egg mixture and put half the well-drained
contents of one 15-ounce can lima beans,
chick peas or cannellini beans on the tart
base before pouring on the milk and egg
mixture. Omit the scallions and parsley
or keep them, as you like. A crushed
garlic clove mixed in with the eggs is also
nice in this, and so are a few juicy black
olives.

STEAMED VEGETABLE PUDDING

This is a vegetarian version of a steamed steak and kidney pudding, with vegetable suet or butter used for the pastry and vegetables in a savory sauce instead of the steak and kidney.

SERVES 4

1¼ cups self-rising whole-wheat flour
½ teaspoon salt
6 tablespoons butter or vegan margarine
2–3 tablespoons cold water
butter for greasing
FOR THE FILLING
1 onion, peeled and chopped
1 tablespoon oil
1 potato, peeled and cut into ½-inch dice
2 carrots, scraped and thinly sliced
½ pound mushrooms
2 tablespoons soy sauce
2 tablespoons water
salt and freshly ground black pepper
TO GARNISH
parsley sprigs

1 Grease a 1-quart pudding mold or heatproof bowl thoroughly with butter or vegan margarine.
2 Sauté the onion in the oil for 5 minutes, then add the potato, carrots and mushrooms, cover and cook gently for 10–15 minutes. Add soy sauce, water and season with salt and pepper.
3 While the vegetables are cooking put the flour into a mixing bowl with the salt, then rub in the butter or vegan margarine with your fingertips, until the mixture looks like fine breadcrumbs. Add enough of the cold water to make a dough.
4 Turn the dough onto a floured board and knead lightly, then roll out two-thirds of it to fit the pudding mold or bowl.
5 Line the mold or bowl, pressing down well, and spoon in the vegetable mixture.
6 Roll out the rest of the dough to fit the top of the pudding. Press down firmly and trim the edges.
7 Prick the top of the pudding several times with a fork, then cover with a piece of pleated greased wax paper and a piece of foil and tie down.
8 Stand the pudding mold or bowl in a baking pan and pour in boiling water to come halfway up the sides. Return to a boil, then simmer gently for 1½ hours. Keep the water level topped up with boiling water as necessary.
9 To serve the pudding, remove the paper coverings, slip a palette knife around the sides of the pudding mold or bowl to loosen the pudding, then turn it out onto a warmed serving plate. Serve immediately, garnished with parsley sprigs.

LIFTING A STEAMED PUDDING OUT OF THE PAN

Steamed Vegetable Pudding

Making Palmiers

These crunchy cookies are an excellent way to use up leftover pieces of puff pastry. Push the pieces of pastry roughly together, and roll out into a rectangle about ⅛ inch thick. Sprinkle thickly with Demerara sugar.

Fold each of the 2 long sides to the center, so that they meet. Then fold the long edges to the middle again. Finally fold one of these rolled edges on top of the other and press down gently.

Cut into slices about ⅛ inch thick and place on a baking sheet. Bake at 450°F for 7–8 minutes, until golden-brown. Cool on a wire rack.

Flaky Pastry

There are three types of flaky pastry:

ROUGH PUFF PASTRY The quickest and easiest of the flaky pastries to make, this rises in flaky layers but does not get as high and light as puff pastry.

FLAKY PASTRY Almost as quick to make as rough puff, this rises higher and looks better. It is also possible to get a good result using 100% whole-wheat flour.

PUFF PASTRY The richest pastry of all, rising in glorious golden flaky layers. It's wonderful for special-occasion cooking: feuilletés, fleurons, bouchées and vol-au-vents. Making your own puff pastry is satisfying and rewarding, though you can also buy excellent frozen puff pastry: look for a brand that does not contain animal fat. Puff pastry made with 100% whole-wheat flour is not very successful; it does not rise any higher than flaky pastry made with 100% whole-wheat flour.

$\boxed{V}$ ROUGH PUFF PASTRY $\boxed{V}$

MAKES ½ pound

1½ cups fine whole-wheat flour
1 teaspoon salt
¼ pound plus 4 tablespoons butter or vegan margarine, chilled
4 teaspoons lemon juice
about ½ cup ice water

1 Put the flour and salt into a mixing bowl and grate in the butter or vegan margarine. Add the lemon juice and water, then mix quickly to a fairly soft dough.
2 Gather the dough into a ball, wrap in plastic wrap and chill in the refrigerator for at least 1 hour.
3 Take the dough out of the refrigerator.

If it's very cold, leave it for 10 minutes to soften a bit, then roll it into a rectangle on a lightly floured board.
4 Mark the oblong lightly into 3 equal sections, then fold the bottom third up and the top third down, to make 3 layers.
5 Seal the edges by pressing them lightly with your rolling pin (to keep the air in), then give the pastry a quarter-turn.
6 Repeat the rolling, folding and turning 4 times. The pastry is then ready to be used, or can be wrapped in plastic wrap and put back into the refrigerator until needed.
7 Roll the pastry out about ¼ inch thick and bake at 425°F.

MAKING ROUGH PUFF PASTRY

1 Grate the butter or vegan margarine into the flour

2 Roll the dough into a rectangle, then fold the bottom third up and the top third down

3 Seal the edges by pressing them lightly with a rolling pin

FLAKY PASTRY

MAKES ½ pound

1½ cups unbleached white flour
pinch of salt
6 tablespoons butter
½ cup (generous) ice water
6 tablespoons white vegetable fat (Crisco)

1 Sift the flour and salt into a mixing bowl. Rub in half the butter. Add enough ice water to make a dough.
2 Turn the dough onto a lightly floured board and knead until smooth. Shape the dough into a rectangle.
3 Roll the dough into a 5 × 10-inch rectangle. Make sure that you have the edges of the pastry straight and the ends square.
4 Cut half the vegetable fat into small pieces and place them in rows over the top two-thirds of the pastry, well clear of the edges of the pastry rectangle.
5 Fold the bottom of the dough (without the fat on it) up and the top third down. Seal the edges by pressing them lightly

with a rolling pin. Give the dough a quarter-turn, so that the folds are at the sides.

6 Roll and fold the pastry once more, without adding any fat.

7 Repeat steps 4, 5 and 6, using the rest of the butter.

8 Repeat steps 4 and 5, using the rest of the vegetable fat.

9 Wrap the dough in plastic wrap and chill in the refrigerator for 15–30 minutes, then roll and fold again without adding any fat. The pastry is now ready for use.

10 Roll the pastry out as required and bake at 450°F.

PUFF PASTRY

[V] [V]

Puff pastry is quite time-consuming but not difficult to make and is very rewarding. Most of the time the dough is resting in the refrigerator between rollings.

MAKES 1 pound

1 1/2 cups unbleached white flour
1/2 pound plus 2 tablespoons butter or vegan margarine, chilled
1/2 teaspoon salt
1/2 cup (generous) ice water
1 1/2 teaspoons lemon juice

1 Put the flour into a mixing bowl with 2 tablespoons of the butter or margarine, and rub it into the flour until the mixture looks like coarse breadcrumbs.

2 Dissolve the salt in the ice water and add to the flour mixture along with the lemon juice. Mix to a dough.

3 Place the dough on a lightly floured surface, knead lightly and shape into a square. Wrap in plastic wrap and chill in the refrigerator for 1 hour. (Have the remaining butter or vegan margarine chilling at the same time.)

4 Put the chilled butter or vegan margarine into a roomy plastic bag and beat with a rolling pin to soften it slightly. Then remove it from the bag, put it onto a floured board and roll it into a square about 6 × 6 inches.

5 Next, roll out the dough on a lightly floured work surface, to make a 10-inch square.

6 Put the square of butter or vegan margarine diagonally on the square of dough and fold the corners of the dough over, overlapping them a little, to make a package that completely encloses the butter or vegan margarine.

7 Put this package of dough on a lightly floured work surface and roll it out, using short, sharp, firm forward and backward strokes, to a rectangle 1/2 inch thick.

8 Mark the dough into thirds. Fold the bottom third up and the top third down. Seal the edges by pressing them lightly with the rolling pin.

9 Now give the dough a quarter-turn so that the folds are at the sides, and roll it out again so that it is about 1/4 inch thick and three times as long as it is wide. Fold the dough in 3 again.

10 The dough has now had 2 foldings, so indicate this by pressing 2 fingers into the dough, then put it into a plastic bag and chill it in the refrigerator for 1 hour (or longer, if this is more convenient).

11 Remove the dough from the refrigerator and unwrap it. If it is very cold, let it rest for 10 minutes before you roll it. Then roll and fold the dough twice as before, and mark it with 4 fingers. Wrap and chill the dough for 1 hour or more as before.

12 Repeat step 11. The dough is then ready for use, or it can be kept in the refrigerator for several days, or frozen for several weeks. When you have rolled out the pastry, chill it again for about 30 minutes before baking at 450°F.

MAKING PUFF PASTRY

1 Roll the dough into a 10-inch square. Place the square of butter or vegan margarine diagonally on the square and fold the corners of the dough over

2 Roll the dough out to a rectangle 1/2 inch thick. Fold the bottom third up and the top third down

3 Seal the edges with a rolling pin

4 Give the pastry a quarter-turn and repeat rolling and folding. Chill. Repeat the whole process twice more

MUSHROOM PÂTÉ EN CROÛTE

*Mushroom Pâté en Croûte; Flaky
Vegetable Pie (p. 271)*

A favorite recipe, this makes a delicious main course served with a Sour Cream and Herb Dressing (p. 156) with cooked vegetables to accompany.

SERVES 6

1 quantity Flaky Pastry (p. 268), or 1 pound frozen puff pastry, thawed
a little raw egg yolk
FOR THE FILLING
1 onion, peeled and chopped
2 tablespoons butter
2 pounds mushrooms, washed and finely chopped
2 garlic cloves, crushed
2 tablespoons chopped parsley
1⅓ cups dried whole-wheat breadcrumbs
2 tablespoons lemon juice
salt and freshly ground black pepper

1 Preheat the oven to 425°F.
2 Sauté the onion in the butter in a large saucepan for 10 minutes. Add the mushrooms and sauté over a medium heat for 20–30 minutes, until all the liquid has evaporated.

3 Remove from the heat and add the garlic, parsley, breadcrumbs, lemon juice and salt and pepper to taste. Allow the mixture to cool.
4 Roll one-third of the pastry into a 6 × 12-inch rectangle. Place on a baking sheet, spoon the mushroom mixture on top, and brush the edges with water.
5 Roll out the remaining pastry to a 9 × 12-inch rectangle.
6 Fold the pastry in half lengthways and make diagonal cuts to give a fancy finish, if you like. Ease the pastry on top of the mushroom mixture.
7 Press the edges together and trim. Make a few steam holes, decorate with pastry trimmings and brush the entire surface with egg yolk. Bake for 30 minutes, until golden-brown. Serve hot or warm.

[V] FLAKY VEGETABLE PIE [V]

SERVES 4–6

½ quantity Rough Puff or Flaky Pastry
 (p. 268), or ½ pound frozen puff pastry,
 thawed
beaten egg to glaze, optional
FOR THE FILLING
1 onion, peeled and chopped
2 tablespoons oil
2 garlic cloves, crushed
4 medium carrots, scraped and diced
2–3 zucchini (about ¾ pound), trimmed and
 diced
1 pound leeks, trimmed, washed and sliced
2 tomatoes, peeled and chopped
2 tablespoons dried breadcrumbs
2 tablespoons chopped parsley
½ teaspoon each dried basil and oregano
salt
⅔ cup dried navy or other white beans,
 soaked, cooked and drained; or one
 15-ounce can cannellini beans, drained
freshly ground black pepper

1 Preheat the oven to 425°F.
2 Make the filling. Sauté the onion in the oil in a large saucepan for 5 minutes, then add the garlic, carrots, zucchini, leeks, tomatos, breadcrumbs and herbs.
3 Season with a little salt, then cook for 10–15 minutes, covered, until the vegetables are tender, stirring occasionally. Add the beans and check the seasoning.
4 Put the vegetable mixture into a 5-cup pie dish and leave to cool.
5 Roll the pastry out 1 inch larger all around than the pie dish. Cut off a strip from all around the pastry. Place the strip around the rim of the pie dish and brush with cold water, then place the rest of the pastry on top.
6 Trim the edges of the pastry and press them together firmly to seal, then crimp the edges with the back of a fork. Make a steam hole in the center. Decorate with pastry trimmings stuck on with cold water.
7 Brush the pie with beaten egg, if used, then bake for 30 minutes, until puffed up and golden-brown. Serve hot.

SHAPING MUSHROOM
PÂTÉ EN CROÛTE

1 Spread out the smaller piece of pastry on a baking sheet and top with the mushroom mixture, heaping it up well

2 Fold the larger piece in half and make diagonal cuts with scissors to within ½ inch of the center

CHOUX PASTRY

Choux pastry works well with either unbleached white or whole-wheat flour, but sometimes with whole-wheat flour the mixture will only take about three-quarters of the egg; more and it would become sloppy, so stop adding it at this point.

MAKES ENOUGH FOR 8 ÉCLAIRS OR 12 PROFITEROLES

4 tablespoons butter or vegan margarine
½ cup (generous) water
½ cup unbleached white or whole-wheat
 flour
2 eggs, lightly beaten

1 Preheat the oven to 400°F.
2 Put the fat and water into a saucepan and heat gently until the fat has melted, then bring to a boil.
3 Remove from the heat and add the flour all at once, beating well with a wooden spoon.
4 Return the pan to the heat and stir with the wooden spoon for 1 minute until the dough leaves the sides of the pan. Tip the dough into a clean bowl.
5 Add about a quarter of the egg, beating vigorously until the dough has absorbed it and become glossy again, then add another quarter of the egg in exactly the same way.
6 Repeat until all the egg has been used and the mixture is glossy and soft but not sloppy. Cover with a plate until needed.

3 Open out and carefully place over the mushroom mixture, being careful to maintain the shape of the mushroom mixture

4 Press the edges together and trim

VEGETABLE GOUGÈRE

An impressive and delicious dish, a big puffed-up ring of golden
choux pastry, the center filled with colorful vegetables.

SERVES 6

double quantity Choux Pastry (p. 271)
a good pinch of cayenne
1½ cups finely grated Cheddar cheese
1 quantity Peperonata (p. 186), or Spring
Vegetable Braise (p. 181), or 1 quantity
Mushrooms in Cream (p. 79)

1 Preheat the oven to 425°F.
2 Make the choux pastry as described on
p. 271. Add the cayenne and 1 cup of the
grated cheese.
3 Spoon or pipe the choux pastry around
the edge of a 12-inch pizza plate or large
shallow ovenproof dish.
4 Sprinkle with the rest of the cheese and
bake for about 40 minutes, until the
gougère is puffed up and golden-brown.
5 Reheat the peperonata or other chosen
filling and spoon this into the center of
the gougère when you remove it from
the oven. Serve hot or warm, and if there
is any filling left over, serve it in a
separate side dish, heated.

WILD MUSHROOMS IN CREAM
WITH PASTRY LEAVES

As the puff pastry is such an important part of this dish, it is best
when made with homemade puff pastry, which has a buttery flavor
lacking in most frozen commercial puff pastry. It makes a beautiful
autumn meal, served with Potato Purée (p. 189) and followed by an
Endive, Watercress and Walnut Salad (p. 161).

SERVES 6

1 quantity Puff Pastry (p. 269) or 1 pound
frozen puff pastry, thawed
beaten egg to glaze
double quantity Wild Mushrooms in Cream
(p. 79)
TO GARNISH
fennel sprigs
thyme sprigs

1 Roll out the pastry ¼ inch thick and cut
into 6 leaf-shaped ovals about 4 × 2
inches. Chill for 1 hour.
2 Preheat the oven to 450°F.
3 Moisten the surface of a baking sheet
with a little water and place the pastry
leaves on it. Make leaf markings on the
top of each with a sharp knife. Brush the

pastry leaves with beaten egg.
4 Bake the leaves for 10 minutes, then
turn down the oven to 375°F and bake for
a further 10–15 minutes, until the pastry
is baked crisply through.
5 Gently reheat the wild mushroom
mixture. Slit the pastry leaves in half
horizontally, using a sharp knife. Place
the bases on a warmed serving dish, or
individual dishes.
6 Spoon an equal quantity of the
mushroom mixture on top of each base,
letting it flow over the edges of the
pastry. Then cover each base with its
own pastry leaf top.
7 Garnish with fennel and thyme sprigs
and serve immediately.

V   # INDIVIDUAL PROVENÇALE   V
TOMATO TARTS

Served warm, these attractive-looking individual tarts make a good
first course.

MAKES 4–6

½ pound puff pastry
2 tablespoons olive oil
1 onion, peeled and very finely
*   chopped*
1 garlic clove, crushed
1 pound tomatoes, skinned, de-seeded
*   and chopped*
salt and freshly ground black pepper
FOR THE TOPPING
½ pound each red cherry tomatoes and
*   yellow cherry tomatoes, or 1 pound*
*   ordinary tomatoes, preferably plum*
olive oil
TO GARNISH
basil sprigs or leaves

1 Preheat the oven to 400°F.
2 Roll the pastry out thinly and cut out
four 6-inch circles or six 4-inch ones. Put
the pastry circles on a cookie sheet and
prick them lightly all over with a fork.
Bake in the preheated oven for 15–20
minutes, until they are crisp and turning
golden.
3 Meanwhile, make the filling. Heat the
olive oil in a medium saucepan, add the
onion and garlic, cover and cook gently
for 5 minutes. Add the tomatoes and
cook, uncovered, for 15–20 minutes,
until the tomatoes are tender and the
mixture is the consistency of a sauce,
with no excess liquid. Season with salt
and pepper.
4 Slice the tomatoes for the topping as
thinly as you can and season them.
Spread some of the cooked tomato mixture carefully over each pastry circle, taking it as close to the edge as you can, then
arrange the sliced tomatoes on top of it,
in circles.
5 Sprinkle with a little olive oil and return to the oven for 15–20 minutes, until
the tomatoes are heated through. Garnish
each tart with a sprig of basil or some torn
basil leaves.

Individual Provençale Tomato Tarts

Variations
TOMATO AND PEPPER TARTS
Use 2 large red and 2 large yellow peppers instead of the tomatoes. Quarter the
peppers and broil for 10–15 minutes,
until blackened. Cool, skin and slice
thinly. Arrange in the cooked tart cases;
sprinkle with olive oil and bake.

ZUCCHINI AND TOMATO TARTS
Replace the cherry tomatoes with ½
pound tender zucchini. Slice thinly,
arrange on top of the tomatoes, brush
well with oil and bake.

SPANIKOPITA

This Greek pie is equally good as a starter or a main course. It's
good served with a Yogurt and Mint Dressing (p. 156).

SERVES 6 AS A MAIN COURSE, 8 AS A FIRST COURSE

10 sheets phyllo pastry
10–12 tablespoons butter, melted
2 pounds fresh spinach or 1 pound frozen
* spinach, cooked, drained and cooled*
1 bunch scallions, trimmed and chopped
¼ pound feta cheese, crumbled
salt and freshly ground black pepper
butter for greasing

1 Preheat the oven to 400°F.
2 Grease a deep pie dish, then place a
single sheet of phyllo pastry in it, allowing the edges of the pastry to hang over
the sides of the dish.
3 Brush with melted butter, then place
another sheet of phyllo pastry on top.
Continue in this way, using 5 sheets of
phyllo pastry. (Keep the rest covered
with a damp cloth, see p. 151.)

4 Chop the spinach and mix with the
scallions, cheese and salt and pepper to
taste. Spoon on top of the pastry.
5 Cover with the rest of the phyllo
pastry sheets, brushing each one with
melted butter as before, and finishing
with melted butter. Neaten the sides;
prick and decorate the top with leaves cut
from pastry trimmings.
6 Bake for 40–45 minutes. Serve hot or
warm.

Variation
VEGAN SPANIKOPITA
Make in the same way, but replace the
cheese with mashed tofu or about 1 cup
pine nuts or slivered almonds. Use vegan
margarine or olive oil for brushing the
pastry instead of butter.

SHAPING A SAMOSA

1 Form a semicircle of pastry into a
cone, pressing the edges together
well

2 Fill with vegetable mixture

3 Fold over the top edge, pressing
down well

 # SAMOSAS

These crisp, spicy little savories are delicious as an accompaniment
to curries or as a snack, with some mango chutney or thick plain
yogurt to dip them into.

MAKES 32

FOR THE PASTRY
2 cups plain whole-wheat flour
1 teaspoon salt
2 teaspoons baking powder
¼ cup oil
½–1 cup ice water
oil for deep frying
FOR THE FILLING
1 large onion, peeled and chopped
2 tablespoons olive oil
1 large garlic clove, crushed
2 teaspoons each mustard seeds, grated fresh
* ginger, ground cumin and ground coriander*
1½ pounds potatoes, cooked and diced
½–¾ cup frozen peas, thawed
salt and freshly ground black pepper

1 First make the filling. Sauté the onion
in the oil for 8 minutes, until soft but not
browned, then add the garlic, mustard
seeds, ginger, cumin and coriander and
cook for a further 2 minutes.
2 Remove from the heat and add the
potatoes and peas. Mix well. Season with
salt and pepper, then cool.
3 Meanwhile, make the pastry. Put the
flour, salt and baking powder into a
bowl, then add the oil and water. Mix to
a soft but not sticky dough.
4 Knead the dough for 5 minutes, then
divide into 16 equal pieces. Roll each into
a circle about 6 inches in diameter, then
cut each circle in half, using a sharp knife,

to make 32 half-circles.

5 Take one of the half-circles of pastry and brush the cut edges with water, then fold it in half and press the moistened cut edges firmly together to form a cone.

6 Fill the cone with about 2 heaping teaspoons of the filling, then moisten the top edges and fold them over to enclose the filling. Fill the rest of the samosas.

7 Heat the oil in a deep fryer to 350°F, then fry the samosas in batches until golden-brown and crispy. Drain on paper towels and keep the samosas warm in a low oven until all are ready.

Phyllo Pastry

Fresh or frozen phyllo pastry can be bought anywhere these days. Frozen phyllo usually comes in 14-ounce packages, containing around 16 sheets pastry. Allow the frozen phyllo to thaw in its package in the refrigerator for up to 2 days.

 # ASPARAGUS STRUDEL

SERVES 6

2 large onions, peeled and finely chopped
¼ pound (1 stick) plus 2 tablespoons butter
   or vegan margarine
1⅓ cups fine fresh breadcrumbs
8 sheets phyllo pastry (p. 151)
1½ pounds trimmed asparagus, washed,
   chopped and cooked until tender (p. 63)
¼ cup finely chopped parsley
TO GARNISH
parsley sprigs
lemon slices
asparagus tips
TO SERVE
1 quantity vegan Yogurt and Herb Dressing
   (p. 156)

1 Preheat the oven to 400°F.

2 Sauté the onions in 2 tablespoons of the butter or vegan margarine for 10 minutes, until soft but not browned.

3 In another pan, heat 4 tablespoons of the butter or vegan margarine and sauté the crumbs until crisp. Melt the remaining butter or vegan margarine in a small saucepan.

4 Spread one phyllo pastry sheet out on a large board and brush with melted butter or vegan margarine. Put another pastry sheet on top and brush with more butter or margarine. Repeat until all the sheets have been used.

5 Spread the onions evenly on top of the pastry, keeping the edges clear.

6 Put the asparagus over the top of the onions and sprinkle with three-quarters of the crumbs and the parsley.

7 Fold over 2 inches all around the pastry, then fold the long edges over to make a roll.

8 Place the roll, seam side down, on a

baking sheet and bend it around into a horseshoe shape.

9 Brush with the remaining melted butter or margarine and sprinkle with the remaining crumbs.

10 Bake for 40 minutes, until golden and crisp. Garnish with parsley sprigs, lemon slices and asparagus tips. Serve with the yogurt and herb dressing.

Asparagus Strudel

MENU
Autumn Dinner Party

SERVES 6

Light Caesar Salad
160

Creamed White Beans with Potato
Pancakes and Broiled Yellow Pepper Strips
206

Julienne of Root Vegetables
184

Wilted Spinach
180

Linzertorte
293

This is a warming dinner party full of fruity, autumn flavors. The salad can be mainly prepared in advance, ready to be finished off with the dressing and croûtons just before you are ready to eat it. The pudding – a deliciously spicy tart – can be prepared in advance, ready for popping into the oven when you start your first course, or it can be cooked ahead of time, covered with foil and simply warmed through before you serve it. The Creamed White Beans and Broiled Yellow Pepper Strips can be done in advance and kept warm, as can the Julienne of Mixed Root Vegetables, leaving just the Potato Pancakes and the Wilted Spinach to do at the last minute. If you fry the Pancakes before you sit down for your first course, they will keep crisp spread on paper towels on a cookie sheet, in the coolest part of the oven.

A sharp, flinty wine would go well with the salad – a Sancerre or a Pouilly Fumé would be ideal – and you could follow this with a medium-dry wine which goes well with vegetables, such as a Savennières, Vouvray or Macon Blanc, or you could serve a red Burgundy.

Desserts

A dessert rounds off a meal perfectly, and even if, like me, you eat them rarely, it is good to have the occasional indulgence. This chapter opens with cold desserts, including cheesecake and sorbets, and progresses to pies, tarts, a hot soufflé, and Christmas pudding. Finally, there are some sweet sauces to serve with fresh and poached fruit, ice cream, pancakes and other desserts. Many more dessert ideas are featured on the fruit pages in the Ingredients section (pp. 84–103), to finish a meal in style.

LITTLE BAKED CUSTARDS

These smooth, velvety custards can be served warm or chilled;
I like them best chilled.

SERVES 6

Tips for Making Custard Sauce

To make life easier for yourself when making a custard sauce, a teaspoon of cornstarch can be mixed in with the egg yolks to stabilize the mixture and prevent it from curdling if it gets too hot.

To prevent a skin from forming on top of custard sauce, sprinkle the top with a thin layer of superfine sugar and whisk in just before serving.

3 eggs
3 egg yolks
¼ cup superfine caster sugar
2 cups milk, half-and-half or light cream
1 vanilla bean or 1 teaspoon vanilla extract
TO DECORATE (OPTIONAL)
whipped cream

1 Preheat the oven to 325°F.
2 Put the eggs, egg yolks and sugar into a bowl and whisk until well combined.
3 Heat the milk or cream with the vanilla bean or extract to just below the boiling point. Remove the vanilla bean if used (rinse, dry and keep for future use).
4 Add the hot milk or cream to the eggs, whisking gently.
5 Strain the custard mixture into a pitcher, then pour into 6 ramekins.
6 Put the ramekins into a baking pan and pour boiling water around them to come about two-thirds of the way up the sides of the ramekins.
7 Bake the custards for 40–45 minutes, until set. Remove from the oven, allow to cool, then chill before serving. Decorate with piped whipped cream if liked.

Variations
POURING EGG CUSTARD
Follow method to end of step 4. Return the mixture to the pan and stir over a gentle heat until thick enough to coat the back of the spoon. Pour into a clean bowl.

LITTLE COFFEE CUSTARDS
For this delicious variation add 2–3 teaspoons continental or espresso instant coffee, dissolved in a little boiling water, to the milk or cream.

CHOCOLATE POTS

This is a versatile recipe, because it can be served chilled or the mixture can be baked, to make Little Chocolate Soufflés (see variation). Both versions are equally good.

SERVES 6

3 ounces sweetened dark chocolate
1/2 cup (generous) heavy cream
3 egg yolks
1 teaspoon regular or espresso instant coffee
4 egg whites
pinch of cream of tartar
2 tablespoons superfine sugar
TO DECORATE
whipped cream
chocolate coffee beans

1 Break the chocolate into pieces and put into a heavy-bottomed saucepan with the cream. Heat gently until melted.
2 Remove from the heat and beat in the egg yolks and coffee.
3 Beat the egg whites with the cream of tartar until stiff, then beat in the sugar.
4 Lightly but thoroughly fold the stiff egg white mixture into the chocolate mixture until the egg white is distributed evenly throughout.
5 Pour the mixture into 6 ramekins. Chill until set. Decorate each pot with a whirl of cream and a chocolate coffee bean.

Variation
LITTLE CHOCOLATE SOUFFLÉS
Fill ramekins to within 1/2 inch of the tops and place on a baking sheet. (This can be done several hours in advance and the mixture covered and refrigerated if convenient. Remove from the refrigerator at least 30 minutes before baking.) Bake at 425°F for 10 minutes, until risen. Sift confectioner's sugar on top. Serve immediately, with whipped cream passed around separately, if you like.

Chocolate for Cooking

You get what you pay for with cooking chocolate. The large bars of "cooking chocolate" are not a good buy because they have a synthetic flavor and fatty consistency. The chocolate which gives the best results is a good quality semi-sweet chocolate with at least 50% cocoa solids, preferably 60–75%.

Chocolate Caraque

These chocolate curls make an attractive garnish for chocolate puddings and cakes and are easy to make. Melt 4 ounces chocolate, pour it in a thin layer onto a baking tray and leave until it is firm enough not to stick to your hand when you touch it lightly. Then, holding a knife in both hands so that the blade is straight, draw it across the chocolate, like a comb, to draw off the chocolate in long curls. Another way to make curls is to shave a block of chocolate with a potato peeler.

Chocolate Shapes and Leaves

Chocolate shapes can be made by cutting a sheet of chocolate, made as described above, with tiny pastry cutters.

For chocolate leaves, dip one side of clean, dry, nonpoisonous leaves, such as rose leaves or small fresh bay leaves, in chocolate. Leave until the chocolate has set, then gently peel away the leaf.

CHOCOLATE TORTE

Although it's luxurious and impressive, this is actually very easy to make and great for a special occasion.

SERVES 6

1/4 pound amaretti biscuits or ratafias
4 tablespoons butter
9 ounces semi-sweet chocolate with at least 75% cocoa solids
1 1/4 cups heavy cream
1 tablespoon rum, brandy or Amaretto

1 Crush the amaretti or ratafias with a rolling pin. Melt the butter and add to the crushed biscuits, mix, then press into the base of an 8 1/2-inch spring-form cake pan. Put into the refrigerator to chill.
2 Break the chocolate into pieces, put them into a bowl and melt over a pan of steaming water. Allow to cool slightly.
3 Put the cream into a bowl and add the melted chocolate and the rum, brandy or amaretto. Whisk until the mixture thickens and turns slightly paler but be careful not to over-whisk to the point where it begins to curdle and break up.
4 Pour the mixture over the crumb base in the cake pan and smooth the top.
5 Put into the refrigerator and chill for at least 2 hours – or overnight – until it is firm to the touch. Then remove the sides of the cake pan, transfer the torte to a plate and serve with some cream.

VANILLA ICE CREAM

How to Make Soy Milk

The soy milk used in the vegan version of ice cream is widely available. However, it is also possible to make a delicious soy milk at home. This takes time, but it works out cheaper than store-bought soy milk, and tastes delicious.

To make soy milk, soak ½ pound soybeans in plenty of water for 2 days, changing the water twice a day. Then purée the beans in a blender with 5 cups fresh water. Line a sieve with a piece of clean cheesecloth, then scald it by pouring boiling water through. Put the sieve over a large saucepan and pour the soy mixture through the sieve, squeezing through as much liquid as possible. Add a vanilla bean, or 1–2 teaspoons vanilla extract. Heat the milk to the boiling point, then remove the vanilla bean (wash, dry and reuse). Then put the milk into a blender or food processor with 1 tablespoon cold-pressed sunflower oil and a little sugar or honey to taste, and whizz. Strain through cheesecloth again, and it's ready.

3 egg yolks
7 tablespoons superfine sugar
½ cup water
2 cups heavy cream
1 teaspoon vanilla extract

1 Whisk the egg yolks until thick and pale.
2 Put the sugar into a heavy-bottomed saucepan with the water. Heat gently until the sugar has dissolved, then bring to a boil and boil for 5 minutes.

3 Add the hot sugar syrup to the egg yolks in a steady stream, beating all the time. (Keep the syrup away from the whisk or it may solidify on this.)
4 Beat until the mixture is thick, pale and mousse-like. Allow the mixture to cool completely.
5 Whip the cream with the vanilla until thick, then fold into the egg yolk mixture. Pour into a plastic container.
6 Freeze until half solid, then beat again and return to the freezer until firm.

QUICK VANILLA ICE CREAM

A simple ice cream, but always popular, especially with children.
Serve with Almond Tuiles (p. 325)

SERVES 8

2½ cups heavy cream
one 14-ounce can sweetened condensed skimmed milk
1 teaspoon vanilla extract

1 Whip the cream until thick, then add the condensed milk and vanilla and whip again until thoroughly blended.
2 Pour the mixture into a plastic container and freeze until firm.

CHOCOLATE ICE CREAM

SERVES 6–8

Vegan Ice Cream

To make a vegan version of Chocolate Ice Cream, use soy milk (see above) instead of dairy milk and replace the evaporated milk or light cream with concentrated soy milk or a nondairy cream.

3¾ cups milk
4 ounces sweetened dark chocolate or carob bar, broken into pieces
5 tablespoons light brown sugar
1 tablespoon cornstarch or potato starch
one 14½-ounce can evaporated milk or 1¼ cups light cream
TO DECORATE
grated chocolate

1 Put all but 4 tablespoons of the milk into a saucepan with the chocolate or carob pieces and sugar and bring gently to a boil.
2 Mix the cornstarch or potato starch to a paste with the rest of the milk in a bowl.
3 Add a little of the boiling milk mixture

to the starch mixture, blend, then pour the starch mixture into the saucepan of hot milk.
4 Stir over moderate heat for 2–3 minutes, until the mixture has thickened a little. Remove from the heat and cool slightly, then add the evaporated milk or light cream and whizz in a blender or food processor, to give a smooth consistency.
5 Pour into a plastic container and allow to cool completely. Freeze until half solid, then beat again and return to the freezer until firm. This ice cream freezes hard; remove from the freezer to room temperature 30–40 minutes before eating. Decorate with grated chocolate.

RASPBERRY ICE CREAM

Fruit ice creams are among the simplest to make, because all you do is fold a sweetened fruit purée into whipped cream, then freeze. Many different types of fruit are suitable; soft fruits only need puréeing (and sieving if necessary to remove seeds), other types should first be stewed gently with the sugar.

SERVES 8–10

Vanilla Ice Cream (p. 280) with Almond Tuiles (p. 325); Raspberry Ice Cream

1 pound fresh raspberries, washed, or frozen
*   raspberries, thawed*
1¼ cups superfine sugar
2½ cups heavy cream
TO SERVE (OPTIONAL)
raspberry leaves
1 quantity Raspberry Coulis (p. 300)

1 Reserve some of the raspberries for decoration. Purée the rest in a blender or food processor, then sieve to remove the seeds. Stir in the sugar.

2 Whip the cream until thick, then gently fold in the raspberry purée.

3 Pour the mixture into a plastic container. Freeze until half solid, then beat well and return to the freezer until firm.

4 Transfer the ice cream from the freezer to the refrigerator 30–40 minutes before you want to serve it. Serve in individual bowls decorated with the reserved raspberries and raspberry leaves, if available. Serve the Raspberry Coulis separately in a pitcher, if you like.

Variations

APPLE ICE CREAM WITH BLACKBERRY SAUCE

Use 1 pound cooking or dessert apples, peeled, cored and stewed with the sugar and 2 tablespoons water. Drain if necessary, then purée and cool before folding into the cream. Taste and add more sugar if you wish. I like to color this ice cream pale green with a little vegetable coloring. Serve with a Blackberry Coulis (p. 300) or Sorbet (p. 282) for a pleasant blend of autumn flavors.

MANGO ICE CREAM

Remove the pits and peel from 2 large mangoes. Purée the flesh in a blender or food processor, then fold into the cream.

APRICOT AND ORANGE FOOL

SERVES 4

Making Fruit Fools

Any soft, puréed fresh fruit, or firmer fruit, stewed, then mashed or puréed, is suitable for making into a fool. Yogurt can be used, or chilled egg custard, or cream, or a mixture of these.

For a richer, special-occasion version of Apricot and Orange Fool fold in ½ cup (generous) heavy cream, whipped, and 2–3 tablespoons apricot brandy or Cointreau before folding in the egg whites.

Try using 1 pound drained, stewed gooseberries. Purée, then sieve if you like, although puréed but unsieved gooseberries produce a fool with a pleasant texture.

Or use 1 pound drained, stewed rhubarb. Mash or purée. This is pleasant with a delicate flavoring of ginger (up to ½ teaspoon added to the rhubarb when stewing it).

½ pound dried apricots, covered with boiling water, soaked overnight, then simmered in the soaking liquid for 20–30 minutes until tender
1 cup strained Greek yogurt, or 1 cup plain yogurt
clear honey or sugar to taste
2 egg whites
grated rind of 1 orange

1 Purée the apricots in a blender or food processor, or mash them very well.
2 Mix the apricot purée with the yogurt. Add honey or sugar to taste.
3 Beat the egg whites until they form stiff peaks. Fold a tablespoon of egg white into the apricot mixture, to loosen, then gently fold in the rest, together with half the orange rind.
4 Spoon the apricot mixture into individual glasses and chill. Sprinkle with the remaining rind before serving.

Vegan Sorbet

Egg whites give a sorbet a particularly light texture, but thorough beating can also achieve this, so they are not essential. Sorbets therefore make a delightful vegan dessert.

Ⓥ PASSION FRUIT SORBET Ⓥ

SERVES 6

1 cup superfine sugar
1¼ cups water
16–18 passion fruits
1 tablespoon lemon juice
2 egg whites (optional)

1 Dissolve the sugar in the water over low heat, then bring to a boil and boil for 3–4 minutes to make a sugar syrup. Remove from the heat and cool.
2 Scoop all the pulp and seeds out of the passion fruits and add to the cooled sugar syrup, through a sieve if you like.
3 Add the lemon juice. Pour the mixture into a plastic container and freeze, uncovered, until half solid.
4 Mash the mixture well to break up the icy particles and return to the freezer until solid. Or beat the egg whites, if used, until they form stiff peaks, then gradually add the mashed frozen mixture, beating all the time. Return to the freezer until solid.
5 Remove the sorbet from the freezer to room temperature 10 minutes before you want to serve it.
6 Mash the sorbet well with a fork to break it up, then spoon it into serving glasses, or mold it as shown on p. 283 and serve on a flat plate.

Variations

BLACK CURRANT SORBET
Cook 1½ pounds black currants without water in a covered saucepan until soft – about 10 minutes. Purée in a blender or food processor, then sieve. Use in place of the passion fruit pulp. 1–2 tablespoons cassis is excellent in this: add before the first freezing. Decorate the sorbet with a few black currants and black currant leaves, if available.

BLACKBERRY SORBET
Make as described for Black Currant Sorbet, using blackberries instead of black currants and adding 1–2 tablespoons orange liqueur, or port, instead of the cassis.

PEAR SORBET
Stew 1½ pounds ripe dessert pears, peeled, in enough water just to cover. Remove the pears from the water; boil the water rapidly to reduce to 1¼ cups, then add the sugar and proceed with the recipe, using the pear purée instead of the passion fruit pulp. 1–2 tablespoons Poire William liqueur stirred into the mixture makes a wonderful addition for a special occasion.

$\boxed{V}$

CHAMPAGNE SORBET WITH
WILD STRAWBERRIES

$\boxed{V}$ *Passion Fruit, Pear and Black Currant Sorbets (p. 282)*

Bringing the champagne to a boil removes the alcohol, which could otherwise prevent the sorbet from freezing properly, but it does not spoil the flavor. This, however, is unnecessary if you're making the sorbet in a sorbetière. Rosé champagne makes the sorbet especially pretty.

SERVES 6

2 1/2 cups champagne
1 3/4 cups granulated sugar
2 cups water
1/4 cup lemon juice
1/4 cup orange juice
3/4 cup wild strawberries or strawberry slices

1 Put three-quarters of the champagne into a saucepan and bring to a boil. Remove from the heat and cool.
2 Heat the sugar and water gently until all the sugar has dissolved, then boil the mixture hard for about 20 minutes, until it becomes syrupy and forms a short thread when you pull a little between your finger and thumb. Remove from the heat immediately.
3 Add the champagne and fruit juices to the sugar syrup and allow to cool.
4 Pour the mixture into a plastic container and freeze until icy. This will take several hours: I leave it overnight.
5 Turn the frozen mixture into a chilled bowl, or the bowl of an electric mixer, and beat until smooth and creamy.
6 Return the mixture to the freezer until firm.
7 When you are ready to serve the sorbet, scoop onto chilled plates or into glasses and quickly decorate with the wild strawberries or strawberry slices. Serve immediately.

SHAPING SORBET FOR
SERVING

1 Fill a tablespoon with sorbet, heaping it up. Cup another tablespoon on top of the sorbet and press down, to mold the sorbet, scraping off excess

2 Repeat this once or twice, moving the sorbet between the two spoons, until you have a smooth oval shape, then place on a plate

Notes on Liqueurs

A dash of liqueur adds a delicious flavor to many sweet dishes. Some of the most popular and useful liqueurs are:

AMARETTO DI SARONNO Almond-flavored liqueur

ANISETTE Aniseed liqueur

BAILEY'S IRISH CREAM Chocolate, heavy cream and whiskey liqueur

CALVADOS An apple brandy

CHARTREUSE Herb-flavored liqueur

COINTREAU Orange curaçao

EAUX-DE-VIE Delicious fruit brandies, including kirsch (cherry), framboise (raspberry), Poire William (pear) and fraise (strawberry)

MARASCHINO Cherry liqueur

TIA MARIA Jamaican liqueur made from coffee, rum and spices

ORANGE PARFAIT WITH GRAND MARNIER AND STRAWBERRIES

A parfait is an extra-rich ice cream which is useful because it can be kept in the freezer until the beginning of the meal, then turned out and served with a flourish.

SERVES 8–10

6 egg yolks
1 cup superfine sugar
finely grated rind of 1 large, well-scrubbed orange
2½ cups heavy cream
1 tablespoon lemon juice
3 tablespoons Grand Marnier
TO DECORATE
¼ pound small sweet strawberries, with their leaves
thinly pared rind of 1 orange, cut into strips
orange sections

Summer Fruit Meringue (p. 285); Orange Parfait with Grand Marnier and Strawberries

1 Beat the egg yolks with the sugar and grated orange rind until thick and pale, then stand the bowl over a saucepan of steaming water off the heat (don't let the bowl touch the water) and continue to beat until the mixture is tepid.
2 Remove the bowl from the heat and beat until the mixture is cold.
3 Beat the cream until standing in soft peaks. Fold into the egg yolk mixture with the lemon juice and Grand Marnier.
4 Pour the mixture into a 5-cup mold or cake pan and freeze until solid.
5 Transfer the parfait from the freezer to the refrigerator 30–40 minutes before you want to serve it.
6 Loosen the sides of the parfait by slipping a knife around the edge.
7 Invert the mold over a serving plate; if it doesn't come out immediately with a slight shake, hold the mold under the hot water faucet for just a second or two; dry the edges of the plate with paper towels. The parfait should slide out easily now.
8 Arrange the strawberries, strips of orange rind and orange sections on top of the parfait and serve at once.

Variations
CHOCOLATE AND ORANGE PARFAIT
Stir 4 ounces coarsely grated sweetened dark chocolate into the parfait before freezing. Decorate with chocolate curls, pared orange rind – and strawberries, too, if you wish.

CHRISTMAS PARFAIT
For this delectable alternative to Christmas pudding, omit the Grand Marnier and grated orange rind. Sprinkle ¾ cup mixed crystallized fruits (including a little ginger, if you like this) with 4–5 tablespoons brandy (or fruit juice or the syrup from the ginger, if children are sharing this). Make the parfait as described, folding the crystallized fruits (and any syrup) into the egg yolks before adding the cream. You can also add ½ cup toasted slivered almonds or crushed hazelnuts. Freeze in a pudding mold.

GINGER TRIFLE

A delicious variation on an old favorite and a great way to use any preserved or candied ginger and ginger wine left from Christmas.

SERVES 6

½ quantity Whisked Sponge Cake (p. 302), unfilled, or 8 lady fingers
½–¾ cup ginger marmalade or preserve
½ cup ginger wine
2 cups Pouring Egg Custard (p. 278) or packet custard, cooled
⅔ cup whipping cream
½ cup preserved or candied ginger, chopped

1 Spread the cake or trifle sponges with the marmalade or preserve, cut into pieces and place in a 2-quart serving dish – a glass one looks attractive.
2 Sprinkle the ginger wine over the top and leave to soak for about 2 hours.
3 Pour the custard on top of the cake mixture. Whip the cream, then spread over the custard, and top with the chopped ginger. Chill until needed.

SUMMER FRUIT MERINGUE

This version of the classic Pavlova makes a stunning centerpiece to any table, and when served with a selection of other desserts at a party, it is always the first one to go.

SERVES 8

4 egg whites
a pinch of cream of tartar
1¼ cups superfine sugar
2 teaspoons vinegar
4 teaspoons cornstarch
½ teaspoon vanilla extract
FOR THE FILLING
1¼ cups heavy cream, whipped
2 kiwi fruits, peeled and sliced into thin rounds, or plums, pitted and sliced
2 nectarines or peaches, peeled, halved and thinly sliced
¾ cup strawberries, hulled and halved, or raspberries or blackberries

1 Preheat the oven to 275°F.
2 Line a baking sheet with nonstick baking parchment.
3 In a clean, grease-free bowl, beat the egg whites and cream of tartar until the egg whites are so stiff that you can turn the bowl upside down without the egg whites falling out.
4 Add a quarter of the sugar to the beaten egg whites and beat again. Then add another quarter. Continue in this way until all the sugar has been added.
5 Mix in the vinegar, cornstarch and vanilla. Pipe or spoon the mixture into a large circle on the prepared baking sheet.
6 Bake the meringue in the coolest part of the oven for 1¼ hours, until crisp. Remove from oven and cool on a wire tray.
7 Just before you are ready to serve, place the meringue on a flat plate and spread most of the cream on top. Arrange circles of kiwi fruit and nectarines or peaches in the center of the meringue. Pipe the remaining cream in rosettes around the edge and arrange the strawberry slices on top. Place a strawberry slice and strawberry leaves in the center.

MENU
Vegetarian Christmas Dinner

Celery and Stilton Soup
132

White Nut Roast with Herb Stuffing
239
Cranberry Sauce
174
Vegetarian Gravy
172
Bread Sauce
175
Roast Potatoes
71
Baby Brussels Sprouts
58
Glazed Carrots
Illustrated on p. 183
182

Christmas Pudding
Illustrated on p. 319
296
or **Christmas Parfait**

PINEAPPLE JELLY

A useful dessert for children. Yogurt Cream (p. 301) or Nut Cream (p. 238) go particularly well with it.

SERVES 6

one 15-ounce can pineapple pieces in
   pineapple juice
2 cups unsweetened pineapple juice
1½ teaspoons agar-agar
a little superfine sugar or clear honey
   (optional)
TO DECORATE
mint sprigs

1 Drain the pineapple, reserving juice.
2 Divide the pineapple between 6 individual serving dishes or glasses.
3 Measure the reserved juice and increase it to 2½ cups with the extra pineapple juice.
4 Put the 2½ cups pineapple juice into a medium saucepan and bring to a boil.

Sprinkle on the agar-agar, a little at a time, whisking constantly.
5 When all the agar-agar has been added, boil for 1 minute. Then remove from the heat. Taste, and sweeten with sugar or honey if necessary. Cool slightly if using glass dishes or glasses.
6 Pour the mixture over the pineapple pieces. Cool, then chill until set. Decorate with mint sprigs.

Variation
RASPBERRY JELLY
Use 1½–2 cups fresh or thawed frozen raspberries instead of the pineapple, and a red fruit juice, such as red currant, instead of the pineapple juice; sweeten to taste.

Fruit Jellies

Other combinations of fruits and juices can be used; try orange juice with orange sections or strawberries; or halved and deseeded grapes with nonsparkling grape juice.

Agar-Agar

Agar-agar is a vegetarian gelatine made from a number of seaweeds and can be obtained in the form of powder, flakes, strips and strands. It should be dissolved in boiling water (2 teaspoons powder or 1 tablespoon flakes to 2½ cups liquid, to give a firm jelly).

 # FRESH FRUIT SALAD

An attractive mixture of colors.

SERVES 4

2 large oranges, peeled and sectioned
   (see p. 99)
1 cup black grapes, halved and deseeded
2 kiwi fruits, peeled and sliced into rounds
2 apples, cored and sliced, unpeeled if skin is
   good
½ cup (generous) orange or apple juice
TO DECORATE
mint sprigs

1 Put all the fruit into a large bowl. Add the orange or apple juice. Mix well.
2 Transfer to a large serving bowl or divide between 4 individual dishes. Chill before serving.

Variations
GREEN FRUIT SALAD
Replace the oranges with a small melon with green flesh: dice the flesh or use a

melon baller to scoop it out of the rind. Use green grapes instead of black.

ORANGE AND KIWI FRUIT SALAD
Use 4 large oranges and 4 kiwi fruits and omit the apples and grapes. Either section the oranges or cut them into thin rings; arrange them alternately with the kiwi fruit in circles on a flat plate, and pour over the orange juice.

TANGERINE AND LICHEE FRUIT
SALAD
A refreshing mixture to serve after a Chinese- or Japanese-style meal. Omit the apples, kiwi fruit and grapes. Use 6–8 tangerines instead of the oranges, peeled and sliced into thin rounds, and the white flesh of 10–12 lichees. One star fruit, sliced, makes an attractive decoration.

Making Fruit Salads and Compotes

For best effect either aim for a real multicolor look, combining five or six colors, or keep it simple and bold, with just one or two colors. For the liquid, you can use a fruit juice such as orange or apricot, or a sugar syrup (p. 85) made from water or wine. Soft fruits will produce their own juice if sprinkled with a little sugar, and treated this way make a delicious red fruit compote.

A fruit salad of prepared pieces of fruit arranged attractively on a coulis of raspberries or blackberries can look jewel-bright and stunning.

Top to bottom: Pashka (p. 288); Pineapple Jelly (p. 286); Fresh Fruit Salad (p. 286)

PASHKA

This traditional Russian Easter dish makes a luscious dessert.
Unless you have a special wooden Russian pashka mold, you'll
need a 6-inch clay flowerpot, scrubbed and baked in a hot oven for
30 minutes or so. Let it cool thoroughly before spooning the
pashka dough into it, however.

SERVES 6

Flower Waters

A little orange-flower water or
rosewater makes a delectable
flavoring for Pashka; add 1–2
tablespoons to the mixture.

When choosing flower waters, look
for the "triple distilled" type; you
can buy these from specialist food
stores, stores specializing in Middle
Eastern foods, and some
pharmacies.

Rosewater is delicious in many
creamy puddings, fillings, toppings
and icings, and can be used to flavor
a delectable jam (p. 338).
Orange-flower water can be used
similarly, but is particularly good, I
think, as a flavoring for a fresh
orange salad, together with a little
orange-blossom honey.

2 egg yolks
7 tablespoons vanilla sugar, or superfine
    sugar and a few drops of vanilla extract
4 tablespoons light cream or half-and-half
1/4 pound unsalted butter, softened
3 cups cottage cheese
1/4 cup whole candied peel, chopped
1/2 cup almonds, blanched and chopped
TO DECORATE
crystallized fruits

1 Beat the egg yolks in a bowl with the
sugar until pale and foamy. Heat the
cream or milk in a saucepan to just below
boiling point, then add to the egg yolks.
Stir well.
2 Return the mixture to the saucepan and
stir until thickened. This only takes a
moment, so watch it carefully: the mixture must not boil, or it will curdle.
Remove from heat and set aside to cool.

3 Beat the butter until light and creamy,
then gradually beat in the egg yolk
mixture.
4 Continuing to beat, add the cottage
cheese, a little at a time, then add the
chopped peel and almonds.
5 Line the flowerpot with a double layer
of paper towels, to extend over the top.
6 Spoon the pashka mixture into the
lined mold and smooth the surface, then
fold the ends of the paper towels over the
top.
7 Put a small plate on top and weight it
down. Stand the pashka on a plate to
catch any moisture that seeps out of the
base. Refrigerate for 6–8 hours or overnight.
8 To serve, invert the container onto a
serving dish, turn out the pashka and
remove the paper towels. Decorate with
crystallized fruits.

QUICK CHERRY AND
LIME CHEESECAKE

SERVES 6

1 1/2 cups crushed graham crackers
6 tablespoons butter, melted
2 cups cottage cheese
1/2 cup (generous) heavy cream
1/4 cup superfine sugar
grated rind and juice of 2 limes or 1 lemon
1 cup (generous) drained canned cherries,
    pitted
TO GLAZE
2–3 tablespoons strawberry jam or red
    currant jelly, melted
TO DECORATE
lime twists

1 Mix the graham cracker crumbs with
the butter. Press the mixture firmly into
the base of an 8-inch springform cake pan
or other suitable shallow dish, using the
base of a clean jam jar.
2 Put the cottage cheese, cream, sugar
and lime or lemon rind and juice into a
bowl and beat together until smooth and
thick. Spoon the mixture on top of the
crumb mixture and level the surface.
3 Arrange the cherries on top. Pour the
jam or jelly over the cherries. Chill well.
Decorate with lime twists to serve.

ROSE CHEESECAKE

This is an exquisite cheesecake. Rose Petal Jam (p. 338) can be made from fragrant roses in the summer, or bought at a shop specializing in Middle Eastern produce.

SERVES 8–12

1½ cups crushed vanilla wafers or graham crackers
4 tablespoons butter, melted
1½ cups rose petal jam
1 cup cottage cheese
½ cup (generous) sour cream
7 tablespoons vanilla sugar or superfine sugar with a few drops of vanilla extract
1 tablespoon cornstarch
1 tablespoon lemon juice
2 large eggs, separated
a pinch of cream of tartar
a little extra butter for greasing
TO DECORATE
crystallized rose petals
pistachio kernels

1 Preheat the oven to 325°F. Grease an 8-inch springform cake pan.
2 First make the crumb crust. Mix together the wafer or cracker crumbs and melted butter. Spoon this mixture into the bottom of the pan. Press down firmly, using the base of a clean jam jar.
3 Spread the rose petal jam evenly on top of the crumbs. Chill.
4 Next make the filling. Put the cottage cheese into a bowl with the sour cream, sugar, cornstarch, lemon juice and egg yolks. Beat until smooth.
5 Beat the egg whites in a clean bowl with the cream of tartar until stiff but not dry. Fold into the cottage cheese mixture and stir carefully but thoroughly.
6 Pour the mixture into the pan on top of the crumb crust. Bake the cheesecake for 1–1½ hours, until firm in the center.
7 Turn off the oven and leave the cheesecake to cool in the still-warm oven for 15–20 minutes, When cool, chill.
8 To serve, decorate with the crystallized rose petals and pistachios.

Cooling Baked Cheesecakes

A cheesecake cracks if it is cooled too quickly; that is the reason for allowing it to cool gently in the turned-off oven.

Freezing Baked Cheesecakes

Baked cheesecakes freeze excellently. Cool the cheesecake thoroughly as described, then remove from the pan. Place on a plate and freeze until solid, then remove from the plate, pack carefully, label and store in the freezer. To use, remove wrappings, place on a wire rack for about 3 hours to thaw, then transfer to a serving plate.

Rose Cheesecake

HOW TO GET
A "TOP HAT" EFFECT

Make a deep groove in the top of the soufflé with the handle of a teaspoon so that it cooks with a "top hat" effect

Hot Black Cherry Soufflé

HOT BLACK CHERRY SOUFFLÉ

A hot soufflé makes an impressive and delicious ending to a meal, yet is very easy to make. The uncooked soufflé will keep perfectly in the freezer, so you can do all the preparation a day (or more) in advance, but use a container that can withstand the extremes of temperature.

SERVES 4

1½ cups drained canned black cherries, pitted
3 tablespoons kirsch
5 egg whites
¼ cup superfine sugar
a little oil for greasing
TO DECORATE (OPTIONAL)
confectioner's sugar
TO SERVE
whipped cream

1 Wrap a double layer of wax paper or foil around a 7-inch soufflé dish so it extends about 2 inches above the top rim. Tie a string around the paper or foil and secure the top with a paper clip. Brush the dish and paper or foil with oil and dust with superfine sugar.
2 Preheat the oven to 375°F.
3 Purée the cherries in a blender or food processor and add the kirsch.
4 Beat the egg whites until they form stiff peaks, then beat in the sugar until stiff and glossy.
5 Fold the cherry purée into the egg whites.
6 Pour the mixture into the soufflé dish, level the top, then draw the handle of a teaspoon around the top about ½ inch from the edge, to make a deep groove.
7 Bake for 30–35 minutes, until the soufflé is firm and doesn't wobble when shaken.
8 Remove the paper or foil, sift a little confectioner's sugar over the soufflé, if you like, and serve with whipped cream.

Variations
RASPBERRY SOUFFLÉ
Make as described, using 1¼ cups puréed and sieved fresh or thawed frozen raspberries. Flavor with a little kirsch or framboise.

APRICOT SOUFFLÉ
Use 1¼ cups stewed and puréed apricots and ¼ cup sugar. Use Cointreau or Grand Marnier instead of kirsch.

BLACK CURRANT SOUFFLÉ
For this excellent variation, use 1¼ cups stewed, puréed and sieved black currants and ½ cup sugar. Use kir instead of kirsch.

LEMON SURPRISE PUDDING

Another old favorite, this mixture separates as it cooks, so that you end up with a light sponge on top of a creamy lemon-flavored sauce.

SERVES 4

2 tablespoons butter
½ cup superfine sugar
grated rind and juice of 1 lemon
2 eggs, separated
½ cup (generous) milk
3 tablespoons unbleached white flour
a little extra butter for greasing

1 Preheat the oven to 375°F. Lightly grease a 2½-cup ovenproof dish. Have ready a roasting pan which is large enough to hold the ovenproof dish.
2 Cream the butter with 2 tablespoons of the sugar, then beat in the lemon rind and juice, egg yolks, milk, flour and the remaining sugar.
3 Beat the egg whites until they are stiff but not dry, then fold carefully into the lemon mixture.
4 Pour the mixture into the prepared dish. Stand the dish in the roasting pan and pour 1 inch boiling water into the pan.
5 Bake for about 40 minutes, until the pudding is risen and golden-brown. Serve immediately.

TARTE AU CITRON

A lovely, refreshing classic tart which needs no accompaniments.

SERVES 4–6

1 cup all-purpose flour
1 tablespoon confectioners' sugar
7 tablespoons butter, cut into pieces
1 egg yolk
2 tablespoons cold water
FOR THE FILLING
3 lemons
3 eggs
scant ½ cup superfine sugar
4 tablespoons unsalted butter, softened

1 Set the oven to 350°F. Sift the flour and confectioners' sugar into a large bowl or the bowl of a food processor and add the butter. Rub the butter into the flour with your fingertips or blend it briefly in the food processor until the mixture looks like coarse breadcrumbs, then add the egg yolk and water and mix again briefly until a dough forms.
2 Turn the dough out onto a lightly floured surface and knead into a smooth round, then roll out to fit an 8-inch loose-bottomed deep tart pan. Trim the edges then place in the refrigerator to chill while you make the filling.
3 Scrub one lemon, then grate the zest finely into a bowl. Add the superfine sugar and eggs and whisk together until thick and pale.
4 Gradually beat in the butter a little at a time. Squeeze the juice out of all the lemons and add to the mixture, then pour it into the pie shell.
5 Bake for about 30 minutes, or until set. Cool, then chill before serving.

Thickening Agents

Cornstarch, which is starch extracted from corn, is just one of the thickening agents available; others are:

ARROWROOT A fine white powder originally made from the *aru* root of the Aruac Indians, arrowroot is less refined than cornstarch and so preferred by wholefood cooks for small thickening jobs, but it loses its thickening powers if cooked for more than 1–2 minutes. Arrowroot is excellent for thickening fruit juice to make a clear glaze for fruit tarts. The proportions are 1 rounded teaspoon to ½ cup liquid.

POTATO FLOUR The gluten-free starch from potato, this can be used in the same way as arrowroot and cornstarch, but as it has a slight potato flavor it is best in savory dishes.

KUZU Made from the roots of a mountain plant in Japan, and gluten-free, kuzu is used in similar ways to the above. In Japan, it is used to prevent colds and as a general digestive tonic.

HOW TO MAKE PÂTE SUCRÉE

1 Sift 1⅔ cups plain 85% whole-wheat flour onto a clean work surface

2 Make a well in the center and into this put ¾ cup superfine sugar, 10 tablespoons softened butter and 4 egg yolks

3 Work these ingredients together with one hand while you push the ingredients to the center with the other hand, to make a dough

4 Knead the dough firmly until smooth, then wrap in plastic wrap and chill for at least 1 hour before use

5 Roll out dough as required, and bake at 375°F

PUMPKIN PIE

Everybody's favorite tradition at Thanksgiving dinner.

SERVES 6

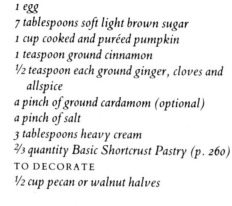

1 egg
7 tablespoons soft light brown sugar
1 cup cooked and puréed pumpkin
1 teaspoon ground cinnamon
½ teaspoon each ground ginger, cloves and
  allspice
a pinch of ground cardamom (optional)
a pinch of salt
3 tablespoons heavy cream
⅔ quantity Basic Shortcrust Pastry (p. 260)
TO DECORATE
½ cup pecan or walnut halves

1 Preheat the oven to 450°F.
2 In a mixing bowl, beat the egg with the sugar until pale and light, then stir in the pumpkin purée, cinnamon, ginger, cloves, allspice, cardamom, salt and cream.
3 Roll out the pastry and use to line an 8-inch pie pan. Trim the edges. Pour in the filling.
4 Bake the pie at 450°F for 7 minutes, then turn down the oven to 325°F and bake for 35–40 minutes more, until a skewer inserted in the center of the pie comes out clean.
5 Remove the pie from the oven and arrange pecan or walnut halves decoratively around the edge, pressing them lightly into the warm filling. Put 2 more pecans or walnuts in the center. Allow the pie to cool completely before cutting into slices.

Ⓥ GLAZED RED FRUIT TART Ⓥ

A luscious, shiny red tart is one of the best things to make from summer strawberries or other red fruit, such as red currants, glazed with a jam or jelly that complements the fruit flavor. I like to use a 12-inch tart pan; for an 8-inch pan, halve all the ingredients. This tart is delicious served with some crème fraîche, sour cream or plain (or vegan) yogurt.

SERVES 8

1 quantity Basic Shortcrust Pastry (p. 260)
  or Pâte Sucrée (left)
2–3 pints strawberries or a mixture of
  strawberries, red currants and raspberries
2 cups red currant jelly
butter for greasing
TO DECORATE
strawberry leaves

1 Preheat the oven to 375°F. Lightly grease a 12-inch tart pan.
2 Roll out the pastry to fit the tart pan. Place in the pan and trim the edges. Prick the base with a fork and bake blind for 20 minutes (p. 266), until pale brown. Set aside to cool.
3 Prepare the fruit. Halve any large strawberries; use smaller berries whole. Arrange in the pastry shell.
4 Melt the jelly gently in a small saucepan and pour over the fruit. Allow to cool and set. Decorate with strawberry leaves before serving.

Variation
JEWELED FRUIT TART
For this very pretty variation, a variety of ripe fruits replace the red fruits. Choose contrasting colors, such as ½ pint each of strawberries or raspberries, sliced peaches or oranges, kiwi fruit, black grapes, bananas or pears. Arrange as shown on p. 23; use sieved apricot jam to glaze instead of red currant jelly.

LINZERTORTE

I'm particularly fond of the combination of flavors in this Austrian tart. It is especially good after a vegetable main course.

SERVES 6

1¼ cups whole-wheat flour
1 teaspoon ground cinnamon
a pinch of ground cloves
1 cup ground almonds
grated rind of 1 lemon
3 tablespoons soft light brown sugar
¼ pound plus 4 tablespoons butter, softened
1 egg yolk, optional
1 cup raspberry, black cherry or black currant preserve
butter for greasing
TO FINISH
confectioner's sugar

1 In a mixing bowl, combine the flour, cinnamon, cloves, ground almonds, lemon rind, sugar, butter and egg yolk, if used, to make a dough.

2 Knead lightly, then wrap in plastic wrap and chill for 30 minutes.
3 Preheat the oven to 400°F. Lightly grease an 8–9-inch pie pan or loose-based tart pan.
4 Roll out three-quarters of the dough, fairly thickly, to fit the pie or tart pan. Ease the pastry into the pan and trim the edges.
5 Spoon the jam evenly over the pastry.
6 Roll out the remaining pastry, again fairly thickly, and cut it into long strips. Arrange in a lattice pattern over the jam.
7 Bake for 25–30 minutes, until the tart is slightly risen and golden-brown. Dredge with sifted confectioner's sugar. Serve hot, warm or cold.

MENU

Bonfire Party

Warming food to come back to!

Leek and Potato Soup
134
Warm Whole-wheat Rolls
Illustrated on p. 331
328

Eggplant Parmigiana
202
Crisp Green Salad

Linzertorte

PITHIVIERS

This delicious almond tart, which originated in the town of Pithiviers, in northern France, is easy to make and delicious served with crème fraîche, whipped cream or thick Greek yogurt. The truly sinful might try vanilla ice cream, too!

SERVES 6

2 tablespoons butter
¼ cup superfine sugar
2 egg yolks
⅔ cup ground almonds
2 tablespoons rum
1 quantity Puff Pastry (p. 269) or 1 pound frozen puff pastry, thawed
beaten egg
confectioner's sugar

1 Preheat the oven to 450°F.
2 Cream together the butter and sugar, then add the egg yolks and beat until creamy. Fold in the ground almonds and rum.
3 Divide the puff pastry into two pieces, one slightly larger than the other. Cut the smaller one into an 8-inch circle. Place on a baking sheet.
4 Spread the almond filling on top of the pastry circle to within ½ inch of the edges.
5 Roll out the second piece of pastry to go on top. Ease into place, trim and decorate the edges. Make a steam hole in the center.
6 Brush with beaten egg and bake for 10 minutes. Turn down the oven to 400°F and bake for 35 minutes more.
7 About 10 minutes before the end of the baking time, remove the tart from the oven and dredge with confectioner's sugar; return it to the oven to melt the sugar to a glaze. Serve warm.

Note on Pithiviers

This is a particularly useful dessert to serve when you're entertaining, because it can be completely prepared, except for cooking, the night before. You can then put it into the oven either when you start your main course, or, if you're serving cheese first, when you start the cheese course, and the tart will be ready, all puffed up, flaky and golden, 25 minutes later. Serve it with light cream.

Ⅴ   OLD-FASHIONED TREACLE TART   Ⅴ

The name of this favorite dessert is really a misnomer, for it uses
not a dark treacly molasses but a light, sweet syrup. It's easy to
make if you pour the syrup straight into the pastry shell on top of
the crumbs, without attempting to mix them.

SERVES 4

⅔ quantity Basic Shortcrust Pastry (p. 260)
1⅓ cups fine fresh whole-wheat breadcrumbs
1 teaspoon lemon juice
1 cup golden syrup or light corn syrup

1 Preheat the oven to 375°F.
2 Roll out the pastry and use it to line an 8-inch tart pan. Trim the edges.
3 Put the crumbs evenly into the pastry shell without pressing them down. Sprinkle with the lemon juice.

4 Pour the golden syrup or corn syrup on top of the crumbs (you can do this straight from the container) so that they are all evenly covered. Don't try to mix them; the crumbs will soak up the syrup as the tart cooks.
5 Roll out the pastry trimmings and cut into strips. Arrange the pastry strips in a lattice pattern on top of the tart.
6 Bake for 25 minutes, until the pastry is crisp and lightly browned. Serve warm.

MENU

Late-Summer Sunday Lunch

Chilled Cucumber and
Yogurt Soup
138

Zucchini with
Hazelnut Stuffing
194
Apple Sauce
84
Vegetarian Gravy
172
Roast Potatoes
71
Carrot Purée
Illustrated on p. 188
189
Green Beans

Country Apple Pie
Illustrated on p. 297

Ⅴ   COUNTRY APPLE PIE   Ⅴ

SERVES 4

⅔ quantity Basic Shortcrust Pastry (p. 260)
1½ pounds cooking apples, peeled, cored and sliced
7 tablespoons soft light brown sugar
3–4 cloves (optional)
TO GLAZE
milk or soy milk
superfine sugar

1 Preheat the oven to 425°F.
2 Roll out the pastry so that it is about 1 inch bigger around than a 4-cup pie dish. Cut a 1-inch wide strip from the pastry.
3 Brush the rim of the pie dish with water and press the pastry strip onto it. Put the apples into the pie dish, sprinkle with the sugar and add the cloves if used.
4 Brush the pastry strip with water, then put the large piece of pastry on top, pressing it down around the edges. Pinch the edges together, trim, and crimp with the back of a fork. Make a steam hole in the center of the pastry.
5 Cut decorations from the pastry trim-

mings, if you like, and stick these onto the pie with water.
6 Brush the pastry with milk or soy milk and sprinkle with a little superfine sugar. Bake for 10 minutes, then turn down the oven to 350°F and bake for 35–40 minutes more.
7 Sprinkle with more superfine sugar and serve hot or cold.

Variations
PLUM PIE
Make as described, using plums instead of apples and omitting the cloves. Halve and pit large plums (small types, such as damsons, can be left whole). Unless the plums are very sweet, increase the amount of sugar to ⅔–¾ cup.

GOOSEBERRY PIE
Make as described, using gooseberries instead of the apples and omitting the cloves. Increase the amount of sugar to ¾ cup or more, depending on how sharp the gooseberries are.

☑ DOUBLE-CRUST BLACK CURRANT PIE ☑

SERVES 4

*1¼–1½ pounds fresh or thawed frozen black
    currants, trimmed*
¾ cup soft light brown or superfine sugar
1 quantity Basic Shortcrust Pastry (p. 260)
butter or vegan margarine for greasing
TO GLAZE
milk or soy milk
superfine sugar

1 Preheat the oven to 400°F. Grease a
9½-inch pie pan.
2 Put the black currants into a heavy-
bottomed saucepan and cook gently for
4–5 minutes, until the juices run. Drain
the fruit to remove excess juice. You can
save this juice in the refrigerator and use it
in another dessert recipe, or add it to your
next batch of jelly.
3 Stir the sugar into the black currants.
Set aside to cool.
4 Roll out just over half the pastry to a
round which will fit the pie pan. Transfer
this to the pie pan, using a board to help
(see p. 260).

5 Put the fruit into the pastry-lined pan
to within ½ inch of the edge. Dampen the
edge with water.
6 Roll out the remaining pastry and place
on top of the fruit. Press the edges
together, trim, and crimp with the back
of a fork. Make a steam hole in the center
of the pastry.
7 Cut decorations from the pastry trimmings, if you like, and stick these onto
the pie with water.
8 Brush the pastry with milk or soy
milk, sprinkle with superfine sugar, and
bake for 30 minutes. Serve hot or cold.

Variations
SUMMER FRUIT PIE
Make as described, but use a mixture of
fresh or frozen raspberries, red currants
and black currants.

APPLE PIE
Use 1½ pounds apples, stewed as
described on p. 84.

DECORATING A
FRUIT PIE

☑ RHUBARB CRUMBLE ☑

I use a shallow French glazed pottery ovenproof dish measuring
10 × 12½ inches, which seems a large quantity for 4, but in my
experience there's never any problem with leftovers!

SERVES 4–6

2 pounds rhubarb, cut into 1-inch lengths
7 tablespoons sugar
butter or vegan margarine for greasing
FOR THE CRUMBLE
1¾ cups self-rising 85% whole-wheat flour
*¼ pound plus 4 tablespoons butter or vegan
    margarine*
1 cup Demerara sugar

1 Preheat the oven to 400°F.
2 Put the fruit into a lightly greased large
shallow ovenproof dish. Mix in the
sugar; make sure the fruit is in an even
layer. Set the dish aside.

3 Put the flour into a mixing bowl and
rub in the butter or vegan margarine with
your fingertips until the mixture looks
like fine breadcrumbs and there are no
lumps of fat showing.
4 Add the Demerara sugar to the bowl
and mix gently. Spoon the crumble topping over the rhubarb in an even layer,
gently spreading it to completely seal the
fruit.
5 Bake for 30–40 minutes, until the
crumble is crisp and lightly browned and
the fruit feels tender when pierced with a
skewer. Serve hot.

TRADITIONAL CHRISTMAS PUDDING

In this pudding, soft butter or margarine replaces the traditional beef suet. The pudding tastes just as good and has a deliciously spicy flavor. It can be made up to 2 months in advance and will keep well (and mature) in a cool, dry place.

SERVES 8

Flaming a Christmas Pudding

Flaming a Christmas pudding with brandy just before serving gives it a wonderful flavor. The important thing is to warm the brandy first. Put ¼ cup brandy into a metal ladle and warm by holding over a gas flame or electric burner, then quickly light the brandy and pour over and around the pudding.

Vegetarian Suet

A vegetarian suet is available from health food stores and can replace animal suet in recipes such as Christmas pudding, mincemeat and suet pudding.

½ pound soft butter or vegan margarine
1¼ cups real Barbados sugar
2 eggs, beaten
¾ cup (generous) 85% or 100%
*   whole-wheat flour*
½ teaspoon salt
½ teaspoon freshly grated nutmeg
½ teaspoon ground ginger
1½ teaspoons mixed spice
1 cup ground almonds
⅓ cup finely grated carrot
¾ cup currants
¾ cup raisins
¾ cup sultanas
½ cup chopped candied peel
½ cup blanched almonds, chopped
1⅓ cups fresh whole-wheat breadcrumbs
grated rind and juice of 1 lemon
1 tablespoon molasses
about 4 tablespoons water or water and rum
*   mixed*
butter for greasing
TO FLAME
4 tablespoons brandy
TO SERVE
holly sprigs
Brandy Butter (below)

1 Grease a 1-quart bowl or pudding mold and have ready a saucepan which is large enough to hold the pudding mold.

2 Cream together the butter or vegan margarine and the sugar until light and fluffy, then whisk in the beaten egg, a little at a time.

3 Sift the flour, salt and spices into the bowl on top of the creamed mixture.

4 Add the remaining ingredients with just enough of the water or water and rum to make a soft mixture that will fall heavily from the spoon when you shake it. Mix well.

5 Spoon the mixture into the prepared pudding mold, cover with a piece of pleated greased wax paper and then a piece of aluminum foil, and tie down securely with string.

6 Put the mold into the saucepan and pour in enough boiling water to come halfway up the sides of the mold.

7 Bring to a boil, then cover the saucepan and steam gently for 4 hours. Check the water level and add more boiling water if necessary.

8 Remove the pudding from the saucepan and allow it to cool, then store it in its mold in a cool, dry place. Steam the pudding again for 3 hours before serving, then remove the paper and foil and turn the pudding out onto a warmed serving plate. Flame with brandy, decorate with holly and serve with brandy butter.

BRANDY BUTTER

SERVES 6

¼ pound unsalted butter
⅔ cup soft light brown sugar
2 tablespoons brandy
TO DECORATE
holly leaves

1 Cream the butter and sugar together until light, pale and fluffy, then gradually beat in the brandy.

2 Transfer the mixture to a serving dish and chill until required. Decorate with holly to serve.

MINCE PIES

This mincemeat is unusual in that it contains no sugar or fat; the dried fruits provide the sweetness. It tastes delicious, but doesn't store in the same way as ordinary mincemeat because of the lack of sugar. This recipe makes 12 mince pies, with enough mincemeat left over for 2 further batches. The mincemeat will keep for up to a week in a covered bowl in the refrigerator. Uncooked mince pies freeze excellently; put them into the muffin tin, freeze, then carefully remove them from the tin and store in a plastic container until required. Return the mince pies to the tin for baking. (They can be baked from frozen, allowing a few extra minutes.)

MAKES 12

Top to bottom: Double-Crust Black Currant Pie (p. 295); Country Apple Pie (p. 294); Mince Pies

1 quantity Basic Shortcrust Pastry (p. 260)
butter or vegan margarine for greasing
TO FINISH
superfine sugar
FOR THE MINCEMEAT
¾ cup currants
¾ cup raisins
¾ cup sultanas
¾ cup pitted unsweetened dates, chopped
¼ cup candied peel, chopped
¼ cup glacé cherries, quartered
½ cup slivered almonds
¼ cup brandy or whiskey
½ teaspoon each ground ginger, mixed spice,
*   freshly grated nutmeg*
1 ripe banana, peeled and mashed

1 To make the mincemeat, put the dried fruit, peel, cherries and almonds into a bowl. Sprinkle with the brandy or whiskey and the spices. Stir, then allow to stand for 1–2 hours, stirring from time to time. Add the banana and mix well.

2 Preheat the oven to 400°F. Grease a 12-hole muffin tin.

3 Roll out the pastry thinly. Using 2 cutters, cut out twelve 3-inch circles and twelve 2½-inch circles.

4 Press the larger circles gently into each section of the muffin tin, then put a heaping teaspoon of mincemeat into each and cover it with a smaller pastry circle.

5 Press down at the edges and make a steam hole in the top of each pie. Bake for 10 minutes, until lightly browned.

6 Cool in the tin, then transfer to a wire rack. Serve the pies warm, sprinkled with a little superfine sugar.

WAFFLES

Waffles are nourishing and make an excellent breakfast, supper or snack at any time. They're particularly popular, in my experience, with children and teenagers. You need a waffle iron to make them.

MAKES 6

Sweet Pancakes

Pancakes are delicious served simply with warmed maple syrup, honey or corn syrup. They are, however, marvelously adaptable, since both the batter and the fillings are infinitely variable.

For chocolate pancakes, replace 2 teaspoons of the flour with 2 teaspoons cocoa powder and add 1 teaspoon vanilla extract or 1 tablespoon rum; serve with warmed black cherry preserve and whipped cream.

For nutty-tasting buckwheat pancakes, replace up to ½ cup of the flour with buckwheat flour. These are good with strongly flavored fillings, either sweet or savory.

For orange pancakes, add grated orange rind and 1 tablespoon Cointreau or Grand Marnier to the batter; try these with pineapple, peaches or apricots.

Fill the pancakes with sliced ripe peaches or nectarines.

For spicy pancakes, add ½ teaspoon cinnamon or ginger to the batter; try filling these with fruits which complement the spicy flavor, such as apples with cinnamon, pears with ginger.

1¾ cups 85% or 100% whole-wheat flour
3 teaspoons baking powder
½ teaspoon salt
3 eggs, separated
2 cups milk
4 tablespoons butter, melted
3 tablespoons superfine sugar

1 Heat the waffle iron according to the manufacturer's instructions.
2 Put the flour, baking powder and salt into a mixing bowl. Add the egg yolks, milk and melted butter. Mix well to make a smooth batter.
3 Beat the egg whites until stiff but not dry, then add the sugar and beat again until glossy.
4 Fold the egg white mixture into the batter.
5 Spread ½ cup batter in the hot waffle iron. Bake for 2–3 minutes, until golden. (If it sticks, cook for a minute longer.)
6 Serve hot, with butter and honey or maple syrup. Or serve the waffles with a jam sauce or cream or ice cream and fresh fruit.

STEAMED PUDDING

Everybody's favorite homely pudding, wonderful to keep out the chill on a winter's day.

SERVES 4

Waffle Irons

Most automatic waffle irons have a thermostat that shows when they are hot enough to add the batter. If yours does not, put a teaspoonful of water into the iron: it is ready when the steaming stops. Since the batter contains fat, you do not need to grease a waffle iron. If the waffle sticks, simply cook for a minute longer. You shouldn't have any trouble with sticking after the first one.

¼ cup jam or light corn syrup
¾ cup (generous) self-rising 85% whole-wheat flour
1 teaspoon baking powder
¼ pound butter, softened
½ cup sugar
2 eggs
extra butter for greasing

1 Grease a 4–5-cup bowl or pudding mold with butter and put the jam or corn syrup into the base.
2 Put the flour, baking powder, butter, sugar and eggs into a large mixing bowl and beat together for 1–2 minutes until the mixture is thick and smooth and looks slightly glossy.

3 Spoon the mixture into the mold on top of the jam or syrup. Cover the mold with a piece of pleated greased wax paper and then with aluminum foil. Tie down securely. Stand the mold in a saucepan and pour in boiling water to come half-way up the sides of the mold.
4 Bring to a boil, cover, then simmer for 1½ hours. Check the water level and add boiling water if necessary.
5 Remove the paper and foil, run a palette knife around the sides of the pudding and turn it out onto a warmed plate. Serve hot.

PANCAKES

Pancakes can be thin and lacy, so that you can almost see through them – these are the elegant French crêpes – or they can be thick and filling, a cheap and comforting homely food. The thick variety were the favorite after-college snack of one of my daughters and her friends, who seemed to arrive at our door on motorbikes in droves. It was then I really learned to make pancakes – fast!

MAKES 12–14

Crêpes Suzette

¾ *cup (generous) 85% whole-wheat flour*
½ *teaspoon salt*
2 eggs
½ *cup (generous) milk*
½ *cup water*
1–2 tablespoons melted butter or sunflower oil
oil or melted butter for frying
TO SERVE
superfine sugar
4 lemons, halved

1 Put the first 6 ingredients into a blender or food processor and whizz until smooth. Or put the flour and salt into a mixing bowl, mix in the eggs, then gradually beat in the milk, water and melted butter.

2 Brush the inside of a small nonstick frying pan with oil or melted butter. Set the frying pan over high heat until a drop of water flicked into it sizzles immediately.

3 Remove the pan from the heat, pour in 1½–2 tablespoons of batter for thin pancakes, more for thick ones, tipping the frying pan as you pour it in, so that the batter runs all over the bottom of the frying pan.

4 Immediately return the pan to the heat and cook the pancake for about 30 seconds, until it is set on top and golden-brown underneath, then flip the pancake over, using your fingers and a small palette knife, and cook the other side until golden-brown.

5 Serve the pancakes immediately, or stack them on a plate and keep them warm until all are ready. Regrease the frying pan as necessary. Serve sprinkled with sugar, along with the halved lemons to squeeze over.

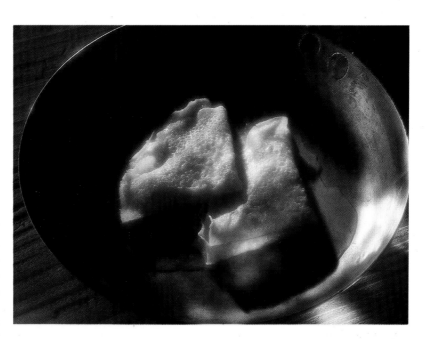

Variation
CRÊPES SUZETTE

This is the favorite dessert of my daughter Katy. Make the batter and cook the pancakes as described. Heat ¼ pound butter, ¾ cup superfine sugar, the grated rind and juice of 3 medium oranges and the grated rind and juice of 1 lemon in a shallow flameproof oven-to-table casserole or attractive frying pan. When the mixture is melted, remove from the heat and dip in the pancakes on both sides, one by one, folding them in half and then in half again to make triangles. When each pancake is coated, push it to the side of the frying pan. When all have been coated, leave them in the frying pan until you're ready to eat, then reheat gently. When all the pancakes are heated through, turn the heat up high for 1 minute to make the sauce really hot, then flame it in the pan with ¼ cup brandy.

Greasing a Pancake Pan

A pastry brush – natural bristle, not nylon, which melts in the heat – is ideal for greasing a pancake pan.

V **RASPBERRY COULIS** V

A delicious sauce for serving with fruit salads, over ice cream or
poached fruits.

SERVES 4

*about 3 cups fresh raspberries, washed, or
frozen raspberries, thawed*
6 teaspoons water
6 teaspoons superfine sugar

*Butterscotch Sauce (p. 301); Raspberry
Coulis; Hot Chocolate Sauce*

1 Blend the raspberries in a blender or
food processor with the water and sugar.
Sieve, then turn into a saucepan. Bring to
a boil and boil for 1 minute, to make the
sauce clear and glossy.
2 Cool and refrigerate until needed.

Variation
BLACKBERRY COULIS
Make exactly as described, using black-
berries instead of raspberries.

Chocolate Fondue

Hot chocolate sauce makes a
delicious sweet fondue, a
special-occasion dessert that children
and students love. Serve surrounded
by prepared fresh fruit for dipping;
pieces of apple, apricot, pineapple,
peach – whatever is available. Some
marshmallows, soft peppermints
and pieces of Turkish delight are also
good for dipping (though not as
healthy).

V **HOT CHOCOLATE SAUCE** V

This sauce is delicious over meringues, profiteroles or ice cream.

SERVES 4

*4 ounces unsweetened dark chocolate, broken
into pieces*
½ cup (generous) light or nondairy cream

1 Put the chocolate and cream into a
small saucepan.
2 Heat gently until the chocolate has
melted. Stir well, then serve.

VEGAN CREAM

V   V

SERVES 4–6

1 teaspoon cornstarch
2/3 cup unsweetened soy milk
1 vanilla bean
7 tablespoons soft pure vegetable margarine
2–3 teaspoons confectioners' sugar
a few drops of vanilla extract (optional)

1 In a small bowl, blend the cornstarch to a paste with a little of the soy milk.
2 Put the rest of the milk into a saucepan with the vanilla bean and bring just to the boil. Pour the milk over the cornstarch mixture, stir, and return to the pan. Stir over a gentle heat for a minute or two until the mixture thickens, then remove from the heat and leave until completely cold. Take out the vanilla bean, which can be rinsed, dried and used again.
3 In another bowl, beat the margarine until it's light and creamy, then gradually whisk in the cooled cornstarch mixture. Add it gradually, whisking well, to produce a beautifully light, whipped cream.
4 Add the confectioners' sugar towards the end, a teaspoonful at a time, tasting the mixture to get it just right. The delicate vanilla flavor can be enhanced with a drop or two of vanilla extract.

YOGURT CREAM

A nice sharp-tasting cream with half the fat content of heavy cream.

SERVES 6–8

2/3 cup heavy cream
2/3 cup non-fat yogurt

Put the cream and yogurt into a bowl and whisk until the mixture forms soft peaks. Chill until needed.

BUTTERSCOTCH SAUCE

MAKES ABOUT 1¼ CUPS

4 tablespoons butter
5 tablespoons soft brown sugar
1/4 cup superfine sugar
2 1/2 tablespoons light corn syrup
2/3 cup heavy cream

1 Put the butter in a saucepan with the sugars and the corn syrup and heat gently for 4–5 minutes.
2 Remove from the heat, stir in the cream and leave to cool.

WHIPPED TOFU TOPPING

V   V

A lovely light topping which is dairy-free and fat-free.

SERVES 4

10-ounce package firm tofu, drained and
    cubed
1 teaspoon real vanilla extract
2 tablespoons maple syrup

Put the tofu into a blender or food processor with the vanilla extract and maple syrup. Blend to a light consistency. Add a drop of water to thin if necessary.

Using Sweet Sauces

A sweet sauce can add the finishing touch to a dessert, transforming a simple dish like homemade ice cream into something special.

Try raspberry coulis with vanilla ice cream; blackberry coulis with apple ice cream; or a coulis made from blackberries or black currants with chocolate ice cream.

For a pretty effect, pour a pool of coulis onto an individual serving plate, top with poached fruit or ice cream, then pour circles of cream on top of the coulis. Make a feather pattern in the circles of cream by drawing a cocktail stick through them, in lines like the spokes of a wheel, first towards the center, then, with the next one, from the center to the outside.

Sweet sauces are excellent with fresh or cooked fruit; try chocolate sauce, raspberry coulis or sabayon sauce with poached pears; or custard sauce with thin circles of juicy tangerines or satsumas (and flavor the custard with some of the grated rind).

Cakes

This chapter contains a medley of favorite cakes, ranging from homely Rock Cakes (p. 308), Parkin (p. 308) and easy All-in-One Sponge (p. 304) to classics such as Carrot Cake (p. 306), Madeira Cake (p. 307), Dundee Cake (p. 311) and Rich Fruit Cake (p. 312), and some sheer indulgences like Meringues (p. 314), Éclairs (p. 314) and the most wonderful chocolate cake of all, Chocolate Roulade (p. 305). At the end of the chapter are some favorite fillings and icings. Among the recipes are several that do not contain eggs or milk, for vegans or for people allergic to dairy products.

Making Assorted Fancy Cakes

A classic sponge cake, baked in a jelly roll pan as described under Swiss Roll, can be cut up to make 12–16 tiny cakes. You can either cover the top of the cake with Glacé Icing (p. 315), before cutting into pieces, or cut the cake into different shapes, using a sharp knife and pastry cutters, then ice and decorate the shapes individually. If you're doing the cakes individually, there is plenty of scope for different colors and flavors; coffee icing decorated with chocolate or walnuts; chocolate icing with chocolate curls; vanilla icing with crystallized rose or violet petals; lemon icing with angelica and yellow sugar cake decorations; orange icing with small pieces of jellied orange sections. If the cake is very crumbly, before putting on the icing or butter icing dip the pieces of cake in a glaze made by boiling 1 cup sieved apricot jam with 3 tablespoons water for a few minutes, until syrupy.

CLASSIC SPONGE CAKE

The lightest sponge of all and comparatively low in calories, because it does not contain fat.

MAKES ONE 8-inch CAKE

4 eggs
½ cup superfine sugar
¾ cup (generous) plain unbleached white flour
a pinch of salt
butter for greasing
FOR THE FILLING
6 tablespoons jam
TO FINISH
superfine sugar

1 Grease two 8-inch shallow cake pans and line the base of each with a circle of greased wax paper.
2 Put the eggs and sugar into a mixing bowl and beat with an electric mixer for about 5 minutes, until the mixture is very pale, has doubled in bulk and leaves a ribbon trail on its surface when the beaters are lifted.
3 Alternatively, put the eggs and sugar into a bowl fitted over a saucepan of gently simmering water (make sure that the bowl does not touch the water) and beat until the same stage is reached. Allow to cool, beating occasionally.
4 Preheat the oven to 350°F.
5 Sift the flour with the salt gently on top of the egg mixture. Then, using a metal spoon, fold it in gently but thoroughly.
6 Pour into the pans. Bake for 30–35 minutes, or until the cakes are shrunk from the sides of the pans and spring back when touched lightly in the center.
7 Cool in the pans for 2–3 minutes, then turn out onto a wire rack and carefully strip off the wax paper.
8 When the cakes are cool, sandwich with the jam and dredge with sugar.

Variations
SWISS ROLL
Use the same mixture, but bake it in a 13 × 9-inch jelly roll pan, lined with greased wax paper, for 10–12 minutes, until golden-brown and firm to a light touch. Turn out onto a piece of wax paper sprinkled with fine sugar. Spread with ½ cup warmed jam and roll up quickly. Cool on a wire rack.

GENOESE SPONGE
This slightly richer whisked sponge is made in exactly the same way, except that 4 tablespoons of very soft (but not melted) butter is added. Pour this around the edge of the bowl after folding in the flour, then carefully fold into mixture.

[V] VEGAN CHOCOLATE SPONGE CAKE [V]

MAKES ONE 8–8½-inch ROUND CAKE

2 cups self-rising 85% whole-wheat flour
¼ cup cocoa powder
3 teaspoons baking powder
1⅓ cups vanilla sugar or superfine sugar
  with 1½ teaspoons vanilla extract
9 tablespoons sunflower oil
1½ cups water
vegan margarine for greasing
TO DECORATE
1 quantity Chocolate Fudge Icing (p. 316) or
  Chocolate Buttercream (p. 316)
coarsely grated sweetened dark chocolate
confectioner's sugar

1 Preheat the oven to 325°F.
2 Grease two 8–8½-inch shallow cake pans and line the base of each with a circle of greased wax paper.
3 Sift the flour, cocoa powder and baking powder into a bowl. Add the sugar, oil and water. Mix well to a batter-like consistency.
4 Pour the mixture into the prepared pans and bake for about 40 minutes, until the cakes spring back to a light touch in the center.
5 Turn the cakes out onto a wire rack and strip off the wax paper. Allow to cool completely.
6 Sandwich the cakes together with half the fudge icing or chocolate buttercream and coat the top with the rest. Sprinkle on a little grated chocolate and confectioner's sugar.

Variation

VEGAN LEMON CAKE

Use 2½ cups flour and omit the cocoa powder. Replace 2 tablespoons of the water with 2 tablespoons lemon juice, and add the grated rind of 1 lemon. Sandwich the cakes together and coat the top with lemon buttercream or fudge icing and decorate the cake with yellow sugar decorations and leaves cut from angelica.

Leavening Agents

BAKING POWDER Consists of a mixture of bicarbonate of soda and cream of tartar in a base of flour. Low-sodium gluten-free baking powder, made from potassium carbonate and potato flour, is also available.

CREAM OF TARTAR A white powder with a slightly sour flavor, cream of tartar is an ingredient in baking powder and can also be used in soft drinks. If you need to make up a baking powder, the proportions are three parts cream of tartar to one part bicarbonate of soda, and they should be added separately to the mixture.

BICARBONATE OF SODA This white powder is one of the ingredients of baking powder and, because of its effervescent qualities, can also be used as a leavening agent on its own. It is usually dissolved in a little acid liquid, such as buttermilk or milk and vinegar, then mixed quickly with the dry ingredients just before baking.

Vegan Chocolate Sponge Cake; Vegan Lemon Cake

ALL-IN-ONE SPONGE CAKE

This is a sponge that you can whip up in no time at all.

MAKES ONE 8-inch CAKE

DECORATING A SPONGE CAKE

Applying a coating of nuts to the sides of a sponge cake

Decorating the top

Making a feather pattern

1½ cups self-rising 85% whole-wheat flour
1½ teaspoons baking powder
1¼ cups soft light brown sugar
½ pound (2 sticks) butter, softened
3 eggs
extra butter for greasing
FOR THE FILLING AND TOPPING
¼ cup warmed jam, preferably the reduced-sugar type
a little superfine sugar

1 Preheat the oven to 325°F. Grease two 8-inch shallow cake pans and line the base of each with a circle of greased wax paper.
2 Sift the flour with the baking powder into a mixing bowl and add the sugar, butter and eggs.
3 Beat with a wooden spoon for 2 minutes, or in an electric mixer for about 1 minute, until the mixture is smooth, thick and glossy.
4 Spoon the mixture into the prepared pans and level the tops.
5 Bake, without opening the oven door, for 30 minutes, until the cakes spring back to a light touch in the center.
6 Leave the cakes in the pans to cool for 1 minute, then turn them out onto a wire rack and carefully remove the wax paper, then leave the cakes to cool completely.
7 Sandwich the cakes together with the warmed jam and sprinkle the top with superfine sugar.

Variations
VICTORIA SANDWICH CAKE

For this traditional version, omit the baking powder. Cream the butter and sugar together until light and fluffy, then gradually add the beaten eggs, beating well after each addition. Fold in the flour in 2 batches. Bake these cakes at a slightly higher temperature, 375°F, for about 30 minutes.

COFFEE AND WALNUT SPONGE CAKE

Dissolve 1 tablespoon of strong good-quality instant coffee in a little boiling water. Add to the rest of the ingredients, together with ½ cup walnut pieces. Sandwich together and coat with a double quantity of Coffee Buttercream (p. 315) and coat the sides of the cake with ½ cup chopped walnuts.

CHOCOLATE SPONGE CAKE

Replace 3 tablespoons of the flour with 2 tablespoons cocoa powder; or, for a rich, gooey cake, add 8 ounces melted unsweetened dark chocolate and bake a little longer. Sandwich together with red currant, cherry or raspberry jam. Coat the top and sides with Seven-Minute Frosting (p. 317) or Chocolate Buttercream (p. 316), then coat the sides with chopped toasted hazelnuts and the top with a generous amount of coarsely grated chocolate or chocolate curls. Dust with confectioner's sugar.

LEMON SPONGE CAKE

Add the grated rind of 1 lemon to the mixture. Sandwich together with Lemon Curd (p. 341) and dust with confectioner's sugar.

ICED SPONGE FINGERS

Make up a half-quantity of the sponge mixture. Bake for 30 minutes in a shallow 11 × 7-inch pan, lined with greased wax paper. Ice with Glacé Icing (p. 315) and cut into 16–20 fingers. Decorate with chopped nuts or glacé cherries.

FRUIT AND ALMOND FINGERS

To a half-quantity of mixture add 1 cup mixed dried fruit or chopped dates and sprinkle on ¼–½ cup slivered almonds before baking. This does not need icing.

CHOCOLATE ROULADE

This needs to be eaten with a fork, and makes an excellent dessert.

SERVES 6–8

5 eggs, separated
1 cup soft light brown sugar
3 tablespoons hot water
6 ounces unsweetened dark chocolate, melted
confectioner's sugar, sifted
butter for greasing
FOR THE FILLING
one 7-ounce can unsweetened chestnut purée
1¼ cups heavy cream
sugar to taste
a few marrons glacés

1 Preheat the oven to 400°F. Grease a 10 × 14-inch jelly roll pan and line with greased wax paper.
2 Put the egg yolks into a bowl with the sugar and beat until thick and pale.
3 Stir the hot water into the melted chocolate, then gently mix this into the egg yolk mixture. Beat the egg whites until stiff, then fold into the mixture.
4 Pour the mixture into the pan, spreading it out to the edges. Bake for 15 minutes. Remove from the oven and leave to cool in the pan for 10 minutes, then cover with a clean damp dishtowel and leave for a further 10 minutes.
5 Have ready a piece of wax paper sprinkled with confectioner's sugar. Remove the dishtowel and turn the roulade out onto the piece of wax paper. Carefully strip off the lining paper and allow to cool completely.
6 To prepare the filling, beat the chestnut purée until soft, then add half the cream and beat until thick. Sweeten to taste.
7 Trim the edges of the roulade and spread with the chestnut cream. Then carefully roll the roulade up from one long end, using the paper to help.
8 Whip the remaining cream and spoon or pipe it on top of the roulade. Decorate with the marrons glacés and sprinkle with confectioner's sugar. This roulade will keep well in the refrigerator for several hours, and it also freezes well. If

you are going to freeze it, don't decorate it until you are ready to serve.

Variation
CHOCOLATE ROULADE WITH ROSEBUDS
Make the chocolate mixture as described. Fill with 1¼ cups heavy cream, and decorate the plate with fresh pink rosebuds. Lovely for a summer birthday!

Freezing Chocolate Roulade

Chocolate roulade freezes excellently; make it completely, open-freeze, then, when solid, wrap carefully. To use, unwrap and place on a serving dish to thaw, allowing 2–3 hours.

All-in-One Sponge Cake (p. 304); Chocolate Roulade

CARROT CAKE

This cake is easy to make, but is best done by hand, rather than in a food processor, which chops up the nuts and fruit too much, spoiling the texture. Properly made, it's delicious, with a moist texture and spicy flavor. Carrot cake is particularly good for serving at picnics and barbecues, but pack carefully and supply forks and paper napkins.

Madeira Cake (p. 307); Carob Brownies (p. 307)

MAKES ONE 9-inch CAKE

¾ cup sunflower oil
1½ cups (scant) soft light brown sugar
2 large eggs
1 teaspoon vanilla extract
¾ cup cold puréed carrot
⅔ cup canned pineapple chunks, drained and roughly chopped
¾ cup walnuts, roughly chopped
1 cup unsweetened desiccated coconut
1⅓ cups 85% whole-wheat flour
½ teaspoon salt
1 teaspoon ground cinnamon
1 teaspoon baking powder
butter for greasing
TO DECORATE
1 quantity Cream Cheese Frosting (p. 316)
a few walnuts

1 Preheat the oven to 350°F. Grease two 9-inch shallow cake pans and line the base of each with greased wax paper.
2 Put the oil into a large mixing bowl and add the sugar. Mix well, until there are no lumpy bits of sugar.
3 Beat in the eggs, then add the vanilla, carrot purée, pineapple, walnuts and coconut.
4 Mix lightly, then sift in the flour, salt, cinnamon and baking powder. Mix together quickly but gently.
5 Spoon the mixture into the prepared pans and level the tops. Bake for 30 minutes, or until a warmed skewer inserted into the center comes out clean.
6 Turn out onto a wire rack, and allow to cool for 10 minutes, then strip off the lining papers.
7 When the cakes have come completely to room temperature, sandwich them together with half the cream cheese frosting. Spread the rest on top. Decorate with walnuts.

MADEIRA CAKE

I like this best made with unbleached white flour, because this
allows the flavors to come through, though I have made it
successfully too with whole-wheat flour.

MAKES ONE 8-inch CAKE

1¼ cups unbleached white flour
1¼ cups self-rising flour
½ pound plus 2 tablespoons butter
1½ cups (scant) superfine sugar with 1½
    teaspoons vanilla extract
4 large eggs, beaten
2–3 tablespoons milk (optional)
extra butter for greasing
TO DECORATE
2–3 thin slices citron peel

1 Preheat the oven to 350°F. Grease an
8-inch round cake pan and line with
greased wax paper.
2 Sift the flours together onto a piece of
wax paper.
3 Cream the butter with the sugar until
pale and fluffy, then add the eggs, a little
at a time, beating well each time.
4 Add the vanilla extract, then fold in the
flour, adding a little milk if necessary to
give the batter a soft consistency, so that
you can drop it by spoonfuls.
5 Spoon the mixture into the prepared
cake pan. Bake for 20 minutes, then carefully lay the citron peel on top of the cake
and bake for a further 1¼ hours, or until a
warmed skewer inserted into the center
of the cake comes out clean.
6 Turn out onto a wire rack and cool.

Serving Madeira Cake

Madeira cake makes, I think, a very
pleasant accompaniment to a fruit
salad or creamy fool; it is
particularly good with Pashka
(p. 288). Serve in thin slices.

Or, for a quick and easy dessert,
serve with some lightly stewed fruit,
such as black currants, and some
cream or thick yogurt.

LINING A ROUND CAKE PAN

CAROB BROWNIES

Sweet and gooey, these brownies have a crisp, cracked top and a
wonderful flavor. Definitely my favorite recipe using carob.

MAKES 12–16

¼ pound (1 stick) butter
2 ounces sweetened carob bar, broken up
2 eggs
1¼ cups soft light brown sugar
½ cup 85% whole-wheat flour, sifted
½ teaspoon vanilla extract
½ cup walnuts or pecans, chopped
extra butter for greasing
TO FINISH
confectioner's sugar, sifted

1 Preheat the oven to 350°F. Line an
8-inch square shallow cake pan with wax
paper and grease the paper well with
butter.
2 Heat the butter and carob bar together

in a small saucepan until melted. Leave
this to cool.
3 Beat the eggs with the sugar until thick
and pale – this takes 10 minutes with an
electric beater.
4 Fold the melted mixture into the
beaten eggs, then the flour, vanilla and
walnuts or pecans. Mix only until all the
ingredients are moistened.
5 Pour the mixture into the prepared
pan. Bake for 40–45 minutes, or until the
center is set. Don't overbake – the inside
should be gooey.
6 Cool in the pan, then dredge with confectioner's sugar, cut into fingers and
remove from the wax paper.

PARKIN

This parkin keeps well and gets stickier the longer it's kept. Wrap in foil to store.

MAKES 12–16 SLICES

Syrups for Sweetening

GOLDEN SYRUP Refined version of molasses (below) but lacking the nutrients

HONEY The sweetening preferred by natural health experts, though others argue that it is just another form of sugar (but lower in calories); many different flavors available

MALT EXTRACT Syrup obtained from malted cereal grains, especially barley

MAPLE SYRUP Smoky-tasting sap of maple trees; be sure to buy the genuine article, not "maple-flavored syrup"

MIRIN A sweet brown liquid made from rice; has been used in Japan for centuries. Boil for 1 minute before using

MOLASSES Dark, treacly syrup left behind when sugar is refined; rich in iron, calcium and B vitamins

TREACLE A blend of refined syrup and molasses

¾ cup (generous) 100% whole-wheat flour
2 teaspoons baking powder
2 teaspoons ground ginger
¾ cup medium oatmeal
¼ cup real Barbados sugar
⅓ cup dark molasses
⅓ cup light molasses or corn syrup
¼ pound butter or vegan margarine
¾ cup milk or soy milk
extra butter or margarine for greasing

LINING A SQUARE CAKE PAN

1 Preheat the oven to 350°F. Line an 8-inch square cake pan with greased wax paper.
2 Sift the flour with the baking powder and ginger into a bowl. Add the bran from the sieve and the oatmeal.
3 Heat the sugar, the light and dark molasses and butter or vegan margarine gently in a saucepan until melted. Cool until you can comfortably put your hand against the pan, then stir in the milk or soy milk.
4 Add the melted mixture to the dry ingredients. Mix thoroughly, then pour the mixture into the prepared cake pan. Bake for 50–60 minutes, until the parkin feels firm on top.
5 Remove from the pan and cool on a wire rack, then cut into slices and carefully remove from the wax paper.

ROCK CAKES

Easy to make, spicy, and delicious eaten while still warm.

MAKES 10

1½ cups self-rising 85% or 100% whole-wheat flour
½ teaspoon mixed spice
¼ pound (1 stick) butter
7 tablespoons raw light-brown sugar
¾ cup mixed dried fruit
1 egg, beaten with 1 tablespoon milk
extra butter for greasing

1 Preheat the oven to 400°F.
2 Sift the flour with the spice into a mixing bowl, add the bran from the sieve, if you're using 100% whole-wheat flour, then rub in the butter with your fingertips until the mixture looks like fine breadcrumbs.
3 Add two-thirds of the sugar, the fruit and the egg and milk mixture, and mix

lightly, so that the mixture just holds together.
4 Spoon heaping tablespoons of the mixture onto a greased baking sheet, leaving room for spreading, then sprinkle with the rest of the sugar.
5 Bake for about 15 minutes, until lightly browned. Remove with a wide spatula, as these rock cakes are fragile while still warm, and cool on a wire rack.

Variation

VEGAN ROCK CAKES
Use vegan margarine instead of butter, add 1 teaspoon baking powder to the flour and use 4 tablespoons soy milk instead of the milk and egg.

Opposite page, clockwise: Vegan Fruit Cake (p. 310); Rock Cakes; Quick Cupcakes (p. 310); Parkin

QUICK CUPCAKES

These cupcakes make an excellent teatime treat for children.

MAKES 18

1¼ cups self-rising 85% or 100%
    whole-wheat flour
¼ pound (1 stick) butter, softened
½ cup soft light brown or superfine sugar
2 eggs
TO DECORATE
Glacé Icing (p. 315), made with ½ cup
    confectioner's sugar
chopped nuts, or a few chocolate dots and
    sliced glacé cherries

1 Preheat the oven to 375°F.
2 Sift the flour into a mixing bowl and add the bran from the sieve, if you're using 100% whole-wheat flour.
3 Add the butter, sugar and eggs and beat well with a wooden spoon or with an electric mixer, until all the ingredients are well blended and the mixture is thick and slightly glossy looking.
4 Drop a heaping teaspoon of mixture into 18 paper cupcake cases. Stand the cases in a deep cupcake or muffin pan, or on a baking sheet.
5 Bake for 15–20 minutes until the cupcakes have risen and feel firm to a light touch.
6 Cool on a wire rack, then ice.

Types of Tea

The natural partner for a piece of cake is a good cup of tea. Many types are available; for instance:

ASSAM Has a strong flavor and is often blended with other teas

CEYLON Good-quality tea with a delicate flavor

DARJEELING Fine-flavored tea from the Himalayan foothills

EARL GREY Tea flavored with oil of bergamot, originally formulated by the second Earl Grey; best without milk

ENGLISH BREAKFAST Generally a blend of Ceylon and Assam teas

GUNPOWDER One of the Chinese green teas with a sharp flavor

JASMINE My favorite; China tea mixed with jasmine flowers, to be taken without milk

KEEMUM The best China tea, with a delicate flavor and fragrance. Can be taken with or without milk

LAPSANG SOUCHONG A black China tea with a large leaf and a distinctive smoked flavor

Ⓥ # VEGAN FRUIT CAKE Ⓥ

This eggless cake is best fresh, but will keep for 7–10 days
in an airtight container.

MAKES ONE 8-inch ROUND CAKE

2½ cups 100% whole-wheat flour
1 teaspoon mixed spice
¼ pound plus 4 tablespoons vegan margarine
1 cup real Barbados sugar
1½ cups mixed dried fruit
¼ cup mixed candied peel
¼ cup glacé cherries, rinsed and halved
grated rind of 1 orange
2 tablespoons ground almonds
¼ cup blanched almonds, chopped
½ cup soy milk or water
2 tablespoons vinegar
¾ teaspoon baking soda
extra vegan margarine for greasing

1 Preheat the oven to 300°F. Grease an 8-inch cake pan and line with a double layer of greased wax paper.
2 Sift the flour with the mixed spice into a mixing bowl.
3 Rub the margarine into the flour with

your fingertips until the mixture looks like fine breadcrumbs, then stir in the sugar, dried fruit, mixed peel, cherries, orange rind, ground and blanched almonds.
4 Warm half the soy milk or water in a small saucepan and add the vinegar. Dissolve the baking soda in the rest of the soy milk or water, then combine the two mixtures.
5 Stir this mixture into the dry ingredients, stirring well so that everything is combined.
6 Spoon the mixture into the prepared pan. Bake for 2–2½ hours, or until a skewer inserted into the center of the cake comes out clean.
7 Leave the cake in the pan to cool, then remove and strip off the wax paper. Transfer to a wire rack and allow the cake to cool completely.

Dundee Cake

DUNDEE CAKE

This cake is good made with unbleached white or
85% whole-wheat flour.

MAKES ONE 8-inch ROUND CAKE

½ pound butter
1¼ cups soft light brown sugar
4 large eggs, beaten
2½ cups flour
1–2 tablespoons milk
1¼ cups sultanas
1¼ cups currants
1¼ cups raisins
½ cup (scant) candied peel, chopped
½ cup (scant) glacé cherries, halved
⅓ cup ground almonds
grated rind of 1 orange or lemon
⅔ cup blanched almonds, split
extra butter for greasing

1 Preheat the oven to 325°F.
2 Grease an 8-inch round cake pan and
line with a double thickness of greased
wax paper.
3 Cream the butter and sugar in a bowl
until light and fluffy, then add the eggs, a
tablespoon at a time, beating well after
each addition.
4 Sift the flour in on top of the butter
mixture, then fold it in gently.
5 If the mixture seems stiff, add a little
milk; it should drop heavily from the
spoon when you bang it against the side
of the bowl.
6 Gently stir in all the other ingredients
except the split almonds.
7 Turn the mixture into the prepared
cake pan. Arrange the split almonds
lightly on top.
8 Bake for about 2½ hours, or until a
warmed skewer inserted into the center
of the cake comes out clean. Cool the
cake in the pan, then turn out onto a wire
rack, strip off the wax paper and allow to
cool completely.

Variation

SUGARLESS DUNDEE CAKE
Replace the sugar with 1½ cups pitted
dates, stewed in about ½ cup water for
about 10 minutes until soft, then beaten
to a purée. Cool, then use in place of the
sugar.

Cake-Making Tips

The most critical part of making
cakes by the traditional creaming
method is the creaming of the butter
and sugar, which should be done
really thoroughly, until they are pale
and fluffy. The beaten egg, which
needs to be at room temperature,
should be added very gradually, a
tablespoon at a time, with thorough
beating after each addition, so that
the mixture doesn't curdle.

If the worst happens and it does
curdle, however, don't despair. Add
a little flour, then continue to add the
egg and flour alternately. The
texture of the cake will not be so
light and crumbly, but it will still
taste good.

If the top of a cake seems to be
browning too quickly, cover it with
a folded piece of aluminum foil, with
a hole cut in it, as described for the
Rich Fruit Cake (p. 312).

Don't open the oven door when a
cake is cooking until nearly the end
of the cooking time, or the cake will
probably sink in the middle. There's
a delicate chemical reaction taking
place which is upset by a blast of
cold air.

Rich Fruit Cake

Alternative Christmas Cake Decorations

Almond paste can be used on its own, attractively fluted around the top of the cake (as you'd flute a pie), and perhaps lightly scored in a crisscross pattern with a knife. Arrange a candle and holly or marzipan fruit around the center and tie a matching or contrasting ribbon around the outside, or try a jewel-bright topping of crystallized fruits and Brazil nuts, halved pecans and whole cashew nuts or blanched almonds. Stick these to the top of the cake in an attractive pattern with warmed clear honey; brush over with more warmed honey to glaze. For a sparkling finish, brush the whole cake over with clear honey, then sprinkle with colored sugar crystals and little silver balls.

Sieved apricot jam is often used to stick the almond paste on a rich fruit cake, but red currant jelly is easier, as no sieving has to be done.

COVERING FRUIT CAKE WITH ALMOND PASTE

RICH FRUIT CAKE

This is a rich, moist fruit cake, and the 8-inch size is excellent for Christmas or special birthdays or celebrations. It can also be made as a wedding cake: for the quantities for different-sized pans, see opposite.

MAKES ONE 8-inch CAKE

1²/₃ cups currants
1²/₃ cups sultanas
1¹/₄ cups raisins
¹/₄ cup glacé cherries
²/₃ cup whole candied peel
2 cups 85% or 100% whole-wheat flour
1 teaspoon baking powder
¹/₂ teaspoon salt
¹/₂ teaspoon mixed spice
¹/₄ teaspoon freshly grated nutmeg
¹/₂ pound plus 2 tablespoons butter
1¹/₄ cups soft light brown sugar
4 eggs, lightly beaten
grated rind of 1 orange
grated rind of 1 lemon
¹/₂ cup ground almonds
²/₃ cup almonds, blanched and chopped
3 tablespoons sherry
2 tablespoons brandy
extra butter for greasing
TO DECORATE
1 quantity Almond Paste (p. 317)
1 quantity Royal Icing (p. 317)
a piece of ribbon
cake decorations

1 Make sure that the dried fruit is clean; wash it if necessary in warm water, dry with paper towels and spread it out on trays lined with paper towels to dry.
2 Wash the cherries to remove the syrup, then dry and cut into quarters. Chop the candied peel.
3 Sift the flour with the baking powder, salt, mixed spice and nutmeg. Set aside.
4 Preheat the oven to 275°F. Grease an 8-inch round cake pan and line with a double thickness of greased aluminum foil.
5 Cream the butter with the sugar thoroughly, until very light and fluffy, then add the eggs, a tablespoon at a time, beating well between each addition.
6 Fold in the sifted flour mixture, then stir in the fruit, orange and lemon rinds, ground and chopped almonds and the sherry.
7 Spoon the mixture into the cake pan, hollowing out the center slightly.
8 Tie a band of brown paper around the outside of the pan and place a folded piece

of aluminum foil, with a 1-inch-diameter circle cut in the middle, over the top of the brown paper to keep the top and sides of the cake from browning before the inside is done.

9 Bake on a low shelf for 4½–5 hours. Do not open the oven door until the cake has been baking for at least 4 hours.

10 The cake is done when a skewer inserted into the center comes out clean. Allow it to cool in the pan, then prick the top all over with a skewer and pour 2 tablespoons brandy over it.

11 Wrap the cake in a double thickness of aluminum foil and store in an airtight container until needed. It will keep well for 2–3 months and mature; prick the top and sprinkle a little more brandy over it occasionally during this time if you wish.

12 A week before you want to ice the cake, trim it to level it, then brush with ¼ cup melted red currant jelly.

13 Roll out two-thirds of the almond paste and cut into 2 pieces to cover the sides of the cake; press them into position.

14 Roll the remaining almond paste into a circle to cover the top; press down and trim. Leave the cake in a dry, airy place for 3–7 days.

15 Put all the icing on top of the cake and roll it backwards and forwards a few times with a palette knife to remove any air bubbles.

16 Spread the icing over the top and sides of the cake. Finally use the blade of the palette knife to flick the icing up into peaks. Arrange decorations on the cake and leave for at least 24 hours to set, then tie a ribbon around the cake.

Simnel Cake

For this traditional Easter cake, put half the rich fruit cake mixture into the pan, then top with a ¼–½-inch-thick circle of almond paste the same size as the pan. Spoon the rest of the mixture on top and bake as usual. Cool, then stick another circle of almond paste on top of the cake and a circle of 11 balls of almond paste (representing the Apostles minus Judas) around the edge. Put the cake briefly under a moderate broiler just to brown the almond paste. Decorate with ribbon, and flowers and Easter chicks, if you like.

Quantities for rich fruit cakes in various pan sizes

Round pan sizes	*6 inches*	*7 inches*	*8 inches*	*9 inches*	*10 inches*	*12 inches*
Square pan sizes	*5 inches*	*6 inches*	*7 inches*	*8 inches*	*9 inches*	*11 inches*
Depth of cake	*2½ inches*	*3 inches*	*3 inches*	*3 inches*	*3½ inches*	*3½ inches*
currants	1 cup	1¼ cups	1⅔ cups	2¼ cups	3 cups	4¾ cups
sultanas	1 cup	1¼ cups	1⅔ cups	2¼ cups	3 cups	4¾ cups
raisins	1 cup	1 cup	1¼ cups	1½ cups	2¼ cups	3⅓ cups
glacé cherries	2 tbs	2 tbs	¼ cup	¼ cup	⅓ cup	½ cup
whole candied peel	¼ cup	½ cup	⅔ cup	¾ cup	1¼ cups	2 cups
flour	1 cup	1½ cups	2 cups	2⅔ cups	3½ cups	5⅔ cups
baking powder	½ tsp	½ tsp	1 tsp	1 tsp	2 tsp	2 tsp
salt	pinch	pinch	½ tsp	⅔ tsp	1 tsp	1 tsp
mixed spice	⅓ tsp	½ tsp	1 tsp	1 tsp	2 tsp	2 tsp
freshly grated nutmeg	pinch	pinch	¼ tsp	½ tsp	1 tsp	1 tsp
butter	10 tbs	14 tbs	18 tbs	¾ pound	1 pound	1⅔ pound
soft brown sugar	¾ cup	1 cup	1¼ cups	1¾ cups	2¼ cups	4 cups
eggs, lightly beaten	2	3	4	5	7	10
grated rind of orange	¼	½	1	1 large	2–3	2–3
grated rind of lemon	¼	½	1	1 large	2–3	2–3
ground almonds	¼ cup	⅓ cup	½ cup	½ cup	¾ cup	1¼ cups
almonds, blanched and chopped	¼ cup	½ cup	⅔ cup	⅔ cup	1⅓ cups	1¾ cups
sherry	1 tbs	2 tbs	3 tbs	3 tbs	5 tbs	6 tbs
brandy	1 tbs	1½ tbs	2 tbs	2 tbs	3–4 tbs	4 tbs
almonds to make paste	1⅔ cups	2½ cups	3¼ cups	4 cups	6¼ cups	8¼ cups
confectioner's sugar for royal icing	1 pound	1½ pounds	2 pounds	2½ pounds	3½ pounds	5 pounds

MERINGUES

MAKES 6 WHOLE MERINGUES

2 egg whites
a pinch of cream of tartar
½ cup superfine sugar
1¼ cups heavy cream

1 Preheat the oven to 300°F. Line a baking sheet with non-stick baking parchment.
2 Put the egg whites into a clean, grease-free bowl with the cream of tartar and beat until stiff and dry. You should be able to turn the bowl upside down without the egg white falling out.
3 Next beat in half the sugar. When this has been absorbed, beat in the remaining sugar, until the meringue is very stiff and glossy.
4 Drop spoonfuls of the mixture onto the prepared baking sheet, making 12 meringues in all.
5 Put the meringues into the oven, then reduce the heat to 200°F. Bake the meringues for 1½–2 hours, until they are dried out.

6 Turn the oven off and leave the meringues to cool in the oven. Remove the meringues from the baking parchment with a palette knife.
7 Whip the cream and use this to sandwich the meringues together in pairs. Serve as soon as possible.

Variations

HAZELNUT MERINGUES
Fold about ½ cup roasted, peeled and finely ground hazelnuts into the meringues after the sugar has been added. These are delicious sandwiched with cream, as described, and served as a dessert, with Hot Chocolate Sauce (p. 300).

MINIATURE MERINGUES
Make as described, but drop heaping teaspoons of the mixture onto the baking sheet; or use a piping bag fitted with a ½-inch shell nozzle to make tiny meringues. Bake for 1½–2 hours. Sandwich together in pairs as described.

Using Broken Meringues

Crush the meringues even more, so that they are in bite-sized pieces, then fold them into whipped cream. Or, to make a wonderful dessert, crush a whole batch of meringues, fold into 1¼ cups lightly whipped heavy cream, then gently mix in a purée made from 1 pint black currants, cooked, sweetened and sieved, to give a ripple effect. Cover and keep in the freezer until required. A useful dessert to have in the freezer, as it can be served without thawing.

Piping Tip

Many people feel nervous about using a piping bag because they get hardly any practice. The way to become an expert is to have on hand a plastic piping bag, fitted with a star nozzle, and every time you're serving cream or have some butter icing left over, have some fun piping it (and let eager children try, too). Or even make up a batch of butter icing and keep practicing with it. It's surprising how quickly you can get the knack, and once you have, it's satisfying to be able to give a cake a professional look quickly and easily.

ÉCLAIRS

MAKES 8

1 quantity Choux Pastry (p. 271)
1¼ cups heavy cream, whipped
4 ounces semisweet dark chocolate, melted

1 Preheat the oven to 400°F.
2 Grease a baking sheet, then moisten it under cold water.
3 Pipe or spoon the choux pastry mixture onto the baking sheet to make strips about 4 inches long and 1 inch wide.
4 Bake for about 35 minutes, until crisp and golden.
5 Make a slit in the side of each éclair, then cool on a wire rack.
6 Just before serving, fill the éclairs with whipped cream, piping it into the slit in

the side of each éclair; then carefully dip each top into the melted chocolate and leave for a few minutes to set.

Variation

PROFITEROLES
Pipe or spoon the choux pastry mixture into small balls, about the size of walnuts. Bake at 400°F on a greased cookie sheet for 15–20 minutes, slit, and cool on a wire rack. Fill each with whipped cream, then heap them up in a pyramid shape on a flat serving dish or cake stand and pour some Hot Chocolate Sauce (p. 300) over the top. Serve the rest of the sauce separately.

GLACÉ ICING

TO TOP AN 8–9 inch ROUND CAKE

1 cup confectioner's sugar
1–2 tablespoons water

1 Sift the confectioner's sugar into a mixing bowl and beat in the water a little at a time. Continue beating in until you have a thick mixture.
2 Use the icing immediately to ice one large cake or 18 cupcakes.

SIMPLE BUTTERCREAM

TO TOP AND FILL, OR COAT, AN 8-inch ROUND CAKE

Meringues and Hazelnut Meringues (p. 314)

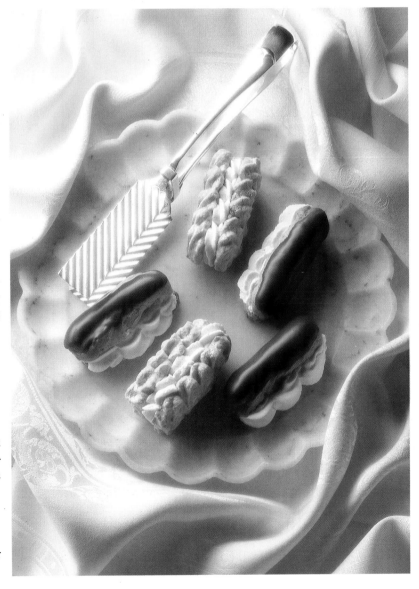

¼ pound butter or vegan margarine
1⅓ cups confectioner's sugar
1–2 tablespoons hot water

1 Beat the butter or vegan margarine in a mixing bowl until creamy, then sift in the confectioner's sugar and beat until light.
2 Add enough hot water to loosen the mixture a little, beating well.

Variations
CHOCOLATE BUTTERCREAM
Melt 2 ounces semisweet dark chocolate, or dissolve 1–2 tablespoons cocoa powder in hot water; beat into the mixture.

COFFEE BUTTERCREAM
Dissolve 2 teaspoons good-quality strong instant coffee (French roast or espresso type) in a little hot water; beat into the mixture.

VANILLA BUTTERCREAM
Add a few drops of vanilla extract.

LEMON OR ORANGE
BUTTERCREAM
Add 1 teaspoon grated orange or lemon rind to the mixture, and replace 1 tablespoon of the water with orange or lemon juice.

REDUCED-SUGAR
BUTTERCREAM
Replace ⅓ cup of the confectioner's sugar with nonfat dry milk. Beat well.

FRENCH BUTTERCREAM

This is light and delicately flavored, worth the extra effort involved, although it isn't difficult to make.

TO TOP AND FILL, OR COAT, AN 8-inch ROUND CAKE

Sugar

Sugar is produced from sugar beets and from sugarcane. Sugarcane contains a rich, sticky sap, which consists of water, molasses and sugar, and this sap goes through a number of refining processes during which the sugar crystals are separated from the molasses. Natural brown sugars, called Light Muscovado, Muscovado and Molasses, are the sugars that retain the natural molasses, light brown sugar having the least, and molasses sugar the most. You can tell a genuine brown cane sugar (as compared to refined white sugar with molasses added later) because it should have the name of the country of origin on the package; this applies to Demerara sugar (raw light brown sugar) as well as the soft brown sugars.

Types of Coffee

A cup of coffee goes particularly well with the richness of desserts such as the Little Baked Custards and Chocolate Pots. There are many varieties to choose from; it is interesting to experiment with different ones and to blend two or more. Some of the best are:

BLUE MOUNTAIN Very rare and expensive; the best, full-bodied, with a fine, sweet flavor

BRAZILIAN Smooth and mild

COLOMBIAN Strong, rich flavor

FRENCH OR ITALIAN ROAST Dark-roasted, with a strong flavor

JAVA A good after-dinner coffee with a mellow flavor

KENYA Mild, has a slightly sharp flavor: another good after-dinner coffee

MOCHA Strong but with a subtle flavor

MYSORE Rich and flavorsome, one of my favorites

VIENNA Smooth and strong

2 egg yolks
¼ cup vanilla sugar, or superfine sugar and a
*   few drops of vanilla extract*
½ cup milk
½ pound plus 2 tablespoons unsalted butter

1 Beat the egg yolks with half the vanilla sugar or superfine sugar until the mixture is pale and light.
2 Heat the milk with the rest of the sugar in a heavy-bottomed saucepan, then pour over the egg yolks. Return the mixture to the pan and stir until it coats the back of the spoon.
3 Remove from the heat and allow to cool, then strain.

4 Beat the butter until light and fluffy, then gradually beat in the custard mixture a little at a time, as well as the vanilla extract, if used.

Variations
COFFEE BUTTERCREAM
Make as described, adding 2 teaspoons good-quality strong instant coffee (French roast or espresso type) to the hot milk and stirring until dissolved. Omit the vanilla.

CHOCOLATE BUTTERCREAM
Melt 2 ounces semisweet dark chocolate and add to the butter with the custard.

CREAM CHEESE FROSTING

TO TOP AND FILL, OR COAT, A 9-inch ROUND CAKE

1 cup cream cheese
4 tablespoons butter, softened
¼ cup soft light brown sugar
a few drops of vanilla extract

1 Put all the ingredients into a mixing bowl.
2 Beat well until thoroughly ·blended, light and fluffy.

Ⅴ   FUDGE ICING   Ⅴ

The flavoring of fudge icing can be varied as suggested for Simple Buttercream (p. 315).

TO TOP AND FILL, OR COAT, AN 8–9-inch ROUND CAKE

4 tablespoons butter or vegan margarine
3 tablespoons water
1⅔ cups confectioner's sugar
a few drops of vanilla extract

1 Heat the butter or vegan margarine and water in a saucepan until melted. Remove from the heat and sift in the confectioner's sugar.
2 Add the vanilla and beat well. The icing will thicken up as it cools.

FONDANT ICING

TO COAT AN 8–9-inch ROUND CAKE

3 cups confectioner's sugar
¼ teaspoon cream of tartar
1 egg white

1 Sift the sugar with the cream of tartar into a mixing bowl.

2 Beat the egg white lightly, just to break it up, then gradually stir it into the sugar mixture, to give a firm but pliable consistency.
3 Roll the icing out on a surface dusted with confectioner's sugar.

Cake Decorations

Fondant icing is easy to use because you simply roll it out. Decorations can be cut out with pastry cutters; children's pastry-making sets have some interesting shapes.

ALMOND PASTE

TO COAT AN 8–9-inch ROUND CAKE

3¼ cups ground almonds
2¼ cups soft light brown or superfine sugar
1 teaspoon lemon juice
a few drops of almond extract
2 eggs, beaten

1 Mix all the ingredients together in a mixing bowl to give a pliable consistency. Do not overwork the mixture or it may become oily.
2 Use immediately, or keep wrapped in plastic wrap.

Crystallized Violets and Rose Petals

A pretty, fragrant garnish for ice cream, cheesecake, sorbet or a special cake. Wash the violets or rose petals gently, shake dry. Beat an egg white until frothy, then dip the rose petals or violets first into this and then into superfine sugar to coat thoroughly. Spread out on baking sheets lined with nonstick baking parchment and bake in a very cool oven (lowest setting) until dry and crisp. Cool completely on wire racks, then store in an airtight container.

ROYAL ICING

TO COAT AN 8-inch ROUND CAKE

4 egg whites
6 cups confectioner's sugar, sifted
1 tablespoon lemon juice
2 tablespoons clear honey (to prevent icing from hardening)

1 Beat the egg whites until frothy, then gradually beat in all the other ingredients.
2 Beat until the mixture thickens and stands in peaks. Use immediately.

SEVEN-MINUTE FROSTING

This icing sets crisp on the outside, with a soft, marshmallowy texture inside.

TO COAT A 9-inch ROUND CAKE

2 large egg whites
1½ cups superfine sugar
¼ cup water
¼ teaspoon salt
¼ teaspoon cream of tartar

1 Put all the ingredients into a mixing bowl and beat until foamy.
2 Set the bowl over a saucepan of simmering water (making sure that the bowl does not touch the water) and beat until the mixture stands in soft peaks – about 7 minutes. Use immediately.

MENU

Christmas Dinner

SERVES 8

Avocado on a Raspberry Coulis
148

Brazil Nut Roast en Croûte
236

Vegetarian Gravy
172

Cranberry Sauce
174

Bread Sauce
175

Julienne of Carrots
184

Brussels Sprouts

Christmas Pudding with Brandy Butter
296

All the traditional Christmas flavors – apart from the turkey, of course – are present in this dinner, and the Brazil Nut Roast en Croûte makes a handsome center-piece. This can be made well in advance and kept in the refrigerator for a day or two, or frozen for up to 4 weeks. The pudding, of course, can also be made several weeks beforehand and kept in a cool, dry place. The cranberry sauce and vegetarian gravy can be made the day before. The raspberry coulis for the first course can be made the day before, too, but the dish needs to be assembled not more than an hour before you want to eat it. Garnish it with holly berries, but remove them before serving.

The nut and herb flavors in the roast need a firm wine to stand up to them, such as a Châteauneuf-du-Pape; or, if you prefer a white, choose a sturdy medium-dry one.

Cookies

Cookies are easy and rewarding to make and delightful for when you want to offer something light with a cup of tea or coffee, or for giving a crisp texture to a smooth dessert such as a fruit fool or ice cream. Cookies also make appealing gifts, packed in pretty boxes or jars, decorated with colored ribbons, fabric or paper flowers and tissue paper. There are many different types, ranging from the quick tray bakes, such as Oatmeal Bars, Easy Shortbread and Date Fingers, in which the mixture goes straight into the baking pan and is cut up after it is cooked, to the more complicated but delicious Brandysnaps (p. 324) and Almond Tuiles (p. 325).

Freezing Cookies

Cookies freeze excellently; cool them thoroughly, then spread them out on a tray and freeze until solid. Pack in a rigid container.

Cookies do not take long to thaw; put them in a single layer on a wire rack and leave at room temperature for 30–60 minutes.

OATMEAL BARS

One of the quickest recipes ever, oatmeal bars keep well in an airtight container.

MAKES 12–16

¼ pound plus 4 tablespoons butter or vegan margarine
1 cup real Barbados sugar
2 tablespoons light molasses
1½ cups rolled oats

1 Preheat the oven to 375°F.
2 Grease a 7 × 11-inch jelly roll pan.
3 Melt the butter or vegan margarine, sugar and syrup gently in a saucepan.

Remove from the heat and mix in the oats.
4 Spread the mixture into the pan and press down evenly with the back of a spoon to make a smooth layer that fills all the corners. Bake for 20–30 minutes, until brown all over.
5 Mark into fingers while still hot, then leave in the pan until cold. The oatmeal bars become firm as they cool.

EASY SHORTBREAD

MAKES 12 PIECES

¼ pound plus 4 tablespoons butter or vegan margarine
7 tablespoons soft light brown sugar
1¾ cups 85% whole-wheat flour

1 Preheat the oven to 300°F.
2 Beat the butter or vegan margarine with the sugar until blended, then add the flour and mix together to form a dough.
3 Knead the dough on a floured surface, then press into an 8-inch tart pan or pie pan and prick the top all over with a fork.

Bake for 1¼–1½ hours until set and just beginning to turn golden.
4 Mark the shortbread into sections with a sharp knife, then leave to cool completely in the pan.

Variation

SHORTBREAD COOKIES
Make the mixture as described, then roll it out about ⅛ inch thick. Cut into circles, place on a baking sheet and bake for about 30 minutes.

ICEBOX COOKIES

MAKES ABOUT 80

¼ pound (1 stick) butter

1 cup vanilla sugar, or superfine sugar and ½
  teaspoon vanilla extract

1 large egg

1½ cups plain 85% whole-wheat flour

2 teaspoons baking powder

a pinch of salt

1 Cream the butter with the sugar and vanilla extract if used.

2 Beat in the egg, then sift the flour with the baking powder and salt on top. Mix well, to make a dough.

3 Turn the dough onto a lightly floured surface and form into a sausage about 2 inches in diameter. Wrap in plastic wrap and chill for several hours.

4 When you're ready to bake the cookies, preheat the oven to 375°F.

5 Using a sharp knife, cut ⅛-inch slices from the cookie roll and place on baking sheets, leaving room for the cookies to spread.

6 Bake for 8–10 minutes, until the cookies are just turning brown at the edges. Remove the cookies from the oven and transfer them to a wire rack to cool completely.

*Icebox Cookies
Tip*

This dough will keep in the freezer for up to 2 weeks, ready for you to cut thin slices off it for baking whenever you want fresh cookies.

V   # DATE FINGERS   V

MAKES 12–16

1½ cups unsweetened pitted dates, chopped

½ cup (generous) water

1½ cups self-rising 85% or 100%
  whole-wheat flour

½ teaspoon salt

¼ pound butter or vegan margarine

3 tablespoons cold water

1 Preheat the oven to 400°F.

2 Put the dates into a saucepan with the ½ cup water and cook gently for 5 minutes until the dates are soft and the liquid is absorbed.

3 Mash the dates, carefully discarding any hard pieces of stem or pit. Cool.

4 Put the flour into a mixing bowl with the salt. Rub in the fat with your fingertips until the mixture looks like fine breadcrumbs.

5 Add the 3 tablespoons water, then press the mixture together to make a dough. Roll out half to fit a 7 × 11-inch jelly roll pan.

6 Spread the date mixture on top of the pastry. Roll out the rest of the pastry to fit the top, press into position and trim the edges.

7 Prick the pastry all over with a fork.

Bake for 30 minutes, until firm and lightly browned.

8 Cool for 30 minutes in the pan, then cut into fingers, ease out of the pan and place on a wire rack to cool completely.

Date Fingers

V # OATCAKES V

These are thin, crisp oatcakes, based on the recipe given in one of my favorite books, *Don't Mix Foods Which Fight*, by Doris Grant and Jean Joice. Make sure the oatmeal smells and tastes really fresh.

MAKES 16

Serving Idea for Cookies

Homemade cookies look wonderful served in a shallow basket; have at least two varieties and pile them up generously. Presented like this, cookies can be served as a quick and easy dessert.

Storing Cookies

Store cookies in an airtight container to keep them fresh and crisp.

½ teaspoon salt
1 teaspoon unsalted butter or vegan margarine
½ cup boiling water
1 cup medium oatmeal
flour for rolling out

1 Preheat the oven to 350°F.
2 Stir the salt and butter or vegan margarine into the boiling water, then add to the oatmeal in a bowl. Mix well, then leave for 2–3 minutes to allow the oatmeal to swell.
3 Turn the oat mixture onto a floured board and knead lightly.
4 Divide the oat mixture into 2 pieces.

Roll each piece into a circle about 4 inches in diameter, then cut each circle into 8 triangles.
5 Roll each triangle as thinly as possible, rolling from cut edge to cut edge (not from the outer edge to the point) to make a good wedge shape.
6 Using a wide spatula or pancake turner, transfer the oatcakes to a lightly greased baking sheet and bake for 20–25 minutes, carefully turning them over halfway through the cooking time, until the oatcakes are pale golden, crisp and curled at the edges.
7 Transfer to a wire rack and allow to cool completely.

CRUNCHY PEANUT COOKIES

These cookies are quick to make and very popular, especially with children. They freeze well and thaw rapidly.

MAKES ABOUT 36

Choosing Peanut Butter

Look for a variety which does not contain emulsifiers and other additives. It may have a layer of oil on top (because of the lack of emulsifiers), but this is normal; just stir the peanut butter before using it.

5 tablespoons butter or vegan margarine
⅓ cup soft light brown sugar
⅓ cup vanilla sugar, or superfine sugar and a few drops of vanilla extract
1 egg
4 tablespoons crunchy peanut butter
¾ cup (generous) 85% whole-wheat flour
1 teaspoon baking powder
½ teaspoon salt
⅓ cup chopped roasted peanuts (if salted, omit the ½ teaspoon salt)

1 Preheat the oven to 350°F.
2 Cream the butter or vegan margarine with the sugars and vanilla, if used, then add the egg and peanut butter and beat again until light.
3 Sift the flour with the baking powder and salt and mix in. Add the peanuts and mix again until the ingredients are thoroughly combined.
4 Roll teaspoonfuls of the mixture into small balls, then place on a greased baking sheet, allowing plenty of room for spreading, and flatten them slightly with the palm of your hand.
5 Bake for 12–15 minutes. Cool slightly, then transfer to a wire rack to cool completely.

Variation
CHOCOLATE OR CAROB CHIP COOKIES
For this delicious variation, leave out the peanut butter and peanuts. Stir in ¼ pound chocolate or carob chips and ¼ cup chopped peeled hazelnuts after adding the flour.

CRUNCHY ORANGE COOKIES

MAKES 20–24

¼ pound (1 stick) butter
7 tablespoons soft light brown sugar
1 egg
grated rind of 1 orange
¾ (generous) cup self-rising 81% or 85%
    whole-wheat flour
crushed wheat flakes, corn flakes or slivered
    almonds for coating
extra butter for greasing

1 Preheat the oven to 350°F.
2 Grease one or two large baking sheets.
3 Cream the butter with the sugar, then beat in the egg and grated orange rind. Add the flour and mix until the ingredients are combined.
4 Roll heaping teaspoonfuls of the mixture in crushed wheat flakes, corn flakes or slivered almonds.
5 Place the little balls on the baking sheets, allowing a little space for spreading, and flatten them slightly with the palm of your hand.
6 Bake for 15 minutes, until golden-brown. Transfer to a wire rack to cool completely.

Left to right: Oatcakes (p. 322);
Crunchy Peanut Cookies (p. 322);
Crunchy Orange Cookies; Gingersnaps
(p. 325)

Ⅴ   CRUMBLY ALMOND COOKIES   Ⅴ

The best cookies of all, in the opinion of my eight-year-old
daughter, Claire. They are excellent for serving with tea or coffee,
or with ice cream or fruit salads.

MAKES 40

9 tablespoons butter or vegan margarine
⅓ cup vanilla sugar or superfine sugar and a
    few drops of vanilla extract
1 cup 85% whole-wheat flour
¼ teaspoon salt
¼ cup slivered almonds, crushed
2 tablespoons slivered almonds
extra butter for greasing

1 Preheat the oven to 325°F.
2 In a medium mixing bowl, cream the butter or vegan margarine with the sugar until light and fluffy.
3 Sift the flour with the salt into the bowl, then stir this into the creamed mixture, with the crushed almonds.
4 Roll teaspoonfuls into small balls, then place on a greased baking sheet, allowing plenty of room for spreading. Flatten the cookies with the prongs of a fork. Decorate with slivered almonds.
5 Bake for 25 minutes, until golden. Cool slightly, then transfer to a wire rack to cool completely.

BRANDYSNAPS

$\boxed{V}$ $\boxed{V}$

A delicious treat on their own, and also an excellent
accompaniment to a creamy dessert or fruit salad, brandysnaps are
easy to make if you use nonstick baking parchment and don't try
to roll them up too soon.

MAKES 20

Serving Ideas for Cookies

Brandysnaps, filled with cream, make a luxurious accompaniment to a simple fruit salad, for a special meal.

Serve fruit salad, ice cream or sorbet in a thin, crisp "cup" made from an almond tuile.

If you haven't time to make a dessert or just want to serve something light, arrange several types of homemade cookies in a pretty basket and offer with coffee or with little bowls of chilled, strained Greek yogurt.

4 tablespoons butter or vegan margarine
½ cup superfine sugar
2 tablespoons light molasses
1 cup 85% whole-wheat flour, sifted
½ teaspoon ground ginger
½ teaspoon grated lemon rind
a little oil
FOR THE FILLING (OPTIONAL)
½ cup (generous) heavy cream whipped with
*   1–2 tablespoons brandy, optional, or*
*   Vegan Cream (p. 301)*

1 Preheat the oven to 350°F.
2 Melt the butter or vegan margarine, sugar and molasses gently in a small saucepan.
3 Remove from the heat and stir in the flour, ginger and lemon rind. Allow the mixture to cool.
4 Line a large baking sheet with nonstick baking parchment.
5 Drop 2 heaping teaspoonfuls of the mixture onto the baking sheet, placing them well apart, then flatten them slightly. Bake for 7–8 minutes, until evenly browned.

6 Cool on the tray for 3–4 minutes, until you can comfortably pick up the brandysnaps. Quickly roll them up by wrapping them around the oiled handle of a wooden spoon. Slide them off onto a wire rack. If the brandysnaps harden before you manage to roll them up, put them back into the oven for a minute or two to soften them up.
7 Make the rest of the brandysnaps in the same way; the same nonstick baking parchment can be used for the whole batch.
8 Serve the brandysnaps plain, or fill them with whipped cream (spiked with brandy if you like). Insert the filling with a teaspoon or a piping bag fitted with a shell nozzle.

Brandysnaps

GINGERSNAPS

These ever-popular ginger cookies are easy to make, crisp and delicious. They keep well either in the freezer or in an airtight container.

MAKES 36

4 tablespoons butter
½ cup superfine sugar
1½ tablespoons light molasses
1 tablespoon beaten egg
1¼ cups self-rising 85% whole-wheat flour
1 teaspoon baking soda
1 teaspoon ground ginger
extra butter for greasing

1 Preheat the oven to 350°F.
2 In a medium mixing bowl cream the butter with the sugar and molasses, then add the egg and beat again until the batter is light.
3 Sift in the whole-wheat flour, baking soda and ginger, then mix to a dough.
4 Divide the dough into 36 small pieces, roll each into a ball and place well apart on greased baking sheets.
5 Bake for 12–15 minutes. Cool slightly, then transfer to a wire rack to cool completely.

Gingersnap Dessert Log

Gingersnaps can be made into a delicious dessert log. Sandwich the cookies together with whipped heavy cream to make a log shape. Cover with more cream and decorate with chopped crystallized ginger. Chill for 3–4 hours to allow the cookies to soften in the cream and for the flavors to blend.

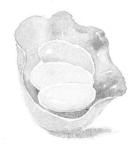

ALMOND TUILES

These thin, crisp cookies make an ideal accompaniment to ice creams and light, fruity desserts. They can also be made larger, to make edible petal cases for holding ice cream.

MAKES 16

2 egg whites
½ cup vanilla sugar, or superfine sugar and
 ½ teaspoon vanilla extract
½ cup 85% whole-wheat flour
4 tablespoons butter, melted
½ cup slivered almonds

1 Preheat the oven to 375°F.
2 Line a large baking sheet with nonstick baking parchment.
3 Beat the egg whites until frothy, then beat in the sugar. Gently mix in the flour, butter and almonds.
4 Spread the mixture on the prepared baking sheet, making circles about 4 inches across. Bake for 7–8 minutes, until flecked with golden-brown.
5 Allow the cookies to stand for a second or two, then immediately lift them off the baking sheet with a spatula and place over the rim of a large empty bowl or over a stick balanced over 2 pans, so that they harden into a curved tuile shape.
6 Make the rest of the tuiles in the same way, reusing the paper. When the cookies are cool, put into an airtight container.

Variations
CIGARETTES RUSSES
Make as described, but omit the almonds. As you take the cookies off the baking tray, roll them tightly around a greased wooden spoon handle. Cool slightly, then ease the rolled cookies off the handle and place on a wire rack.

FLOWER CUPS FOR HOLDING ICE CREAM
To make these, draw 6-inch circles on nonstick baking parchment and spread the uncooked mixture into these. Bake for about 10–15 minutes. As you take the cookies off the baking sheet, put them over a lightly oiled upturned tumbler, pressing them down with your hands to make a cup shape and pulling the edges out slightly to give a petal effect.

Cookie-Making Tips

Make the cookies the same size and thickness so that they take the same amount of time to cook.

Use a flat baking pan or sheet to enable the heat of the oven to reach the sides of the cookies.

Baking sticky cookies like brandysnaps on a pan lined with nonstick paper makes it easy to lift them off when they are done.

Leave space around the cookies to allow them to spread during cooking. Some cookies, such as brandysnaps, spread considerably.

Let the cookies cool for a few minutes on the pan before removing with a spatula and placing on a wire rack to cool.

Cookies that are to be rolled or shaped after baking, such as brandysnaps and almond tuiles, need to cool on the baking sheet until they are firm enough to lift but still pliable. Once you've made the first batch, you soon recognize this stage. If the cookies harden too much, they will soften again if you pop them back into the oven for a minute or two.

Bread and Scones

Nothing ensures your reputation as a good cook more quickly than making your own bread, and there is something particularly satisfying about being able to offer friends and family your own home-baked bread. Yet making bread from a simple recipe is no more difficult than making a cake. This chapter contains my favorite recipes for yeast breads together with a selection of non-yeast breads, muffins and scones, which are also easy to bake and make a pleasant change. If you like bread, you can easily make a bigger batch of the Quick and Easy Whole-Wheat Bread (p. 328); simply double or triple all the ingredients.

Making Tea and Herb Tea

The method for making tea is the same, whether you are using herb or flower tea, or traditional tea leaves. Warm the pot and, if you like normally strong tea, put in a teaspoon of tea for each person and, if it's for more than three people, an extra spoon for the pot. If, like me, you like weak tea without milk, use less tea. I use just 1 teaspoon to the pot; it's a question of personal taste. Bring a kettle of fresh cold water to a boil, then pour this onto the tea. Leave to infuse for 2–3 minutes for China or herb tea, 4–5 minutes for Indian tea, then strain into cups. Add milk or slices of lemon as required. For herb teas, try adding a little cinnamon or a dash of honey.

Herb Teas

Many different herb teas are available; buy in small quantities and experiment until you find the ones that you like. Try serving scones, muffins and tea breads with herb teas instead of ordinary tea. Individual herb teas have healing properties:

PEPPERMINT Helps digestive upsets

COMFREY Has cleansing properties

CAMOMILE Calming and sleep-inducing

LEMON VERBENA and LEMON GRASS Good as tonics

GOLDENROD A natural diuretic

LINDEN FLOWER Helps you relax

EASY WHOLE-WHEAT SCONES

Serve with butter and clear honey, or with jam and cream.

MAKES 10

1½ cups 100% whole-wheat flour
2 teaspoons baking powder
4 tablespoons butter
2 tablespoons sugar
1 egg, beaten, with milk added to equal ½ cup (generous)

1 Preheat the oven to 425°F.
2 Sift the flour with the baking powder into a mixing bowl, then add the butter and rub in with your fingertips. Mix in the sugar. Add the egg and milk and mix to a soft but not sticky dough.
3 Turn the dough out onto a floured board and knead lightly, then press out to a depth of at least ½ inch.
4 Cut the scones out with a 2-inch round cutter and place them on a floured baking sheet.
5 Bake for 12–15 minutes, until the scones are golden-brown and the sides spring back when lightly pressed. Cool on a wire rack, or serve immediately so that the butter melts right into them.

Variations
VEGAN SCONES
Use ½ cup (generous) soy milk instead of the egg and milk, and 6 tablespoons vegan margarine instead of the butter, for extra richness.

CHEESE SCONES
These are delicious to eat warm from the oven, for a quick lunch or supper. They're good buttered, with a little salad, and some fresh, firm tomatoes and crisp celery sticks. Omit the sugar. Add ½ teaspoon mustard powder and ½ cup (scant) grated cheese to the mixture. Sprinkle another ½ cup (scant) grated cheese on top of the scones before baking.

RAISIN SCONES
Add ¾ cup raisins to the mixture. Half a teaspoon mixed spice or cinnamon is also a pleasant addition.

LIGHT BROWN SCONES
Replace the flour with 85% whole-wheat flour, or half whole-wheat and half plain unbleached flour.

CRANBERRY SCONES
For this Christmas version, add 1 cup cooked sweetened cranberries to the mixture and a good pinch of ground cloves. Cook as above.

[V]

BRAN, HONEY AND SULTANA MUFFINS

[V] *Clockwise from top: Whole-Wheat Banana Tea Bread (p. 330); Bran, Honey and Sultana Muffins; Easy Whole-Wheat Scones (p. 326)*

These healthy muffins are quick and easy to make and are delicious served warm from the oven. You can use raisins instead of sultanas or a mixture of both, if preferred.

MAKES 12

²/₃ cup 100% whole-wheat flour
¼ cup bran
1 tablespoon baking powder
a pinch of salt
²/₃ cup sultanas
2 tablespoons clear honey
¼ cup sunflower oil
⅓–½ cup water
a little extra oil for greasing

1 Preheat the oven to 350°F. Grease a 12-section muffin pan.

2 Put the flour and bran into a mixing bowl with the baking powder, salt and sultanas. Add the honey, sunflower oil and water.

3 Mix well to make a batter-like consistency.

4 Spoon the mixture into the muffin pan, dividing it equally among the 12 sections.

5 Bake for 15–20 minutes, until the muffins have risen and feel firm to a light touch. Serve warm.

Making Coffee

The traditional way to make coffee is to put coarse grounds into a pot, pour on almost boiling water, cover, allow to infuse for 4 minutes, then strain into cups. Allow ½ cup coffee to 2½ cups water.

My favorite ways of making coffee are the filter method, pouring almost boiling water onto finely ground coffee in a filter and letting it drip through into a pot; and the cafetière method, where you put medium-ground coffee into the cafetière, pour on the water, allow to infuse for 4 minutes, then push the plunger down into the coffee, pushing the coffee grounds to the bottom of the pot.

⟨V⟩ QUICK AND EASY WHOLE-WHEAT ⟨V⟩ BREAD

This bread can be made in a variety of shapes.

MAKES ONE 1-pound LOAF

SHAPING BREAD DOUGH IN A LOAF PAN

1 Press out the dough so that its width is the same as the length of the pan

2 Form the dough into a loose roll

3 Place the roll of dough into the pan, seam side down

4 Push the dough down well into the corners and sides of the pan, to encourage it to form a dome-shaped loaf

1–1¼ cups tepid water
1 teaspoon sugar
2 teaspoons dried yeast
3½ cups 100% whole-wheat flour or
    2½ cups whole-wheat flour and 1 cup
    unbleached white flour
2 teaspoons salt
butter or oil for greasing
TOPPING
sesame seeds
rolled oats
poppy seeds
cracked wheat or
whole-wheat flour

1 Put half the water into a measuring cup with half the sugar and the yeast; mix, then leave for 5–10 minutes to froth.
2 Grease a 1-pound loaf pan generously with butter or oil.
3 Put the flour into a bowl with the remaining sugar and the salt and make a well in the center.
4 Pour in the frothed-up yeast, add the rest of the water and mix to a dough.
5 Turn out onto a clean work surface and knead for 10 minutes, until the dough is smooth, supple and silky.
6 Flatten the dough into a rectangle and gently roll it up to fit the pan. Put the roll into the pan with the fold underneath. Push it down to make sure that it fills all the sides and corners. This will give a nice domed shape to the loaf.
7 Cover with a clean dishtowel wrung out in hot water and put in a warm place for about 30 minutes to rise.
8 Preheat the oven to 350°F.
9 When the dough has doubled in size and risen above the rim of the pan, sprinkle with any of topping ingredients and bake for 40–45 minutes.
10 Turn the loaf out of the pan. It should sound hollow when you bang it on the base. Cool on a wire rack.

Variations

HERB AND ONION BREAD
Add 1 small finely chopped onion and ½ teaspoon each of oregano (or dill) and rosemary. Serve this bread warm.

THE GRANT LOAF
For this extra-speedy variation, increase the water to 1½ cups to make a soft mixture. Don't knead; divide the mixture in two, shape the pieces as described at left and put each into a greased 1-pound pan. Allow to rise until the sides of the loaves are about ¼ inch from the top of the pans. Bake the loaves for 30 minutes at 400°F.

QUICK WHOLE-WHEAT ROLLS
Rub 4 tablespoons butter or vegan margarine into the flour, then use ½ cup (generous) each of milk (or soy milk) and water to make the dough. Knead for 5 minutes, then put the dough into a clean, lightly oiled bowl, cover and leave in a warm place for about 1 hour, until doubled in bulk. Shape into 8–10 rolls, or rounds, plaits, knots, tricorns or miniature cottage loaves, and place well apart on a floured baking sheet. Cover and leave in a warm place for 15–20 minutes, until well risen. Bake the rolls for 15–20 minutes at 425°F.

HOT CROSS BUNS
Make the dough as described for quick rolls. After the first rising, knead into the dough ½ teaspoon each of mixed spice, cinnamon and grated nutmeg, ¾ cup currants, ¼ cup chopped mixed candied peel and 2 tablespoons sugar. Form the dough into rolls; then cut crosses out of ¼ pound shortcrust pastry and place on top. Bake for 20 minutes. Heat 2 tablespoons superfine sugar in 2 tablespoons milk until dissolved; brush over the buns.

Guide to Bread-Rising Times

Place	First rising times	Second rising times	Place	First rising times	Second rising times
In a warm (74°F) place, such as a cupboard, by a pilot light, near a radiator	45–60 mins	30 mins	In a refrigerator (brush with oil and cover bowl with plastic wrap to prevent hard crust forming; leave at room temperature for 15 minutes before baking)	up to 24 hrs	up to 12 hrs
At room temperature, 65–70°F	1½–2 hrs	40–50 mins			
In a cool room or larder	8–12 hrs	2–3 hrs			

Proving Bread Dough

Bread will "prove" or rise slowly in the refrigerator. Brush it with oil and cover with plastic wrap. Leave for 12 hours. Let the bread stand at room temperature for 30 minutes before baking, while the oven heats up, to allow it to "come to."

POPPY-SEED BRAID

This is an attractive bread with a delicate flavor and a golden crust coated with poppy seeds.

MAKES 1 LARGE BRAID

1 ounce fresh yeast or 1 package active dry yeast plus ½ teaspoon sugar
2 cups (scant) warm milk
5¼ cups unbleached white flour
1½ teaspoons salt
1½ teaspoons sugar
4 tablespoons butter
TO GLAZE
1 small egg, beaten
poppy seeds

1 Blend the yeast into the milk; for dried yeast, add the sugar, too, and leave for 10–15 minutes until frothy.
2 Put the flour, salt and sugar into a large mixing bowl and rub in the butter with your fingertips. Add the frothed-up yeast liquid and mix to a dough.
3 Knead for 10 minutes, put into a bowl, cover with plastic wrap and leave in a warm place until doubled in bulk. This should take about 1 hour.
4 Punch down the dough, knead briefly, then make a braid: divide the dough into 3 equal pieces, roll each into a sausage about 12 inches long, fat in the middle and tapering at the ends. Start braiding from the center, finishing each end of the braid by pinching the dough together into a neat point.
5 Place on a greased baking sheet, cover and leave to prove for 30 minutes, until puffy. Preheat the oven to 450°F.
6 Brush the braid with beaten egg, sprinkle with poppy seeds and bake for about 35 minutes. Cool on a wire rack.

Variations

VEGAN POPPY-SEED BRAID
Use soy milk instead of dairy milk and vegan margarine instead of butter. Brush the loaf with soy milk instead of egg.

SWEDISH TEA RING
Make the dough as described and let it rise in the bowl. Instead of making a braid, roll out to a rectangle 9 × 12 inches. Brush with melted butter, then roll up like a jelly roll and join the ends to make a ring. Place on a baking sheet and, using kitchen scissors, make diagonal slashes 1 inch apart. Pull open the cut sections. Leave to prove for 30 minutes, then bake at 375°F for 30–35 minutes. Decorate with icing, glacé cherries and slivered almonds.

SHAPING POPPY-SEED BRAID

WHOLE-WHEAT BANANA TEA BREAD

Serve this tea bread sliced and buttered.

MAKES ONE 1-pound LOAF

Clockwise from top right: Jasmine Tea; Camomile Tea; Peppermint Tea

4 tablespoons butter
¼ cup real Barbados sugar
3 tablespoons light molasses or clear honey
1½ cups self-rising 100% whole-wheat flour
¾ cup walnuts, chopped
2 ripe bananas, peeled and mashed
1 egg, beaten
extra butter for greasing

1 Preheat the oven to 350°F. Grease a 1-pound loaf pan and line with a strip of greased wax paper to cover the base of the pan and extend up the narrow sides.
2 Heat the butter, sugar and light molasses or honey gently in a small saucepan until melted. Set aside to cool until you can comfortably put your hand against the saucepan: stand the pan in a bowl of cold water if you're in a hurry.
3 Put the flour into a mixing bowl with the chopped walnuts and mashed bananas. Add the cooled melted mixture and the egg. Mix well.
4 Spoon the mixture into the prepared pan. Bake for 40 minutes, or until a warmed skewer inserted into the center of the loaf comes out clean.
5 Turn out on to a wire rack to cool. Strip off the wax paper.

Variations

VEGAN BANANA TEA BREAD
Use vegan margarine and 1 extra teaspoon baking powder. Replace the egg with 2 tablespoons soy milk.

DATE AND WALNUT LOAF
Make as described, using ¾ cup chopped cooking dates and 2–3 tablespoons milk, instead of the bananas.

SODA BREAD

Soda bread needs to be eaten the day it is made, although it makes good toast the next day. I like it particularly with clear honey.

MAKES ONE 1-pound LOAF

Measuring Light Molasses or Honey

If you can set your scale, place your mixing bowl or saucepan on the scale, set to zero, and pour in the molasses or honey until you have the right weight.

Or put the jar of honey or molasses on the scale and remove some from the jar until the scale shows you've taken out the quantity you need. Use a heated spoon to remove the honey or molasses from the jar, and flour the inside of your scale pan if you wish to transfer the honey or molasses to another container.

3½ cups whole-wheat and unbleached white flour mixed, or plain whole-wheat flour
1 teaspoon salt
2 teaspoons baking soda
2 tablespoons butter, softened
1¼ cups buttermilk, or milk warmed with 1 tablespoon vinegar to sour it

1 Preheat the oven to 425°F. Flour a baking sheet.
2 Sift the flour, salt and baking soda into a mixing bowl. Add the butter and rub in with the fingertips until the mixture resembles fine breadcrumbs.
3 Make a well in the center and pour in the milk, then gradually mix together to make a dough.
4 Turn the dough onto a floured board and knead it lightly, then form it into a round loaf.
5 Put the loaf on the prepared baking sheet and cut a cross shape in the top, using a sharp knife.
6 Bake the loaf for 30–35 minutes until it has risen and is golden-brown and crusty. Cool on a wire rack.

[V]   # CHAPATIS   [V]

These round unleavened breads make an excellent accompaniment
to curry or a lentil soup. Brush with a little melted butter or ghee
before serving, if you like.

MAKES 12

1½ cups (generous) 100% whole-wheat flour
1½ teaspoons vegetable oil or ghee
1 teaspoon salt
about ½ cup cold water

1 Put the flour into a mixing bowl with
the oil or ghee, salt and water and mix to
a soft dough.
2 Turn the dough out onto a floured
surface and knead for 5 minutes. Cover
the dough with a damp cloth and leave
for 2–3 hours, then knead again for a few
minutes.
3 Divide the dough into 12 equal pieces.
Form each into a ball, then roll out to a
circle 6–8 inches in diameter.
4 Fry the chapatis on both sides in an
ungreased frying pan until set and lightly
flecked with brown.
5 Pile the chapatis up on a plate as they're
cooked, covering with a piece of foil to
prevent them from drying out.

Ghee

A cooking fat which is much used in
Indian cookery. To make ghee, melt
¼–½ pound unsalted butter slowly
in a saucepan, then cook it very
gently for 30–45 minutes, until the
sediment at the bottom of the pan
has become a golden-brown. Strain
the butter through a sieve lined with
surgical gauze. Ghee can also be
bought from supermarkets and
Indian shops, and vegetable oil ghee
is available.

*Left to right: Quick Whole-Wheat Rolls
(p. 328); Soda Bread (p. 330); Quick
and Easy Whole-Wheat Bread (p. 328)*

Quick Snacks

Topped and filled breads in various forms make sophisticated hot and cold snacks and an exciting alternative to the sandwich. Crostini and bruschetta are different kinds of Italian toast: crostini, cut from a baguette, are usually lighter and more delicate, while bruschetta are made from coarse country bread, rubbed lightly with a garlic clove and drizzled with some olive oil after broiling. French baguettes and Italian ciabatta loaves can be sliced horizontally, piled up with your choice of filling and pressed down. And pita breads are slit open and warmed under the broiler before being packed with a variety of tasty ingredients and salad.

Serving Crostini and Bruschetta

Both crostini and bruschetta can be served plain, to accompany soup, salads, dips or other dishes. Or they can be topped with all kinds of delicious ingredients to make hors d'oeuvres, quick snacks or light meals. If you're making a meal of them, they're good served with some salad. You can make crostini from a small or large baguette, depending on how big you want the finished pieces to be. One baguette makes 50–60 slices, so you only need a small piece to make a snack or meal for 2 people.

Crostini Toppings

- Radiccio, Guacamole (p. 73) or mashed avocado, pink peppercorns
- Lettuce, scrambled egg, asparagus spears, parsley
- Watercress, sliced Lentil Loaf (p. 213), cranberry mayonnaise or mango chutney
- Lettuce, Hummus (p. 41), paprika, black olives and a drizzling of olive oil
- Lettuce, farmer's cheese, sliced ripe pear, halved black grapes
- Lettuce, slices of cheese and tomato, chopped parsley, stuffed green olives
- Watercress, coarsely grated carrot, mayonnaise, sliced tomato, Black Olive Pâté (p. 258)

Ⅴ BASIC CROSTINI AND BRUSCHETTA Ⅴ

1 baguette for crostini or 1 country-style loaf for bruschetta
olive oil
1 garlic clove, peeled and halved

1 Cut the baguette into slices ¼ inch thick, or slice the country bread.
2 Toast the bread until dried out and slightly golden on one side, then turn it over and repeat with the second side.
3 For crostini, brush the slices lightly with olive oil if you wish – I prefer them without. For bruschetta, rub the garlic lightly over the surface and brush or drizzle with some olive oil.

CROSTINI WITH SCRAMBLED EGG, ASPARAGUS AND DILL

1 tablespoon butter
1 egg, beaten
salt and freshly ground black pepper
4 small or 2 large crostini (see above)
4 asparagus spears, cooked
sprigs of dill

1 Heat the butter in a small pan, add the egg and cook gently, stirring, until scrambled. Remove from heat; season.
2 Spoon the egg on the crostini and arrange the asparagus and dill on top.

CROSTINI WITH SOFT GOAT'S CHEESE AND SUN-DRIED TOMATOES

4 small or 2 large crostini (see above)
¼ cup white goat's cheese
4 sun-dried tomatoes in oil, sliced
freshly ground black pepper

1 Spread the goat's cheese thickly on top of the crostini.
2 Arrange the sun-dried tomatoes on top of the goat's cheese, then coarsely grind some black pepper over the top.

Ⅴ RED AND YELLOW PEPPER CROSTINI Ⅴ

½ yellow pepper
½ red pepper
4 small or 2 large crostini (see above)
salt and freshly ground black pepper
4 capers, on stems if possible
sprigs of basil

1 Cut the peppers into quarters and place under a hot broiler for about 10 minutes or until the skin has blistered and blackened in places. Remove from the broiler and, when cool enough to handle, peel off the skin. Remove the seeds and stem and slice the peppers.
2 Arrange the strips of pepper on the crostini. Season with salt and pepper, then garnish with the capers and basil.

V CROSTINI WITH HUMMUS, BLACK OLIVES AND CORIANDER V

1/3 cup hummus
4 small or 2 large crostini (see above)
4 black olives
a few sprigs of coriander
a little paprika

1 Spread hummus thickly on the crostini.
2 Decorate with the black olives, sprigs of coriander and a dusting of paprika.

BRUSCHETTA WITH PLUM TOMATOES, MOZZARELLA AND BASIL

2 plum tomatoes, sliced
salt and freshly ground black pepper
a little olive oil
1 ounce fresh mozzarella cheese
2 bruschetta (see above)
4 basil leaves

1 Sprinkle the tomato slices with salt, pepper and a few drops of olive oil.
2 Cut the cheese into small pieces.
3 Put tomatoes on top of the bruschetta, dot with the pieces of mozzarella and tear the basil over the top. Grind some more pepper over dish and serve.

BRUSCHETTA WITH AVOCADO, TOMATO AND PARMESAN SLIVERS

½ avocado, peeled and sliced
1 tablespoon lemon juice
2 bruschetta (see above)
1 tomato, sliced
salt and freshly ground black pepper
a few slivers of Parmesan cheese
a little torn basil

1 Toss the avocado slices in the lemon juice, then arrange on top of the bruschetta with the tomato. Season.
2 Top with the Parmesan and basil.

Bruschetta with Avocado, Tomato and Parmesan Slivers; Crostini with Hummus, Black Olives and Coriander; Crostini with Soft Goat's Cheese and Sun-dried Tomatoes; Red and Yellow Pepper Crostini; Crostini with Scrambled Egg, Asparagus and Dill; Pita with Salad and Chick Peas (p. 334); Pita with Chili Eggplant (p. 334); Filled Pita Pocket (p. 334).

French Bread, Tacos and Pita Bread Fillings

Build these up into glorious colorful extravaganzas with your choice of:

- ☐ Shredded crisp lettuce, sliced tomato, scallion, cucumber
- ☐ Cubes of cold nut or lentil loaf
- ☐ Sliced, grated or diced cheese
- ☐ Wedges of hard-boiled egg
- ☐ Favorite Coleslaw (p. 161)
- ☐ Sliced red or green pepper, avocado pear, cooked asparagus tips or artichoke hearts
- ☐ Grated carrot, cauliflower, cooked or raw button mushrooms, sliced or whole
- ☐ Mayonnaise (p. 155), Guacamole (p. 73), Pepper and Almond Sauce (p. 230)
- ☐ Juicy black olives, chopped fresh herbs, walnuts or pecans

Elegant Sandwich Fillings

- ☐ Scrambled egg with asparagus tips
- ☐ Duxelles or mushroom pâté
- ☐ Cream cheese or farmer's cheese with chopped herbs or nuts
- ☐ Yeast extract or a thin spreading of light miso and wafer-thin cucumber slices
- ☐ Ripe avocado mashed with a little vinaigrette
- ☐ Finely grated cheese blended with cream, milk or farmer's cheese
- ☐ Herb butters (p. 118)
- ☐ Hummus (p. 41) with a little Black Olive Pâté (p. 258)

Ⅴ FILLED PITA POCKET

SERVES 1

1 whole-wheat pita bread
2 lettuce leaves, shredded
1 tomato, sliced
¼ quantity French Lentil and Walnut Salad (p. 158)

1 Slit the pita bread at the top and ease it open, to make a pocket for the filling.
2 Fill the pita bread with the lettuce, tomato and lentil salad.

Ⅴ PITA WITH SALAD AND CHICK PEAS

a few salad leaves, torn
1 tablespoon Vinaigrette (p. 154)
⅔ cup cooked and drained chick peas
a few coriander leaves
1 wholewheat pita bread, slit open and warmed under the broiler
salt and freshly ground black pepper

Pack all the ingredients into the pita bread and serve at once. You can use freshly cooked felafel instead of chick peas for a delicious variation (p. 208).

Ⅴ PITA WITH CHILI EGGPLANT Ⅴ

½ medium eggplant, cut into slices about ⅛ inch thick
a little olive oil
a few drops of Tabasco or other chili sauce
salt and freshly ground black pepper
1 wholewheat pita bread, slit open and warmed under the broiler

1 Brush the eggplant with olive oil, then broil on both sides until golden brown and tender

2 Mix the eggplant with the chili sauce and salt and pepper to taste. Pack into the pita bread and serve at once.

Ⅴ FILLED CIABATTA

SERVES 2

1 ciabatta loaf, halved lengthwise
2–4 lettuce leaves
1 beefsteak tomato, sliced
¼ pound mozzarella cheese, sliced
1 small avocado, peeled, pitted and sliced
a few basil leaves
salt and freshly ground black pepper

Layer the ingredients on the bottom half of the ciabatta, seasoning as you go. Put the other half on top, press down firmly, cut in half and serve.

Ⅴ FILLED FRENCH Ⅴ BREAD

SERVES 4

2 wholewheat French sticks
butter, vegan margarine, mustard or mayonnaise
1 lettuce, washed and shredded
225 g/8 oz tomatoes, sliced
100 g/4 oz beansprouts
1 onion, peeled and sliced
1 × 425-g/15-oz can red kidney beans, drained
salt and freshly ground black pepper

1 Make a slit down the side of each French stick and scoop out a little of the crumb.
2 Spread the inside of each French loaf thinly with butter, vegan margarine, mustard or mayonnaise.
3 Fill each loaf with the vegetables and beans, and season with salt and pepper.
4 Press the slits together, wrap the loaves tightly in foil and chill until required, then cut each in half.

QUICK BREAD PIZZA

SERVES 4

*1 round or oval wholewheat loaf, about
450 g/1 lb
olive oil
2 large onions, peeled and sliced
2 garlic cloves, crushed
1 × 425-g/15-oz can chopped tomatoes
oregano
salt and freshly ground black pepper
100 g/4 oz cheese, grated
8 black olives*

1 Preheat the oven to 220 C/425 F/Gas
Mark 7. Cut the loaf in half horizontally
and scoop out some of the crumbs. Brush
inside and outside the halved loaf with oil
and place on a baking sheet.
2 Fry the onions in a tablespoon of oil for
10 minutes, then add the garlic and fry for
a further minute or two.
3 Remove from heat and add tomatoes
and a little oregano, salt and pepper.
4 Spoon the mixture on to the bread
halves and sprinkle with grated cheese.
5 Bake for 15 minutes, then put on the
olives and bake for a further 5–10
minutes. Serve hot.

V ASPARAGUS V ROLLS

A pleasant tea-time or drinks'
party nibble.

MAKES ABOUT 40

*½ sliced large wholewheat loaf
butter or vegan margarine
1 × 225-g/8-oz packet frozen asparagus
    spears, cooked and drained, or
1 × 350-g/12-oz can asparagus spears,
    drained*

1 Cut the crusts off the bread, then
flatten each slice with a rolling pin.
2 Spread the slices thinly with butter or

vegan margarine, then wrap each piece of
bread round an asparagus spear, cutting
off any spare bread, so that the edges
meet but do not overlap.
3 Cut each roll into 2 or 3 pieces so that
they are a manageable size for eating.
4 Cover with clingfilm and keep in a
cool place until needed.

CHEESE ON TOAST

SERVES 1

*1–2 slices wholewheat bread
75–100 g/3–4 oz cheese, grated
1–2 tablespoons milk
freshly ground black pepper*

1 Heat the grill to high. Toast the bread
on one side.
2 Blend the cheese to a paste with the
milk, and season with pepper.
3 Spread the cheese mixture on the un-
toasted side of the bread and grill until
puffed up and golden-brown. Serve
immediately.

MOZZARELLA IN CARROZZA

SERVES 2

*1 Mozzarella cheese
4 slices bread, crusts removed
2 eggs
oil for shallow frying*

1 Cut the cheese into thin slices and
arrange on 2 of the slices of bread. Top
with the remaining slices.
2 Beat the eggs, then strain them into a
shallow dish.
3 Put the sandwiches in the egg, leaving
them to soak it up, and turning them over
once.
4 Shallow-fry the sandwiches on both
sides in a little oil, until golden-brown
and crisp. Drain on kitchen paper and
serve immediately.

School Lunch Box Sandwich Fillings

Children have their own definite
ideas about these – one of my
daughters would only ever eat plain
yeast extract sandwiches – and they
generally like their sandwiches to
look as much like everyone else's as
possible. Here are some ideas:
☐ Yeast extract, miso, mayonnaise,
  peanut butter, sesame spread,
  cottage or cream cheese with
  cucumber, lettuce, bean sprouts,
  tomato or grated carrot
☐ Cottage or cream cheese with
  finely chopped nuts or dates
☐ Mashed cooked red kidney beans
  with salad
☐ Chopped hard-boiled egg mixed
  with salad cream or milk, or
  scrambled egg, with watercress
☐ Grated carrot mixed with
  mayonnaise and chopped herbs or
  raisins
☐ Sliced or grated cheese with
  lettuce, tomato or cucumber
☐ Sliced banana, with or without
  peanut butter or sesame spread
☐ Honey and finely ground nuts

Iced Tea

Make the tea as described on
page 326, then strain and chill. Serve
with crushed ice and a slice of lemon
and a sprig of mint or lemon balm, if
you wish. Iced herb teas make a
specially good summer drink. For a
fruity flavor, try adding a sliced
peach to the tea before chilling.

Iced Coffee

Make coffee by the filter method,
then chill. Serve in tall glasses with
ice. Top with a spoonful of whipped
cream, if you like, and pass sugar
separately

MENU
Children's Tea

SERVES 4–6

Little Basket of Crudités
143

Yogurt and Herb Dressing
156

Potato and Cheese Layer
200

Fresh Tomato Sauce
170

Peas

*Chocolate Ice Cream with Crumbly
Almond Cookies*
280 and 323

This is a substantial meal for children arriving home from school ravenous, and features dishes which in my experience are always popular. The Potato and Cheese Layer is easy to make, but allow time for it to cook. It is served with a tomato sauce, crudités and a yogurt and herb dressing – many children will eat vegetables raw that they wouldn't eat cooked!

I've never quite been able to understand why children like the Chocolate Ice Cream so much, but they always do, and as it's a low-fat, low-sugar one, I'm not arguing! The Crumbly Almond cookies go well with it, or you could serve some slices of fresh fruit. To drink, whatever is your child's favorite healthy drink of the moment; apple cider or grape juice is usually popular, or apple-juice concentrate (p. 340) diluted with water or soda water.

Preserves and Chutneys

Homemade jams, jellies, preserves and chutneys add a delightful touch of luxury to a meal, yet are both easy and satisfying to make. If you're lucky enough to have fruit trees and bushes, a cheap source of fruit is readily available; but even if you have to buy them, at the peak of their season fruit and vegetables are likely to be inexpensive. Delicious with homemade bread and scones, jams and jellies also make excellent fillings and toppings. Chutneys and pickles, with their piquant, sweet-and-sour flavors, are excellent with cold nut and lentil roasts and burgers.

Preserving Pan

You need a preserving pan, or an extra-large saucepan or saucepan part of a pressure cooker, because the mixture needs plenty of room. Because of this, it's best not to make too much at a time. If you're using a microwave – a very clean way to make preserves – it's best to make even smaller quantities (see recipe, p. 339) and to use a large bowl.

Preparing Jam Jars

Wash jam jars thoroughly and sterilize them by drying them off in a cool oven, 275°F. Fill the jars while they are still warm.

Jam Jars and Covers

Use special preserving jars with metal screwbands and flat metal lids edged with a sealing compound. Wipe the jars after filling while still warm, but stick on the labels when the jars have cooled.

Sugar for Preserves

Granulated sugar is the cheapest and just as good as the more expensive preserving sugars (which give a particularly clear jelly) for normal use. Real brown sugar can be used, and gives a dark color and mellow flavor to chutney and marmalade, but is not successful in jam, in my opinion. Whatever kind of sugar you use, make sure it is completely dissolved before the jam is boiled, or it may not set properly.

Ⓥ ROSE PETAL JAM Ⓥ

Use petals from unsprayed roses which have not been growing near a busy road. Cut away the white triangle at the base of each petal.

MAKES 1 quart

5 ounces scented rose petals, washed and trimmed
2¾ cups water
¾ cup lemon juice
2½ cups sugar
5 tablespoons commercial pectin
3 tablespoons rosewater

1 Put the petals, water, lemon juice and sugar into a large saucepan and heat gently until the sugar has dissolved.
2 Bring to a boil, then cover and simmer gently for 30 minutes.
3 Add the pectin and rosewater, stir well, then boil hard for 5 minutes.
4 Test for a set (p. 339); if the jam is not ready, test again in 2 minutes, and keep testing until a set is reached.
5 Cool slightly, then pour into warmed, sterilized jars (left). Cover, seal and label when completely cold.

PLUM JAM

Do not use any bruised or over-ripe plums for making jam, as they will not give a good set and could cause the jam to ferment.

MAKES 2½ quarts

3 pounds plums
2 cups water
6 cups sugar
a knob of butter

1 Wash the plums, then put them into a preserving pan with the water and simmer for about 30 minutes, until the fruit is soft.
2 Remove the pan from the heat and stir in the sugar. Stir well until the sugar has completely dissolved.
3 Bring to a boil, then boil hard for 10–15 minutes, stirring often.
4 Test for a set (p. 339) then, when this point is reached, stir in the butter.
5 Using a slotted spoon, remove the plum pits from the top of the jam.
6 Let the jam stand for 15 minutes to settle, then pour it into warmed, sterilized jars (left). Cover, seal and label when completely cold.

Variations
DAMSON JAM
Use the same recipe but you'll only need 2½ pounds of fruit. Test for a set after 7–10 minutes.

BLACK CURRANT JAM

Use about 2 pints black currants, about 1 quart water and 6 cups sugar. Simmer the black currants for 45 minutes, until the skins are really tender, before adding the sugar.

GOOSEBERRY JAM

Use about 3 pints gooseberries, 2½ cups water and 6 cups sugar. Cook the gooseberries in the water for 30 minutes, until soft, then add the sugar.

STRAWBERRY JAM

MAKES 2½ quarts

3 pints small, slightly underripe strawberries, hulled and wiped
7 cups sugar
3 tablespoons fresh lemon juice
a small knob of butter

1 Put the strawberries into an enamel or stainless steel preserving pan with the sugar and leave for an hour or so, or overnight if convenient.
2 Add the lemon juice and heat slowly, over very low heat, until the sugar has dissolved.
3 Return to the heat, bring to a boil and boil rapidly for 7–8 minutes, then remove from the heat and test for a set (see right).
4 If the jam isn't ready, return to the heat and test again in 2–3 minutes' time. Keep on testing until a set is reached.
5 Remove from the heat and stir in the butter.
6 Let the jam stand for 30 minutes, for the fruit to settle, then stir gently and pour into warmed, sterilized jars (p. 338). Cover, seal and label when cold.

Variation
RASPBERRY JAM
Make this in the same way, omitting the lemon juice, and using about 4 pints raspberries and 8 cups sugar. After adding the sugar, boil the jam for about 30 minutes. Test for a set, then add the butter. Cover, seal and label when cold.

Ⅴ MICROWAVE Ⅴ STRAWBERRY JAM

MAKES 3 cups

1⅓ pints strawberries, washed and hulled
¼ cup fresh lemon juice
1¾ cups superfine sugar

1 Put the strawberries into a 2½-quart bowl with the lemon juice. Cook, uncovered, at full heat for 5–6 minutes, until the strawberries are soft.
2 Add the sugar, stirring until it has completely dissolved.
3 Return the bowl to the oven and cook at full heat for 20 minutes, stirring at the end of every 5 minutes.
4 Test for a set (see right); if the jam has not yet reached setting point, return the bowl to the oven for a further 1½ minutes, then test again. Continue this process until the jam sets.
5 Leave the jam to cool until tepid, then pour it into warmed, sterilized jars.
6 Cover, seal and label when cold.

Testing for a Set

Setting point is reached when the jam or jelly reaches 220°F on a sugar thermometer, or when a teaspoon of the mixture put on a chilled saucer, and chilled for a few minutes in the freezing compartment of the refrigerator, wrinkles at the edges and does not run together again when you run your finger through it. It's important to take the pan off the heat while you test for a set, to avoid overcooking.

Descumming Jam

Stirring in a knob of butter after the setting point is reached helps disperse the surface scum on jam.

Clockwise from top right: Rose Petal Jam (p. 338); Lemon Curd (p. 341); Strawberry Jam; Mary's Marmalade (p. 341)

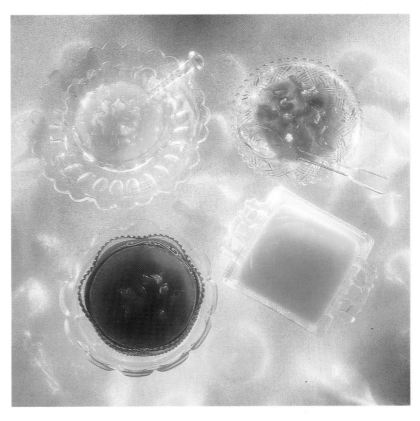

Fruit–Sugar Proportions in Jam

For fruits rich in pectin and acid, such as cooking apples, red and black currants and gooseberries, the proportions are 2½–3 cups sugar to each 1 pound of fruit. For fruits with a moderate amount of pectin and acid, such as blackberries, loganberries and raspberries, allow 2 cups sugar to 1 pound fruit.

Fruit–Sugar Proportions in Jelly

Basic proportions are 2 cups sugar to each 2½ cups fruit juice.

Sugarless Jam and Jelly

I'm indebted to Jackie Applebee, of the Wholefood Cookery School, for this information on making sugarless jams and jellies, and for the sugarless jam recipes included in this book. The basic proportions are 1–1½ pounds fruit to 1 cup concentrated apple juice weighed in a plastic container. You cook the fruit in just enough water to prevent sticking (soft fruits such as raspberries and strawberries can be puréed in a blender or food processor and heated gently without water), then add the apple juice concentrate and boil until a set is reached. Make this jam in small quantities and store in the refrigerator.

Apple Juice Concentrate

Concentrated apple juice can be bought at health food shops. As well as its use in preserves, and, well diluted, as a drink, concentrated apple juice makes a healthy sugar replacement in cakes, desserts and other sweet treats.

Ⅴ SUGAR-FREE Ⅴ MIXED BERRY JAM

Although this delicious, fruity jam should be made in small quantities and kept in the refrigerator, it can be made from frozen berries throughout the year.

MAKES 3 cups

¾ pint strawberries, hulled
¾ pint blackberries
¾ pint gooseberries, trimmed
1 cup apple juice concentrate

1 Wash the berries, then purée half of them in a blender or food processor and place in a large saucepan with the rest of the fruit.
2 Simmer gently until the fruit is cooked.
3 Add the apple juice concentrate and boil for 15 minutes, then test to see if it has reached setting point (p. 339). If this has not been achieved, continue to boil, testing frequently, until setting point is reached.
4 Remove from the heat and cool slightly, then pour into warmed, sterilized jars (p. 338). Cover, seal and label when cold.
5 Store in a cool place for up to 4 weeks, or in the refrigerator.

Ⅴ CRAB APPLE Ⅴ JELLY

A delightful, sharp-tasting jelly, good with nut roasts.

MAKES 1–1½ quarts

4 pounds crab apples
5 cups water
4–6 cups sugar

1 Wash the fruit, then cut away any damaged parts, and cut any large fruits into halves or quarters, so that they are all about the same size.
2 Put the crab apples into a saucepan with the water and boil gently until the fruit is soft and pulpy.
3 Have ready a large sieve lined with some cheesecloth or surgical gauze and set over a large bowl.
4 Tip the apple mixture into the sieve and leave overnight to drip through.
5 Measure the liquid and put it into a saucepan with 2 cups sugar for every 2½ cups liquid.
6 Heat gently, stirring, until the sugar has dissolved, then bring to a boil.
7 Boil for 10–15 minutes. Test for a set (p. 339), and when this point is reached, remove from the heat and pour into warmed, sterilized jars (p. 338). Cover, seal and label when cold.

Pectin Content of Fruits and Vegetables

*high in acid

High	Medium	Low
*Cooking and crab apples	Underripe apricots	Cherries
*Cranberries	*Bilberries	Elderberries
*Currants, black, red and white	Blackberries	Japonica
*Damsons	*Greengages	Loquats
*Gooseberries (should be underripe)	*Loganberries	Peaches (dried ones are best)
*Grapefruit	*Mulberries	
*Lemons	Nectarines	
*Limes		
*Oranges		
Plums, if underripe,* especially yellow ones	Ripe plums	
	*Underripe raspberries	Rhubarb
Quinces	*Sloes	Underripe strawberries

LEMON CURD

Tangy and delicious, and very easy to make.

MAKES 3 cups

6 tablespoons butter
grated rind and juice of 2 large, well-scrubbed lemons
1¼ cups superfine sugar
3 eggs, beaten

1 Put all the ingredients into the top of a double boiler or a heatproof bowl set over a saucepan of boiling water, making sure the base of the bowl does not touch the water.
2 Stir until the sugar has dissolved, then continue to cook gently for about 20 minutes, stirring often, until the curd thickens.
3 Strain into jars. Cover, seal and label when cold, then store in a cool, dry place.

MARY'S MARMALADE

This recipe, which was given to me by a friend who is an expert marmalade maker, makes a light marmalade with a tangy flavor. It's easy to make with a blender or food processor.

MAKES ABOUT 5 quarts

12 Seville oranges
1 sweet orange
2 small lemons
2 quarts water
5 pounds sugar
a knob of butter

1 Scrub the oranges and lemons well, then quarter them and remove the seeds.
2 Put the seeds into a piece of cheesecloth and tie loosely with string.
3 Purée the oranges and lemons with the water in a blender or food processor. Put into a bowl with the bag of seeds; leave overnight.

4 Next day, transfer the mixture to a pan and simmer, uncovered, for 2 hours.
5 Put the puréed orange and lemon mixture into a large saucepan or preserving pan, strain in the seed liquid and bring to a boil. Add the sugar and cook, stirring often, until setting point is reached (p. 339).
6 Remove from the heat and stir in the butter. Cool slightly, then pour into warmed, sterilized jars (p. 338). Cover, seal and label when cold.

V PRESSURE-COOKER MARMALADE V

Pressure cooking cuts out messy preparation.

MAKES ABOUT 10 cups

12 Seville oranges
2 lemons
3 quarts cold water
6–7 pounds sugar
a knob of butter

1 Scrub the oranges and lemons, then put them into a pressure cooker with 5 cups of the water. Cook at 15 pounds pressure for 25 minutes, or until the oranges are completely soft.
2 Drain juice into a nonmetal bowl.
3 When the fruit is cool enough to handle, scoop the insides of the fruit away from the skin, using a teaspoon.
4 Sieve the pulp and add the purée to the bowl of juice.
5 Cut the peel into shreds and add this to the bowl, with the remaining water. Cover and leave overnight.
6 Next day, measure the mixture into a preserving pan. Bring to a boil, then add 2 cups sugar for every 2½ cups liquid.
7 Heat gently until the sugar has dissolved, then bring to a boil and boil until setting point is reached (p. 339).
8 Remove from heat, stir in the butter, and allow to settle 15 minutes. Pour into warmed, sterilized jars (p. 338). Cover, seal and label when cold.

Canning Jam

Put circles of wax paper on top of the jam immediately after you've poured it into the jars, when it is still very hot, or wait until it is completely cold. This will act as a seal between the top of the jam and the lid, and help prevent mold.

Making Reduced-Sugar Jams and Jellies

The sugar in standard recipes can be reduced by 20 percent without affecting the set. This jam will not keep for more than about a month in a cool place, or 6–8 weeks in a refrigerator.

A few sprigs of sweet cicely cooked with acid fruit counteracts the sharpness so that less sugar is needed.

Sugar-Free Marmalade

Use 2 cups freshly squeezed orange juice (ready-squeezed orange juice is not suitable) and the thinly pared rind of 1 orange and 1 lemon, well scrubbed. Make as for Sugar-free Mixed Berry Jam (p. 340), boiling the mixture until the rind is soft before adding the apple juice concentrate.

Pectin

Pectin is a carbohydrate found in the cell walls of plants. It is important for the setting of jams and jellies. The pectin content of fruits varies (p. 340). Pectin can be bought and is useful for making preserves from ingredients with a low pectin content, such as rose petals in Rose Petal Jam (p. 338). It is widely available in liquid form from supermarkets.

Basic Chutney Making

To make chutney, cook together a mixture of chopped fruits and vegetables, including onions and dried fruit such as raisins or chopped dates, with vinegar, sugar and spices. The chutney should be simmered gently, uncovered, for 1–3 hours, until nearly all the vinegar has disappeared and when you part the mixture with a spoon the channel does not immediately fill with liquid. The chutney will thicken up more as it cools.

The covers for chutney and pickles are important, as the vinegar may corrode metal, and will evaporate through paper coverings. So use plastic caps or synthetic covering material, or line metal covers with vinegar-proof paper.

Pieces cut from a wide (4-inch) bandage or some surgical gauze can be used for tying up the pickling spices. Secure with string, then loop this around the handle of the pan, for easy removal.

Chutneys vary a good deal in spiciness, fruitiness and the balance of sweet and sour. Therefore it's a good idea to make up a new recipe in a small quantity, to try. But remember most chutneys, pickles and relishes need at least 6–8 weeks to mature before you can judge their true flavor.

Ⅴ SWEET SPICED Ⅴ
APRICOT CHUTNEY

This is a sweet, spicy chutney, rather like mango chutney. It can be made with peaches or plums instead of apricots.

MAKES 6 cups

4 pounds fresh apricots or 1½ pounds dried apricots, soaked in water overnight, then drained
2 small cooking apples, peeled, cored and chopped
¾ cup raisins
2½ cups white distilled vinegar
1⅓ cups granulated or raw light brown sugar
1 tablespoon ground ginger
3 garlic cloves, crushed
1 teaspoon freshly grated nutmeg
¼ teaspoon cayenne
1 teaspoon salt

1 Put all the ingredients into a large saucepan or preserving pan.
2 Bring to a boil, then cook gently, uncovered, stirring occasionally, for about 1½ hours, until the mixture is thick and no excess liquid appears when it is parted with the spoon.
3 Spoon the mixture into warmed, sterilized jars (p. 338) and cover immediately with airtight, vinegar-proof tops. Label when cold. Store in a cool, dry place.

Ⅴ APPLE CHUTNEY Ⅴ

An easy chutney to make, with a deliciously spicy flavor.

MAKES ABOUT 8 cups

3 pounds cooking apples, peeled, cored and diced
3 pounds onions, peeled and chopped
3 cups sultanas
1¾ cups soft dark brown sugar
2½ cups malt vinegar
2 tablespoons ground ginger
2 tablespoons salt
½ teaspoon cayenne

1 Put all the ingredients into a preserving pan and bring to a boil.
2 Reduce the heat and simmer gently, uncovered, for about 1½–2 hours, stirring occasionally, until the mixture is very thick and no excess liquid appears when it is parted with a wooden spoon.
3 Spoon the mixture into warmed, sterilized jars (p. 338) and cover immediately with airtight covers (snap-on plastic covers are ideal; avoid metal, which the vinegar may corrode). Label when cold.
4 This chutney improves with keeping, stored in a cool, dry place.

Ⅴ BREAD AND Ⅴ
BUTTER PICKLES

Delicious on bread and butter, and very easy to make.

MAKES ABOUT 6 cups

2 pounds cucumbers, washed and sliced
2 large onions, peeled and sliced
1 large green pepper, deseeded and chopped
2 tablespoons salt
2 cups (scant) white wine vinegar or cider vinegar
1 cup (scant) soft light brown sugar
½ teaspoon ground turmeric
½ teaspoon ground cloves
2 teaspoons mustard seeds
½ teaspoon celery seeds

1 Put the cucumber into a bowl with the onion and pepper. Sprinkle with the salt, mix well, and leave for at least 3 hours.
2 Rinse the vegetables thoroughly under cold water. Drain well and put into a large saucepan with the vinegar.
3 Bring to a boil and simmer for about 20 minutes until vegetables are tender.
4 Add the sugar and spices to the pan and heat gently until the sugar has dissolved.
5 Bring to a boil, then remove from the heat, pour into a bowl, cover and leave until cold.
6 Spoon the mixture into warmed, sterilized jars (p. 338) and immediately cover with airtight, vinegar-proof tops. Label when cold and store in a cool, dry place.

Ⓥ PRESERVED Ⓥ KUMQUATS

This is an attractive way to use baby kumquats. They are delicious spooned over ice cream, or served as they are, chilled, with some whipped cream and a scattering of almonds. Packed into pretty jars, they make good presents, and they will keep well for up to 6 months.

MAKES five 1-cup JARS

1½ pounds kumquats
2 cups granulated sugar
2½ cups water
6 tablespoons brandy

1 Scrub the kumquats, then prick them all over with a fine skewer.
2 Put the sugar and water into a saucepan and heat gently until the sugar has dissolved, then bring to a boil.
3 Add the kumquats, cover and cook gently for about 15 minutes, or until they are very tender and almost transparent.
4 Using a slotted spoon, take the kumquats out of the syrup and place in warmed, sterilized jars (p. 338).
5 Add the brandy, then pour in enough of the cooking syrup to cover the kumquats. Cover, seal and label when cold, then store in a cool, dry place.

Ⓥ SPICED ORANGE Ⓥ SLICES

These spicy orange slices are good with cold nut or lentil roasts.

MAKES ABOUT 15 cups

12 thin-skinned oranges
6¼ cups soft light brown sugar
2½ cups white wine vinegar or cider vinegar
12 whole cloves
4 inches cinnamon stick
½ teaspoon ground mace or 6–8 mace blades

Left to right: Preserved Kumquats; Bread and Butter Pickles (p. 342); Sweet Spiced Apricot Chutney (p. 342); Spiced Orange Slices

1 Scrub and dry the oranges. Slice them about ⅛ inch thick; remove the seeds.
2 Put the orange slices into a large saucepan and cover with cold water. Bring to a boil and simmer gently, covered, until the orange skin is just tender – about 20–30 minutes.
3 Put the remaining ingredients into another large saucepan and heat gently until the sugar has dissolved, then boil for 3 minutes.
4 Using a slotted spoon, remove the orange slices from the pan and add to the vinegar mixture.
5 Add enough of the orange cooking liquid to cover the orange slices, then simmer them gently until tender but not disintegrated – 35–45 minutes.
6 Remove from the heat and leave the oranges in the syrup for 24 hours.
7 Remove the orange slices with a slotted spoon and place in warmed, sterilized jars (p. 338), filling them no more than half full.
8 Heat the syrup to boiling, then continue to boil for a few minutes to reduce it slightly.
9 Cool for 15 minutes, then pour the syrup into the jars, filling them to the top. Cover immediately with airtight, vinegar-proof tops. Label the jars when cold. Store them in a cool, dry place for 4 weeks before using.

Spiced Vinegar

This is used for some chutneys and pickles. Tie ½ ounce each of blade mace, cinnamon stick, allspice and cloves, and a few peppercorns in a piece of cheesecloth. Put into a saucepan with 2½ quarts vinegar and 1 tablespoon salt. Bring to a boil, then cover and simmer for 5 minutes. Strain and use immediately, or cool, bottle and store. For sweet pickles, add sugar to the vinegar, allowing 2 cups sugar to 2½ cups vinegar, and add a few strips of lemon rind. For pickled pears, poach 2 pounds peeled cooking pears (whole if small, halved or quartered if larger) in spiced vinegar with 2½ cups soft brown sugar, for 30–40 minutes. Bottle and keep for 6 weeks before using.

Candies and Confections

Making candies and confections is frivolous but fun, and, as with desserts, I'm all for the occasional indulgence. The ones in this section are those I find most popular and easy to make, without the need for any special equipment. Homemade sweets make a delightful treat; they can be served as petits fours at the end of a meal and they also make attractive gifts and bazaar items. If you're giving them away, they will look especially festive in fluted paper cups, jars and pretty boxes, or in cones made of colored light-weight card or twists of colored cellophane, with decorations of hearts, flowers and ribbons.

Healthy Sweet Ideas for Children

Dried fruits make natural sweets; add a mixture of sun-dried raisins, dates and apricots in a twist of plastic wrap to a child's lunch box. For children over six, replace the pit in dates with a whole almond or small Brazil nut. For younger children, replace the pit with a paste of ground almonds and honey.

Coat peeled banana chunks first in clear honey, then in carob powder and chopped nuts. Freeze until firm. Eat as frozen sweets, or insert sticks before freezing and eat as lollipops.

Cleaning a Toffee Pan

To clean a sticky toffee pan, fill the pan with water and bring to a boil. The toffee will melt and can be poured away with the water.

Sweets for Gifts

Homemade sweets make delightful gifts, but packaging makes all the difference. Pack candy or cookies in pretty jars, in small baskets lined with a doily and covered with plastic wrap, or in pretty boxes you've saved, along with a twist of scrunchy cellophane. Decorate with colored ribbon, small fabric flowers, colored labels.

Ⓥ FRUIT SNACK BITES

A healthy sweet that contains no added sugar. In my experience children like these as long as they don't have them too often!

MAKES 64

3–4 cups mixed dried fruit, such as dates, apricots, peaches and raisins
about 1 cup Brazil nuts
1⅓ cups desiccated coconut (unsweetened)
grated rind of 1 orange or lemon
1–2 tablespoons fresh orange juice
a little extra desiccated coconut for coating

1 Put the dried fruit and Brazil nuts into a food processor and whizz until finely chopped. Or chop the dried fruits very finely by hand, grind the nuts and mix together.
2 Add the 1⅓ cups desiccated coconut, grated citrus rind and enough orange juice to make the mixture stick together, and process again, or mix the ingredients very well by hand.
3 Put the rest of the desiccated coconut into a shallow bowl. Roll the dried fruit mixture into small balls and toss in the coconut until they are thoroughly coated.
4 Place on trays and chill the fruit snack bites in the refrigerator for 1–2 hours, until they have firmed up.

Ⓥ Ⓥ CAROB, CASHEW Ⓥ AND HONEY SWEETS

Another healthy sweet that children like in moderation. These sweets are rich and nourishing: a little goes a long way.

MAKES 21 PIECES

about 1 cup cashew nuts
1 tablespoon carob powder
a few drops of vanilla extract
1 tablespoon thick honey

1 Put the cashew nuts, carob and vanilla into a food processor and whizz to a powder. Or grind the nuts finely, then put into a bowl with the carob and vanilla.
2 Add the honey and process the mixture again (or mix by hand) until it forms a stiff paste.
3 Put the mixture into an 8-inch square pan and press it out so that it is ½ inch thick (it will fill only about a third of the pan).
4 Chill in the refrigerator until firm, then cut into squares.

Variation
CAROB, BRAZIL NUT AND HONEY SWEETS
Use Brazil nuts instead of the cashew nuts, if preferred, and make the sweets as described above.

⩔ TREACLE TOFFEE ⩔

MAKES ABOUT 1¼ pounds

1 cup raw light brown (Demerara) sugar
6 tablespoons butter or vegan margarine
½ cup molasses
3 tablespoons water
¼ teaspoon cream of tartar
extra butter for greasing

1 Grease an 8-inch square pan, then line with nonstick baking parchment.
2 Put the sugar, butter or vegan margarine, molasses and water into a heavy-bottomed saucepan. Heat gently until sugar has dissolved, then bring to a boil, remove from the heat and add the cream of tartar.
3 Return the pan to the heat and boil until the mixture reaches 246–252°F, the hard ball stage (see right), stirring from time to time.
4 Pour the mixture into the prepared pan. Leave until nearly set, then mark into squares.
5 When the toffee is completely cold, remove from pan and break into squares.

CHOCOLATE RUM TRUFFLES

MAKES 36

8 ounces semisweet dark chocolate
1¼ cups heavy cream
2 tablespoons rum
cocoa powder for coating

1 Break the chocolate into pieces and put it into a heavy-bottomed saucepan with the cream.
2 Heat very gently until the chocolate has melted, then remove from the heat, transfer to a bowl and cool.
3 Add the rum, then beat until pale and thick. Chill in the refrigerator until firm enough to handle.
4 Sprinkle some cocoa on a plate, then put heaped teaspoonfuls of the mixture onto this and sprinkle with more cocoa.

5 Roll each piece of mixture in cocoa to make a truffle, and place in a fluted paper cup or on a small serving dish.
6 Chill until ready to serve.

CREAMY FUDGE

I've tried many fudge recipes, and this one I always find the best.

MAKES ABOUT 2¼ pounds

¼ pound (1 stick) butter
one 15-ounce can condensed milk
2 cups superfine sugar

1 Line an 8-inch square pan with nonstick baking parchment.
2 Put the butter, milk and sugar into a large, heavy-bottomed saucepan.
3 Heat gently, stirring, over a low heat, until the sugar has dissolved.
4 Raise the heat and boil for 5 minutes, stirring all the time, until the mixture starts to come away from the sides of the saucepan.
5 Pour the mixture into the prepared pan. Allow to cool to room temperature, then mark into squares.
6 When the fudge is completely cool, cut it into squares with a sharp knife.

Sugar Boiling Stages

A cooking thermometer is useful for candy making, but not essential, because the mixture behaves quite distinctively at different temperatures:

Thread (225°F): a little of the mixture forms a short thread when placed between finger and thumb and pulled apart

Soft ball (240°F): a little of the syrup put into a cup of cold water forms a small soft ball

Hard ball (255°F): a little of the mixture forms a hard ball when dropped into a cup of cold water

Crack (280°F): a drop of the syrup put into cold water becomes brittle

Caramel (312°F): the syrup turns a dark brown color

When testing the sugar syrup, remove it from the heat to prevent further cooking.

Creamy Fudge; Fruit Snack Bites (p. 344); Chocolate Rum Truffles; Carob, Cashew and Honey Sweets (p. 344)

Index